Marxism and Historical Practice
VOLUME II

Historical Materialism Book Series

The Historical Materialism Book Series is a major publishing initiative of the radical left. The capitalist crisis of the twenty-first century has been met by a resurgence of interest in critical Marxist theory. At the same time, the publishing institutions committed to Marxism have contracted markedly since the high point of the 1970s. The Historical Materialism Book Series is dedicated to addressing this situation by making available important works of Marxist theory. The aim of the series is to publish important theoretical contributions as the basis for vigorous intellectual debate and exchange on the left.

The peer-reviewed series publishes original monographs, translated texts, and reprints of classics across the bounds of academic disciplinary agendas and across the divisions of the left. The series is particularly concerned to encourage the internationalization of Marxist debate and aims to translate significant studies from beyond the English-speaking world.

For a full list of titles in the Historical Materialism Book Series
available in paperback from Haymarket Books, visit:
https://www.haymarketbooks.org/series_collections/1-historical-materialism

Marxism and Historical Practice

Interventions and Appreciations

VOLUME II

Bryan D. Palmer

Haymarket Books
Chicago, IL

First published in 2015 by Brill Academic Publishers, The Netherlands
© 2015 Koninklijke Brill NV, Leiden, The Netherlands

Published in paperback in 2017 by
Haymarket Books
P.O. Box 180165
Chicago, IL 60618
773-583-7884
www.haymarketbooks.org

ISBN: 978-1-60846-689-4

Trade distribution:
In the US, Consortium Book Sales, www.cbsd.com
In Canada, Publishers Group Canada, www.pgcbooks.ca
In the UK, Turnaround Publisher Services, www.turnaround-uk.com
In all other countries, Ingram Publisher Services International,
intlsales@perseusbooks.com

Cover design by Jamie Kerry of Belle Étoile Studios and Ragina Johnson.

This book was published with the generous support of Lannan Foundation
and the Wallace Action Fund.

Printed in Canada by union labor.

10 9 8 7 6 5 4 3 2 1

Library of Congress Cataloging-in-Publication data is available.

To all the 'beautiful and ineffectual utopians and hissing factionalists' who make life on the revolutionary left exciting, challenging, and rewarding.

∴

Contents

Acknowledgements

Permission to republish material that first appeared elsewhere is gratefully acknowledged. I am indebted to the scholarly journals *Labour/Le Travail*, formerly known as *Labour/Le Travailleur*, *Histoire Sociale/Social History*, *The Review of Radical Political Economics*, *Osgoode Hall Law Journal*, *International Review of Social History*, *Online Journal of the Canadian Historical Association*, *Left History*, *Historical Materialism*, *American Communist History*; to the left-wing publications *Against the Current* and *Monthly Review*; and to the publishers McGill-Queen's University Press, Oxford University Press, Verso, Academic Press, Merlin Press, Escuela Nacional de Antopolígia e Historia, Jaca Book, and Manchester University Press. In the order in which they appear in this volume of *Marxism and Historical Practice* specific permissions to reprint are as follows:

Palmer, Bryan D. 1993, 'Critical Theory, Historical Materialism, and the Ostensible End of Marxism: The Poverty of Theory Revisited', *International Review of Social History*, 38 (August), Part II, 133–62.

———— 2006, 'Historical Materialism and the Writing of Canadian History: A Dialectical View', *Online Journal of the Canadian Historical Association*, New Series, 17, 33–60.

———— 2010, 'Canada', in *Histories of Labour: National and International Perspectives*, edited by Joan Allen, Alan Campbell and John McIlroy, Pontypool, Wales: Merlin Press, 196–230. Published here under the title 'Writing about Canadian Workers: A Historiographic Overview'.

———— 1997, 'Night in the Capitalist, Cold War City: Noir and the Cultural Politics of Darkness', *Left History*, 5, 57–76.

———— 2003, 'The Hands that Built America: A Class-Politics Appreciation of Martin Scorcese's *The Gangs of New York*', *Historical Materialism*, 11, 317–45.

———— 2013, 'A Life Beyond Imagination: The Artist Formerly, and Again, Known as Rodriguez', *Against the Current*, 162, 31–35, 44. Published here in an adapted form as 'Sugar Man's Sweet Kiss: The Artist Formerly, and Now Again, Known as Rodriguez'.

———— 2003, 'Rethinking the Historiography of United States Communism', *American Communist History*, 2, 139–73.

———— 1999, 'Before Braverman: Harry Frankel and the American Workers' Movement', *Monthly Review*, 50, 33–46.

———— 2010, 'The Personal, the Political, and Permanent Revolution: Ernest Mandel and the Conflicted Legacies of Trotskyism', *International Review of Social History*, 55, 117–32.

———— 2006, 'Marxismo Metropolitano y Amplitud Analitca en la historia de Hobsbawm', in *Los Historiadores y La Historia para el Sigo XXI: Homenaje a Eric J. Hobs-bawm*, edited by Gumersindo Vera Hernandez and José Patoja, Mexico City: Escuela Nacional de Antropolígia e Historia, 145–58. Published here under the title 'Hobs-bawm's History: Metropolitan Marxism and Analytic Breadth'.

————— 2006, 'Las politicas de Hobsbawm: se ha detnindo la marcha hacia adelante del Frente Popular', in *Los Historioadores y La Historia para el Sigo XXI: Homenaje a Eric J. Hobsbawm*, edited by Gumersindo Vera Hernandez and José Patoja, Mexico City: Escuela Nacional de Antropolíga e Historia, 93–104. Published here under the title 'Hobsbawm's Politics: The Forward March of the Popular Front Halted'.

————— 2013, 'James Patrick Cannon: Revolutionary Continuity and Class Struggle Politics in the United States, 1890–1974', originally published in Italian in *The Other Twentieth Century: Heretical Communism and Critical Thinking*, edited by Michele de Gregorio, Milan: Jaca Book.

————— 2013, 'Paradox and the Thompson "School of Awkwardness"', in *E.P. Thompson and English Radicalism*, edited by Roger Fieldhouse and Richard Taylor, Manchester: Manchester University Press, 205–28.

Introduction

I am not sure what makes some people historians. But I have concluded that there are those predisposed to think historically and inclined to take an interest in the past. It is, often, a matter of environment and the stimulations of family and surroundings. Readings are encouraged and things old are layered in meanings, invested with intrinsic value rather than calculated in terms of market considerations.[1]

With others this attraction to history can seem almost *sui generis*. Brought up in a house without books, by parents whose educations were either truncated by dropping out of high school or being streamed into practical, gendered employment and living in what could have been considered a suburban retreat from any traditions that connected the present and its antecedents, my privileging of the historical was not so much learned as it was resourced, held as a kind of antidote against what I came instinctually to regard as a barren, philistine upbringing. So I suppose I was *always* a historian, at least in terms of basic inclinations.

But what *kind* of historian one becomes is what really matters. This has less to do with instincts and much more to do with industry. Yet there is also more than a bit of the accidental in this production of orientation. This labour of becoming is inevitably about time, place and happenings of various kinds, of influences in part serendipitous. The context in which sensibilities are forged, paths started down and tendencies taken up is always, in some ways, fortuitous. And then possibilities harden into outcomes.[2] The consequences of consequences lead us to where we end up, a process in which we have made our personal histories, but never exactly and only as we might have chosen – if choice was ever a simple, clear-cut option. It is all reminiscent of a passage from William Morris's *A Dream of John Ball* (1888):

> [M]en fight and lose the battle, and the thing that they fought for comes about in spite of their defeat, and when it comes turns out not to be what they meant, and other men have to fight for what they meant under another name.[3]

---

1 Stedman Jones 2001.

2 See the exchange on 'deciding to be a historian' between Michael Merrill and E.P. Thompson in Abelove et al., 1983, p. 13.

3 Quoted in E.P. Thompson 1976a, p. 722.

What is crucial in this Morris quote is not just the chance outcome that results from a series of decisions and actions, but the importance of conflict, of a clash of thought, a struggle of positions.

Or so it has been with me. My childhood interest in history came of a certain age in the 1960s, although I was still too young to consider becoming a historian. Then, after largely missing the turmoil of 1968 – I was barely 17 at the time and lived in a medium-sized Canadian city not galvanised by youthful rebellion – I was drawn to the radicalism of the New Left, and from there into a variety of causes and a course of reading. My apprenticeship in Marxist history commenced in the late 1960s and intensified in the 1970s, originating in non-academic encounters with theories and texts as well as mobilisations and movements. All of this unfolded as I dropped out of university in Canada after only one year, and lived for a time in the heady atmosphere of New York City. There I tested the waters of dissidence, as what had once been the headline-catching Students for a Democratic Society imploded. Crashing lecture halls at the New School (where I was not officially enrolled and was eventually asked politely to leave by Robert L. Heilbroner, whose chapter on Marx in *The Worldly Philosophers* from 1953 I considered scandalous), immersed in late-night study and affinity groups, arguing with all manner of leftists in a radical educational experiment known as Alternate U (where Murray Bookchin and Revolutionary Youth Movement II leaders debated the nature and meaning of the Russian Revolution and American slavery), struggling unsuccessfully to read Hegel and spending a part of every day either working in or frequenting bookstores, was more of an education than I would later receive in any formal university setting. There were leaflets to prepare, protests to organise and demonstrations to attend. But there was always time to pore over books. I first read historians such as Moshe Lewin, W.E.B. Du Bois, E.P. Thompson, C.L.R. James and Eugene Genovese, not to mention Marx, Engels, Lenin, Mao, Stalin, Gramsci, Luxemburg and Trotsky, as well as writers like Kate Millett, Shulamith Firestone and Malcolm X, in the intellectually and politically intoxicating atmosphere of the aftermath of May '68. Inebriated discussions often broke out in dug-out cellar bars of the East Village, now almost all gone, such as the Frog Pond; to this day I remember fiercely contested clashes in which anarchism, Maoism and Trotskyism were argued through, often with allusions to historical events. My 'classrooms' had no formally credentialed professors and involved no grades; positions seldom involved 'sucking up' to any credentialed authority.

When, after an exhilarating year of this, I decided to return to my hometown of London, Ontario, and complete the undergraduate degree I had abandoned with my departure for New York, sitting in staid lectures, prodding through the syllabus and writing term papers seemed rather anti-climactic. Fast-tracking myself through it all, I paused to participate in a summer student works project on the labour history of London, then struck out for the State University of New York at Binghamton, enrolling in a master's and then a PhD programme. I was soon part of a loose network of graduate students affiliated with the history department or the Braudel Center, amongst whom Art Hirsch, Peter Friedlander and Phil McMichael were my best friends. We were all Marxists then![4]

That Marxism, however, was worn in scholarly settings with a genuine humility. I know that I was no wallflower in graduate seminars, and the baptism of fire that I had received in movement discussions where forceful argument was valued rather than questioned made me partial to polemic, always striving for strong stands. But I was nonetheless reluctant to decisively declare myself a Marxist. I felt I had a lot to learn and needed to earn the right to proclaim myself a Marxist historian. It was not until sometime in the early 1980s that I began to associate myself publicly in published work with Marxism. At that point, after roughly 15 years of growing familiarity with Marxism, I was apparently willing to acknowledge that my apprenticeship had come to its close and could actually name myself politically.

Far easier was considering oneself a working-class or labour historian. The vocation of studying the history of class formation and detailing the nature of class struggle was, in fact, embedded in the guild that I had joined by virtue of embarking on graduate studies. And with the large numbers of nascent working-class historians who had flocked to seminars run by professors like David Montgomery, Herbert G. Gutman and my supervisor Melvyn Dubofsky, it was easy to situate yourself in the mid-1970s within a cohort for whom study of workers defined a significant slice of the entirety of the past, that illusory totality we then aspired to explore and explicate. As social historians of labour, those of us doing working-class history considered ourselves to be moving from a privileged part of social history into the history of society.[5]

The essays that appear in these two volumes are a reflection of the parallel processes of becoming a Marxist *and* becoming a working-class historian. In my case, these makings were reciprocal endeavours. They were not bifurcated into the theoretical and the empirical but were always linked, as the process of conceptualisation wrestled with the discoveries of the archives or the exploration of bodies of evidence that could be gleaned from newspapers, government reports or statistical series. If my area of inquiry focussed on the tensions gen-

---

4   For a brief autobiographical statement, see B. Palmer 2005.
5   Hobsbawm 1971a.

erated around capitalist class formation, this is not to say that I necessarily considered labour to be a subject studied always in the same way and regarded from the same vantage point. To be sure, my approach was, I think, always that of the historical materialist, but how and in what ways historical materialism addressed class formation and class struggle necessarily exhibited subtle shifts over time. Again, this is precisely because the theoretical informed the empirical – not only in terms of what was researched and why, but how evidence was examined, what questions were asked of it and why it was interpreted in specific ways. Conceptual priorities, while exhibiting basic continuities, also experienced change according to the intellectual and political climate of the moment. *Marxism and Historical Practice*, then, is about doing history in ways informed by Marxism. This project has always been about making histories in 'circumstances directly encountered, given and transmitted from the past'.[6] All of the writing republished here was very much influenced by the particular context in which each piece was written. Discrete circumstances of political economy, social struggle, the politics of power and its exercise and the nature and possibilities of dissent all had their impact.

So too did the shifting contours of historiography, especially the changing accent placed on aspects of class formation in writing on the past. It is for this reason that these volumes are arranged thematically, bringing together articles, contributions to edited collections, components of particular books that I now offer as free-standing chapters and review essays – all of which are aligned in specific sections that might bring together writing concentrated within a few years or spread over as much as three decades of time. The themes explored in particular sections of these volumes, as well as the volumes themselves, convey both common concerns and divergences in perspective and orientation. In specific short introductions to the designated parts of each volume, all of which contain from two to four essays, I locate briefly the impetus behind particular writings.

If it is imperative to recognise the extent to which all of the writing in these two volumes emerged at the interface of Marxism or historical materialism as a particular animating theoretical framework and the place of class within both history and historiography, event and analysis, it should also be noted that the two volumes each privilege a particular side of this duality. Volume I draws together interpretive essays on class formation and class struggle; the components of various sections address particularities of working-class experience in Canada and United States in the 19th and 20th centuries. That volume accents

---

6   Marx 1968, p. 97.

the historical practice of Marxism. Volume II, in contrast, is composed of essays that are meant to highlight Marxism's insights as they can be brought to bear on how history is written, presented visually and embodied in the lives and writings of specific movements and individuals. While the focus is once more on Canada and the United States, the reach of particular interventions and appreciations in Volume II extends also to Europe and the United Kingdom.

The developing world is, admittedly, an understated presence in these volumes. Such original research as I have done has been conducted overwhelmingly in English-language sources. This is, I acknowledge freely and with a large sense of limitation, inhibiting. That said, I have been the beneficiary of translations of theoretical work and rich historical studies, and in both *Descent into Discourse: The Reification of Language and the Writing of Social History* (1990) and *Cultures of Darkness: Night Travels in the Histories of Transgression* (2000), my concerns in theory and in historical interpretation have been anything but narrow. Both works, as well as other writings on historiography such as *E.P. Thompson: Objections and Oppositions* (1994), have appeared in Korean, Greek, Portuguese and Spanish editions, with articles translated into Chinese, Italian and other languages. Nothing has pleased me more than exchanges across borders, languages and cultures with historical materialists engaged in the critical scrutiny of the past and active involvement in the present, all of us drawn to the different ways in which analysis and activity animated by Marxism can bridge divides and build new ways of seeing human possibility realised.

A proper accounting of the debts incurred over the course of more than three decades of historical writing is not possible. The colleagues, friends, students and comrades who have shared with me a sensibility of the politics of our times, from the late 1960s to the present, are too numerous to mention, and the risk of leaving unacknowledged a particular individual of importance too great, for me to attempt anything approximating adequate acknowledgements. I have also benefitted enormously from the institutional support of the universities with which I have been affiliated in Canada – Queen's, McGill, Simon Fraser and Trent – all of which provided hospitable climates for writing and reflection. The journal *Labour/Le Travail*, in which the lead article in the first issue of 1976 was one of my earlier publications, has been a mainstay of my intellectual life for the better part of four decades, 30 years of which I have spent as either book review editor or editor, often working closely with Gregory S. Kealey, whose initiative was responsible for bringing *LLT* into being. Since 2000 I have the Canada Research Chairs programme to thank for supporting my research, which has been located within the Canadian Studies Department at Trent University. Two women in my life, my daughter Beth and my partner Joan, each in their different ways, are the stars that light my dark nights and the suns that bring new meanings and hopes every morning.

This collection of essays owes a great deal to two of the mainstays of the *Historical Materialism* project, Peter Thomas and Sebastian Budgen. The latter, with his indefatigable attentiveness to email lists, latched on to a seemingly inconsequential response to an obscure posting seeking suggestions of what might be read on class formation in the United States of the 19th century. Forwarding me an email in which it was suggested that my 1983 essay 'Social Formation and Class Formation in 19th-Century North America' remained a good guide to a particular way of approaching the problem, Sebastian wrote, economically, 'Perhaps time for a collection of your essays'. What resulted was anything but economical, and I must thank Sean Carleton and Julia Smith, two doctoral candidates at Trent University's Frost Centre for Canadian Studies and Indigenous Studies, for their laborious efforts in reformatting a disparate collection of writings for re-publication. I benefitted greatly from the help and diligent editorial advice of an extremely able trio of Historical Materialism Book Series mainstays: David Broder, Danny Hayward and Sarah Grey. The essays that follow were improved by their interventions, although I alone bear responsibility for their contents. I am indebted to Martin Schoots-McAlpine for preparing the index.

These volumes of essays constitute something of an imperfect and faint representation of how I have tried to depict the legacies of working-class struggle and the rich reservoir of Marxist understandings that I consider timeless in its relevance. T.S. Eliot's 'The Hollow Men' (1925) seems an appropriate note leading in to what follows:

> Between the idea
>   And the reality
>   Between the motion
>   And the act
>   Falls the shadow.[7]

As a shadow crossing the chasm separating theory and practice, mobilisation and historical activity, the essays collected here struggle, inevitably somewhat incompletely, to link Marxism and historical practice, a conception of the past with an appreciation of the necessity of changing our present and realising a better future. They can, at this point, fall where they may.

---

7   Eliot 1971, p. 58.

PART 1

Theoretical and Historiographic Interventions

∴

Introduction to Part 1

Materialist social histories abounded in the 1970s, which is not to suggest that all of this work was Marxist. That said, cavalier dismissal of Marxism within social-history circles (of the kind that has come, sadly, to be all too common) was distinctly out of fashion. There was a sense that Marxism and historical practice were certainly congruent undertakings. In the 1980s, however, there was a change in this climate of tolerance, even possibly acceptance and acknowledgement of Marxism's contribution to the production of invaluable materialist accounts of the past. Specific factors contributed to the changing relationship of Marxism and historical practice, with the fortunes of historical materialism in definite decline.

The generalised climate of radicalism associated with the 1960s, through which many historians apprenticing in Marxism of one kind or another passed throughout the early to mid-1970s, gave way to an entirely different political sensibility. In the political economies and cultural cauldrons of the advanced capitalist West, the revival of class struggle and the promise of socialist possibility that had dawned in youthful mobilisations of workplace militancy and street protests waned. Nineteen sixty-eight and its slogans of defiance gave way, by 1978 and certainly by 1988, to a less bellicose and challenging context. Capitalism's apparent victories trumped the momentum of left-wing, class-based, alternative-ordered challenge.

These triumphs registered not only over capitalism's global adversary, Soviet communism, but also over its domestic critics. The 1980s dawned with the Solidarność upheaval in Poland, which prefigured the eventual implosion of the Soviet Union and its hegemonic hold over the Iron Curtain 'socialism' of Eastern and Central Europe. In the United States and the United Kingdom, the fortunes of class war, which showed signs of significant revival in the late 1960s and early to mid-1970s, witnessed a turning of the tide. Miners' strikes in 1972 and 1974 contributed, along with shop-steward militancy in the auto sector, to the collapse of the Tory government of Edward Heath, creating the possibility of the Labour Party coming to power under the admittedly tepid social-democratic leadership of Harold Wilson. Since the mid-1960s young workers in the Fordist vanguard of American production in auto plants in Lordstown, Ohio, and Detroit, Michigan, had been charting a course of resistance fed by alienation and overt class anger. But the 1980s opened in the United States with Ronald Reagan's declaration of war against the labour movement, decisively sounded in his 1981 defeat of the Professional Air Traffic Controllers Organization, and the blue-collar blues and Leagues of Revolutionary Black Workers that had seemed pivotally important in the late 1960s and early 1970s were all-too-distant memories. Reagan's British equivalent, Margaret Thatcher, was not about to repeat Heath's dance of death with the miners: she battled this seemingly archaic class enemy into the ground of the barren coal fields in a 1984 strike that proved to be the colliers' last stand.

As this class war waged from above took its toll, the entire political spectrum shifted to the right. The drive to a new ideological consensus, gathering momentum as a revanchist conservatism, rebranded itself 'neoliberalism'; components of it were disciplining and domesticating the unions, marginalising the left, and proclaiming a final and unambiguous routing of what passed for communism. This was more easily done than at any previous time in history, because the contradictory internal dynamic of 'actually existing socialism' was tending towards implosion. This is precisely what happened in the Soviet sphere, when the political caste that stood astride the social order opted to try to 'reform' the ossified structures of production *and* governance simultaneously, unleashing too many demons for even the rigid Stalinist apparatus to contain. The result was an unpredictably precipitous implosion of the old order and a chaotic descent into capitalist barbarism, in which new hordes of profit seekers pillaged the socialised property forms of what had once contained some semblances of a workers' state. In the ensuing dismantling of popular protections, the primitive accumulation of new class formations took on the trappings of a disorderly frontier of acquisitive individualism. Socialism seemed a historical impossibility. In China, the market's incursions into the rigidities of a mechanically planned economy that allowed no leeway for workers' control were more managed and less rapacious because the state refused to concede democratisation of politics. It retained its capacity to suppress dissent and to cultivate or coerce conformity. As this reached its violent apex with the 1989 suppression of student protests in Tiananmen Square, Stalinism's capacity to present itself as progressive took yet another nose dive.

For many New Left-influenced historians, reared on the 1960s belief that the old left was dying and that revolutionary possibility could be rekindled in new mobilisations and a politics of participatory democracy, Marxism could not survive this 1980s onslaught. Too much blood had now passed under the bridge that supposedly connected workers, as Marx's gravediggers of capitalism, and their past struggles to a better future.

Looking back on the becalmed protest possibilities of the 1960s, the jaded realities of the 1970s, and the hard defeats of the 1980s, a generation of social historians whose original interests lay in exploring the histories and possibilities of class and its struggles retreated politically. They were increasingly drawn to new ways of seeing the world. Through aging eyes, these interpretive innovations looked less and less likely to be conceived of and formulated in old categories of analysis, like class, that had ostensibly produced so little in the way of tangible successes. Political and intellectual convictions changed with the trend of contemporary developments; old insights weakened.

Into this political breach marched a proselytising intellectual current, one that proclaimed the end of all master narratives, a refusal of all paradigms centred in the determinative influence of specific categories of analysis, and a suspicion of claims that power could be located in particular locales, rather than being discursively dispersed. As conservative critics proclaimed that the fall of the Soviet Union constituted 'the end of history', a termination of the contest between capitalism and communism, with the former triumphant,[1] a *nouvelle vague* of critical theory declared a similar end of history by insisting that everything thought to have been known about the past needed to be jettisoned in recognition that the insights of the post-modern moment questioned all past understandings.[2] 'All that is solid melts into air', Marx and Engels had written in 1848.[3] For historical materialists, the 1980s and 1990s reflected how destabilisation in the realm of political economy could produce a reconfigured intellectual climate, one in which what had long been considered gains in knowledge were suddenly challenged and interrogated to the point of undermining the validity of rational thought itself.

Marxists grasped, as Trotsky had stressed in 1940, that 'those who cannot defend old positions will never conquer new ones'.[4] They responded to the interpretive trajectory of the times by refusing, in particular, the specific analytic assault on class as a critically important basis on which societies, past and present, were ordered, just as they resisted the more generalised attempt to repudiate the Enlightenment project of rational thought which the worst postmodernists advocated.[5] I lent my voice to this 'defence of history' and 'Marxist metanarrative' in *Descent into Discourse: The Reification of Language and the Writing of Social History*, as well as in articles in the *Socialist Register* and elsewhere.[6] Much of this writing was subsequently translated into Spanish, Korean, and other languages.[7] The lead article in this volume, 'Critical Theory, Historical

---

1   See, for interest, Fukuyama 1989.
2   For a selection of relevant statements that touch on many of the influential texts of the 1980s and 1990s, see Jenkins 1997.
3   Marx and Engels 1968, p. 38.
4   Trotsky 1973, p. 178.
5   See, among other important statements, Wood 1986 and Wood and Foster 1997.
6   B. Palmer 1990a; 1990b; 1993a; 1993b; 1993c; 1997.
7   B. Palmer 1994a; 2004.

Materialism, and the Ostensible End of Marxism: The Poverty of Theory Revisited', which originally appeared in the *International Review of Social History*, was thus one of many statements that addressed the post-modern challenge to Marxism and historical practice.

Two later historiographic interventions step slightly outside of this context to attempt overviews of historical materialism, the writing of Canadian history, and writing on Canadian workers. But both of these essays return, inevitably, to ways in which Marxism and historical practice can be brought together, seeing in writing on the past a contribution, whatever its limitations, to envisioning and creating a different present and a better future.

CHAPTER 1

Critical Theory, Historical Materialism and the Ostensible End of Marxism: The Poverty of Theory Revisited*

It is now a decade and one-half since Edward Thompson penned *The Poverty of Theory: or an Orrery of Errors*, and ten times as many years have passed since the publication of Marx's *The Poverty of Philosophy*.[1] Whatever one may think about the advances in *knowledge* associated with historical materialism and Marxism, particularly in terms of the practice of historical writing, there is no denying that this sesquicentennial has been a problematic period in the making of communist society; the last 15 years, moreover, are associated with the bleak end of socialism and the passing of Marxism as an intellectual force.

Indeed, it is a curious conjuncture of our times that the much-proclaimed end of Marxism is somehow related to the end of history as we know it. Who would have thought that history, both as an unfolding process and a set of interpretive writings, would come to an end when Marxism as a ruling ideology in what has passed for 'socialist' political economies crumbled and lost its appeal to many academics? No Marxist ever accorded his or her world view the apparent force or influence – in theory or practice – that this current coupled understanding of the early 1990s end of Marxism/history suggests.[2]

For those who revel in the discursive identities and endlessly fluctuating subjectivities of post-structuralism as theory and post-modernism as condition, the instabilities of the current moment – analytical and political – are absolute advantages, realities in an age that refuses acknowledgement of 'the real', substance to be celebrated and championed in times when resistance has been,

---

* 'Critical Theory, Historical Materialism, and the Ostensible End of Marxism: The Poverty of Theory Revisited', *International Review of Social History*, 38 (August 1993), Part II, 133–62.

1 E.P. Thompson 1978c; Marx n.d.

2 Associated with the much-publicised 1989 pronouncement of Francis Fukuyama that 'What we may be witnessing is not just the end of the Cold War, or the passing of a particular period of post-war history, but the end of history as such', this position has gained much credence. For a journalistic statement see Richard Bernstein, 'Judging "Post-History", the End to All Theories', *New York Times*, 27 August 1989. Responses from the Marxist left include the essays in Miliband and Panitch 1990.

thankfully, replaced by play and pun. To be a Marxist in these times is obviously neither easy nor pleasant, but it does offer certain securities. Amongst the most significant, perhaps, is the insight that what we are witnessing now, however seemingly novel and debilitating, has parallels and, perhaps, direct precedent in past struggles over questions of theory and interpretation, battles that were seldom divorced from that touchstone of the human condition, history.[3] 'With man we enter *history*', proclaimed Engels.[4]

And yet if we are to appreciate current intellectual trends, it is apparent that history is precisely what is not being 'entered'. This essay takes as its central concern the extent to which a rather uncritical adoption of what has come to be known as critical theory has resulted in the wholesale jettisoning of historical materialist assumptions and understandings, to the detriment of historical sensitivities and the denigration of the actual experience of historically situated men, women, and children. To make this claim is not to suggest that there can be no engagement with this critical theory and that it has nothing to tell us. Rather, this ground of refusal can be claimed for Marxism and historical materialism precisely because the value of critical theory can be assimilated, enriching historical investigation and interpretation, but only if the cavalierly unthinking and patently ideological anti-Marxism so pervasive amongst former leftists in the 1990s is identified and rejected for what it is: the opportunism and apostasy of a particular political climate.[5]

This essay proceeds in particular directions. First, it notes briefly the extent to which post-structuralism and post-modernism have *generally* espoused a particular hostility to historical materialism[6] and, in identifying this hostility, it provides indications of what the theoretical literature in these areas espouses and contributes to a potentially analytic historiography. In this brief definitional and descriptive preface there will be occasion to comment on the nature of the relationship of post-structuralism/post-modernism and Marxism, especially the validity and quality of much of critical theory's dismissal of historical materialism. Second, contemporary developments in historiography related to the critical theory of the 1980s and 1990s will be addressed and a critique of arguments dismissive of historical materialism elaborated. An attempt will be

---

3 Note, for instance, the argument in Wood 1986.
4 Engels 1968, p. 353.
5 Again, this has historical parallels. See E.P. Thompson 1978c, pp. 1–34; 1969, pp. 149–81. Note as well Geras 1990, p. 62.
6 Fredric Jameson notes, 'One's occasional feeling that, for poststructuralism, all enemies are on the left, and that the principal target always turns out to be this or that form of *historical* thinking' (Jameson 1991, p. 217).

made to explore the contemporary relevancy of Marxist historical analysis and its capacity actually to ground the often important insights of critical theory in materially embedded social relations and experiences of struggle and subordination, power and resistance, accumulation and accommodation. Third, and finally, the essay closes with an explanation of the ironies and potency of an anti-Marxist critical theory in the context of the 1990s.

Ideology and Epoch

Ideology, as Terry Eagleton has recently reminded us, is a complex term with an even more complicated historical evolution.[7] It is also rather suspect in most intellectual circles at the moment, a process of denigration that Eagleton notes is not unrelated to the current fashion of post-structuralist thought and the contemporary assumptions and trends of post-modernity as a peculiarly distinct *fin-de-siècle*. It is nevertheless useful, both in terms of situating post-structuralism and post-modernism as particular meanings in the present of the 1990s and in locating them historically, to adopt a conception of ideology drawn from those who both founded historical materialism and inaugurated our modern understanding of ideology as a central category in the linked projects of interpreting *and* changing the world.

At the risk of sliding over many qualifications and eliding not a few problematic writings, Marx and Engels nevertheless developed an appreciation of ideology as a material constraint on the possibility of revolution. As in much of the elaboration of the concepts of historical materialism, their method was polemical, striking out at what was inadequate and *ideological* in the philosophical conventions of their time. Against the idealised advances of Enlightenment thought (which marked a turning point away from blind obedience to superstition, illusion, and divine authority), Marx and Engels propounded a radicalised extension of Enlightenment reason, insisting not on the liberatory potential of de-historicised ideas and abstractions, but rather on the powerful determination of profane social activity. In *The German Ideology* Marx and Engels assailed as ideological the idealism that refused acknowledgement of the primacy of actual humanity, the determining power of social relations over the consciousness of those relations.[8] For Marx and Engels, then, ideology was originally and fundamentally the construction of false consciousness, the obscuring of

---

7   Eagleton 1991.
8   Marx and Engels 1947, pp. 6–7, 14–15.

the primacy of social practice, and the reification of ideas and categories as ruling forces in history. Much muddled in later years, as the term came to be associated with varied meanings associated with different movements and personalities of revolutionary opposition, ideology's tangled history as a concept parallels the history of Marxism: relatively coherent throughout the years of the Second International, it fragments in the aftermath of World War I.[9]

It is the fundamental premise of this essay that post-structuralism is the ideology of a particular historical epoch now associated with post-modernity. Alex Callinicos has recently argued, with considerable conviction and force, that post-modernity does not exist as some sharp and fundamental break from 'the modern', a scepticism also at the core of Marshall Berman's exploration of the experience of modernity.[10] They may be right, although for the purposes of this essay the matter is somewhat beside the point. It is perfectly plausible to accept that the late 20th century has witnessed a series of shifts in the cultural arena, even perhaps in the realm of political economy, without, of course, seeing this as a fundamental transformation of the mode of production. Many sites of 'representation' and related fields of 'design', by which the spatial and cultural aspects of our lives are ordered through the reconstruction of modernism's locale, the urban landscape, can be scrutinised in ways that suggest recent change in literary genres, art and architecture, cinema and the technology of cultural diffusion, the case of video being undoubtedly the most dramatic. I see no necessity to deny that all of this means something culturally and is related to material structural transformation, most markedly the rise and fall of what some social theorists designate a Fordist regime of capitalist accumulation.[11] Contra Callinicos (who does strike some telling blows) are the resolutely historicised and materialist recent texts of Fredric Jameson and David Harvey. Taken together, Jameson's *Postmodernism, or, the Cultural Logic of Late Capitalism* and Harvey's *The Condition of Postmodernity: An Enquiry into the Origin of Cultural Change* present a complementary account of the remaking of a capitalist cultural order in the late 20th century. But unlike most post-modernists, these Marxists refuse to see this restructuring of fundamental features of the non-biological reproductive realm as a remaking of the capitalist mode of production. Post-modernity, for Jameson and Harvey, whatever differences in emphasis they choose to accentuate, is an epoch of *capitalism*, as fundamentally continuous with the exploitation and accumulation of earlier

9   For an overly brief statement see the entry on 'ideology' in Bottomore 1983, pp. 219–23.
10   Callinicos 1990; Berman 1982.
11   See, among other writings, Mike Davis 1986.

times as it is discontinuous in its forms of representational expression.[12] And, like the Los Angeles of Mike Davis's *City of Quartz*, this post-modernity as capitalist condition is made not outside of history, but inside its relations of power and challenge, struggle and subordination.[13]

What a Marxist reading of post-modernism rejects, then, is not the *condition* of contemporary cultural life, which, admittedly, is open to many contending historical materialist readings, one of which might well lay stress on the cultural movement into post-modernity. Rather, Marxism rejects the *ideological* project of rationalising and legitimating this post-modern order as something above and beyond the social relations of a capitalist political economy. In the words of the American advocate of post-structuralism Mark Poster, this notion of post-modernism is not unrelated to the dismissal of Marxism:

> In the first half of the twentieth century marxist theory suffered three set-backs: (1) the establishment of bureaucratic socialism in Eastern Europe; (2) the rise of fascism in Central Europe; and (3) the birth of the 'culture industry' in Western Europe and the United States. These massive phenomena reshuffled the dialectical deck of cards. No longer could it be said that the working class is the standard-bearer of freedom, the living negation of domination, the progressive side in the contemporary class struggles that would surely end in a utopian community.

For post-structuralists such as Poster these 'truths' (which, it must be pointed out, are eminently explainable through Marxist theory and have not shaken Marxism as a project of understanding) are only reinforced by even more recent events and developments, amongst them the decolonisation and feminist movements and the rise of an ostensible information order.[14]

The making of post-structuralism as an ideological reaction to the failures of what was once a Stalinised, actually existing, socialism is thus fairly clear. As the working class is arbitrarily and conceptually displaced as the agent of social transformation, a seemingly unassailable dismissal following logically from the degeneration of the first workers' state, Marxism is overtaken by both its own political failures and the arrival of new social forces (the feminist and decolonisation movements, to which could be added other sectors: peace, ecology, Aboriginal, and 'national' rights) and social formations, none of which

---

12   Jameson 1991; Harvey 1989. For comment on these texts see B. Palmer 1993.
13   Mike Davis 1992.
14   Poster 1989, pp. 1–3.

are actually situated in anything approximating an elementary relationship to *actually existing capitalism*. In the process, any sense of objective 'reality' and its social relations is lost in the swirl of subjectivity that forces a retreat from class and an embrace of almost any and all other 'identities', which are understood as expansive, discursive, and positively plural. It is the contention of this chapter that post-structuralism is thus a project of mystification and obfuscation particularly attuned to the often submerged, occasionally explicit, politics of the moment; post-structuralism as theory is to post-modernity as epoch what idealism as philosophy was to the Enlightenment. This does not mean that it contains no insights or potential, only that left to its own ultimatist trajectory it will inevitably collapse into ideology.

What is post-structuralism? What is this new critical theory? This is a large question, answering which demands an understanding of much of the intellectual history of the last century.[15] But, bluntly put, post-structuralism emerged out of the theoretical implosions associated with Parisian intellectual life in the 1960s, most particularly 1968. By that date a French theoretical turn had concentrated the social anthropology of Claude Lévi-Strauss, Lacanian psychoanalysis and a textually focussed Althusserian Marxism in a paradigm known as structuralism. What united these components of the French theoretical turn was a deep commitment to a scientific explication of the structural systems of human existence. In the cases of Lévi-Strauss and Lacan, interpretation of these structural systems was explicitly scaffolded on insistence that language was the foundation of all human activity, which was therefore understandable only in terms of the laws of linguistics as propounded by Saussure. From kinship systems to the unconscious, structuralism proclaimed a linguistic apprehension of reality. 'All the anthropologist can do is say to his colleagues in other branches of study that the real question is the question of language', claimed Lévi-Strauss. 'If you solve the problem of the nature and origin of language, we can explain the rest: what culture is, and how it made its appearance; what art is and what technological skills, law, philosophy and religion are'.[16] For his part, Lacan 'Saussurianised' psychoanalysis, declaring that 'the unconscious is the discourse of the other ... the symptom resolves itself entirely in a Language analysis, because the symptom itself is structured like a Language, because the symptom is a Language from which the Word must be liberated'.[17] This linguistic scientism

---

15   I have attempted to offer a brief overview of some of the salient intellectual developments in B. Palmer 1990a, pp. 3–47.

16   Charbonnier 1973, pp. 154–5.

17   See, for instance, Lacan 1968, especially pp. 7–8, 27, 32.

scorched Parisian Marxism in the 1960s, culminating in what Thompson and Norman Geras dubbed 'the final idealism' of Althusser.[18] In the Althusserian reading of ideology 'the only interests at work in the development of knowledge are interests internal to knowledge'.[19]

With the Parisian events of 1968 a curtain descended on the analytic stage of structuralism. Its players experienced a certain banishment. With them went various projects – the Lévi-Straussian imposition of classifications and order, the Lacanian stress on the historicised subject, the Althusserian insistence on ideology's rootedness in class *interests* – although the swept stage, now occupied by post-structuralism, remained littered with the residue of structuralism, most particularly language as the site of meaning, power and resistance. Post-structuralism was thus born of structuralism's demise. It carried a part of structuralism's legacy, most acutely in terms of the stress on language, but it refused many of structuralism's assumptions and purposes. In the writings of Michel Foucault, Jacques Derrida, Jean Baudrillard, Gilles Deleuze and Jean-François Lyotard a re-evaluation of language and its meanings culminated in an intense interrogation of 'the real', a relentless exposure of the ways in which knowledge/reason masked domination, and a blunt rejection of any and all projects – emancipatory or otherwise – that sought to impose or locate centres of power or resistance. To the structuralist interpretive order was orchestrated, a conscious construction of the human mind. For the post-structuralist, however, such order/orchestration was to be deconstructed. In the words of Derrida, drawing upon Montaigne, the post-structuralist project was 'to interpret interpretations more than things', a constant unravelling of language that easily slipped into a positioning that 'everything became [or was] language'. History, for Derrida, has always been conceived as but 'a detour between two presences'.[20]

Post-structuralist thought is extremely difficult to pin down and define with clarity precisely because it celebrates discursiveness, difference, and destabilisations: it develops, not as a unified theory, but as constantly moving sets of concentric circles, connected at points of congruence, but capable of claiming new and uncharted interpretive territory at any moment. Like the architectural innovations of the post-modern age, post-structuralist theory is defiant of boundaries, resists notions of the analytic equivalent of a spatial centre in the

18   E.P. Thompson 1978c; Geras 1978, pp. 232–72.
19   Geras 1978, pp. 266, 268.
20   Note, especially, the important article 'Structure, Sign, and Play in the Discourse of the Human Sciences', in Derrida 1978, pp. 279–80, 291–2.

celebration of discursiveness and proliferating subjectivities and elevates the untidy to a virtue in a principled refusal of causality. Post-structuralism thus rationalises, legitimises and indeed sanctifies the post-modern condition. Its role as ideology secures the present; in the process it severs this present from the past and limits the possibilities of its future.

In its beginnings, one of post-structuralism's attractions was undoubtedly what Callinicos has referred to as its 'openness to the contingencies, the uncertainties, the instabilities of history'.[21] But ideologies, always dependent on their capacity to illuminate *a part* of experience at the same time as they mystify it, have a tendency to overreach themselves in moments of extremist overconfidence. Post-modernity, an age of excess if there ever was one, pushes ideology masquerading as theory in precisely this direction.

This point has recently been made with great force in Robert Young's insistence that history has never been anything but problematic inasmuch as it has always been an outcome of imperialistic plunder and the subordination of specific peoples of colour. Drawn to the 'post-colonialist' wing of critical theory, Young regards 'History' as but one expression of the Eurocentric premises of Western knowledge, a flattened exercise in shoring up 'the concept, the authority, and assumed primacy of, the category of "the West"'. He finds great solace in post-structuralism's questioning of history – which, abstractly, poses no problem for historical materialism, engaged as it is in the same project – and, more to the point, in post-modernism's achievements in precipitating us into a period of dissolution:

> Contrary, then, to some of its more overreaching definitions, postmodernism itself could be said to mark not just the cultural effects of a new stage of 'late' capitalism, but the sense of the loss of European history and culture as History and Culture, the loss of their unquestioned place at the centre of the world. We could say that if ... the centrality of 'Man' dissolved at the end of the eighteenth century as the 'Classical Order' gave way to 'History', today at the end of the twentieth century, as 'History' gives way to the 'Postmodern', we are witnessing the dissolution of the 'West'.[22]

The problem with this passage, and the book of which it is a part, is *not* that it alerts us to the need to scrutinise the making of history in ways sensitive to colonialism and its immense human costs. Rather, the difficulty with Young's

---

21   Callinicos 1988, p. 3.
22   Young 1990, esp. p. 20.

deconstruction of 'history' is its partial, amazingly self-selecting account of what constitutes the text of a highly differentiated historical practice: Toynbee, Trotsky and E.P. Thompson are at least alluded to once or twice (although, amazingly, Victor Kiernan merits nary a nod), but only in passing, and in ways that homogenise historiographies designated 'white'; C.L.R. James, Walter Rodney and Jean Chesneaux are absent from this account, allowing Young to bypass histories made at particular points of intersection in which First and Third Worlds meet and white, black, brown, and yellow connect.

To be sure, Young's post-structuralist assault on 'History' contains the kernel of challenge attractive to many who want to right the wrongs of a historiography rooted in racism. But it does so in ways that actually stifle the project of emancipation, suffocating it in an ideology of illusion. For the 'West', as the site of capitalism's late-20th-century power, is not, in any meaningful sense, in the throes of dissolution. Whatever the cultural reconstructions of post-modernity as a period of capitalist accumulation, 'History' has hardly been displaced. Mere months after the publication of Young's words, the carnage of the Gulf War exposed the Achilles heel of this kind of ideological trumpeting to the unequivocal and technologically superior blows of a 'West' as bellicose and militantly militaristic as other, ostensibly long-buried capitalist social formations. Small wonder that Marxists such as Ellen Meiksins Wood, attentive to the history of capitalism, have thrown up their hands in despair at what post-structuralism as ideology has accomplished in a few short years. 'At the very moment when the world is coming ever more within the totalizing logic of capitalism and its homogenizing impulses, at the very moment when we have the greatest need for conceptual tools to apprehend that global totality', protests Wood, 'the fashionable intellectual trends, from historical "revisionism" to cultural "postmodernism", are carving up the world into fragments of "difference".'[23]

My sympathies obviously lie with Wood, and with a host of other Marxist and feminist commentary that has grappled with the rise of post-structuralism, but that is almost universally ignored by those championing the new critical theory.[24] This is not to say that Marxists need ignore the extent to which post-structuralist thought forces our sometimes partially closed eyes open to specific problems that have received perhaps less than adequate attention within the many streams of a highly variegated Marxist tradition, including the very 'difference' Wood seems to castigate. The importance of subjectivity and the self, of identities not reducible to class, of representation and discourse, of

---

23   Wood 1991, p. 93.

24   Among many exemplary texts that could be cited see Dews 1987; Geras 1990; Soper 1990.

the problematic ambivalence of 'knowledge' canonised within particular social formations where thought and power are not unrelated – all of which post-structuralism alerts us to even as it over-determines analysis of this terrain off of its material referents – Marxists need not denigrate. Indeed, it is possible to actually explore specific texts of historical materialism to argue that attention to discourse, even to the point of materialising it and exploring its role in determination, is not necessarily foreign to the Marxist project.[25]

In Defence of Marxist Historiography

Moreover, neither structuralism nor post-structuralism, as theory, have produced actual histories of substance and sensitivity. Whatever the merits of the Richard Johnson-led Centre for Contemporary Cultural Studies forays into making histories, the fundamental gulf dividing this collective project of historiographic *critique* and the actual histories produced out of the insights of such critical readings is both wide and obvious.[26] Second, in the absence of 'theory writing better history', it is important to restate the fundamental contribution of the English Marxist historians – especially the 1950s, 1960s and 1970s writings of Hill, Hobsbawm, Hilton and Thompson – and to point to the impact of historical materialism in generating reconsiderations of such central matters as the transition from feudalism to capitalism.[27] Far from refusing theory, this historical writing is poised at the fruitful conjuncture of conceptualisation *and* empirical explorations of the admittedly problematic evidence generated out of the past, a practice that demands the integration of structure and agency, being and consciousness, past and present, subject and interpretation, and the self-reflective elaboration of the relationships amongst these linked processes.

There was a time when these *histories* were recognised as contributions to historiography and theory, as one proof of historical materialism's richness. Over the course of the 1980s, however, that contribution and richness have been repeatedly questioned. Post-structuralism as ideology in the guise of theory has been persistent in its challenge to Marxist historiography, but precisely because it rarely deals with actual historical texts, preferring instead a theoret-

---

25   As one example see B. Palmer 1990a, pp. 48–86.

26   See, for instance, Clarke, Critcher and Johnson 1979; Johnson et al. 1982.

27   For a brief introduction to the English Marxists see Kaye 1984; for a specific comment on American Marxist historiography, Anderson 1984.

ical gloss on what theorists have said of history, or rather glib characterisations of specific historiographic traditions, entirely in line with its own penchant for conceptual absolutism, this has not proven a particularly destructive critique. More destabilising have been those who have chosen to jump the ship of historical materialism. For if post-structuralist theorists have exhibited markedly little actual engagement with either the content of the past or its interpretation by practising historians, there have been those within the range of historical materialism's practice who have gravitated towards the determinations of discourse and representation and, in the process, struck specific blows at the validity of Marxist historiography.

It is virtually mandatory to begin the dissection of this process with Gareth Stedman Jones's reconsideration of Chartism and his brief introductory remarks to the collection of essays, *Languages of Class*, which gave that article an appropriate home.[28] I will indeed commence with this text, but in doing so suggest that it has achieved the status of an unwarranted, albeit negative, canon: under-theorised, ahistorical in its de-contextualisation of Chartism, and rather old-fashioned in its reduction of discourse to the published accounts of the labour press (a kind of nostalgic return to the syllabus of 'Political Thought', as Dorothy Thompson has noted); 'Rethinking Chartism' and the injunctions of the Stedman Jones introduction have achieved a certain notoriety precisely because they signalled the *acceptability* of a retreat from historical materialism premised not on the reasoned labours of theory *and* research, but on assertion congruent with the ideology of the times. Stedman Jones laid great stress on the ways in which a language of 18th-century radicalism over-determined the struggles of the 1830s and 1840s to the point that they were less about what materialist histories said they meant, class conflict embedded in the socio-economic transformations associated with the Industrial Revolution, and more about the continuity in populist discontent with the state, expressed in a particular discourse. This was an insightful, but extremely limited, reading of Chartist rhetoric; it by no means established the autonomy of language and its overshadowing of class experience asserted aggressively by Stedman Jones. As literally a score of materialist critiques of 'Rethinking Chartism' establish, the history of English class relations and conflicts in the third quarter of the 19th century is not one in which class formation and language, economics and politics, mobilisation and programme, challenge and cultural continuity can be so neatly categorised and dichotomised.[29]

---

28   See Stedman Jones 1983, esp. pp. 1–24, 90–178.

29   The literature on Stedman Jones's essay, much of it cast in materialist opposition, is now

The Stedman Jones essay thus introduces us to the ways in which historical materialism has been undermined from within its own ranks. But in this
introduction two points must be made, before moving on to consider a more
substantive statement on the reconsideration of class as it is made materially
and historically.

First, Stedman Jones's article, with its revisionist tilt away from the traditional orthodox materialist reading of Chartist experience, registered such a
profound impact amongst social historians precisely because it came from an
author long recognised as a Marxist historian with an acute sense of theory. But
what was missed within an appreciation of Stedman Jones's Marxist credentials
was the extent to which his Marxist theory had long been a captive of the aestheticism of 'Western Marxism', a process of political and intellectual formation
that moved Stedman Jones easily in the direction of post-structuralism's *ideological* framing of ideology.[30] Signs of this could be seen not only in Stedman
Jones's explicit theoretical statements, but also in his more resolutely historical
examination of class relations in Victorian society.[31] By the time of the writing of the Chartist essay, this trajectory had run its course in a series of blunt
statements that demanded nothing less than a reconsideration not so much
of Chartism, but of Marxist method and theory. Insisting implicitly on a trans-
historical conception of class consciousness as the programmatic direction of
'a class for itself', 'Rethinking Chartism' proclaims the non-existence of this
programme in the published statements of the labour press of the 1830s and
1840s. Stedman Jones was now convinced of 'the impossibility of abstracting
experience from the language which structures its articulation'. His aestheticism was voiced in his insistence that it was the terms and propositions within
language that demanded systematic exploration, rather than 'a putative experi-
ential reality of which they were assumed to be the expression'. On this 'contemporary intellectual terrain', claimed Stedman Jones, history must renew itself.
And this renewal, of course, was to stand in opposition to 'economic determ-

---

considerable. See, for instance, B. Palmer 1990a, pp. 128–33; Wood 1986, pp. 102–15; Foster
1985, pp. 29–46; Pickering 1986, pp. 144–62; Scott 1987, pp. 1–13, and the responses to Scott
by Palmer (B. Palmer 1987, pp. 14–23), Stansell (Stansell 1987, pp. 24–9), and Rabinbach
(Rabinbach 1987, pp. 30–6); D. Thompson 1986, pp. 54–7; Kirk 1987, pp. 2–47; Gray 1986,
pp. 363–73; Epstein 1986, pp. 195–208; 1989, pp. 75–118; Rogers 1987, pp. 143–52; Clark 1986,
pp. 78–86.

30   On aestheticism and 'Western Marxism' see the discussions in Anderson 1976; Megill
1985.

31   Stedman Jones 1973, pp. 96–115; 1978, pp. 11–60; 1971.

inism' and 'mechanical Marxism' and to proceed on the basis of the 'broader significance' of post-Saussurian linguistic analysis and its implicit critique of any assumed causal relationship between being and consciousness.[32]

As the materialist response to Stedman Jones pointed out with some regularity, this embrace of Saussure and the resulting linguistic turn were made abruptly and with little in the way of developed theoretical elaboration or justification. 'Deconstructing' Stedman Jones, however, suggests the possibility of reading his revisionism in interesting ways. For there lies between the lines of 'Rethinking Chartism', not unlike a Derridean 'trace', the high structuralism of the Stedman Jones of the 1960s and 1970s: ordering each layer of his argument in this linguistic analysis is an idealised understanding of class consciousness that the actual socio-economic and historical relations of the Chartist moment ensured would never become a practical and mass possibility. It is understandable that given the continuing, if deteriorating, hold of merchant capital, outwork and sweated metropolitan and country forms of petty production, many segments of the labouring poor would not see their plight in terms of a Marxist grasp of the way surplus value was extracted from them. Therefore, the call for a new proletarian order that would overturn the *state* as a central foundation of capitalist power was inevitably premature. The language of class necessarily spoke of state power in terms of an 'old corruption'. It contextualised class relations within a system in which the inadequacy of the price that producers could command for their output proved fundamental in the development of popular grievance. As such, resentment against governing authority turned on the pivotal role of a parasitic political caste in perpetuating such a political economy of inequality. An historical analysis of the economic context, acknowledging national patterns and local divergences, might well suggest, ironically, the lack of materialist justification for insisting that an incompletely formed working class speak in the words and meaning of a Marxist kind of class consciousness that was not quite yet firmly placed on the historically constituted agenda of class struggle. This does not mean, of course, as Stedman Jones claims, that language determines political being, but that material life sets the boundaries within which language and politics develop. Nor does it understate the importance of the state, which must be granted its relative autonomy at the same time as it is located in relation to the development of the economy. But this is not the lesson that Stedman Jones's revisionism draws out of the experience of Chartism. Instead, he simultaneously stands Peter's ground of denial

---

32   Stedman Jones 1983, esp. pp. 13, 20–1, 24.

and Solomon's ground of dichotomisation. This also has the advantage of making it clear that he's not denying Peter or dichotomising Solomon: 'Attention to the language of Chartism suggests that its rise and fall is to be related in the first instance not to movements in the economy, divisions in the movement, or an immature class consciousness, but to the changing character and policies of the state – the principal enemy upon whose actions radicals had always found that their credibility depended'.[33]

What such a conclusion suggests is that class is immaterial where a fully elaborated class consciousness cannot be unambiguously located. The elevation of the state to the status of prime determinant, as opposed to the exploitative and oppressive relations of a class order that conditions a particular kind of state apparatus and practice, thus moves Stedman Jones into a particular politics of resistance. Or perhaps it is the other way around: a political reading of the contemporary moment may well be conditioning a specific interpretation of Chartism's meaning, for the second point that needs to be made in regarding Stedman Jones as an introduction to the current displacement of historical materialism is more crudely political. In response to the many replies to the 'Rethinking Chartism' essay, all of which call for more theoretical clarity, Stedman Jones has offered not a single line of elaboration. Rather, it would seem that the justification, for Stedman Jones, of the retreat from historical materialism and of class as one of its major conceptual foundations is the politics of the moment. Against Thatcherism, he proposed taking the Labour Party out of its antiquated class politics and forging a genuine popular front of all progressives.[34] Against the 'crisis of communism', Stedman Jones proposes the failure of the political language of 'marxism-leninism', now at 'the end of the road, both in word and deed'.[35] It is hard to read political writings such as these and not be struck with the extent to which being does determine consciousness, that in a political moment of profoundly anti-Marxist tenor, the conscious identification with Marxism fades and falters within a layer of intellectuals who see little to be gained from staying with a ship that fashion and fatalism have seemingly sunk.

The assumptions and direction of Stedman Jones have been developed in a more sustained effort to comment on industrial England and the question of class in the period 1848–1914. Patrick Joyce's recently published *Visions of the People* is a lengthy essay that oscillates between historiographic critique

---

33   Stedman Jones 1983, p. 178.
34   Stedman Jones 1983, p. 256.
35   Stedman Jones 1989b, pp. 230–6.

and synthetic statement. Drawing far less on original research than on Joyce's reading of journal literature and published monographs, the text ranges across the cultural landscape of 19th-century England, exploring the moral and organisational discourses of labour, the significant place of custom, symbolism, and language (as dialect and sense of the past), and the ways in which mass entertainment – centred in the music hall, the broadside ballad, and the popular theatre – orchestrated specific understandings of collective experience. Much of what Joyce has to say is welcome and useful. What is at issue here is his insistence that the history of these years constantly returns to repudiations of class and, in place of this seemingly simple economistic and conflictual identity, the presence of a populist sense of 'them' and 'us' that is both more discursive and less constricting than the usual Marxist-imposed conceptual edifice.

At the foundation of this historical materialist project Joyce finds nothing less than 'the tarnished idol of class'. What Joyce means by this, like Stedman Jones, is actually not class as a structural relationship to the means of production, a relationship into which men and women are born and, with time, enter into through their subsistence activities, but rather class consciousness. *Visions of the People* turns on a ubiquitous insistence that 'the consciousness of *a class* and the consciousness of *class*' are not always the same thing, as if any Marxist ever said they were. The language of labour just 'did not add up to "class consciousness"'. Because the English proletariat did not embrace a language of unadulterated class consciousness, a dialect of Marxism, Joyce wants to move historians away from class: 'The notion of "languages of class" carries great dangers'. But inasmuch as there is a constant refrain throughout the period of industrial-capitalist consolidation of class *difference*, Joyce cannot quite bring himself to jettison the term 'class'. Instead, he undercuts it on virtually every page, only to bring it in as a kind of obscured image, conceptually over-shadowed by the somehow more robust rhetoric of populism: 'Rich and poor, the people and the ruling class, were the dominant elements, rather than considerations of class'. In this curious sentence the problematic fence-sitting and conceptual overdrive of the Joyce volume are summed up in two lines: a language of populism overrides not only instances of class consciousness, but class as a structural relation to production, and it does so in ways as tyrannically totalising and 'essentialist' as those now uniformly associated with the use of the concept of class. Populism is such a useful interpretive container because anything can be poured into it, while so much else can be shut out by arbitrary adjustment of the lid. This kind of analytic latitude proves particularly useful to an account that cannot escape class even as it is immersing the reader in a narrative of denial. How is it possible for an historian such as Joyce to speak of 'the ruling class' and yet insist that 'considerations of class' were subdued?[36]

Without seeming to know it, Joyce has offered a fascinating exploration of the multi-faceted construction of an ideology obscuring class all the more effectively because it resonates with class divisions, accepts the inevitable recognition of class difference, but masks the actualities of class power, commenting on how this ideology was also internalised and propagated by the working class itself. Joyce then confirms this ideology as 'real', taking the failure of the working class to identify the economic bedrock of class relations and consciousness as proof that notions of station, nation, and honour were somehow separate and dichotomised from class *and* more resilient as sources of identification. Small wonder that Joyce introduces his book with the statement that '[t]he vested interest workers and employers have in co-operation is at least as great as any tendency toward conflict', or that he insists that '[t]he stuff of class was the stuff of deference'.[37] Inspired by the recent work of William Reddy, who has been at pains to banish class from the vocabulary of historical scholarship, Joyce paints the experience of workplace tension as driven by superstructural engines somehow severed from the base of crude economic relations: 'Industrial conflicts were about mastership and authority, respect and honour, as much as they were about material considerations'. With labour's values and language cast in conceptions of justice and honest remuneration, Joyce expresses the view that 'little or no sense of labour and capital as the basic social dichotomies' existed in Victorian England, where the people looked to 'moral and not economic realms' as decisive, ensuring that 'an explicitly class vocabulary is notable by its absence'.[38]

Typical of most post-structuralist histories that retreat from class, *Visions of the People* commences with an assertive, unquestioning embrace of the ideology of post-modernism, replete with the mandatory dismissals and caricatures: there is no need to 'retain the fig-leaf of Marxist decencies'; the supposedly Marxist preoccupation with '"struggle" as the defining mark of class' is jettisoned. (No matter that this is *not* universally the point of departure in

---

36   Joyce 1991, esp. pp. 97, 113, 254.

37   Joyce 1991, pp. 3, 133. It is not that deference and the ideology of labour-capital harmony need be denied by historians, only that they need be situated, contextualised, and explored, rather than reified. This was more successfully scrutinised in Joyce's earlier work, although there is no mistaking the connection between that text and his current concerns. See Joyce 1980.

38   Joyce 1991, pp. 110, 246. The laudatory assessment of Reddy 1987, is counter-posed to the discussion in B. Palmer 1990a, pp. 134–44.

a Marxist appreciation of class origins, but rather the inevitable outcome of social relations ordered by the logic of exploitation, accumulation, and alienation.) Joyce commences with the blunt statement that received wisdom (Marxist?) 'has in fact become a dead weight', and in joining the ranks of those attacking the inappropriate and inadequate concept of class he has produced a book that is 'at least in part ... a product of its post-structuralist times'. Not conflict and class, but 'extra-proletarian identifications such as those of "people" and "nation" are involved ... notions combining social justice and social reconciliation'. 'The accent on social concord and human fellowship is very strong', concludes Joyce, in an echo of the German true socialism of the 1840s. Joyce's post-structuralism is thus simultaneously ideological and under-theorised. Deconstruction means little more than acknowledgement of the proliferating identities of people, post-structuralism a 'theoretical' gesture to the determinations of language. And with this kind of substantive skirting of the conceptual foundations of his study, Joyce is able to lapse into the very problematic oppositions that his own proclaimed 'theory' would question. Class consciousness is cast in oppositional ultimatism to class; economy and morality are dichotomised; populism, as an expansive politics of rhetoric and identity, replaces the more rigidly closed Marxist understanding of class, which has contained both too much and too little. Joyce concedes that populism as such an all-embracing interpretive concept is 'too baggy but that it is a necessary and useful heuristic device' (unlike, apparently, class).[39]

The result is a book that tells us a great deal, mystifies those findings unnecessarily, and loses its moorings in a tendency to scrutinise class for evidence of a fully formed class consciousness at the same time that populism is recognised to clasp a part of class (in differential social structural terms that translate into values and world views as likely to be fatalistic as conflictual) within its reach while closing its fist against expressions of anything approximating its conscious realisation. What could have been an important statement about the making of class as a presence in an English society characterised by the partial and problematic non-making of class consciousness withdraws into textual and analytic waffling in which class is acknowledged at the same time as it is displaced in the accentuation of rhetoric and representation, which hover above material structures of power, authority, and dominance. As befits an historian obviously adrift in the complex maze of ideology and structure, consciousness and being, Joyce offers up a grand statement nullifying class that can, nevertheless, only conclude on a note of postured balance: 'Class contin-

---

39   Joyce 1991, pp. 1, 3, 5, 11–12.

ued to be only one of the many ways in which the social order was envisaged, though in the integrity of the self-created traditions of the 19th-century labouring poor one can unmistakably detect more than the semblance of a class talking, if not of class talk'.[40]

Much historical writing influenced by post-structuralist thought thus assimilates a kind of instinctual anti-Marxism that, not surprisingly, understates class in a perfunctory defiance of 'economism' that results in little more than a reified representationalism. Stedman Jones and Joyce can well stand as surrogates for two distinct paths converging, in the 1980s and 1990s, on this intellectual end.

The first path is travelled by those Marxists once sympathetic to structuralist critiques of so-called Thompsonian socialist-humanist historiography. Evident in the case of Stedman Jones, this trajectory can also be discerned in the movement of other historians away from the classificatory scholasticism of the 1970s, usually associated with one or another European Marxist 'theorist', towards the new-found explanatory power of language, discourse, subjectivity, and identity, little of which is acknowledged to be embedded in material relations. Ironically enough, historians who have walked this path of analytic development often commenced their journey decidedly hostile to 'culturalism', but now find themselves embracing the political and interpretive significance of culture far more self-assuredly and uncritically than did Thompson or his supposed followers.[41]

The second path, of which Joyce is a prime example, encompasses those historians who were never all that much at home within Marxist analysis and who have found in the celebration of discursive identities a theoretical rationale for their discomfort with class not available to them as little as ten years ago. This process culminates in a loosening of the materialist moorings which bound fruitfully most social history of the 1970s. Joyce's first book, for instance, was a sustained critical *engagement* with the notion of the labour aristocracy, a term that Marxist historians developed through studies that advanced our understanding of class experience conceptually and empirically. With *Visions of the People*, however, this need to relate to a particular historiography is quietly deflated: 'The labour aristocrat so beloved of recent historiography was rather more a rhetorical than an economic construct'.[42] When entire layers of

40   Joyce 1991, p. 342.
41   See, for instance, Stedman Jones 1989a, pp. 272–324. In the case of Canada I would situate Ian McKay similarly. Note, for an early statement hostile to 'culturalism' and paying homage to the wisdom of Stedman Jones, McKay 1981–2, pp. 185–241.
42   Joyce 1980; Joyce 1991, p. 57.

working-class life can be reduced to the rhetorical, social history enters a particular kind of free-fall, propelled, quite often, by the ideological whirlwind of
post-modernity.

This is evident in what is perhaps the most sustained and serious historiographic breakthrough of the last two decades. Feminist history, pivoting on
gender relations (and admittedly highly variegated) is simultaneously Marxism's most serious challenge and social history's greatest advance. Not surprisingly, it registers its most profound impact in terms of our understanding of
class. Nowhere in the historiography, moreover, has post-structuralist thought
made comparable inroads, and post-modernist feminist theory and historical
writing are now metaphorically cross-referenced.[43]

As in the case of Stedman Jones, Joan Wallach Scott has attained a particular
stature as central to the making of a new, post-structuralist feminist historiography. Unlike Stedman Jones, Scott never embraced the theoretical aestheticism of Western Marxism, opting instead for a pragmatic radical engagement
with the terrain of American politics. In her formative years as an historian
this translated into a robust, if occasionally naïve, attachment to Thompson's
Making of the English Working Class. But as the possibilities of *class* politics
appeared to fade in the 1980s, Scott turned her back on workers as historical
subjects and offered a series of curt and cavalier dismissals of Marxism. She
moved decidedly to women as subjects and insisted increasingly on the importance of gender as the central category of social history. While her earlier historical writing had been fairly traditional in its subdued espousal of theory, by
the later 1980s Scott was unambiguously post-structuralist, perhaps the most
ardent proponent of a deconstructive, Foucauldian feminist historiography
outside of France. When her collection of essays, *Gender and the Politics of History*, appeared in 1988 it was hailed by Lynn Hunt, author of a post-structurally
inclined history of the politics of the French Revolution, as a major breakthrough ensuring that 'our reading of Marx and our understanding of class
differentiation will never again be the same'.[44]

Whatever the merits of Scott's essays, they most emphatically do not contain
a sophisticated interrogation of Marx and Marxist historiography or theory.
Marxism is in fact caricatured in the pages of Scott's book, described as 'a fixed
set of definitional categories that must be applied to historical events in the
same way every time'. Engels's *Origins of the Family* is dismissed in a few lines
and the only direct quote from Marx appears in a footnote and relates to the

---

43   For a brief introduction see B. Palmer 1990b, pp. 126–37.
44   Dust-jacket promotional statement on Scott 1988.

relationship of prostitution as the commodification of sexuality and of labour power. Scott misunderstands the work of Juliet Mitchell and assumes that her defence of the psychoanalytic tradition must somehow be dichotomised from materialist analyses of gender, when in fact Mitchell's work is a sustained effort to explore the materiality of the unconscious.[45] To appreciate the impact of Scott, then, it is necessary to look in directions other than those that relate to a substantial appreciation of Marxism.

Scott's appeal lies in her timely elaboration of gender as a useful category of historical analysis. She provided a summary of the literatures and positions consolidating around gender at precisely the moment that historians recognised the need to move beyond narrative stories of women's involvement *in* history. The very necessity of those stories testified to the process of exclusion that was characteristic of historical practice throughout most of the 20th century. In doing this, Scott provided no fundamental theoretical restructuring of women's experience or gender relations, but summarised the developments within social history and feminist theory up to the early 1980s. Politically, Scott lent this project her professional reputation, detailing as well the experience of women in the American university. These narrations of a process of silencing and the attempt to break out of it with written histories and concrete involvement in the academic job market were, however, presented alongside a parallel commitment to post-structuralism as a theoretical agenda that would empower women through its capacity to address discursive identities long suffocated under the weight of patriarchal power. Scott grasped post-structuralism, especially Derridean deconstruction and Foucauldian approaches to knowledge as power, as keys capable of unlocking a closed historiographic door. To make her point she took to task Thompson's *Making* and its gendered – masculinised – notion of class.[46]

The result is not so much a powerful indictment of Thompson's text as it is an indication of how post-structuralism, in the hands of those paying lip-service to its premises, can simply provide theoretical window-dressing for projects that have no need for it or, worse, collapse inward in a politics of dubious character. Thus Scott has some useful things to say concerning the ways in which class was metaphorically gendered in the language of Jacobinism, just as she explores with sensitivity the extent to which statistical representations of work in 19th-century Paris constructed the meaning of labour in gendered ways. As insightful as these and other points are, they hardly require the theoretical

---

45   Scott 1988, pp. 35, 69, 207, 223.
46   For a detailed discussion see B. Palmer 1990a, esp. pp. 78–86.

foundation of post-structuralism to shore them up. What does get erected on that foundation, however, is a troublingly aestheticised politics. Historically, this collapses into an oddly essentialising opposition in which the fantastic prophet Joanna Southcott serves as an example of sexual difference, domesticity and spirituality, while Mary Wollstonecraft and others are in Scott's terms little more than 'fitting partners for Radical men', their secular, combative and rational make-up being only a cosmetic politics of accommodation.[47] This fixation on sexual difference as the pivot of politics translates into Scott's insistence that women struggling in the courts to fight inequality and wage discrimination would do well to arm themselves with the works of Derrida and Foucault. This aestheticisation of politics in the name of a post-structuralist understanding of gender has led one commentator to remark: 'It defies common sense to think that a fully articulated deconstructive position, presented in the language of academic theory, would ever persuade a reactionary judge to rule in favor of women claiming discrimination ... The message seems clear: *Cherchez la femme* and leave real women on the side'.[48]

What the problematically under-theorised post-structuralism of Scott's work exposes is the tendency for a feminist analytic post-modernism to collapse inward on the very same troubling oppositions and essentialisms it supposedly decries. Adept at pointing to the tendency of particular social formations to construct women categorically and then extending that construction into widening spheres of power and authority, thus imposing gendered understandings on whole realms of seemingly 'neutral' relations within civil and economic society, post-structuralist feminism has the decided tendency to *stop* the analytic exercise at this point, reifying the almost Weberian ideal typologies of women and failing to explore the actual diversity of the history of gender relations.[49] In short, post-structuralist feminism, proclaiming the materiality of representation, denigrates the material as merely representational. Class, surely a social relationship and structural presence made as much historically and economically as it is forged in language, image and rhetoric (however much these forces are indeed interrelated), inevitably gets shunted aside in explorations of the past resting theoretically on this feminist post-structuralism, or, as in the case of Joyce, the material meaning of class is constantly dodged in a project that can only be understood as analytic waffling.

---

47   Scott 1988, esp. p. 78.
48   Koonz 1989, pp. 19, 20.
49   This, I would argue, is precisely the strength *and* weakness of Riley 1988.

Stedman Jones, Joyce and Scott thus stand as particular signs of the times. They are representative of the extent to which a post-structuralism that situates itself in problematic ways to historical materialism and its understandings of class and ideology has insinuated itself into the project of interpreting the past. Marxists given to structuralist and aestheticised stands, social historians uncomfortable with the Marxist insistence on determination and feminists of various kinds have all found something to embrace in the eclectically proliferating theoretical implosion of post-structuralism. Much of value has indeed come out of this project. Post-structurally inclined historians rightly stress the need for closer attention to language and representation, demand scrutiny of the unreflective construction of analytic categories within the master codes of dominant ideologies both past and present and justifiably call for research into the discursive identities that surround the social space of class and consciousness. No Marxist should react in blind opposition to this kind of challenging expansion of the terrain of study and explanation.

But as the commentary on the above texts indicates, historical materialism is not incapable of addressing these issues. Indeed, it is apparent that only with Marxism's analytic insistence on material referentiality can the free-fall of post-structuralism into an ideological rationale of post-modernity's continuous, albeit agitated, connection to capitalist forms of exploitation and oppression be halted. Stedman Jones and Joyce, for instance, may well present important findings of the languages of class and its limitations, but it requires the hard labours of historical materialist theory and empirical research to explain just why it was that class consciousness could not break through the actual walls of political thought, dialect, sectional trade attachments and the dialogues of music-hall ballads and popular broadsides. The answers to the dilemmas of class as a process of consciousness lie not in divorcing the material place of labour from its conception of itself, as Stedman Jones and Joyce are prone to do, but rather in excavating that structure of being, the better to understand and *materialise* the structure of feeling that at times accompanied it and at other times seemed strikingly out of step.[50] That their project rejects this balance is a product of the politics of post-modernity, of disillusion and despair, on the one hand, and of proud anti-Marxist defiance, now finally legitimated by 'theory', on the other.

This, too, is central to feminism's varied responses of rejection of the Marxist project. But feminist theoretical and historical writing also needs, desperately

---

50   This I take to have been the project of Raymond Williams. For an introduction see
      R. Williams 1976; 1979; 1980; 1989.

so, the checks of historical materialism if it is to work its way through the fundamental dilemmas of its own making.[51] For as the range of post-structurally informed writing on class and gender suggests, feminist histories that take the ideological cues of the post-modern age as a theoretical guide find themselves at best waffling on the question of class and, at their worst, caught up in the massive contradiction of repudiating the essentialising category *woman* at the same time that they reproduce it in their pages, denying the concrete validity and meaning of binary oppositions as they are embedded in Western thought only to recast them as lived experience.[52]

There are those feminist theorists who are resisting this movement at the related levels of theory, interpretation and politics.[53] But the drift of the last decade has not been in this direction. Michèle Barrett's introduction to the 1988 edition of *Women's Oppression Today* captures the trajectory of feminist theory over the course of the 1980s. Once committed to Marxism and materialist analysis, the Barrett of the late 1980s is a captive of the ideological ensemble of post-structuralist theoretical positions associated with the supposed political and cultural ruptures of post-modernity:

> Post-modernism is not something that you can be for or against: the reiteration of old knowledges will not make it vanish. For it is a cultural climate as well as an intellectual position, a political reality as well as an academic fashion. The arguments of post-modernism already represent, I think, a key position around which feminist theoretical work in the future is likely to revolve ... I want to add a word about the general philosophical climate of today in comparison with the one that informed the book's premises. Just as it would be impossible to write such a book without integrating a consideration of racism and ethnicity, so it would, I think, be impossible to write in such a confidently materialist vein. At the very least one would

---

51   The work of Juliet Mitchell is just such an attempt to take the valuable insights of feminist theory – such as attention to the subject and to the importance of the personal – and materialise them. But her early work on psychoanalysis remains anathema to many feminists convinced that Freud is, simply put, the enemy; her later call to appreciate economic determination and limitation has been misconceived as a retreat. See Mitchell 1974 and Mitchell 1986, pp. 34–49.

52   In 'Feminism, Humanism, Post-modernism' (in Soper 1990, pp. 228–45), Kate Soper offers a way out of this dilemma, but it is not one embraced by many post-structuralist feminist theorists or historians. For an approach of feminist literary theorists to the problem of essentialism see the volume of *Tessera* (AA.VV. 1991) devoted to this issue.

53   See, for instance, the underappreciated Segal 1987 and 1990.

have to defend the assumptions made about epistemology, the concept of ideology, the purchase of Marxist materialism, and the definition of the subject. Thus there would have to be a consideration of whether, for example, Foucault's suspension of epistemology and substitution of 'discourse' and 'regimes of truth' for a theory of ideology was to be accepted or not. There would have to be a consideration of arguments, put forward by Ernesto Laclau and Chantal Mouffe, that the substantive arguments of a Marxist analysis of capitalism must be superseded. There would have to be an engagement with the arguments that the theory of the subject embodied in the text was, whilst not the universal male identification of bourgeois ideology, nevertheless still a conception unacceptably tainted by a humanist perspective.[54]

Passages such as this return us, but in new ways all the more threatening, to historical materialism, to the ground of 'The Poverty of Theory'.[55]

The Irony of Ideology

The Marxist literary critic Franco Moretti has insisted that a century of modernism has taught us that 'irony, extraordinary cultural achievement though it is, has to recover some kind of problematic relationship with responsibility and decision – or else, it will have to surrender history altogether'.[56] Edward Thompson said much the same thing decades earlier when he stressed the importance of the 'consequences of consequences' and the need to understand the contradictory character of human development, in which 'opposing tendencies and potentialities can interpenetrate within the same tradition'. This he saw as 'the stuff of history'.[57] In this concluding section I want to address these questions of irony, responsibility and the consequences of consequences, not in order to apportion blame but to understand the ironic authority of post-structuralism as the ideology of post-modernity, especially as this pertains to the practice of historical materialism.

---

54   M. Barrett 1988, pp. xxxiii–iv. Discerning readers will note that although Barrett did not alter her text, she did change her subtitle. Originally published under the heading 'Problems in Marxist Feminist Analysis', the reprinted edition proclaims itself a text in 'The Marxist/Feminist Encounter'. This is a far distance to travel in eight years.

55   See Soper 1990, pp. 89–125.

56   Moretti 1988, p. 248.

57   E.P. Thompson 1958, p. 106.

It is my contention that the fundamental *advances* of historical materialist historiography were registered throughout the 1960s and 1970s, ironically, in
ways that have filtered through the class defeats and disillusionments of our
time, only to be re-filtered, as a consequence of this separation of theory and
practice, through the ideological prism of post-modernism in the 1980s and
1990s. The result is an ironic but understandable set of reversals, registered as
'theory' but in fact comprehensible – in terms of a political project of changing the world as opposed to glorying in its ever more complex interpretive
possibilities – as retreat. This was not necessarily the fault of those historical
materialists of an earlier generation but was, instead, a 'theoretical' end over-
determined by a series of necessary political refusals that failed, by and large,
to be followed by positive political developments capable of generating the
kind of practical Marxist endorsements that could relight the cooling embers
of the theoretical fires of historical materialism. When these fires burned less
brightly in the suffocating darkness of the political defeats of the late 20th century, the epoch of post-modernity was there to be proclaimed as a new dawn,
the ideology of post-structuralism raining down in a steady and dampening
drizzle.

To understand this process it is necessary to return, once again, to Thompson's 'Poverty of Theory', for it was this text that reiterated that the theoretical
rupture within historical materialism that produced *The Making of the English Working Class* and a host of other important writings was, in its origins, a
political rupture, symbolised by '1956' and fiercely oppositional to Stalinism. It
was in that moment of Marxist reassessment and realignment that Thompson
and others, such as John Saville, articulated the need for a socialist humanism that would stand as stark contrast – theoretically and practically – to
the moral nihilism, anti-intellectualism, and denial of the creative agency of
human labour and the value of the individual that many claimed 1956 exposed
as fundamental to Stalinism. Theoretically, Thompson translated this political
break into a direct repudiation of the base/superstructure metaphor central to
orthodox Marxism. He saw the crude determinism of this dichotomised coup-
ling, with its ideological caricature of conscious human agency as nothing more
than a reflection of humanity's social being, as a political rationale for Stalinism and a theoretical justification for historical materialist writing that reduced
class formation to the equation of 'so many factories + so many peasants driven
from the land = the proletariat'.[58] Concerned with the silences in Marx, and the

---

58   See, for instance, E.P. Thompson 1957, pp. 105–43; B. Palmer 1981a; Wood 1990, pp. 125–52;
      Abelove et al. 1983, pp. 3–26.

subsequent reproduction and indeed legitimation of those silences in Marxist historiography, Thompson conceived of *The Making of the English Working Class* as an extension of Marxism, as a rehabilitation of 'lost categories and a lost vocabulary', an attempt to find a voice for the 'unarticulated assumptions and unrealised mediations' of an actual experience Marx too often bypassed in his engagement with the terrain and categories of bourgeois political economy.[59] Out of this rupture – simultaneously political and theoretical – Thompson offered his historical writings of the 1960s and 1970s, in which class formation was never simply collapsed into the formulae of economism but, rather, was lived out at the intersection of agency and structure as a web of determination that set the limits of what was possible, limits within which society and economy, culture and politics, developed and changed. Three points, however, need be remembered and placed alongside the developing edifice of what has been called 'socialist-humanist history'.[60]

First, Thompson always conceived of the project of historical materialist histor*ies* as a collective endeavour. Growing out of the collaborations of the British Communist Party Historians Group, this project was never meant to produce all-encompassing texts; rather, it was comprised of different writings and, above all else, differing historical sensitivities and tones of presentation, most especially those associated with a more closely *economic* argument. For Thompson, his own writings were always to be placed alongside those of others, such as Hill, Saville, Dorothy Thompson and, even, the one major historian who remained loyal to the Party after 1956, E.J. Hobsbawm.[61] Parallel to this grouping, Raymond Williams was increasingly to address theoretical issues central to Thompson's project, albeit in a language more congenial to orthodox Marxism.[62] Second, while unambiguously hostile to the notion of base/superstructure, Thompson *never* abandoned the notion of economic determination. In the last instance, as it were, he remained very much the materialist. 'I hope', Thompson stated clearly in 1978, 'that nothing I have written above has given rise to the notion that I suppose that the formation of class is independent of objective determinations, that class can be defined simply as a cultural formation'.[63] Third, as this engagement with Marxist theory and historical materialism developed, a New Left Thompson had helped to initiate drifted increasingly

---

59   Abelove et al. 1983, p. 21; E.P. Thompson 1978c, pp. 251–2.

60   R. Johnson 1978, pp. 79–100.

61   See, for instance, Hobsbawm 1978a, pp. 21–48; Abelove et al. 1983, esp. p. 22.

62   See, for instance, R. Williams 1973, pp. 3–16; 1977, esp. pp. 75–89.

63   E.P. Thompson 1978a, p. 149.

in directions he deplored. In these years the aestheticisation of British Marxism paved the way for the Althusserian structuralism he would later pillory in 'The Poverty of Theory'. Alongside the historical materialist advances of Marxism as history, Marxism as a political practice registered no corresponding victories, an interpretive point of agreement shared, interestingly, by both Thompson and Perry Anderson.[64] Some on the left saw this aestheticisation as rampant enough to decry the rise of 'a coterie of marxist swots at the mercy of their own intellectual crazes, and prizing theory more as evidence of their own cleverness than for its possible relevance in the struggle for socialism'.[65]

Indeed, this kind of overly harsh dismissal of the trajectory of those Perry Anderson gathered around him at the new *New Left Review* (a journal Thompson, Saville, and others helped to found only to find themselves rather quickly displaced) had early been thrown in the face of Thompson himself by the Trotskyist Peter Fryer. Fryer, like Thompson, made his exit from the Communist Party in 1956, but he refused to follow Thompson in his insistence that Stalinism was linked to Lenin's base/superstructure-derived understanding of knowledge as a reflection of being. This comprised, for Fryer, 'an assault on the philosophy of dialectical materialism' leading 'into the swamp of subjectivism and solipsism'.[66]

It is the ironic conclusion of this essay that while Fryer's assessment of Thompson was wrong and one-sided, it nevertheless speaks to the authority of post-structuralism as the ideology of the contemporary post-modernist moment. Lacking the disciplined connection to Marxism as a *political* practice that had, in good measure, constructed Thompson and others as dissident leftists, many historians who came to maturity in the New Left mobilisations of the 1960s and early 1970s experienced their leftism as – a further irony – culture rather than as politics. Their staying power as leftists, as well as their discipline as Marxists, was in no way comparable to those of Thompson and his generation. As Thompson notes in 'The Poverty of Theory', whatever the battles waged and remembrances of struggles past fondly recalled, 'there has never been a generation of socialist intellectuals in the West with *less* experience of practical struggle, with less sense of the initiatives thrown up in mass movements, with less sense of what the intellectual can learn from men and women of practical experience, and the proper dues of humility which the intellect must owe to this'. Any sense of current critical theory and Marxism thus commences, for

---

64   E.P. Thompson 1978c, p. 376; Anderson 1980, p. 150.
65   Sedgwick 1976, pp. 131–53.
66   Fryer 1957, pp. 136–47.

Thompson, 'with a *de facto* sociological and intellectual segregation of theory and practice'.[67]

This is, as the history of Western Marxism has shown for much of the 20th century, a heavy burden to shoulder. Given the immense class defeats of the last quarter of the 20th century – from the implosion of the first workers' state to the bellicose triumphalism of a reinvigorated American imperialism, evident in the grotesquely one-sided war in the Gulf to the New Right-orchestrated assault on Western trade unionism crippled by economic restructuring – this weight is made all the more onerous. In this political context many social historians have assimilated Thompson's message of the silences in Marx and in historical materialism, but they have done so in ways that have little to do with Thompson's two-sided engagement with Marxism. Thompson's creative rethinking of Marx was always rooted in a passionate rupture from Stalinism that refused, categorically, to succumb to the capitulationist ideology of capitalism in its mid-20th-century ascendance. Thus his critique of Marx was never anti-Marxist in the ways that the movement away from the Communism of a previous generation associated with Koestler and 'the god that failed' proved to be. At the end of the century, however, critical theory has too often taken on the trappings of a uni-dimensional repudiation of Marx which owes more to Koestler than to Thompson.

This one-sidedness has indeed taken on some of the character of, in Fryer's words of the late 1950s, a swamp of subjectivism and solipsism. Many social historians drawn, however cavalierly, to critical theory, deconstruction and discourse have historically passed through a 'Thompsonian' moment or continue to rationalise their repudiation of historical materialism and class through recourse to what they designate the insights of Thompsonian texts. This is no fault of Thompson himself, who did what he could with 'The Poverty of Theory' to stem the tide of 'idealist irrationalism' and, subsequently, has offered a Swiftian satire pointedly addressing the follies of the reification of language.[68] But the process exposes how a particular consequence of a specific political and theoretical motion can, in an entirely different milieu and in the hands of a markedly divergent appreciation of experience and its meanings, result in consequences that reverse direction and stall, if not stop, specific developments.

Evidence of this particular process amongst social historians is now abundant, surveyed through the pages of the *History Workshop Journal* by a Raphael

---

67   E.P. Thompson 1978c, p. 376.

68   E.P. Thompson 1978c, p. 384; 1988; and, for comment on this later text, B. Palmer 1990a, pp. 211–14; Buhle 1989, pp. 24–6.

Samuel who displays a curious apolitical resignation to what seems to him a kind of intellectual over-determination. Refreshing in its range and idiosyncrasies, Samuel's historiographic commentary concludes on a note strikingly congruent with the argument of the centrality of Thompson and the ruptures of 1956:

> Discourse analysis, as practiced by the French post-Marxists and their latter-day American followers, is another way of writing about the social order. In the hands of Foucault himself, a wayward but inspired historian, posing as a theorist, it is a kind of Marxism without the economics. His 'discursive formations' are base and superstructure, theory and practice rolled into one ... Foucault refuses the Marxist notion of ideology and distances himself from the idea of general theory ... His 'epistemes' evidently involve both a master signifier and a community of meanings; his 'discursive formations' are by definition cultural wholes ... The insistence on radical heterogeneity goes hand in hand with a considerable appetite for the identification of the generic; for the reconstitution of symbolic essences ... and for the designation of transhistorical, or meta-historical, forces.

Given the language of this passage, one can be excused for mistaking its author for Hayden White and substituting Thompson for Foucault. But one would err seriously, as Samuel well knows, for in Foucault 'class [has] ... been dismantled as a collective subject ... its place taken by a whole series of unified categories which serve as the common currency of critical discourse'.[69] With the refusal of this jettisoning of class we are back, once again, with 'The Poverty of Theory'.

The pages of *History Workshop* are as good a place as any to locate the historiographic fashion of the moment. On American campuses, writes Irving Howe, what we are witnessing today 'is a strange mixture of American populist sentiment and French critical theorizing as they come together in behalf of "changing the subject"'. Reminiscent of Joyce's *Visions of the People*, Howe concludes: 'The populism provides an underlying structure of feeling and the theorizing provides a dash of intellectual panache'. As Bruce Robbins comments in an extension of Howe's claim, class is what has been lost in this subjectivist shuffle.[70] But as Howe (and Russell Jacoby) well know, the populist appeal to

---

69   Samuel 1991, pp. 105–7. I have shifted the place of the last sentences in the block quote to enhance coherence. For White on Thompson see White 1978, pp. 14–19.

70   Howe 1991, p. 42, quoted in and commented on in Robbins 1991, p. 156.

the oppressed (which takes the form of addressing the subject as it is constructed in racial and gendered forms, but not as a class collectivity) is divorced from any substantive engagement with an audience, let alone a mass political base, precisely because its predominantly post-structuralist theoretical moorings are nothing if not a seductively sticky barrier inhibiting a politics of engagement and change.[71]

The ostensible, and much-proclaimed, end of Marxism is thus nothing more than a powerfully orchestrated ideological mobilisation. Historical materialism has lost neither its power to interpret the past nor its relevance to the contemporary intellectual terrain. What has happened, and undeniably so, is something quite different. The current political context is one of profound malaise for a left lacking roots in political struggles. Situated at the historic conjuncture of the disintegration of what remains of the workers' states of the Soviet Union, Eastern Europe, Indo-China and the so-called Third World after three-quarters of a century of Stalinist degenerations and deformations and the retreats of the labour movements of the capitalist West, this period presents a serious impediment to the project of extending the reach and purchase of historical materialism. These are not good times to be a Marxist.

Yet they are times when being a Marxist remains, arguably, of fundamental importance. For at no time in the history of the 20th century have Marxism and the practice of historical materialism been on shakier ground; at no time has the threat to the practice of Marxism – political and theoretical – been so great. Marxist social historians will play, at best, a small role in the revival of a genuinely proletarian politics. But even a small role, in these times, is well worth playing. It will not be played, however, by adapting to the ideological climate of the moment. Historical materialism, as the post-1956 texts of Marxist historiography reveal, can indeed address silences in Marx's writing, but only if the audible accomplishments of Marx and subsequent Marxists remain. Poststructuralism is too often a reification of such silences, a reading of history and politics that throws these silences into the arena of interpretation and action, the better to create a deafening din drowning out the voice of Marxism, the analytic sentences of historical materialism, the presence and capacity of class to speak. To keep the practice of historical materialism alive, to refuse to succumb to the current wave of subjectivism, but rather to reassert the necessity of historicising and materialising both our analysis and activity as Marxists, will be no mean achievement in the years to come. Doing this cannot help but contrib-

71   Jacoby 1987.

ute, in however limited ways, to the revival of a mass class politics of resistance that is the only force capable of turning back the destructive tides evident in both the intellectual and economic histories of our time.

CHAPTER 2

Historical Materialism and the Writing of Canadian History: A Dialectical View*

Some time ago, with a couple of hours to kill in London, I wandered into a pub, pulled out a copy of Paul Buhle's *Marxism in the USA: From 1870 to the Present Day* (1987),[1] and proceeded quietly and unobtrusively to turn its pages. As the bartender plopped down a pint, he glanced at the title, raised his eyebrows, looked at me with a jaundiced air of superiority and commented, 'I'd have thought that would be a rather short book, mate'. The traditional class dichotomy of British society – 'them' and 'us' – took on new meaning as an Old World understanding of materially embedded division posed itself against the exceptionalism of the New World order. In this commonsensical appreciation of difference, historical antagonisms bred of exploitation and struggle, as well as the ideas of liberatory possibility that accompany such deep structures of being, tend to be stripped away from the English-speaking experience of North America. I offered something in the way of rejoinder and went back to my beer and my book, and the caustic server sauntered to his perch at the end of the bar, trading quips with customers of more familiarity than me, offering a running commentary on a televised soccer match.

The debate that periodically rises and falls over American exceptionalism is an old one, reaching back to Werner Sombart and, in Canada, echoing in the first sustained scholarly attack on the potential realisation of a proletarian state in O.D. Skelton's *Socialism: A Critical Analysis* (1911).[2] For Skelton, Canada was perhaps the original site of exceptionalism's foothold, a primitive accumulation of conditions anything but conducive to socialism's emergence. In the view of the Sir John A. Macdonald Professor of Political Science at Queen's University, socialism in the British Dominion was both 'sporadic' (being materially inhib-

---

* 'Historical Materialism and the Writing of Canadian History: A Dialectical View', *Online Journal of the Canadian Historical Association*, New Series, 17 (2006), 33–60.

1   Buhle 1987.

2   For contemporary discussions see Wilentz 1984a, pp. 1–24; Foner 1984, pp. 57–80; Katznelson and Zolberg 1986; Heffer and Rovet 1988; Friedman 1998; Kirk 2000, pp. 1–26; and AA.VV. 2003. For two classic statements see Sombart 1976, reprinting the original 1906 German publication, and Skelton 1911.

ited by the lack of concentrated industrial development, except in the Pacific mining sector) and 'exotic' (restricted to the immigrant workforces of locales like Winnipeg, where 'the motley foreign quarter' exercised undue influence).[3]

The irony of Skelton's immediate pre-World War I statement, of course, is that Canada would, in the inter-war period and into the 1960s, come to be conceived by some social scientists as an oppositional rejoinder to a solitary United States exceptionalism. With its Co-operative Commonwealth Federation (CCF) and New Democratic Party (NDP) party formations, its agrarian populism that challenged liberal individualism, its Hartzian-fragment socio-political culture, characterised by Tory and socialist 'touches' of bourgeois imperfection that could unite the conservative (George Grant) and the radical (Gad Horowitz) in a traditionalist collectivism that seeded the Canadian ground with socialist possibility, Canada confirmed the United States as the last exceptionalist stand of a pristine capitalist society. Whereas Skelton, in 1911, saw Canada as insulated from socialism, Lipset, Hartz, Grant and Horowitz – all in different ways – saw Canadian identity as intricately related to socialist possibility and, in its essence, differentiated from the political culture and nation-state formation of the United States.[4] So, too, did the revived and increasingly left-nationalist radical political economy that emerged in the late 1960s, which built on the uniquely Canadian insights of Harold Adams Innis.[5] From this quarter would come calls for an 'independent socialist Canada'[6] as well as an on-going radicalisation of Canadian political economy that would encompass not only a

---

3 Skelton 1911, pp. 309–10. Ian McKay suggests that Skelton regarded 'the Quebec population' (seemingly in its essentialised entirety) as 'one of the great barriers that would shield a fortunate Canada from the waves of socialism sweeping the world', but this is an exaggerated claim. Skelton wrote that '[t]he power of the Catholic Church in Quebec erects a solid barrier in the path of socialism', a statement rather different in its meaning than the blanket generalisation McKay attributed to Skelton. See McKay 2005, p. 192.

4 Lipset 1971; McHenry 1950; Hartz 1964; Horowitz 1968, pp. 3–57; Grant 2005.

5 As an introduction only see Watkins 1972, pp. 68–92; Drache 1976, pp. 3–18; and for a stimulating recent introduction to Innis, reviewed with insight by Watkins, Watson 2006, pp. 45–7.

6 Among the pivotal texts that appeared out of a late 1960s ferment that grew out of the New Democratic Party's Waffle (the Movement for an Independent Socialist Canada) and other critical left nationalist spheres would be: Levitt 1970; Lumsden 1970; Teeple 1972; Laxer 1973. One of the best statements of this trajectory was G. Williams 1976, which grew into G. Williams 1983. The significance of left nationalism in Canadian radical political economy into the 1980s and 1990s – as well, perhaps, as its displacement in the current focus on identity, gender, social movements and globalisation – can be gleaned from three texts: Clement and Williams 1989; Clement 1997; and Clement and Vosko 2003.

sophisticated Marxist body of writing on the state, but also a resolutely historical materialist critique of the Innisian origins of the field.[7] All of this belatedly
makes a point already obvious in the 1940s: it would have been incongruous
for Victor Gollancz's Left Book Club to publish a volume entitled *Left Turn,
United States* in its mass-circulation, orange-covered British series, but this was
indeed how M.J. Coldwell titled his Canadian social-democratic statement of
1945.[8]

This has the feel of the dialectic about it, as a historical process culminates in new creations emerging out of older processes that seemed destined to
produce something quite different than what actually surfaces in the give and
take of development. In all of this, socialism has, sadly, been locatable more
in the shadows than in the substance of Canada, discernible here and there
in utopian idealism and, on occasion, as a practical politics. Its conceptions,
categories of analysis and ways of thinking, seeing and doing have been chimer-
ical rather than central to Canadian experience, yet they have left their mark
nonetheless, largely as a force mediating liberalism's electoral agendas in the
era of welfare state attainment. But that, after all, was a relatively abbreviated
moment in the *longue durée* of Canada's historical evolution, developing in the
1940s with the first regional achievements of provincial social-democratic legis-
lative power, attaining its programmatic zenith in the 1960s of Trudeau's 'Just

---

7   I do not address seriously in this essay the important Canadian Marxist political economy
    that has developed over the course of the last three-and-a-half decades, often in opposition
    to more nationalist strains of the new political economy. Suffice it to say, however, that it is
    an analytically differentiated field. On the one hand, the influential state theorist Leo Panitch
    played a significant role in the development of the journal *Studies in Political Economy* and
    has taken over the co-editorship of *Socialist Register* from Ralph Miliband and John Saville,
    as well as developing connections with the United States radical publication *Monthly Review*.
    Panitch has worked with a broad array of younger radical political economists influenced by
    the traditions of historical materialism, many of whom address issues of Canadian class form-
    ation and comparative labour studies as they intersect with international political economy.
    The contribution of Panitch and a subsequent cohort of Marxist political economists has been
    considerable. But it remains somewhat distinct from another, if smaller and less influential,
    analytic school of Marxist political economy, one in which the laws of motion of capitalist
    accumulation are granted central interpretive place. To the extent that both of these Marxist
    strains of political economy challenge dependency theory and radical nationalist schools of
    political economy, they are similar, but the sharpness of critique and the interpretive accents
    nevertheless differ. For Panitch, see Panitch 1977; 1981, pp. 7–33; and for political economies of
    capitalist accumulation and harder-edged critiques of radical nationalist thought see Murray
    Smith 1994; 2000, pp. 343–68; McNally 1981, pp. 35–63.

8   Coldwell 1945.

Society' and beginning the slow march of demise in the mid-1970s with a glob-ally induced fiscal crisis of the state that reverberated throughout Canadian political-economic relations in the 1980s and 1990s.[9]

Curiously enough, or perhaps predictably, the actual *history* of historical materialism in Canada, a historiography that remains to be written and that is as brief as it is (to use a word advisedly) *tragic*, is not unrelated to this context of political economy and the centrality of left-leaning publications in the post-1945 years. It can be argued that the 1960s represented the first serious stirrings of historical materialism in Canadian historical writing, and that this bore some fruit in the 1970s and early 1980s, only to succumb to pressures of conceptual and political hostility and material setbacks to the cause of Marxism on a global scale that unfolded over the course of the 1980s. These gathered momentum with the implosion of actually existing Soviet socialism in 1989; socialism's (and Marxism's) fortunes have been on a downward trajectory ever since.[10]

Prior to the 1960s, there is barely a hint of historical materialism present in Canadian historical writing. There were, of course, historical materialists such as the so-called revolutionary impossiblist E.T. Kingsley, whose agitational tracts were didactic efforts to cultivate within the working class a sense of his-torical materialism's capacity to serve as a key for unlocking it from incarcera-tion.[11] But even when a topic such as labour was broached, it was more often examined and written about in ways that were anything but historical mater-

---

9   See, as an introduction only, Struthers 1994; Owram 1996; Panitch and Swartz 2003. The overly elastic terminology of 'liberal order' animating McKay's *Rebels, Reds, and Radicals* is thus, to my way of thinking, problematic precisely because it is insufficiently historically materialist in its conceptualisation. I can appreciate McKay's point that Marx is read dif-ferently by new generations of leftists. It is nevertheless troubling to see McKay embrace Marx as 'a dynamic and changing cultural code' (McKay 2005, p. 15). This licenses much that is conceptually vague and, in McKay's reading of historical developments, not a little that is idiosyncratic. Few historians of the Canadian left, for instance, will accept McKay's unsubstantiated assertions that virtually the entirety of all past writing is compromised by a sectarianism that he alone has transcended. Moreover, this transcendence is often achieved by bypassing acute differences on the left, such as those separating Communists and social democrats in the 1940s. It does historical materialism no service to marshal it against a rigorous reading of such differences, however much the aim is to create a unified left in our time.

10   Discussions of this global context can be found in Miliband and Panitch 1990; Panitch and Leys 2005; Wood and Foster 1997; Sanbonmatsu 2004.

11   Kingsley 1916. Unfortunately, our knowledge of Kingsley's importance has not been ad-vanced substantially since the publication of McCormack 1977.

ialist, as Gregory S. Kealey's overview of 'writing about labour' from the 1880s
through the 1950s suggests.[12] There were inevitably iconoclastic commentators
on Canadian historical development, such as H.C. Pentland, whose materialist inclinations and refusal to take up conventional anti-Marxist shibboleths
lulled many into thinking of themselves as Marxists when in fact they were
not,[13] and others, like the political theorist C.B. Macpherson, whose ambigu-
ously rich writings promised to open out into a historical materialist analysis
of Canada only to find their final outlet in non-Canadian argument.[14]

   There is no denying, then, that prior to the 1960s Marxist ideas and, in particular, a theoretical elaboration of what constituted historical materialism were
largely the stuff of Communist study groups and the Party press and journals,
not university classrooms.[15] For all of the homage now paid to Stanley Ryerson, he was read seriously only on the fringes of Canadian scholarship, which
did not so much marginalise Marxism as method as ignore it until vilifica-
tion seemed necessary, which was not all that often.[16] Moreover, even acknowledging Ryerson's accomplishments and appreciating his philosophical training and inclination, it is apparent that the steeply uphill battle of conveying
a sense of Canadian historical development in terms of class antagonism and
national oppression was a difficult enough climb that the patrician Communist
rarely elaborated on the theoretical foundations of his labours of interpretation
and recovery. Like many historians, he wore his conceptual clothing loosely
and undoubtedly thought that its daring and dash would be evident in the fit

12   G. Kealey 1995, pp. 3–31.
13   Precisely because Pentland refused to be anti-Marxist, he was often regarded as Marxist,
     which may explain why he was largely ignored among economists and read partially and
     idiosyncratically among left-nationalist political economists. His most enthusiastic read-
     ers were working-class historians. For the complexity of Pentland see the posthumously
     published Pentland 1981, edited and introduced by Paul Phillips; Pentland 1974, pp. 26–8;
     and for a somewhat simplified assimilation of Pentland to Marxism, Watkins 1977, esp.
     p. 95, n. 49. See as well G. Kealey 1995, pp. 32–47; Drache 1976.
14   Macpherson 1953; 1962.
15   See, as examples only, Ryerson 1947, pp. 46–51; 1946; Vance 1962, pp. 26–42.
16   D. Wright 2005, p. 125; Berger 1976, pp. 183–4, 217. For discussions of Ryerson from com-
     mentators of the left see the favourable G. Kealey 1995, pp. 48–100 and the more critical
     McDougall 1981. For one of the few positive gestures towards Ryerson's early historical
     writing see Guillet 1938, p. 242, but Guillet was hardly at the centre of the Canadian profes-
     sional historical milieu. Regarded more as an 'amateur' and an 'archivist' than a historian,
     Guillet's marginalisation has continued; studies of professional historical writing by Ber-
     ger and Wright bypass him. See, as well, Greer 1995, pp. 1–18.

and flair of his moving narrative, rather than in a stationary, ostentatious display of theoretical erudition. Ryerson's first historical studies of popular revolt and French Canadian democracy offered little in the way of overt comment on historical materialism, not a surprising omission given their gestation in the problematic suppressions of the Popular Front.[17] Later, in books first published in the 1960s and reprinted into the 1970s, Ryerson's self-conscious articulation of historical materialism was more pronounced, but it developed within these texts largely as quotes from Marx and Engels on the significance of material forces and class relations and as polemical postscripts in which the substance of broad interpretive overview was posed against the narrowing empiricist conventional wisdoms of the professional historical mainstream.[18]

Within this intellectual stratum few had a sophisticated understanding of historical materialism. Undoubtedly many thought that to be an historian and to be concerned with the material or the economic was to flirt with being a historical materialist. This could well explain a part of the reception accorded D.G. Creighton's *The Commercial Empire of the St. Lawrence, 1760–1850* (1937). Reviewing the book in the *Canadian Journal of Economics and Political Science*, Herbert Heaton was reminded of Friedrich Engels, Karl Marx, *The Communist Manifesto*, and what he indiscriminately referred to as 'the economic interpretation of history'. He thought Creighton's text would be well recommended to the Left Book Club! More than 25 years later, Stanley Mealing saw Innis and Creighton as inspiring interpretations of Lower Canada from the Conquest to Confederation that seriously entertained the idea that class was a motive force in Canadian history.[19]

Historical materialism, of course, involves more than the historical approach, more than the appreciation of the economic factor, more than an accent on class as a significant component of everyday life, social relations, and change. Historians in Canada have split few hairs in understanding what constitutes a Marxist historical materialist approach. Little effort has gone into either explicating the categories of historical materialist analysis and their meaning or defending these conceptual building blocks when they have come under attack.[20] The fundamental question that animates this essay is a relatively

---

17   Ryerson 1937; 1943.

18   See especially Ryerson 1963, pp. 326–9; 1973, pp. 424–35. See also Ryerson 1947; 1962, pp. 46–64.

19   Creighton 1937; Heaton 1938, pp. 565–70; Berger 1976, p. 216; Mealing 1965, p. 211.

20   As a beginning only, see the varied positions in Cohen 1978; E.P. Thompson 1978c, pp. 193–398.

straightforward one: how did historical materialism come to be such a non-entity in contemporary Canadian historical practice when, for some of us, it was a touchstone of our identity in the 1970s and early 1980s?[21] To answer these queries it is necessary to begin at the beginning.

Marxism is often seen, somewhat mechanically, as a fusion of German philosophy, French socialism and British political economy.[22] In terms of historical materialism these influences were conjoined in various ways. In their intermingling, of course, all were altered from what they had been as developments of bourgeois thought or specific, often utopian, struggles against it. British political economy *and* the history of class struggle in France, culminating in socialist developments in the 19th century, were by definition historicised subject realms. But it was as a springboard into the analytic richness of historical materialism that Marx made them more than studied episodes of the past.[23]

As Isaiah Berlin (certainly a critical reader of Marx, not given to acceptance of Marxist premises) noted in 1963, the theory of history and society Marx propounded was 'wholly original; the combination of elements [did] not in this case lead to syncretism, but form[ed] a bold, clear, coherent system, with the wide range and the massive architectonic quality' that marked it as decisively Hegelian. If historical materialism could not be reduced to a merely empirical undertaking, it was nonetheless 'not guilty of Hegel's reckless and contemptuous attitude towards the results of the scientific research of his time', but rather 'attempts to follow the direction indicated by the empirical sciences, and to incorporate their general results'. Yet, for all of this attraction to scientific method and empirical research, historical materialism refused to confine itself to mere description of phenomena, rejected mechanical understandings of

21   It is critical to recall that the international renaissance of social history that grew out of the 1960s and that bloomed in its political aftermath was, if not always Marxist, almost always engaged with Marxism in ways that meant Marxism was never easily caricatured and dismissed. This seems an eternity away from the current politico-intellectual moment. Thus many social historians of the 1990s who have come to be associated with critiques of Marxism and in particular Marxist social history were themselves advocates of Marxism and of Marxist social history, of a sort, in the 1960s, 1970s and early 1980s. This is evident, for instance, in the personal trajectory of the highly influential feminist historian and theorist Joan Scott, although she has never discussed it in anything resembling an autocritique. Compare, for instance, J.W. Scott 1974; 1988.

22   Among the legion of texts that address this three-tiered nature of Marxism's origins, see Lenin's 1913 biographical statement on Marx in Lenin 1960, p. 33; Anderson 1984, p. 86; and for more elaboration, Lichtheim 1965; or Berlin 1963.

23   For a classic statement see Marx 1941. But note as well Engels 1943; Marx 1968, pp. 97–180; and of course Marx 1959.

what constituted adequate 'proof' in the search for and appreciation of causality in accounts of the past and instead proposed a doctrine of 'movement in dialectical collisions'. As such, it 'turned into truisms, what had previously been paradoxes', and as its originator, Berlin claimed, Marx achieved a kind of genius.[24]

As Berlin's comments suggest, the development of historical materialism drew productively on Marx's encounter with German philosophy and his engagement with Hegelian idealism, in which he took Hegel at his best, in order, as he said, to stand him on his head, a project that also centrally involved his co-thinker Friedrich Engels.[25] The resulting materialism developed in Marx's first stage of intellectual explorations, the philosophical studies of his youth, in contradiction to thinkers such as Feuerbach, who sought to understand the essence of humanity through a conventional materialism governed by the insights of the ruling ideas of his epoch, featuring individualism, abstract conceptualisation, and, consequently, of thought divorced from practical human activity. In his brief theses on Feuerbach Marx indicated that a revolutionary materialism whose point was not just to interpret the world but to change it was inherently historicised. The eighth, ninth, and tenth theses provide something of a guide to Marx's and Engels's method:[26]

> Social life is essentially *practical*. All mysteries which mislead theory to mysticism find their rational solution in human practice and in the comprehension of this practice.
>
> The highest point attained by contemplative materialism, i.e., materialism which does not understand sensuousness as practical activity, is the outlook of single individuals in 'civil society'.
>
> The standpoint of the old materialism is 'civil society'; the standpoint of the new is *human society* or socialized humanity.[27]

These passages illuminate what was critical for Marx and Engels: that humanity is understood as a collective historicised social undertaking, with a past, gov-

---

24   Berlin 1963, pp. 127–30.

25   Central texts are Marx and Engels 1947; Engels 1941; Marx and Engels 1956; Marx 1980.

26   I use the term 'method' in this chapter to denote something more than merely a way of doing research. Rather as Marx noted: 'Now metaphysics – indeed all philosophy – can be summed up, according to Hegel, in method'. Marx n.d., p. 87. See, for fuller elaboration, McLennan 1981.

27   Karl Marx, 'Theses on Feuerbach', in Engels 1941, p. 84. This text contains a number of important statements on dialectical materialism, French materialism, etc.

erned by sensuous practical activity, in which figures prominently, of course, labour. Labour and human beings' relationship to it is for Marx one of the quintessential experiences of collective humanity, and for this reason Marx's historical materialism is embedded in his understanding of class. 'The history of all hitherto existing society is the history of class struggles', he would write with Engels in the 1848 *Manifesto of the Communist Party*.[28]

Class is thus central to Marx's understanding of historical materialism because it is the pivotal driving force of sensuous practical human activity at its highest level, the revolutionary remaking of social possibility. And in this we see how Marx's historical materialism was decidedly different than a mere pairing of historical method and materialist understanding would suggest. There are, after all, legions of bourgeois thinkers who embrace an historical approach. To be historical may be a necessary condition of being a Marxist – 'Always historicize!' is perhaps Fredric Jameson's favoured maxim.[29] But to be historical in and of itself, shorn of other premises of Marx's method, means little in terms of revolutionary thought. Nor, of course, is materialism per se, in and of itself, radical, Marxist or transformative. The bourgeoisie is an eminently materialist class; the right wing of our times, ensconced in positions of global imperialist authority, is a thoroughly materialist ideological and political force; my cats are materialist beings to their core, demanding their morning and early evening feedings with the regularity of the sun's rise and set.

What made historical materialism Marxist was the formative fusion of the systematic and critical approaches/meanings of political economy, philosophy and socialism. If Marx's method was rooted in the bourgeois thought of the Enlightenment, in the dialectical analytic approach, which, building on Hegel, posits 'the grasping of opposites in their unity or of the positive in the negative',[30] it moved beyond origins to occupy entirely new, disruptive and revolutionary terrain. It was itself a confirmation of dialectics. As Marx stressed in *The German Ideology*,

> Proletariat and Wealth are opposites. As such they form a whole. They are both formations of the world of private property. What concerns us here is to define the particular position they take within the opposition. It is not enough to state that they are two sides of a whole.[31]

---

28   Marx and Engels 1968, p. 35.
29   Jameson 1981, p. 9.
30   For the broader discussion see Hegel 1961, Volume II, pp. 63–70.
31   Marx 1947, pp. xii–xiii.

In Hegel, dialectical insight truncates at the level of the idea, seeing in history only the animating authority of the spirit, of essentialised categories, of civil society's supremacy as an ordered formation, rather than of struggle and practical, sensuous human endeavour as it is lived in the messy conflictual relations of class and its hierarchicalisation of power. Marx's dialectic differed from Hegel's in that historicised political economy placed a practical and analytic emphasis on the great contending class confrontations – the unity of opposites – bounded by the determinations of productive life. As Marx wrote to J.B. Schweizer on 24 January 1865, the secret of scientific dialectics lies in comprehending economic categories as 'the theoretical expression of historic relations of production, corresponding to a particular stage of development in material production'.[32] Class is, for Marx, not an inert social structure but a movement of clashing social antagonists embedded in irreconcilable difference, a structure of oppositions that deforms civil society's potential. Only through the ultimate negation, the transcendence of class that is the final, necessary possibility of socialism, can capitalism's inevitable limits be revealed and redefined not as actualities of exploitation and oppression, but as histories superseded by struggle and overcome by the present. 'No antagonism, no progress', as Marx succinctly summed it up in *The Poverty of Philosophy*.[33]

It is thus the contribution of Marxism to revolutionise bourgeois thought, to transform the dialectic of Hegel into something other than what it was and, in the process, to transcend the historicism and materialism central to the Enlightenment's ideological project. The outcome was historical materialism, a weapon of analysis that owed its origins to the class struggles it would argue advanced humanity's on-going social change. Thus Marxism as idea and method, as well as practice, was itself a confirmation of the ever-present dance of the dialectic. 'The ideas of the ruling class are in every epoch the ruling ideas, i.e., the class which is the ruling material force of society is at the same time its ruling intellectual force'.[34] But with the ascent of capitalist property forms and the inevitability of class struggle, ideas of opposition were in gestation: their triumph would register as class struggle culminated in a new social order.

Like most of Marx's maxims, this one appears, on the surface, to be impossible to sustain. There are always ideas of dissent and opposition and, especially in academic life, we like to believe that they matter, because they are the stuff of

32   Marx and Engels 1935, p. 172.
33   Marx n.d., p. 53.
34   Marx 1947, p. 39.

our lives. But how, if Marx is right, does historical change happen? How do the ideas of one epoch become the discarded and antiquated thought of another phase of human development?

The answer lies in the insights of historical materialism. Ideas do not, contrary to Hegel and much of the sensibility of our times, make history, although they often greatly influence its development. In the relational clash of forces that is historical change, material being (which is always in a state of dialectical dependency on the past and disruptive destabilisation of the future) shifts the ground on which men and women sensuously walk. Neither change nor the foundations of human existence that move with it are *individual*, and these historicised phenomena are rarely pre-eminently governed by grand *ideas*, however much such ermine-gowned thought bows in humbly proclaiming its high influence over humankind:

> Social relations are closely bound up with productive forces. In acquiring new productive forces men change their mode of production; and in changing their mode of production, in changing the way of earning their living, they change all their social relations. The hand-mill gives you society with the feudal lord; the steam-mill, society with the industrial capitalist.

As Marx insisted, ideas emerged in conformity with their social relations and were necessarily transitory: 'The only immutable thing is the abstraction of movement'.[35]

Ideas change like the social structures in which they are embedded. And in the clash of change, the ruling ideas of one epoch are challenged by ideas of opposition. Historical materialism is an analytic approach that highlights change, that sees ideas as critically important in making history, but always within boundaries of determination.[36] The analytic insight of Marxism's development of historical materialism was, I am suggesting, the infusion of dialectical thinking into understandings of determination. This opened out into a conceptual richness that was able to grasp historical process in motion in ways that mainstream empiricist historical study could never quite appreciate. With his elaboration of historical materialism, for instance, Marx shattered forever

---

35   Marx n.d., pp. 92–3.

36   On determination see, for instance, the once highly influential writings of Raymond Williams, especially 'Base and Superstructure in Marxist Cultural Theory', originally appearing in *New Left Review*, but reprinted in R. Williams 1980, pp. 31–49; 1976, pp. 98–102.

the settled complacencies of 19th-century empiricist notions of historical interpretation, in which historical practice was a descriptive exercise of accumu-
lating and ordering the factual progression of events that were themselves the
final articulation of history's often linear march. Historical materialism demanded new interrogations – which facts, outcomes and developments? – and
insisted on posing in more complex ways questions of why the past happened
as it did and how it came to culminate in the present. It is for exactly this reason
that historical materialism was in some senses a prefatory analytic movement
into post-modern thought (which is precisely why most of the major theorists
of critical theory have their origins in relations with Marxism), for it opened
important chapters in destabilising conventional intellectual wisdoms.[37]

The destabilising contribution of historical materialism registered forcefully
in the Anglo-American academic world in the immediate post-World War II
years.[38] Perhaps no set of wide-ranging discussions from the 1950s to the 1980s
illuminated this reach of historical materialism more than the richly productive debate over the transition from feudalism to capitalism. In this scholarship,
which saw Marxist creative historical argument at its best trump liberal and
conservative writers, the analytic sweep of historical materialism prodded the
founding of the journal *Past & Present* and revived a discipline – economic
history – that was brought out of the interpretive doldrums of its retreat into
the mind-numbing cul-de-sac of cliometrics by the Brenner debate.[39] Animated by feminist concerns and insights, a Canadian Marxist sociologist, Wally
Seccombe, made a major contribution to both historical materialism *and* the
transition debate in his brilliantly original insistence that the dynamics of population – the unexplored 'science' of demography – demanded consideration
as an important stimulus in the transition to capitalism.[40]

---

37   It is of course ironic that some of the best writing cognisant of Marxism's intuitive grasp of
      modernity's eventual inevitable foundering on the shoals of its own immutable destabil-
      isation fed into conceptualisations of postmodernity as a condition of late capitalism,
      when an ideology of that cultural logic, postmodern*ism*, would then often assail histor-
      ical materialism as yet another discarded remnant of outmoded modernist thought. See,
      for instance, Berman 1982; Harvey 1989; Jameson 1991. On critical theory's debt to historical
      materialism see Derrida 1994.

38   For a brief introduction only, see B. Palmer 2001, pp. 49–60.

39   As introduction only, see Trevor-Roper 1968; Hilton 1978; Ashton and Philpin 1987.

40   Seccombe's original brief statement appeared as Seccombe 1983, pp. 22–47, and for an
      appreciative tribute see Anderson 1984, p. 88. See, for a fuller elaboration, Seccombe 1992;
      1993.

Nothing so momentous happened in reconfiguring the history of Canada. Yet regardless of how one views Stanley Ryerson's understandings of the meaning of Confederation, outlined in his *Unequal Union*, there is no denying that his approach to a central event in Canadian historical development differs dramatically from the empiricist accounts that had prevailed in mainstream historiographic circles up to the 1960s. In the place of a rhetoric of regional debate articulating specific essentialised geo-economic interests and the manoeuvres and manipulations of particular individuals ('Fathers of Confederation'), we have an accounting that accents the material determinations of colonialism and capitalism, confounded by the tensions that proliferated in the midst of class formation and the exercise of state-building. Along the way we are treated to accounts of the growing impact of ideas of democracy and self-determination; appreciations of land and labour and their place in circumscribing the possibilities of the period; understandings of developing thought in the natural and social sciences; and appreciations of regionally based movements of protest. Old debates over whether Confederation was an 'Act' or a 'Pact' could indeed be situated within an historical materialist reading of a cornerstone in the making of Canadian nationhood, but never in the same routinised ways as had been common in conventional scholarship.[41]

As a New Left historiography of 19th-century Canadian class formation emerged in the late 1970s and early 1980s with the publication of my study of Hamilton workers, *A Culture in Conflict*, Gregory S. Kealey's *Toronto Workers Respond to Industrial Capitalism*, and our co-authored treatment of the Knights of Labor and the Great Upheaval, the possibilities of a historical materialist labour history now became apparent. These studies shifted analytic sensibilities to working-class life. They did this because of their research as well as their conceptualisation, which, in the words of the major non-Marxist historiographic commentator Carl Berger, constituted 'significant achievements' contributing markedly to 'the ultimate clarification of class – and class in history'.[42]

---

41   Ryerson 1973. For a stimulating recent non-Marxist discussion of the Act vs. Pact debate over Confederation, see Romney 1999.

42   B. Palmer 1979; G. Kealey 1980; Kealey and Palmer 1982. Note, as well as Berger's assessment, R. Cook 1983, pp. 115–26. For Berger's comment see Berger 1986, p. 307, which also stressed what he saw as the confusing and capricious polemical debates surrounding 1970s and 1980s writing in the field of working-class history. No doubt Berger simply did not understand polemic, which as Perry Anderson has pointed out 'is a literary form whose history has yet to be written ... Polemic is a discourse conflict, whose effect depends on a delicate

In retrospect, the accomplishments of historical materialist writing in Canada, viewed through a reading of, on the one hand, Ryerson on the national question and 19th-century state-building and, on the other, Kealey and Palmer on 19th-century class formation, were both considerable *and* limited. In both cases, significant forces of opposition and containment constrained the development of historical materialism's possibilities. This was a matter of influences embraced and accepted willingly, as well as forces of constraint that challenged and cajoled both overtly and tacitly. To understand this context, it is important to appreciate something of the history of historical materialism's making in the period reaching from the late 19th century into the second and third quarters of the 20th century and beyond, culminating in a series of exchanges and debates that erupted in the 1970s.

The complicated relations of dialectics, historical materialism, and Marxist writing from the Second International through the degeneration of the Russian Revolution in the 1920s had raised innumerable issues about science, nature, economism, and humanism. They take us from Engels's *Dialectics of Nature* and *Anti-Dühring* through Lenin's *Materialism and Empirio-Criticism* and into a troubled attempt to address Stalinism in the revival of Hegelianism by theorists such as Lukács and Korsch. Strains of this intellectual history echo in Gramsci, are certainly central to Marcuse's stature as a leading analytic voice in the emergence of a 1960s New Left, and are unmistakable in the E.P. Thompson versus Louis Althusser debate of the 1970s, in which historical materialism figured centrally. As Western Marxism, its Hegelianising influences given free rein by the defeats of the revolutionary left in the inter-war period, came to be counter-posed to a Soviet Marxism increasingly reduced to more wooden and mechanical conceptualisation under the pressures of Stalinisation, historical materialism bifurcated. As Perry Anderson has suggested, it divided into camps of increasingly abstract philosophical textualism, on the one hand, and, on the other, rote repetitions of 'last instance', economistic short-hand for dialectical materialism. The quintessential statement of what came to be known in 'Party' circles as 'diamat' was presented under the ultimate authority of Stalin's widely diffused and elementary primer, *Dialectical and Historical Materialism*, first

---

balance between the requirements of truth and the enticements of anger, the duty to argue and the zest to inflame'. Canadian historians of Berger's generation had no sense of such enticements, duties and zests. Indeed, it can be argued that very few academics in Canada, at any time, up to and including the present, embrace these sensibilities, which, of course, have often been central to historical materialism's making, from Marx to the current period. On polemic, see Anderson 2005, pp. 178–9.

published in English in 1940. This impasse pressured the 1948 reflections of C.L.R. James, *Notes on Dialectics: Hegel, Marx, Lenin*, but by the 1960s and 1970s it was perhaps more starkly evident in the forceful attacks on Hegelianism by theorists such as Louis Althusser, Galvano Della Volpe and, with more subtlety, Sebastiano Timpanaro and Lucio Colletti.[43]

The complexity of this divide within historical materialism in the 1920 to 1970 period never registered forcefully in Canada, largely because the notion of Marxist historical practice, of Marxism as method, was almost entirely translated, prior to the 1960s, through Party functionaries such as Stanley Ryerson. His truncated theoretical and polemical passages tended, for all their strengths, to be summaries of Soviet Marxist diamat. As the opportunity to transcend this limitation appeared, it proved stillborn. Kealey, other New Left historians, and I emerged out of the 1960s and early 1970s in Canada embracing historical materialism in our studies of labour, but the resulting scrutiny of Marxism and our capacity to elaborate on its applicability to the study of the past were to prove quite limited. One cause of this, certainly, was that in the uphill battle to secure for Marxist ideas some measure of acceptance in the academy, a kind of 'popular front' of all seemingly Marxist scholars consolidated, to the point that differences *within* Marxism were, with small exceptions, suppressed and silenced. Without a doubt the peculiarly vehement reaction of certain liberal-social democratic historians, who were stridently vocal in their opposition to Marxism, reinforced this tendency to keep dissent amongst Marxists bottled up. The development of historical materialism as method was thus constrained by the peculiarly Canadian boundaries of an *ideological* debate that pitted old

---

43   This complicated intellectual history of Marxism is best introduced by the brilliant exposition in Anderson 1976, and, at its endnote, in the robust polemic of E.P. Thompson 1978c or in a subsequent summary, Anderson 1984, pp. 9–31. But along the way it generated an immense output of philosophically inclined commentary of relevance to historical materialism in general and of central importance in the formation of a New Left historiography emerging out of the 1960s. For some of the most pivotal texts, see Lukács 1968, and the (at the time unknown) Lukács 2000; James 1980; Marcuse 1960; 1961; Gramsci 1971. For the anti-Hegelianism of Timpanaro and Colletti see Timpanaro 1975; Colletti 1972; 1973. Timpanaro, whose Marxism and materialism were resolute and above concession to fashion, remained steadfast in his politics, while Colletti failed to stay the course. As the 1970s wound down, he lapsed into what Anderson (1984, pp. 28–9) designated 'a shrill enemy of Marxism and staunch defender of a more or less conventional liberalism'. Anderson's affectionate recollection of Timpanaro appears in Anderson 2005, pp. 188–209. The primary document of diamat is Stalin 1940.

guard, empiricist, *and* mildly left historians against a seemingly coherent *nouvelle vague* of Marxist historical practitioners.[44]

Moreover, because the most rigorously promoted innovations in historical methodology of this period turned in class directions and embraced materialist premises, but did so in ways that shied away from culture and the concerns of many so-called 'new' working-class historians, further divisions unfolded in complex ways. Michael B. Katz and his students turned tantalisingly in the direction of historical materialism as their Hamilton Social History Project shifted gears from its focus on mobility to an accent on class formation. But this interesting movement always twisted in the winds of a reification of quantitative methodology, as Katz et al. explored important questions of social structure and the emergence of industrial capitalism that too often restricted analysis according to the accessibility of certain kinds of evidence. Class struggle, workplace relations, the cultural intricacies of everyday life – these seemed distant from what Katz insisted was important in historical process, which was invariably what could be measured out in the records of a methodologically privileged discernment: manuscript census tracts and tax assessment rolls.[45]

---

44 For a taste of the anti-Marxism of the liberal and social democratic critique of the so-called new working-class history, see, for instance, McNaught 1981, pp. 141–68, a knock-about polemic commissioned by the *Canadian Historical Review* and awarded its annual prize for the best essay appearing in the journal's pages; Bercuson 1981, pp. 95–112; Nelles 1980, p. 6; Bercuson 1983, pp. 589–91. Attacks on Marxists as vituperative appeared in J.L. Granatstein, 'No Hostages Taken in War Between Historians', *Toronto Star*, Saturday Magazine, 24 June 1989, repeated later in Granatstein 1998, p. 61. The response of established Canadian historians to a New Left, class-based historiography was harsher than in other national settings. See, for a brief discussion of this, Palmer 2000b, pp. 107–17. Ironically, as McNaught's intervention indicates, it was perhaps the strength of a social democratic presence in Canadian intellectual life during the 1960s and 1970s that explains the vehemence with which the mainstream reacted to Marxist initiatives. McNaught, but also even Bercuson and Granatstein, had liberal/social democratic roots in the 1960s, and if this is difficult to grasp in 2006 after years of their movement to the right it is nevertheless crucial to keep in mind as we historicise the development of historiographic difference. It was only *because* some of these people could be perceived as left or understood to be experts in the study of labour that they had something of a platform from which to address the nascent development of historical materialism in Canada.

45 Katz's 1970s Canadian sojourn produced much of value, but in terms of the relationship of this work to historical materialism it must be said that the accomplishment was limited. It also unconsciously helped to isolate historical materialist study of the working class by elaborating and justifying quantitative *methodology* as opposed to developing Marxist method. See Katz 1975; Katz, Doucet, and Stern 1982, with the most explicit attempt

From within historical materialism more properly, a sophisticated, but quite solitary, critique by Ian McKay gravitated in similar directions in its useful, if somewhat caricatured, insistence that culture was a problematic category of analysis. McKay, who recognised that the intellectual-political impasse of 'old' versus 'new' working-class history was in actuality a complicated morass of positions and debates, nevertheless sided resolutely with anti-Hegelian theorists such as Colletti, insisting that '[w]e close the logical and political circles only by a return to the concrete: to the determinate abstractions of *Capital* and to a logical political practice'. Written in some ways as a rejoinder to E.P. Thompson's *The Poverty of Theory* as well as a riposte against the far more nascent analytics of the Canadian so-called new working-class history, McKay's embrace of Colletti reduced the possibility of exploring historical materialism to a dichotomous challenge: 'for or against culture'. In retrospect, what this opposition misses is the shifting nature and meaning of culture within Marxist scholarship, which in turn illuminates well the differences between the 1960s and 1970s and the 1990s and the opening decade of the 21st century. Those historical materialists, in Canada as well as in England and the United States, who were assailed as 'culturalists' in 1979 and 1980 were of course anything but advocates of the determining influence of culture. That Richard Johnson labelled them as such did not necessarily mean that writers like E.P. Thompson were guilty of taking historical materialism in the problematic directions some theorists identified. A quarter of a century later, it is obvious that those historical materialists of the 1970s who utilised the study of culture to recover lost aspects of class formation and re-situate class struggle did so in ways that developed Marxism and class analysis, unlike much of the study of culture in the post-1990 years. If cultural study has proliferated in our times, it has done so in ways increasingly wrenched from anything akin to material moorings, concerning itself only obliquely and idiosyncratically with historical materialism.[46]

---

to develop a Marxist analysis in Katz 1978, pp. 6–23. Early critique appeared in two review essays: B. Palmer 1976, pp. 16–25; 1984a, pp. 190–7. The project of quantitative historical method in Canada has been carried on, often in quite stimulating ways, by Peter Baskerville and Eric W. Sager (1998).

46   For McKay's Colletti-inspired critique see McKay 1981–2, pp. 185–241. This essay sits uneasily with McKay's later writing, starting with McKay 1994 and extending into McKay 2000, pp. 617–45, and even McKay 2005. Little in these later texts addresses the determinative abstractions of *Capital*, but then the intellectual and political climate of McKay's original critique was decidedly different than the current moment. (Compare, for instance, Heron 1988 and Heron 2003.) Moreover, if we take a text that *was* congruent with McKay's hostil-

As Terry Eagleton notes, the shift that has taken place in the last three decades around cultural questions has been both monumental and decisively debilitating for radical thought. 'Culture had been among other things a way of keeping radical politics warm', he writes with colloquial insight,

> a continuation of it by other means. Increasingly, however, it was to become a substitute for it. In some ways, the 1980s were like the 1880s or the 1960s without the politics. As leftist political hopes faded, cultural studies came to the fore.[47]

On reflection, those of us who struggled to develop historical materialism in Canada made some advances, but also missed some opportunities. We thought we were all historical materialists in the small circles of left historians that debated various questions, and in retrospect we probably let slip away the chance for a much-needed sharpening of our theoretical swords. We possibly lost the conceptual momentum of a moment when we could have both sustained our historical projects of recovery and reinterpretation *and* developed and deepened our sense of historical materialism. Little did we know, in the 1970s, that the implosion of actually existing socialism and the fall of the Soviet Union would unfold over the course of the 1980s and that this about-face in the world of global *realpolitik* would unleash the ideological hounds, turning the tables decisively on the loosely Marxist analytics that seemed hegemonic amongst social historians as historical materialism was struggling to secure a place in Canadian historiography. Even less predictable would be the related explosion of 'critical theory', in which the cultural logic of late capitalism, labelled 'post-modernism', would soon come to be understood as the interpret-

---

ity to culture (McKay 1978, pp. 63–108) it is apparent that it is richest in its elaboration of business history. Its conception of working-class history and formation was both unduly schematic and given to interpretive extremism, evident in the assertion that 'at no time during "the making of the Canadian working class" (1850–1914) was there a serious possibility of generalized class conflict and that this is the central problem of labour history that must be explored. Such an absence of national class conflict made Canada unusual among the industrialized countries' (McKay 1978, p. 66). For the Richard Johnson-led critique of culturalism, which influenced much discussion in the late 1970s and early 1980s, see R. Johnson 1978, pp. 79–100; Clarke, Critcher, and Johnson 1979. Thompson's brief rejoinder and refusal of the label of culturalism is in E.P. Thompson 1981, pp. 396–408.

47   Eagleton 2003, p. 45. Note as well the comments of Perry Anderson on arguably the most important Marxist cultural theorist of the late 20th century, Fredric Jameson, in Anderson 1998, pp. 134–7.

ive canon of our time, its ideas of discursiveness and what Perry Anderson has designated the 'exorbitation of language' and the 'randomization of history' striking repeated blows at the edifice of historical materialism. That these blows came not from the hands of conservatives but often from quarters that had been linked to Marxist historians of the 1970s, such as erstwhile socialist feminists, progressives in gay and lesbian studies, and those demanding that the special oppression of race be addressed frontally, only complicated matters further.[48]

Historical materialism thus proved insufficiently rooted amongst a layer of radical Canadian historians. As a collectivity, the Canadian Marxist cohort that emerged within the discipline of history in the 1970s proved ill-prepared to confront a new and aggressively self-confident theoretical challenge that, in effect, denied that there was all that much of analytic interest in the historical materialist tradition and that was soon given to caricature of Marx and Engels, on the one hand, as architects of 'vulgar economism' or, on the other, as little more than another radical voice of mainstream, conservative thought incarcerated in the prison house of a language of class. Many were no doubt numbed by the cavalier repudiation of historical materialism as somehow an Anti-Theory and, when statements of an extreme sort challenged them directly, simply wilted in silence or claimed that the arguments were too ill-considered to merit response. Others clearly moved on to cultural terrain that was now judged more attractive and avant-garde than the materialist subjects of another seemingly rather spent and tired era.[49]

The immediate post-1960s cohort of radical Canadian historians thus spent a youthful decade of decisive productivity in the 1970s and early 1980s developing Marxism in Canada. The accomplishments, to be sure, were impressive. Yet there is no doubt that this work placed the necessity of elaborating a sophisticated conceptualisation of historical materialism on the lower shelf of

---

48   See Jameson 1991; Anderson 1984, pp. 40, 48.

49   I am struggling to be fair-minded here and to appreciate the shortcomings of a collectivity in which I myself must be situated. That remains my belief. Nevertheless, it is of course true that some of us made efforts to turn the tide. See B. Palmer 1990a; Leier 1996b, pp. 61–75. It will be argued that the belief that the tide had to be turned was itself mistaken, especially by those who were either swept along or who stood on the sidelines enjoying the view. Such arguments are generally being made, I contend, by those who have taken a detour away from the historical materialist sensibilities and political edge of the 1970s. For a disturbing statement on Canadian historiography that contained much that anyone embracing historical materialism could have responded to (but did not), see Valverde 2000, pp. 59–77.

priorities. This may well have been inevitable, the first task being to recover important dimensions of the Canadian historical past. So little had been written on class formation in the 19th century; on family history and the importance of the household; on cultural rituals that revealed the shared relations of private life, age and community; on major upheavals of working-class opposition other than the Winnipeg General Strike; on sexuality, market society and social mores; on women and the left or, indeed, on the history of communism, socialism or anarchism that it is not surprising that historical materialists sunk their research teeth into the project of recreating a past largely lost.[50] Canadian historians, sociologists and political economists of the Marxist left made their mark in refining and developing important analytic points with respect to the Braverman thesis on the degradation of work[51] or, in the case of socialist feminists, in charting a particularly important gendered appreciation of *both* paid work and household production. The role of the Women's Press in sustaining a socialist-feminist politics in Toronto and Canada in the years from the early 1970s to the mid-1980s is under-appreciated; the unique contribution this publishing house made enlivened historical materialism by infusing it with appreciations of women's experience and gender struggles, securing international reputations for its writers.[52] But in the main, these invaluable statements were for all their importance insufficiently rigorous in premising and elaborating their findings on the *theory* of historical materialism. Then, too, some of us were involved in the actual class struggles of the time and bent our pens to produce critical histories of moments of dissent that were channelled towards defeat through leaderships animated by anything but historical

---

50   The above is only a partial list of what could be considered. For review essays that highlight such accomplishments of historical materialist scholarship, consider, for instance: G. Kealey 1981a, pp. 95–126; Bradbury 1987, pp. 23–44. Among countless studies that could be cited see Bradbury 1993; B. Palmer 1978, pp. 5–62; B. Palmer 1984b, pp. 229–308; Lévesque 1989; Kinsman 1987. On the history of the Canadian left, consider the following fundamental works of significant recovery: Angus 1981; Lévesque 1984; Sangster 1989; D. Frank 1999; Hobbs and Sangster 1999.

51   See, for instance, Heron and Storey 1986; B. Palmer 1975, pp. 31–49; Heron and Palmer 1977, pp. 423–58. Braverman 1974 had a significant impact among Canadian working-class historians in the 1970s.

52   Among the works that could be cited, Sangster 1995b; Steedman 1997; Fox 1980; Luxton 1980; Briskin and Yanz 1983. This feminist project was never defined within the disciplinary niche of historical studies. Rather, it was interdisciplinary in nature and often developed out of the political economy tradition, but it was nonetheless often usually framed within a historical *and* a Marxist perspective. See, for instance, Maroney and Luxton 1987; C. Yates 1993.

materialist premises. Such writing, an engagement with the political setbacks
of our times meant to be read by a broad audience and tip the balance of class
forces in new directions, did not necessarily easily lend itself to articulations of
theoretical refinement.[53]

By the early 1990s, then, the 1960s and 1970s seemed a long way away. The
deluge of change registered in the obliteration of an epoch in which radical,
even revolutionary, thought was both exhilaratingly appreciated in specific
niche sectors of Canadian academic life and valued as contributing to the
political possibilities of social transformation that seemed vibrant and very
much of the times. Marxism and historical materialism flourished and captured
the hearts and minds of so many precisely because, in the 1960s and into the
1970s, capitalism appeared to have lost its authority to govern. Major struggles
erupted.

Quebec seemed on the precipitous edge of revolution, and not only because
of the activities of the Front de Libération du Québec from 1963 to 1970: in
the aftermath of the October Crisis, an explosion of the francophone dispossessed culminated in the galvanising La Presse strike of 1971 and the Common
Front 'Crise Sociale' of March through May 1972, which saw 210,000 public-
sector workers take to the streets, authorities jail union leaders and strikers
defiantly occupy workplaces and such information conduits as radio stations.
'La Belle Province' had become notorious as North America's centre of revolutionary syndicalist upheaval. Within the Canadian working class as a whole,
developments were less momentous but nonetheless quite noteworthy. Violent
wildcat strikes rocked the settled relations of rank-and-file workers, their trade-
union officialdoms, Canadian employers and the state during 1965 and 1966.
Pitched battles continued into the mid-1970s, with threatened general strikes
and massive militant work stoppages throwing provincial governments into
disarray and assailing the Liberal state's containment strategy of wage and price
controls. A revival of Canadian feminism snake-danced its way across the country in abortion caravans and women's consciousness-raising groups, marching
into Royal Commissions, out of university classrooms and onto picket lines and
trade-union executives. Campus revolts shook the pillars of university administrations from George Williams and McGill to Simon Fraser, while anti-racist
actions, peace mobilisations and the drum beats of Aboriginal dissent echoed
throughout the 1970s. As late as 1983, when British Columbia was faced with one

---

53   See, for instance, B. Palmer 1988b; and for a historical study related to such developments,
      Leier 1995. For a similar kind of study written by Marxists in the political economy
      tradition, see the highly influential Panitch and Swartz 1988.

of the first and most decisive all-out cut-back assaults of a New Right government, the forces of opposition could still summon something of the spirit of the
1960s, orchestrating a massive protest movement that threatened to culminate
in shutting down the entire province had not the timid trade-union tops folded
up the tent of protest before it filled to the bursting point with angry militants
howling their derision of the Social Credit Party's dismantling of the welfare
state.[54]

By this late date, however, capitalism's rising ascendancy, now a decade
strong, and actually existing socialism's on-going demise had swept the scholarly deck of old positions, reducing historical materialism's attractiveness decisively. Students in undergraduate programmes in the 1990s barely got to
engage Marx, in part because in some quarters he was being reduced to merely
a radical appendage to Eurocentric thought.[55] Left organisations that had been
strong and vibrant in the 1970s and that had provided an alternative education
in basic principles of Marxist analysis were now largely defunct, torn asunder
by campaigns of disinformation orchestrated by the Canadian security apparatus, bitter internal wars of factional position and the general cooling of the
climate of dissent.[56] The social movements of post-modern times are not galvanised so much by Marxist theory as they are moved by other critical traditions, most of which have their origins in an engagement with – but ultimately
a break from – historical materialism and socialist principles.[57]

There are of course developments of considerable importance, including
ones with much promise for the left and for historical materialist analysis.
In Latin America, for instance, popular mobilisations are opening new doors

---

54   This history is both too detailed and too complex to reference adequately in an article of
      this nature. I explore some of the 1960s events in a forthcoming study: *Canada in the 1960s:
      The Ironies of Identity*. For a sense of the tumultuous events in Quebec and the attendant
      transformation of consciousness, see Vallières 1971; Fournier 1984; Drache 1972. For an
      abbreviated overview of the labour scene in this period see B. Palmer 2003, pp. 37–9, and
      for feminism, class and the women's movement, Luxton 2001, pp. 63–88; Adamson, Briskin,
      and McPhail 1988; Rebick 2005.

55   See Young 1990. For a counter to this reductionism, see the critically important defence of
      historical materialism in Ahmad 1992 and the important essays in Bartolovich and Lazarus
      2002.

56   See, for instance, AA.VV. 1980; B. Palmer 1981b, pp. 28–41; 1988a; Hewitt 2002; and the not
      entirely reliable O'Toole 1977.

57   See Carroll 1997, and especially Adam 1997, pp. 39–56, which commences with the state-
      ment, 'Much of the recent social theory generated around understanding the 1990s has
      turned from political economy to culture in identifying the forces for social change'.

many thought closed. Nevertheless, in Canadian historical circles, defence of basic tenets of historical materialism is not exactly resolute. A recent poll of the editorial board members of the Canadian journal *Left History*, in which they were asked to answer the question 'What is left history?', revealed little concern with the theoretical issues posed in the development of historical materialism.[58] Trotsky's maxim, 'Those who cannot defend old positions will never conquer new ones', is judged little more than a traditionalist albatross weighing down the creativity of contemporary scholarship.[59] Sebastiano Timpanaro's closing 1979 postscript to *On Materialism* falls largely, it seems to me, on deaf ears: 'The renovation of socialism, however much it may diverge, even in important respects, from the vision of Marx, Engels, Lenin, and Trotsky will not be able to ignore some of their teachings that remain fundamental. Whoever speaks of socialism that must be "reinvented wholly anew" winds up inventing something very old: capitalism'.[60]

If those who want to reinterpret the world radically as well as change it are to avoid reinventing this wheel of capitalism, which threatens to roll over the entire world in its destructive march to accumulate more and more for fewer and fewer, we will need the analytic insights and practical political engagements historical materialism has always offered and encouraged. For a century and a half, this historical materialism has enriched the politics of the left and the analysis of society. It has opened into new interpretive vistas, engaging productively with understandings of feminism,[61] language, productive life and all

---

58   See AA.VV. 2006, pp. 12–68.

59   Trotsky 1973, p. 178. For an elaboration of the price paid for jettisoning tradition, an all-too-common occurrence among contemporary labour and social historians, see B. Palmer 2006, pp. 195–226.

60   Timpanaro 1975, p. 261. Ellen Wood makes a congruent point in some of her commentary on the 'retreat from class' and other developments of the 1980s and 1990s, as does Terry Eagleton in a range of writings including Eagleton 2003. See Wood 1986; 1997, pp. 1–16.

61   Feminist socialists made significant contributions to historical materialism as theory and as the practice of expanding the subject of inquiry of historical reinterpretation in the period I have been addressing. But as is evident in the contrasting subtitles of Michele Barrett's 1980 and 1988 editions of her pivotally important text, *Women's Oppression Today: Problems in Marxist Feminist Analysis* (M. Barrett 1980) vs. *Women's Oppression Today: The Marxist/Feminist Encounter* (M. Barrett 1988), the toll taken on the linked projects of Marxism and feminism over the 1980s was considerable. Still, in Canada, advances in historical materialism that developed out of the productive engagement of feminist theory and research with Marxist analysis included important contributions to debates over productive/reproductive labour, significant expansion of the terrain of inquiry in critical disciplines such as political economy, the transformation of fields such as working-class

manner of critically important subjects. It does not so much centre class and the dominant relations of production as *the* categories of analysis as it insists that they be related, with due consideration given to their significant place in the complexities of determination, to a host of other developments, increasingly important in the shifting gears of modernity's movement: gender, race, empire and imperialism, social movements, identity and subjectivity, national states and the collectivities of struggles localised and generalised.

Even before the epoch of identity's acute fragmentation under the living conditions of late capitalism, Marx understood that 'unequal individuals' made up the entirety of the working class, just as they composed the differentiated nature of society. In 1875, he chastised those in the workers' movement who insisted that the proletarian material of class society could be 'measurable only by an equal standard in so far as they are brought under an equal point of view ... regarded *only as workers* and nothing more is seen in them, everything else being ignored'. Central to this insight, however, was the *materialist* boundary of determination that hemmed in the differentiation of class individuals: the realisation of humanity could 'never be higher than the economic structure of society and its cultural development conditioned thereby'. As a consequence, only with society's attainment of a higher plane, in which communist relations finally abolish 'the antithesis between mental and physical labour', making work 'life's prime want' and freeing the flow of 'co-operative wealth ... more abundantly', could 'the narrow horizon of bourgeois right be crossed in its entirety and society inscribe on its banners: From each according to his ability, to each according to his needs'.[62]

In a famous letter of 1877 Marx answered those who saw his method as overly deterministic and narrowly reductionist. He denied propounding 'any historico-philosophical theory of the *marche général* imposed by fate upon every people'.[63] But in elaborating, through his development of historical materialism, the general analytic framework of how historical change takes place through the development of the productive forces – how class antagonisms and the logic of specific modes of production and their regimes of accumulation drive historical transformation, situating the men and women and chil-

---

history and decisive interventions in the area of critical race studies. On these general developments, as an introduction only, see Hamilton and Barrett 1986; Maroney and Luxton 1987; Luxton 2001; Clement and Vosko 2003; Sangster 2000, pp. 127–65; Bannerji 2000.

62   Marx 1962, p. 24. See also the different but highly important discussions in Sen 2006; Ahmad 1992.

63   Marx and Engels 1938, p. 354.

dren who make history, but never quite as they please, within materialised ensembles of relations – Marx provided a theory *and* a politics capable of realising humanity's ultimate movement into a new stage of development in which antagonism is not the structured premise of social being. 'The tradition of all the dead generations weighs like a nightmare on the brains of the living', Marx wrote in his most resolutely historical materialist work, *The Eighteenth Brumaire of Louis Bonaparte*. He ended that historical discussion of bourgeois power corrupted with this historical materialist insight:

> Driven by the contradictory demands of the situation and being at the same time, like a conjurer, under the necessity of keeping the gaze fixed on himself ... by springing constant surprises, that is to say, under the necessity of executing a *coup d'état en miniature* every day, Bonaparte throws the entire bourgeois economy into confusion, violates everything that seemed inviolable ... makes some tolerant of revolution, others desirous of revolution, and produces actual anarchy in the name of order, while at the same time stripping its halo from the entire state machine, profanes it and makes it once loathsome and ridiculous.[64]

How timely such a statement appears today!

From Bonaparte to George Bush, history is indeed understandable through the lens of historical materialism, a lens in which the dialectical view focusses, clarifies and magnifies the intricate process of change. Neither the final denouement of Stalinism nor the related rise of 'post'-critical theory changes this actuality, especially for those times past that predate the arrival of a postmodern cultural logic associated with late capitalism. To keep to this interpretive course, associated with 150 years of historical materialist theory, insight and research, reminds us that the present is not humanity's jail cell but rather only a confining construction, the walls of which are a specific set of historically conditioned determinations that demand transcendence.

---

64   Marx 1968, pp. 97, 180.

CHAPTER 3

Writing about Canadian Workers:
A Historiographic Overview*

The writing of Canadian labour history has always unfolded at the intersection of national specificity and international currents of influence, be they in the realm of analysis or activism. Yet an assessment of Canadian working-class history's rise and reconfiguration also highlights some 'peculiarities of the Canadians'. First, Canada is a big country, but its academic culture is decidedly small. This means that debates within Canadian labour history can be, and have easily become, quite sharp and even personalised. Second, with a weak communist tradition but a strong social-democratic presence, a scholarly field such as labour history tends to concentrate attention on contentious differences within the left, especially as these were evident, initially, in social history's rise and, subsequently, in cultural history's later challenges. Third, for these and other reasons, working-class history in Canada has arguably had a much greater influence on more general historiographic debates and trends than in other countries, where study of workers' past may well be more insulated from the hegemonic mainstream. Fourth, and finally, labour historians have played an important role in the upper reaches of the academic profession in Canada, perhaps more so than in any other country. All things considered, labour history in Canada has led a charmed life. And yet it is both relatively young and not without something of a tumultuous past.

The Past as Prologue

Until the modern labour historiography of Canada emerged out of the ferment of the 1960s, professional historians played second fiddle to a band of economists, political scientists and even specialists in English literature in writing on the country's workers and their labour movement.[1] Paralleling these academic developments were radical and Communist commentaries, but such writing

---

* 'Canada', in *Histories of Labour: National and International Perspectives*, edited by Joan Allen, Alan Campbell and John McIlroy (Pontypool, Wales: Merlin Press, 2010), 196–230. Published here under the title 'Writing about Canadian Workers: A Historiographic Overview'.

1 For detailed accounts of this early writing, see G. Kealey 1995, pp. 3–47; 1981b, pp. 213–22.

was hardly influential, especially in comparison with other English-speaking settings.[2] By the 1960s, Communist publications that addressed the history of class formation in Canada and the development of the trade-union movement included Charles Lipton's *Trade Union Movement of Canada, 1827–1959* (1966) and Stanley Ryerson's *Unequal Union: Confederation and the Roots of Conflict in the Canadas, 1815–1873* (1968). An autodidactic dissident communist, Jack Scott, expelled from the Communist Party of Canada (CPC) in 1962, also produced a series of labour history studies in the 1960s and early 1970s. He opened one study with the declaration that: 'Historians – with a few honourable exceptions – take virtually no note of the existence of workers in society'.[3]

Lipton, Ryerson and Scott resonated with an emerging contingent of New Left-influenced students in the 1960s, to be sure.[4] As a mid-1960s historiographic article in the *Canadian Historical Review* by Stanley Mealing indicated, however, mainstream historians were by no means convinced that 'the concept of social class' was highly relevant to understanding national identity and the country's history.[5] Canada lacked anything comparable to the influence of the Hammonds, the Webbs and G.D.H. Cole in England, where the Fabian and moderate socialist analytic stream ran historically deep, with specific currents having a pronounced impact on disciplines and fields such as economics, history and political thought. Nothing comparable to the American Wisconsin School, associated with the substantial researches of John R. Commons, Richard T. Ely and Selig Perlman existed north of the 49th parallel. Liberal individualism, on the one hand, and patrician sensibilities, on the other, incarcerated most Canadian historians in an academic aesthetics that shunned approaching the nation and its past in class ways as troublingly base. '[T]he study of the common, or common-place man', wrote Arthur R.M. Lower in 1929, 'if overdone, would no doubt make for common-place history'.[6]

Kenneth McNaught presented a similar barrier to new approaches to labour within the small 'left' of academic historiography. McNaught, a committed social democrat associated with the Co-operative Commonwealth Federation (CCF), had been schooled in the late-1940s variants of the contemporary 'culture wars'. This education was a battleground that pitted moderate socialists

---

2   Note, for comparative purposes, Irving and Seager 1996, pp. 239–77; Hobsbawm 1978a, pp. 21–48; J. Barrett 2004, pp. 23–54.

3   For discussion of Communist labour history, see G. Kealey 1982a and 1982b. Jack Scott's writings are discussed in B. Palmer 1988a; and Scott is quoted from Jack Scott 1974, p. 1.

4   See, for instance, Teeple 1972.

5   Mealing 1965, pp. 217–18.

6   Lower 1929, p. 66.

of the parliamentary road against the nefarious 'reds', who threatened to bore from within essential democratic institutions, in the process contaminating if not destroying them. So small were the concentric circles of Canadian labour studies in this period that McNaught would leave his mark indelibly on what came to be a post-1960s rupture of two intimately forged research cohorts. They began to create modern working-class history in the aftermath of what was arguably the country's most tumultuous decade.[7]

The Layered 1960s: Modern Labour Historiography and Its Divergent Camps

One significant difference separating the historiography of Canadian workers from that of research and writing in other national contexts was that Canadian labour history gave rise to two roughly identifiable orientations to the study of class in English Canada in a relatively short time frame. In French Canada, a distinct labour historiography also appeared in the same period. These metaphorical 'generations' of scholarship were marked by decidedly different impulses and engagements, but all emerged from the cauldron of the 1960s.[8]

The first English Canadian contingent, which entered PhD programmes mostly in the early to mid-1960s, was largely untouched by Marxism and was either liberal or 'liberal in a hurry' (moderately social-democratic). Arguably the most significant of its authors – David J. Bercuson and Irving Martin Abella – were trained at the University of Toronto by McNaught. The conception of the working class that animated this loose grouping was one of institution, episodic conflict, material inequality, the forward march of labour as enshrined in the realisation of trade-union entitlements such as collective bargaining and an accent on labour politics that privileged the social-democratic/labourist traditions. Framed very much within a national discourse, the scholarship of this cohort set new standards of professionalism in the writing of Canadian labour history.[9]

This initial production of modern labour history was recognisable in the moderation of its analytic directions as well as in its focus on the more modern period. Bercuson's history of the Winnipeg General Strike, for instance, concluded by stressing the 'futility and tragedy of massive confrontation combined

---

7   McNaught 1959; 1999.
8   B. Palmer 1979–80, pp. 594–616.
9   Abella 1973; Bercuson 1974; Bercuson and McNaught 1974; McCormack 1977.

with hysteria and intransigence', casting a plague on both the houses of the militant labour left and the state ideologues and agencies of repression.[10] Abella's discussion of the Canadian Congress of Industrial Organizations (CIO) unions, the CCF and the CPC acknowledged the often heavy-handed tactics adopted to drive the reds from the unions, pointing out that the expulsion of the left wing served the workers' movement poorly. Nonetheless, in Abella's view, the main story of the CIO in Canada was the achievement of 'an industrial union movement', albeit one dominated from without, not by Communists but by Americans.[11]

All of this was most emphatically a 20th-century story. It was not uncommon for historians to suggest, as did Abella in an edited collection on major Canadian strikes, that '[l]abour's trauma started in Winnipeg in 1919. Until then its horizons had seemed unclouded and propitious'.[12] The struggle to achieve working-class rights was thus telescoped into a frame where state-labour relations dominated and victories were won in terms of trade-union development, the achievement of collective bargaining rights and political advances registered in the rise of parties willing to promote the cause of 'ordinary Canadians'. Studies of poverty in the industrial city and immigrant radicals complicated this Whiggish narrative somewhat, but most Canadian labour history was increasingly understandable against the backdrop of socialism's so-called 'golden age' in the early to mid-1940s, when the CCF achieved electoral breakthroughs.[13]

One early figure who problematised this emerging, respectable face of labour history was Michael S. Cross. Cross studied the 19th century rather than the 20th (in which he also had an interest) and was more concerned with the history of riot and raucous confrontation than he was in hitching the cart of workers' revolt to the wagon of social democracy.[14] In his exploration of the timber workers' social and ethnocultural conflict, articulated in a pioneering discussion of the Ottawa Valley Shiners' Wars of the 1830s, Cross addressed class less as an institution and more as a messy historical happening.[15] He thus linked metaphorical arms not only with his generational colleagues, who implicitly championed the study of the respectable faces of labour history, but also with

---

10   Bercuson 1974, p. 174. Cf. Penner 1973.
11   Abella 1973, esp. pp. 1, 222.
12   Abella 1975, p. xii.
13   Copp 1974; Piva 1979; Avery 1979.
14   See Cross 1974a.
15   Cross 1973, pp. 1–26.

a second, loose grouping of social historians whose connections to the 1960s were more activist than accidental.

For members of this new contingent, their experience was often one of engagement with politics to the left of the now-renamed social-democratic successor to the CCF, the New Democratic Party (NDP). Never the tightly knit, coherent collectivity that some imagined it to be, members of this soon-to-be-misnamed 'school' of 'new labour history' gravitated to one another not so much out of an understanding of what they were *for* as on the basis of a shared appreciation of what they were *against*.[16] There was relatively common agreement that the history of class formation, rather than conventional accounts of the trade union and the political party, was what working-class history was all about. This was not to say, of course, that institutions and politics were unimportant, only that they were *part of* a larger process. In general, much of the initial research and writing of this cohort addressed the years from 1860 to 1930. Many of these emerging historians of the working class went to graduate schools in the United States, where they were educated in the break from the consensus historiography of Richard Hofstadter and other prominent figures of the 1950s. Others studied at Warwick University in England in the mid- to late 1970s. All read widely in the international literature that was, from the mid-1960s onwards, making working-class history an exciting field, alive with new ideas and fresh perspectives.

E.P. Thompson's *The Making of the English Working Class* (1963) was, for many, an inspiring text, while others found in the circulation of Herbert G. Gutman's unpublished articles of the late 1960s a *samizdat*-like body of writing that opened new interpretive possibilities about ways to write about workers and their presence within and influence on civil society. Theory animated this new research agenda, perhaps as it never had before in the writing of Canadian history. Marx was read, of course, but so too were anthropologists like Claude Lévi-Strauss; subterranean thinkers such as Antonio Gramsci and Georg Lukács; commentators on the culture of everyday life, from Georges Lefebvre to Raymond Williams; and young New Leftists from both sides of the Atlantic: the sociologist C. Wright Mills, the feminist historian Sheila Rowbotham and the impressively wide-ranging editor of the *New Left Review*, Perry Anderson.[17]

By the time the first major statements of this loose historiographic approach appeared in the late 1970s and early 1980s, it was apparent that the now-

---

16   Nelles 1989, p. 6; D. Morton 2000, pp. 11–36, refers to working-class historians as 'one of the most homogeneous and influential groups in the disparate crowd of Canadian historians' (p. 21).

17   Note, for comparative purposes, Jones 2001, pp. 103–24.

contentious field of labour history had in some ways rocked historians of Canada out of a complacent somnolence. My own *A Culture in Conflict: Skilled Workers and Industrial Capitalism in Hamilton, Ontario, 1860–1914* (1979), Gregory S. Kealey's *Toronto Workers Respond to Industrial Capitalism, 1867–1892* (1980), and our jointly authored *Dreaming of What Might Be: The Knights of Labor in Ontario, 1880–1900* (1982), were all either nominated for major academic prizes or won such awards. Fair-minded commentators such as Ramsay Cook assessed such studies as significant breakthroughs.[18] Others were less generous. David Bercuson, for instance, took aim at *Dreaming of What Might Be* and characterised it as 'pretentious, problematic, and tedious ... a Sunday sermon ... dry, boring, and devoid of any feeling for the workers'.[19]

Debates may well have been, in the words of the country's foremost historiographic commentator, Carl Berger, 'captious, intemperate, and confusing'. They also revealed the analytic fault lines that could run through *all* historical interpretation, whatever the claims to objectivity, however different the attachment to divergent understandings of political engagement. Berger was generous in his acknowledgement that writing influenced by Thompson's 'humanistic Marxism' had 'recovered copious and scarcely suspected details on social life in the Victorian period ... [helping] move to the centre of attention the social conflict that accompanied the arrival of industrial society, ... [according] a place to ideas and attitudes in history that belied the commonplace image of Marxist scholarship as materialistic'. Referring to the importance of quantitative methods and their significance within methodological debates in the 1970s, Berger also added – in a comparison that contrasted the approaches of Michael Katz and his highly funded and team-researched social history of stratification and inequality in Hamilton, Ontario, with the social histories of workers' struggle – that writing on late 19th-century class formation 'contributed far more to the ultimate clarification of class – and class in history – than the statisticians of social mobility'.[20]

---

18   B. Palmer 1979; G. Kealey 1980; Kealey and Palmer 1982. These works had been preceded by surveys of archival holdings and an early collection of essays: Hann, Kealey, Kealey, and Warrian 1973; Kealey and Warrian 1976. Shortly after the appearance of the major monographs on Hamilton and Toronto I published an overview of Canadian working-class history: B. Palmer 1983. Ramsay Cook was among the most generous of mainstream, liberal commentators on this writing: see R. Cook 1983, pp. 115–26.

19   Bercuson 1983, pp. 589–91.

20   Berger 1986, pp. 306–7. For the important work of Katz and his colleagues, see Katz 1975; Katz, Doucet, and Stern 1982.

At the pinnacle of the national historical culture, the *Canadian Historical Review*, edited in 1981 by Bercuson and J.L. Granatstein, commissioned a lead article on writing about labour and the left by the doyen of a patrician, social-democratic approach to working-class studies, Kenneth McNaught. McNaught suggested that 'those young researchers who have been lovingly adapting E.P. Thompson to the mines, production lines, and even the countryside of Canada's past' needed to get back to appreciating how much the 'smart union leadership' of the 1930s and 1940s (which had extracted concessions from the employers, beaten back the reds and negotiated a place in the state-orchestrated system of post-World War II industrial pluralism) needed study and emulation. The goal of that sophisticated layer of union builders, McNaught stressed in the last line of his essay, 'was not to defend an Archie Bunker-charivari culture, but, rather, to liberate those who had been entrapped by the economic-cultural constraints imposed by political capitalists'. The CHR promptly awarded McNaught's essay, commissioned by partisans and itself a highly partisan statement, the journal's annual prize as the best article published in its pages.[21]

Years later, Granatstein, increasingly a spokesman for the view that Canadian historiography had overspecialised to the point of trivialising the country's past as the study of insignificant servant girls when there were important prime ministers to write about and momentous events such as wars and elections to commemorate, would conclude that 'the struggle for the past' began in Canada in labour history. 'The old-style institutional labour historians were either driven out of the field or left the field to seek new areas to work in', Granatstein wrote in 1998, adding: 'The Marxists had complete control of the labour history field, including the journals and the students, and they maintain it still, notwithstanding the discrediting of Marxism everywhere in the world. The universities, sheltered from the real world, continue to protect their Marxists'.[22] This was Canada's 'end of history'.[23]

---

21   McNaught 1981, pp. 141–68. Lest those unfamiliar with Canadian historical writing be perplexed with a reference to Archie Bunker-charivari culture, I had just published an article in *Labour/Le Travail* on the ritual of charivari, relating it to class formation and its varied tensions and antagonisms. See Palmer 1978, pp. 5–62. See also Morton 1983, pp. 165–84.

22   Granatstein 1998, pp. 60–1. Marxist labour historians also attracted the attention of the Royal Canadian Mounted Police, which received reports from a spy. See G. Kealey 1999, pp. 3–18.

23   Fukuyama 1992. Insightful commentary appeared in Anderson 1992b, pp. 279–375.

Francophone historians of Quebec's working class were, for the most part, uninvolved in these historiographic controversies, nor was their work all that much referred to in the debates. This reflected the undeniable reality of Canada's 'two solitudes', which historians of the country struggled to bridge. To be sure, there was evidence of conceptual convergence. One of Kealey's first forays into the social history of 19th-century workers was an abridged edition of the critically important workers' testimony before the first Canadian Royal Commission investigating the conditions of labour and capital in the decade of Knights of Labor upheaval, the 1880s. This subject also captivated the attentions of Quebec's leading sociological commentator on class formation in this period, Fernand Harvey.[24] Abella's counterpart amongst Francophone historians was the prolific Jacques Rouillard, who charted the nationalist course of Quebec's institutional labour history over the course of the 20th century.[25] In both French and English Canada, the early 1970s preface to a spate of new histories was important bibliographic work.[26]

Yet the historiography of Quebec workers had indeed developed differently than had the study of labour in English Canada. Quebec historians, in general, looked more to interpretive trends associated with France, where the Annales School was prominent,[27] than they did to the British Marxists, such as E.P. Thompson, Christopher Hill and Eric Hobsbawm, or American social historians of working-class life such as Gutman or David Montgomery.[28] Working-class history in Quebec had long borne the imprint of Laval University's Jean Hamelin. His 1950s sojourn at the École Pratique des Hautes Études in Paris had schooled Hamelin in the unique structuralist blend of the materialism of Marxism and an *Annaliste* concern with the *longue durée*, especially as it was manifested in the economic conditions of the *menu peuple*. It was in many ways this intellectual interface that animated the work of Ernest Labrousse who, in turn, decidedly influenced both Hamelin and his most precocious collaborator, Fernand Ouellet. Ouellet was not so much concerned with *labour* and *workers* as he was with a class analysis that did not sidestep Quebec's limitations. He

---

24   See G. Kealey 1973b; F. Harvey 1978. An early gendered reading is Trofimenkoff 1977, pp. 67–82.

25   See Rouillard 1974; 1979; 1981.

26   Hann, Kealey, Kealey, and Warrian 1973; LeBlanc and Thwaites 1973.

27   Note particularly Dubuc 1978; F. Harvey 1979, pp. 9–43.

28   Contrast the accent on North American traditions and the British Marxists evident in Hann and Kealey 1977, pp. 92–114, and the discussion of theory and 'the state of the question' in Belanger et al. 1975.

was himself somewhat disappointed that the social history of Quebec's workers seemed routinised in institutional studies of trade unions and accounts of labour politics, most of which were firmly situated within conventional understandings of *la question nationale*.[29]

The Labroussian accent on long-term trends in the economic formation of society, in which particular points of demarcation were delineated as *conjonctures*, would factor in Quebec labour history's early attempts to address strike trends and patterns of class formation.[30] However much 20th-century studies in Quebec tended to highlight the peculiarities of leadership and organisation associated with the province's Catholic unions,[31] there was nevertheless significantly more attention paid to the pre-industrial capitalist era in Quebec than in English Canada, although Judith Fingard had sensitively explored maritime labour and early 19th-century poverty.[32] Stimulating studies of early artisans and apprenticeship resulted in publications founded upon the different kinds of documents relating to contracted craft training, which proliferated because of French Canada's legal system and the importance of notarial records. They revealed an economic history premised on something other than the staples trade in fur pelts, fish and timber that had long been regarded as central to the ostensibly dominant mercantile order.[33] As the insightful work of Joanne Burgess suggested, the young cohort of working-class historians emerging in French Canada concentrated their interests on issues of labour recruitment processes and trade training.[34]

---

29   Ouellet 1985, pp. 11–83. On institutions and ideas as the subject of work of the late 1960s and early 1970s, see L.-M. Tremblay 1968 and 1972; Dofny and Bernard 1968; Hamelin and Harvey 1976.

30   Hamelin, Larocque, and Rouillard 1979; Belanger et al. 1975.

31   Aside from Rouillard's important work, see, for suggestive statements from union activists, Francoeur, Lefebvre, Vadeboncoeur and Roux 1963; Charpentier 1971.

32   The opening statements of this research would be Fingard 1974, pp. 65–94; 1977, pp. 35–53. But see also Fingard 1982, critiqued in Rice 1983, pp. 154–68.

33   Consider, for instance, the number of relatively early articles and studies that addressed the pre-1850 years, among them: Espeset, Hardy and Ruddel 1972, pp. 499–539; Moogk 1971, pp. 65–83; Hardy and Ruddel 1977; R. Tremblay 1979, pp. 301–35. Note, on the early economy, Dechêne 1992.

34   Compare G. Kealey 1973a, pp. 137–57; G. Kealey 1976, pp. 32–68; Burgess 1977, pp. 187–210.

Ironic Interlude: Labour History's Canadian Institutional Formation

Trends in working-class history thus diverged within English Canada, just as the nature of the first sustained waves of labour scholarship in Quebec and the rest of the country seemed differentiated.[35] In spite of heated debates which focussed on institutional versus social accents in the writing of history, this was also a period in which the formal apparatus of a labour history *society* was established and consolidated. Marxists and non-Marxists, social democrats and dissident communist oppositionists, Anglophone and Francophone, westerners, easterners, and those in the Ontario 'centre' – all collaborated and worked together to establish the Committee on Canadian Labour History (CCLH). Historians such as Robert Babcock whose research was decidedly institutional worked closely and productively with younger, more socially and culturally attuned colleagues.[36] On occasion this coming together was expressed in textbooks, as in the documentary collections on workers in the 19th and 20th centuries edited by Cross, on the one hand, and Abella and David Millar, on the other.[37]

A subsection of the Canadian Historical Association (CHA), the CCLH's initial meeting took place at Winnipeg in June 1970. Shortly thereafter, the CCLH produced a biannual, bilingual newsletter/bulletin. Discussions ensued about establishing a formal journal of Canadian labour studies. Founded as an annual in 1976 under the editorship of Gregory S. Kealey and James D. Thwaites, *Labour/Le Travailleur* was launched as the official journal of the CHA-affiliated CCLH. Its membership was constituted through subscription to the annual publication and it met once a year during the meeting times of various Canadian academic discipline associations in an annual late-May/early-June gathering. Published yearly from 1976 to 1980, *Labour/Le Travailleur* would soon be edited solely by Kealey. Incorporating a range of material in its pages, the journal quickly supplanted the *Bulletin*, which was allowed to lapse. Becoming a biannual in 1980, and changing its name to *Labour/Le Travail* in 1983 in order to transcend the gender-specific nature of its original title, the journal and the CCLH (renamed the Canadian Committee on Labour History in 1991 in order to incorporate broad, transnational interests) came, by the mid-1980s, to symbolise the coming of age of working-class history in Canada. CCLH presid-

---

35   Burgess 1990, pp. 149–73; Rudin 1997, pp. 193–4.
36   See Babcock 1974.
37   Cross 1974b and Abella and Millar 1978.

ent Irving Abella proclaimed with enthusiasm in 1982: 'Canadian labour history has finally arrived!'[38]

That arrival was the product of scholarship contributed by varying camps. The mainstays of the early CCLH executive were Abella and Kealey, representatives of divergent analytic streams in Canada's developing field of working-class history. If Kealey provided much of the energy and enterprise in the founding of the journal, its editorial board always reflected the breadth of the contentious field. Debates and discussions of what to publish and how to do it were often heated and disagreements were many, but there was never, in my recollection, a point where the project itself was felt to be either compromised or on the brink of some destructive implosion.

Stabilisation and Diversity: *Fin-de-siècle* Triumphs and Testings

A measure of labour history's consolidation was the explosion of graduate theses written in the field in the late 1970s. Whereas in 1966 the Canadian Historical Association's *Register of Post-Graduate Dissertations in Progress in History and Related Disciplines* recorded a total of nine MA and PhD theses in labour and working-class history, a decade later the comparable figure was a whopping 99.[39]

Labour had become one of those 'limited identities' much discussed as vanguard topics of consideration in the late 1960s.[40] In barely a decade and a half such subjects managed to find an institutional niche in professional historical circles, where journals, conferences and societies proliferated on the periphery of a still fairly traditional historiographic mainstream. But that periphery was encroaching upon the centres of conventional historical interpretation, where research tended to concentrate on orthodox political history and narratives of national development. Topics once considered marginal were becoming increasingly difficult to ignore and now encompassed women's history, robust studies of regionalism's significance on the national canvas, consideration of ethnicity and, unmistakably, the study of class. Moreover, it was in these years that Canadian working-class history consolidated transnational connections, cultivating ties with other societies dedicated to the study of labour history

---

38   Abella 1982, pp. 114–36 (p. 114).

39   D. Morton 2000, p. 36.

40   R. Cook 1967, p. 663; Careless 1969, pp. 1–10.

and engaging in dialogue over comparative studies of workers in Canada, the United Kingdom, Wales and Australia.[41]

To complicate matters, however, the last two decades of the 20th century would be marked by new developments that constantly reconfigured the nature of the historiography of Canadian workers in this period. In what follows immediately below I address the significance of the changing *personnel* involved in the writing of labour history in the 1980s and beyond.

First, an older contingent of once-influential figures began to vacate the field in the late 1970s, moving away from labour studies to take up research and writing in such areas as military history (Bercuson, Terry Copp and, to some extent, Desmond Morton, who had always oscillated between histories of the military, the labour movement and social-democratic politics) or ethnicity (Abella). Second, as the playing field of labour history in Canada seemed to be levelled in ways that left Kealey and Palmer standing firm in a specific interpretive direction, a new research agenda surfaced. It differentiated itself from the institutional-political orientation of the McNaught-Bercuson-Abella approach at the same time as it voiced growing concerns with the ostensible 'romanticism' of their original critics. To some extent this was merely the articulation of analytic differences that had long existed within a broad contingent of historians, all of whom were charting new directions, many of them highly cognisant of fissiparous relations and contentious understandings of what constituted a politics of the left.

At issue, again, was the vantage point of 20th-century/19th-century difference, which in particular posed the 'crisis of the craftsman' in ways that suggested a divergent politics of understanding. Looked at from the perspective of the 1880s, framed within a research vision that addressed the period from 1860 to 1914, a number of skilled workers often seemed to be on the cutting edge of class mobilisation, robust architects of resilient mechanisms of shop-floor structures of workers' control and leading spokesmen in bodies like the Knights of Labor, which for all of its limitations struggled to promote the politics of labour reform as had no other working-class organisation of the 19th century. Peering backward at this experience, analysing it in terms of skill dilution and the workplace transformations associated with the early 20th-century Second

---

41   The first such jointly sponsored endeavour was the September 1981 Commonwealth Labour History Conference at Warwick University, involving scholars from Australia, Canada and the United Kingdom. Later conferences resulted in publications. See Hopkin and Kealey, 1989; Kealey and Patmore 1990; and *Labour/Le Travail*, 38 (1996), also issued as *Labour History*, 71 (1996).

Industrial Revolution, as well as awareness of the programmatic clarifications of revolutionary politics in the years 1917 to 1925, conditioned a different perspective. Craig Heron thus accented 'the ambivalence of artisanal culture' and the persistent 'defence of craft privilege' that the British historian James Hinton had labelled 'the clinging dross of exclusivism'.[42] Wayne Roberts tried to bridge this chronological and political chasm, suggesting that sectors of the skilled straddled the traditions of the past and the tendencies of the future, harbouring consciousnesses of craft distinctiveness as well as the politics of revolution, but his subtle appreciations of complexity tended to be lost in the hardening view that one was either *for* or *against* the craftsman.[43]

An orientation stressing the possible significance of aristocratic divisions within the working class dovetailed nicely with research increasingly attentive to the labour process, work segmentation and the fragmentation of labour in the 20th century.[44] Canadian studies animated by such concerns brought much of the scholarship together in an engagement with and refinement of the arguments of Harry Braverman, whose 1974 *Labor and Monopoly Capital* had unleashed a plethora of studies and productive debates in the United States, Canada and the UK. This labour process literature highlighted generalised alignments in the study of Canadian workers as well as subtle but emerging interpretive fissures.[45]

Of these fissures, the most significant was, as it had been in the early charge McNaught and Bercuson had led against the supposed Thompsonians, the issue of culture. But the debate now leaned left, relying not on atheoretical and rhetorical labelling of ostensible class-ordered cultural autonomies, as it had in the Bercuson and McNaught critiques, but on a revived Marxist attachment to base-superstructure distinctions, an insistence on the rigours of political economy and a refusal to concede anything to the 'dogmas of culture'. Ian McKay led the offensive against what he dismissed as a culturalist 'retrospective anthropology'. Along the way, McKay deplored the theoretical cost of accommodating what he presented as the indiscriminate conceptual meanderings of Raymond Williams. In McKay's words, these had 'allowed social historians to indulge in retrospective cheerleading for progressive ideas', enabling 'them to forget that "emergent" socialist values, did not, in fact, "emerge" and

42   Heron 1980, pp. 7–49, esp. p. 72, quoting Hinton.
43   Roberts 1976a, pp. 92–121; 1980, pp. 49–72.
44   McKay 1978, pp. 63–108.
45   Among many writings see, for instance, Heron and Storey (eds.) 1986; Radforth 1987; Heron 1988.

win the acceptance of the majority'. With Thompson's *The Poverty of Theory* (1978) fresh in his mind, McKay railed against Thompson's capacity to reel out culture after culture, concluding that conceptually 'culture' was little more than a non-explanatory buzzword designating whatever happened to engage academic interest. 'Rather than making this inability to explain a merit in itself', McKay argued, 'we should envisage the creation of logico-historical models by which this realm of consciousness may be made the object of scientific discourse ... We close the logical and political circles only by a return to the concrete: to the determinate abstractions of *Capital* and to a logical political practice'.[46]

This was heady stuff, but it did not quite manage to capture the historiographic moment. For the most part, the differentiations that emerged in the 1980s played themselves out less at the level of advancing Canadian labour history through recourse to more rigorous scientific Marxist analysis, which was what McKay was attempting to encourage. Rather, more mundane separations ensued. Bercuson's attempt to understate the voices of Canadian working-class revolutionaries by downplaying the subjective, conscious adherence to anti-capitalist ideas and affiliations in the era of the Winnipeg General Strike explained the labour revolt of these years in deterministic terms, placing interpretive accent on the environment of the western industrial frontier. This approach was challenged decisively in Kealey's pan-Canadian account of the 1919 labour revolt. Most labour historians, by the late 1980s, accepted Kealey's claims that the upheaval of the post-World War I years had been national, as opposed to regional. But the developing scholarship tended to accent more 'labourist', ballot-box orientations and, with considerable subtlety and sophistication, drew a picture of the rising of the workers that concentrated less on Kealey's outline of general and sympathetic strikes as rooted in a new adherence to revolutionary programme than it did on elaborating the cracks in the walls of working-class solidarity.[47]

---

46   McKay 1987, pp. 172–9; 1981–2, pp. 185–241 (especially pp. 185–6, 216, 223, 225, 240–1).
     Contrast these early 1980s reflections on Williams with McKay's more recent efforts to
     present an overarching history of emergent socialist thought in Canada. See, for instance,
     McKay 2005, in which Marx is presented as 'a dynamic and changing cultural code' (p. 15),
     and McKay 2008.

47   Bercuson 1977, pp. 154–75; and his historiographic afterword in the reprint of Bercuson's
     Confrontation at Winnipeg: Labour, Industrial Relations, and the General Strike (Bercuson
     1990, pp. 196–205). For Kealey's rejoinder see G. Kealey 1984, pp. 11–44. Other writing of a
     slightly different accent includes Heron 1984, pp. 45–76; Naylor 1991; Heron 1998.

Increasingly under fire was Kealey and Palmer's suggestion that the 1880s had been a significant moment of class mobilisation, in which the Noble and Holy Order of the Knights of Labor had played a major and, certain limitations aside, laudatory role.[48] An entire collection of essays was produced to in some ways offset what volume editor Paul Craven and his assembled contributors regarded as a consolidating metropolitan focus on labour in Toronto and Hamilton, Ontario's pre-eminent industrial cities. This Kealey and Palmer writing was associated with the Thompsonian-influenced historiography emerging out of the 'debate between institutional labour historians and the New Left'. Not surprisingly, the essays in Craven's *Labouring Lives: Work & workers in Nineteenth-Century Ontario* (1995) highlighted the importance of paternalism, religion and other cross-class components of plebeian life, stressed the linkages of home and work and detailed the limitations of craft organisation.[49] Echoes of the McNaught-Bercuson position reverberated in this criticism. Those earlier attacks rebounded more forcefully in a shot fired across the Kealey-Palmer bow by a left-nationalist political economist, Daniel Drache, in a 1984 *Studies in Political Economy* article. Drache downplayed industrial-capitalist development in Canada, drawing on Harold Innis's fixation on the resource economy's reliance on a series of staples: fish, fur, timber, wheat and, later in the 20th century, oil and gas. He depicted craft unions as little more than vehicles of working-class colonialism constituting a reactionary élite and insisted that Canadian labour had been historically mired in its internal fragmentations.[50]

By the 1990s and into the first decade of the 21st century, then, there were certainly those who sought to define themselves against what they considered a problematic reading of the 19th-century working-class past. Concentrated at York University, these critics tended to understate class tensions, conflicts and struggles and instead focussed on experiences of a cross-class character. Thus, Lynne Marks's account of working-class life in Victorian Ontario used the small town as a prism through which to envision workers' place in society. She argued that class, as an analytic category, had been 'privileged' to the point that it had become unduly 'fundamental'. If this approach had the potential to interpretively moderate some of the analytics of enthusiasm characteristic of earlier writing and to develop the historiography by addressing areas long understud-

---

48 An early challenge focused on the quantitative evidence relating to the Knights of Labor local assemblies. See Piva 1983, and Kealey and Palmer 1983, pp. 169–89. Piva was responding to Kealey and Palmer 1981, pp. 369–411.

49 Craven 1995.

50 Drache's article and my rejoinder appear in Bercuson and Bright 1984, pp. 6–75.

ied in class ways, such as religion, Marks too often relied on misrepresentation of the actual positions she was at pains to overturn and read too much into evidence that was at best ambiguous and thin.[51]

A contemporary of Marks, Robert B. Kristofferson, later challenged what he referred to as 'the dispossession model' of 'the proletarianization of the crafts-worker', associated in Canada with Kealey and Palmer. Kristofferson researched assiduously in records that allowed him to produce a statement on how, in Hamilton, Ontario, the mid-century years witnessed the march of Marx's 'really revolutionizing path to industrial capitalism', craft capital transforming itself into industrial capital. Yet he also ignored evidence and interpretive issues inconvenient to his argument. Importantly, he awkwardly sidestepped the quantitatively derived perspectives on inequality Michael Katz and his associates had marshalled, as well as fundamental issues of periodisation in which the class-struggle perspectives of work addressing peak labour mobilisations in the 1880s offer a diametrically different chronology from Kristofferson's, which was generated out of the 1850s and 1860s. The result was a book that unnecessarily understated the complexities and meanings of the first stages of class struggle in Canada. As a perceptive review by Douglas McCalla in the *American Historical Review* noted, Kristofferson too readily caricatures positions in the scholarly literature he is critiquing. McCalla holds up my own book, *A Culture in Conflict*, as a 'particular target' that is mishandled in a variety of ways. Most readers of Kristofferson's book will rightly wonder what the point is in battling over this old ground, misrepresenting a book published almost 30 years ago, when something new and fresh could have emerged out of his research.[52]

From other quarters, the graduate seminars of the 1980s yielded different results. An eclectic mix of graduate students at Queen's University in the 1980s and 1990s tackled a diversity of research subjects. Peter S. McInnis took up the challenge of McNaught, Morton and others to develop a sophisticated reconsideration of the reconstruction of Canadian society in the aftermath of World War II, when labour militancy, the emergence of the welfare state and strategies of incorporation evident in certain government and business circles culminated in a post-war compromise that set the stage for future decades of class relations.[53] Karen Dubinsky, Steven Maynard, and Annalee [Golz] Lepp produced stimulating studies of 19th- and early-20th-century sexuality in which readings

51   Marks 1996. I raised a number of issues about evidence and interpretation in Marks's writings in Palmer 2000b, pp. 105–44, which was responded to by Marks 2001, pp. 169–86.

52   Kristofferson 2007, esp. pp. 8–9, 246, 202, 15–16, 112; McCalla 2008, pp. 1513–14.

53   McInnis 2002.

of violence against women, familial disorder and male same-sex relations were framed within analyses attentive to the importance of a class-divided society.[54] In one of the more creative readings of the history of dispossession associated with the Great Depression, Todd McCallum drew on Paul Lafargue's *The Right to be Lazy* and the critical practice of the hobo to reframe analysis of the human meaning of capitalist 'unemployment'.[55] At the intersection of the history of workers, the history of ideas and the mobilisations of the left, Peter Campbell charted a discussion of strands of Canadian Marxism from 1900 to 1940 that separated themselves out from the dominant, and bifurcated, party allegiances of social democracy and Communism.[56]

Equally eclectic were the researches of graduate students emanating from Memorial University in the same period. Much of this work understandably addressed a political economy of material constraint and marginalisation, yielding impressive new perspectives on the resource sector (especially the fishery), the colonial condition and the last province to enter into Confederation, Newfoundland, which only joined Canada in 1949.[57] Undoubtedly the most influential of this revisionist work has been that of Sean Cadigan. His articles, critiques and books include a recent synthetic statement on the history of Newfoundland from prehistoric times to the present. Cadigan argues a case for seeing the history of one of Canada's most unique regions as a struggle against environmental odds that have been even further loaded against the masses of Newfoundlanders by the undeniable class inequalities of specific political and economic formations.[58] Miriam Wright's *A Fishery for Modern Times* (2001) added a gender dimension to this kind of rewriting of Newfoundland history; the book was complemented by a growing body of feminist Atlantic Canada writing.[59]

Other graduate students of these years made significant interventions into vital issues of national and international significance. Mark Leier was among the first wave of this cohort. Arguably he is its most prolific player, producing studies that historicise appreciation of the making of the trade-union bureaucracy as well as an imaginative and pedagogically inspired text on the case of

---

54   Among a number of studies, see Dubinsky 1993; Maynard 1997, pp. 191–235; 1994, pp. 207–42; Golz 1993, pp. 9–50.

55   McCallum 2005, pp. 51–88; 2006, pp. 79–107; 2007, pp. 43–68.

56   J.P. Campbell 1999.

57   For the scope of much of this work, see Frank and Kealey 1995.

58   Among many possible statements, see especially Cadigan 1995; 1990, pp. 125–50; 2009.

59   M. Wright 2001; M. Porter 1985, pp. 105–23; Neis 1993, pp. 185–202.

a notable and intricately complicated West Coast labour spy, Robert Gosden.[60] Amongst the second wave, Andrew Parnaby looked at the dock workers of the West Coast and, in the process, aligned labour history and Aboriginal history, outlining an encounter of 'Indians at work' that had first been broached seriously decades earlier by the maverick anthropologist Rolf Knight.[61] Important studies on Canadian communism appeared at the end of the 1990s, realising the promise of scholars such as David Frank and John Manley.[62]

Working-class history's developing level of sophistication registered in the quantity of articles published in *Labour/Le Travail*, as well as the publication programme and on-going annual workshops of the CCLH. By 2000 the Committee had published almost 20 volumes, most of them oral biographies and memoirs, as well as eight volumes of the Royal Canadian Mounted Police Security Bulletins.[63] In addition, the CCLH organised a Secretary of State-sponsored lecture series on labour history at four Canadian universities in 1983 and 1984, publishing a selection of the popularly pitched talks in *Lectures in Canadian Labour and Working-Class History* (1985) and also making available six of the videotaped lectures. By the 1990s, its annual workshop brought together trade-union activists and labour studies academics in day-long events which drew audiences of 100 participants and more. Three 'surveys' of labour history were published over the course of the 1980s, and by the 1990s all had been reprinted in revised editions. A 1999 publication of the CCLH, *The Woman Worker, 1926–1929*, edited by Margaret Hobbs and Joan Sangster, gathered together articles from the official newspaper of the CPC-affiliated Canadian Federation of Women's Labor Leagues. These articles provide commentary from the late 1920s on women and wage work, protective legislation, social reform, war and peace, women and the sex trade, family, domestic labour and birth control. The volume suggested how central women had become to the project of labour history.[64]

---

60   Leier 1995; 1999.

61   Parnaby 2008; Knight 1978; High 1996, pp. 243–64.

62   Frank 1999; Manley 1992, pp. 65–114; Frank and Manley 1992, pp. 115–34; Manley 2005, pp. 9–50.

63   For background to the interest in state security issues, see G. Kealey 1992, pp. 281–314.

64   Cherwinski and Kealey 1985; Hobbs and Sangster 1999. The three surveys of Canadian labour history offered readers highly different accounts and analytic accents, and here I cite three 1990s issues: D. Morton 1990; B. Palmer 1992; Heron 1996.

Paradigm Shift 1: Women's History Reconfigures the Labouring Subject

In Canada, women's history and working-class history emerged in tandem. The institutional consolidation of these fields, with their societies, professional networks and journals, overlapped. Women were present on the editorial board of *Labour/Le Travailleur* from its inception, but it would be wrong to discount the extent to which the journal's making as a durable project and its original intellectual content were largely male enterprises. By 1990, however, fully eight of the fifteen-member editorial *équipe* responsible for *Labour/Le Travail* were women (the comparable figure for the United States journal *Labor History* was *two*). Morton's content analysis of *Labour/Le Travail* from 1976 to 1999 confirms the significance of this shift. In the 1970s two articles addressed gender issues; by the 1980s that number had climbed to 12; and over the course of the 1990s fully 26 articles could be placed in the gender category, making women's and gender issues the single most prominent subject written about amongst studies of industrial relations, strikes, unions, working lives, ethnicity and politics. Looking back on these years, Sangster later commented:

> Labour history generally welcomed feminist research exploring gender and class. Though *some* (usually, but not always, male) practitioners saw class as definitive, gender a critical additive, they were always willing to contest this issue with those of us who disagreed. If tensions were there, between class and gender, feminism and socialism, debating 'who was on top', in which theory, and why, they were not necessarily negative: they could be productive.[65]

Research on labouring women often addressed the seemingly perennial question, asked most forcefully in the United States by Alice Kessler-Harris, of what barriers existed in Canada to women working for wages and joining the trade-union movement.[66] The answers varied from the cultural to the structural.[67] Interpretive developments in the 1970s and 1980s produced writing that, in its

---

65   Sangster 2000, pp. 127–65; D. Morton 2000, p. 35.

66   Kessler-Harris 1975, pp. 92–110. Much of the research and writing of this period addressed women's waged work, on the one hand, and middle-class women's reform movements, on the other. See L. Kealey 1979; Lavigne and Pinard 1983; Briskin and Yanz 1983.

67   Roberts and Klein 1974, pp. 211–60, strikes a structural note of explanation as opposed to the 'ideological' and 'cultural' analysis evident in other essays in the same edited collection. See also Roberts 1976b.

unambiguous and often rigorous debate over socialist-feminist labour studies and Marxist conceptualisations, catapulted Canadian scholarship into a critically important exchange of views on the meaning and significance of reproductive labour.[68] As feminism transformed political economy, countless studies began to address women's work – in the present as well as in the past – in new and rigorous ways.[69] This helped stamp the Canadian women's movement of this period with a radical, socialist-feminist edge and a working-class content that situated it to the left of many of its international counterparts.[70]

Bettina Bradbury charted a new course of appreciation of working-class families, her quantitatively derived discussions of Victorian Montreal emphasising the complexity of the labouring poor's domestic economy and the significant contributions made to it by the unpaid labour of women and children. In establishing definitively the precarious nature of the working-class household, she established the gendered nature of everyday lives bifurcated by public/private and productive/reproductive social constructions.[71] Feminist historians of the organised left provided a range of studies that demonstrated the extent to which orthodox parties of communism and social democracy had understated women's oppression at the same time as they had nurtured a vocal contingent of female organisers, writers and activists who insisted on bringing the women's question into the politics of revolution and reform.[72] Histories of specific occupational sectors or unions in which women's work predominated and leftist politics proved influential, such as the garment trades or the United Electrical, Radio, and Machine Workers union, might well produce discussions of the organised left *and* workplace-familial relations.[73] Increasingly, moreover, such research emphasised the reciprocities of gender, ethnicity and occupation. Immigrant women laboured at various jobs, both waged and unwaged, and in a myriad of ways they exposed how fragile were supposedly entrenched adherences to the middle-class ideal of domesticity.[74] Indeed, two books that situated their subjects in different ways in the world of the 1920s and 1930s native-born Canadian women revealed that the domestic ideal for working-class women of *any* ethnic background was more fiction and faith than fact.[75]

---

68   Fox 1980; Luxton 1980; Barrett and Hamilton 1986; Seccombe 1992; 1993.

69   See Maroney and Luxton 1987.

70   See Luxton 2001, pp. 63–88; Maroney 1983, pp. 51–71.

71   Bradbury 1993. See also Baskerville and Sager 1998.

72   Sangster 1989; Newton 1995; L. Kealey 1998; Lévesque 1984; 1999.

73   Frager 1992; Steedman 1997; Guard 1996, pp. 149–77.

74   Best 1988; Iacovetta 1992.

75   Strong-Boag 1988; S. Morton 1995.

More and more, the study of women was subsumed within a *theoretical* insistence on studying gender as a system of social organisation demarcating the sexes, a project that dovetailed with the emergence of critical thinking at the *fin-de-siècle*. As Canadian historians gravitated to gender as, in Joan Scott's words, 'a useful category of historical analysis', they were also drawn into the complex swirl of conceptualisation associated with the rise of post-modernism and discourse analysis.[76]

Paradigm Shift 11: Labour History and the 'Linguistic Turn'

What I will designate (largely because it is the most eclectic and open-ended of terminologies) 'the linguistic turn' shifted historians' perspectives on mean- ing. Against the ostensible determinative fix of social history's loose association with materialism in general and Marxism in particular, in which the *struc- tures* of political economy established boundaries within which human agency unfolded, 'the linguistic turn' instead suggested the need to complicate ana- lysis by recognising that all language, including that of individual authors, has shaped both understandings of events and the nature of interpretation in the past and subsequent 'readings' and 'representations' of such happenings. That this intellectual movement into new understandings of more discursive appre- ciations of determination and causality took place at the same time that the Soviet Union imploded, and that complex debates about the 'end of history' were reconfiguring not only the liberal, mainstream 'centre' but also the left, was of course noteworthy. In Canada the context was complicated further by an intensification of reaction against the entire oeuvre of social history, as cer- tain well-placed, mainstream historians attacked labour, women's and regional historians for narrowing Canadian history to a trivialising focus on the insigni- ficant and ignoring the grandeur of the politics of nation-building. The result was a popular front-like unity of all progressives against 'the Granatsteinian enemy'. In a supreme irony, this was constructed with a rhetorical flourish that papered over quite significant differences amongst the ranks of seemingly like- minded advocates of an undifferentiated social history.[77]

---

76   J.W. Scott 1986, pp. 1053–75. For the impact of Scott's article see the 2008 forum, 'Revisiting "Gender: A Useful Category of Historical Analysis"' (AA.VV. 2008, pp. 1344–430).

77   A major statement of mainstream animosity was Bliss 1991–2, pp. 5–17; for a drawing together of some of his previous thoughts, Granatstein 1998. The most sustained response appeared in McKillop 1999, pp. 269–99. I offered a complicating rejoinder to McKillop in B. Palmer 1999, pp. 676–86.

Gendered labour histories became the site where 'the linguistic turn' played itself out most clearly within Canadian historical writing. Over the course of the 1990s gender histories attentive to class subjects abounded and included studies of nursing, agricultural labour, skill and labour reform, working girls and networks of urban leisure, and politics in the automobile industry.[78] Collections of essays on 'gendered pasts' contained, of course, much that did not touch down on working-class history, but in most cases such texts – whether they brought together previously unpublished contributions or reprinted articles – featured labouring lives prominently.[79]

Joy Parr's *The Gender of Breadwinners: Women, Men, and Change in Two Industrial Towns, 1880–1950* (1990) was arguably one of the more influential of a host of 1990s writings. Suggesting that past interpretations of labouring life had been incarcerated in a constrained interpretive failure to explore simultaneously the ways in which class *and* gender ordered being, Parr provided Canadian historians with an admonition that would orchestrate much scholarship for the next decade and a half:

> The challenge now plainly is to think beyond this history of dualisms and its accompanying assertion of an ahistorical hierarchy of oppressions. We need to problematize and unmake the chain of binary oppositions – masculine/feminine, market/non-market, public/private, waged/non-waged – and rethink the categoricalism that cantonizes gender, class, race, ethnicity, and nationality, so as to see past the conceptual signage, which has illuminated the previously invisible but now threatens to obstruct our view of the living space beyond.

Oddly enough, the important empirical findings of Parr's study relating to labour recruitment, work processes and the gendered nature of labour-capital relations and class conflict often seemed to emerge against the grain of the book's insistence on the need to transcend binary oppositions. Indeed, Parr's organising framework *was* just such a powerful dualism, dependent as it was on the contrasting outlines of work in an ostensible 'men's town' of furniture production and in a 'women's town' of knitting mills. Theoretical structures aside, gender's significance usually over-shadowed class in Parr's interpretive history.[80]

---

78   McPherson 1996; Danysk 1995; Burr 1999; Strange 1995; Sugiman 1994.

79   Parr and Rosenfeld 1996; McPherson, Morgan, and Forestell 1999.

80   Parr 1990, especially pp. 11, 8, 119; 1995, pp. 354–76.

Different in tone and orientation was Sangster's volume of Peterborough-based studies of working women in a manufacturing town. Sangster eschewed the more grandiose promises of post-modernism and settled instead for an exploration of gender *at work*, concentrating her conceptualisation at the conjuncture, rather than the disjuncture, of Marxism, feminism and productive suggestions of 'the linguistic turn'. The result was a book that looked primarily at women's experience, concentrating on how working women were socialised into their gender and class roles, how they adapted to the gendered division of labour in the home and in the waged workplace, and how they managed, over time, to straddle the fence of accommodation and resistance, embracing understandings of respectability and trade-union principles, being mothers and militants. Sangster's studies thus convey a sense of gender difference and class solidarity that is attentive to what is distinctive in women's experience as well as what crosses the boundaries of masculine and feminine in a generalised framing of the relations of labour and capital.[81] Sangster's approach led to her refusal of the tendency, evident in positions articulated by some gender historians, that women's history was passé and that only the study of an all-encompassing gender order, constitutive of the normative identities of masculine and feminine, could unlock the meaning of the past.[82] Revealingly, Sangster brought one young historian, Steve Penfold, to task for stating bluntly, perhaps licenced by the climate of dismissal that was becoming commonplace, that '[u]ntil recently, paying attention to gender meant nothing more than discussing women. But under the influence of post-modern theorists, historians (even those who would reject much of post-modern philosophy) have begun to advance a more complex understanding of gender which focuses on the interplay of ideals of femininity and masculinity'.[83] Sangster's understandable rejoinder – 'a revealing pejorative comment, as if this was *nothing*' – received a reply from Penfold. He claimed that his statement had been directed at 'the intellectual posture of gender-blind labour historians'.[84] This seemingly inconsequential exchange captured a certain development of the 1990s in which gender history, 'the linguistic turn' and working-class history could, in the hands of particular practitioners, separate. The more sharply and polemically historians took 'the linguistic turn', the more likely it was that they would

---

81   Sangster 1995b; 2004, pp. 47–88.
82   Sangster 1995a, pp. 109–21. This article was replied to in force by two teams of historians, with Sangster responding in AA.VV. 1995–6, pp. 205–48.
83   Penfold 1994, p. 23.
84   Penfold 1995–6, p. 238; Sangster 1995–6, p. 241.

misrepresent and caricature past writing in the field of working-class history.[85] Small wonder that one working-class historian posted the question 'w[h]ither class' in writing on his region's history.[86]

Nonetheless, labour history in Canada has not died, and 'the linguistic turn', while certainly influential, has perhaps slowed of late. On the one hand, its insights have been absorbed, while an earlier aggressive challenge to a material-ist social history of class has softened.[87] On the other, attentiveness to language and the social constructions so evident in the past has prodded historians to rethink a range of important dimensions of working-class experience, includ-ing its gendered and racialised nature. Indeed, 'the linguistic turn' has been foundational in stimulating new studies of racialised otherness that are cent-ral to understanding class formation. Many of them spring from concerns with gender, and *Labour/Le Travail* has often been an original forum in which to showcase research before developing it into a monograph.[88]

If working-class history in Canada has not yet quite achieved the totalising articulation of the interlocking hierarchies of class, ethnicity, race and gender Ruth Frager called for in 1999, then it has travelled a considerable distance in the right direction.[89] Ethnicity, class and gender coalesce, for instance, in the many edited collections on immigrants, transnational diasporas and state policy emanating from the on-going research and collaborative study of Franca Iacovetta.[90] A reader designed for use in labour history courses and first published in 1992 reflected this advance, reprinting a plethora of articles that addressed the nature and meaning of workers' lives in Canada, especially in terms of how class, race and gender intersected.[91]

85   Note the particularly personalised and often wrong-headed commentary in Valverde 2000, pp. 59–77, especially pp. 64–5.
86   Leier 1996b, pp. 61–75, with responses by me (B. Palmer 1996, pp. 76–84), Strong-Boag (1996, pp. 84–7), and McDonald (1996, pp. 88–92), and a rejoinder by Leier (1996a).
87   This is how I read a trend in contemporary historiographic reflection. Note, for instance, Sewell 2005; Eley and Nield 2007.
88   Muszynski 1996; Creese 1999; Guard 2004, pp. 117–40.
89   Frager 1999, pp. 217–47.
90   Gabaccia and Iacovetta 2002; Iacovetta 2006.
91   Radforth and Sefton 1992.

Labour History at the Current Conjuncture

A variety of monographs suggest Canadian labour history's diversity in the 21st century. Steven High's *Industrial Sunset: The Making of North America's Rust Belt, 1969–1984* (2003) uses a cross-border comparison of de-industrialisation in Canada and the United States to outline the continuing relevance of combining working-class history and political economy. This peculiarly Canadian marriage has spawned considerable comment on the 'revolution from above' which has reconfigured contemporary industrial relations. Leo Panitch's and Donald Swartz's many editions of what is now titled *From Consent to Coercion: The Assault on Trade Union Freedoms* (2003) is arguably the most stimulating, politically effective and widely read of a number of important studies.[92] Equally important, Canadian political economy and gendered labour studies have recast the analytic stage on which working-class histories of struggle and resistance are rethought in light of the importance of fundamental structures such as state power and policy, family and economy.[93] Legal scholars, in turn, have situated labour's history in relation to changes in the law.[94]

   The most recent course-designed reader, Palmer and Sangster's *Labouring Canada: Class, Gender, and Race in Canadian Working-Class History* (2008), gathers together 28 articles that introduce students to class formation from early colonisation and Aboriginal dispossession to the state of the unions in an epoch of neoliberal assault and working-class retrenchment. Gender and race receive considerable coverage, as do state policies, household economies and class struggles and their advocates. In but one indication of how the field has expanded its inclusiveness, it reprints an important discussion of sex work, Becki L. Ross's critical reflection on exotic dancing, 'Bumping and Grinding on the Line: Making Nudity Pay', which originally appeared in a special 'millennium edition' of *Labour/Le Travail*.[95]

   Labour history in Canada, then, has long left behind a debate over whether its focus would be institutions and politics or the social life and cultural experience of working people. On one level this debate was always more of a *political* disagreement than it was a discussion of the substance and content of actual

---

92   Panitch and Swartz 2003 has gone through many printings and revisions, and is now in its third edition. Its origins lie in an article published in *Labour/Le Travail* (Panitch and Swartz 1984, pp. 133–57). See also Reshef and Rastin 2003.

93   See especially Luxton and Corman 2001; A. Porter 2003.

94   Fudge and Tucker 2001.

95   Palmer and Sangster 2008; B. Ross 2000, pp. 221–50.

research and study, as subsequent commentary defending industrial legality as an unambiguous advance would make abundantly clear.[96] This political divide remains, surviving in often complicated ways, even as new work addressing 'the cultural' is now seemingly much in vogue.[97] Those of us who, decades ago, suggested that there was a need to attend to the cultural realm (which did not, of course, imply that other realms were insignificant and not worthy of study) did so because we conceived of culture as something of a web of 'connective tissues of an ambiguous realm of everyday life that bridged the chasm separating class as a silent structure and class as a potential force for revolutionary change'. Such 'tissues were never, however, simply one-way threads tying class place to the realization of class consciousness; more often than not they wrapped themselves around class experience in ways that produced web-like mazes in which little was direct and obvious'.[98] Labour history, in this understanding of the moment of a particular birth in the 1970s, was indeed about grappling with class as an agent of social transformation. Those who charted this analytic path 'self-identified' as 'working-class historians' and in so doing consciously separated themselves from those who, while they wrote labour history, named themselves differently and would soon be drawn to other fields.

The political and economic conjuncture in which modern Canadian labour history was formed, however, differs markedly from the current conjuncture. Intellectually, 1970s scholarship was forged in the crucible of the 1960s, and it rested, as had that decade, on New Left visions and a boundless sense of the possibility of dissidence. Today's moment can barely remember such a time, coming after decades of coerced left retreats and material assault on working-class well-being on the one hand, and, on the other, waves of academic fashion that have called into question class-based politics. Marxism had become, by the early 1970s, a viable answer for many New Leftists who discovered, as their movements wound down or fractured into factions, much to appreciate and emulate in an older left's programmatic grasp of the traditions associated not only with Marx and Engels but with Lenin and Trotsky. The turn to class was, in Canada as elsewhere, a logical political and intellectual move. In 2009, no such grasp is easily within reach. A new generation of progressive scholars turns to proliferating identities, discursive practices and a less singular subject. Someone like Ian McKay, whose original studies of the 1970s and 1980s

---

96   See, for instance, the arguments of MacDowell 2001, p. 295.
97   Contrast contemporary treatment of the 'cultural' aspects of working-class life with studies of the late 1970s and 1980s. See, for instance, Heron 2003; and Heron and Penfold 2006.
98   B. Palmer 1992, pp. 11–28 (pp. 13, 20).

addressed workers, has now turned to the history of the Canadian left enlightenment, which he is at pains to claim is not about 'a death-defying mastery
of Marx's *Capital*, or defeating rivals in theoretical and political combat in the
ritualized dialectical duels for which Marxist men have long been famous'. Well,
no, to be sure, no reasonable human being would want to be associated with
that! Instead, what McKay suggests is needed is a 'life commitment to shared
conversations and collective acts that hasten the day of a more generous democracy'. And in this conversation, 'Canadian leftism cannot be seen as the passive
reflection of the working class', just as, of course, it cannot write the workers off
entirely either. Class matters in the current conjuncture, but the project of our
times, the making not of working-class power but of 'a more generous democracy', cannot be reduced to proletarian initiative.[99]

Leaving aside the politics of such strictures, with which it is possible to both
agree to some extent and disagree in other ways, my point in concluding this
discussion of the historiography of Canadian workers is that this positioning
serves as a useful suggestion about the actual environment in which labour history now exists. The surroundings of our time are stimulating and productive
and have generated important and fresh perspectives on the lives of Canada's
labouring men, women and children. But new studies that are doing this are
not, for the most part, framed as labour history. Class of course figures in this
writing, but *not* decisively so. The material social histories of class formation
and struggle of the 1970s and 1980s are long separated from the gendered,
classed, raced and largely cultural histories that have begun to appear since
2005.[100] There are very few, if any, 'new' working-class historians in Canada
precisely because it is rare indeed for graduate students to name themselves
'labour historians'. To the extent that new scholars consciously append 'labour'
to their self-identifications, they tend to come from disciplines such as sociology, political economy and, most emphatically, labour studies, spheres that
are welcoming to but different from working-class *history*.

Of course this is *precisely* the kind of interdisciplinary crossing of conceptual
and investigative borders that takes working-class history in new directions and
enlivens the field. *Labour/Le Travail*, which has been something of a bellwether
of working-class history in Canada, is now very much an illustration of this
process. The articles that appear in its pages are seldom easily and narrowly
categorised as 'labour history', although there are, inevitably, specific pieces
of this kind. For the most part, the journal is now what might be designated

---

99   McKay 2005, pp. 47–8.
100   Fahrni 2005; Rudy 2005; Dummitt 2007.

a 'cross-over' publication. Many of the articles that make their way through our peer review process into print do so as examinations of working-class life that conjoin labour being a *class* with a host of other considerations, amongst them gender, race, region, age, sexual orientation, etc. This is to the good. And yet it should also raise concerns. Because if 'labour history' is advanced by its integration into larger analyses of social, cultural, political and economic life, so too is it the case that when a subject cannot sustain its name, it is in danger of losing itself amongst those many other subjects that have no shyness proclaiming *their* identity.

In this sense labour history needs perhaps to revitalise itself not in some defensive posture of asserting its claims against other subjects and identities, but in stepping up a sense of the contributions it can make and what it is that is uniquely significant about the working-class past and its legacies. We need the history of the working class now more than ever. Given the challenges that workers as a class face in the current period of capitalist-imposed austerity, its institutions, traditions, and well-being threatened by crises *not* of its making but most emphatically dire in its consequences for labouring people, it is arguably the case that *class politics from below* need reviving in the face of the onslaught of destructive *class politics from above*. Just as those class politics from below will never be reinvigorated without an appreciation of the ways in which working-class life and struggle involve dimensions of experience beyond the wage and the workplace, so too is the history of labour's combativity and defence of its material circumstances centrally important in charting a new politics of resistance. Such a politics, to be sure, demands much more than a nuanced and radical sense of the past, but such an understanding has its own small role to play in mobilising a future.

PART 2

Reel History: Comment on the Cinematic

∴

Introduction to Part 2

Historians like films. They are especially drawn to the cinematic if its content is directly situated in the past. But historians are also able to claim, with justification, that a film that does not have historical moorings is something of a rarity. If 'all the world's a stage', the theatre inevitably rests on the foundations of the past.

Since the 1970s, moreover, historians have become involved with film in a plethora of ways: they review films, serve as consultants to filmmakers and even make films themselves.[1] History and film has become a scholarly field and history departments, eager for enrolments, are increasingly offering courses which explore the relationship of cinema and history. Texts such as Natalie Zemon Davis's *Slaves on Screen: Film and Historical Vision* suggest how vividly specific historical experiences can be portrayed cinematically, while historians like Robert A. Rosenstone have written on how film challenges understandings of history and provides a medium that forces researchers to reconsider the limitations of conventional sources and of the literary narrative as a mode of historical representation.[2] Films such as *The Godfather* (1972), *Reds* (1981), *The Return of Martin Guerre* (1982) and *Glory* (1989) captured historians' imaginations in the 1970s and 1980s, while Oliver Stone's 1989–95 trilogy of an America at war with its enemies and with itself (*Born on the Fourth of July*, *JFK* and *Nixon*) offered an explosive commentary on power and its discontents.[3] With the release of each new historical dramatisation historians are precipitated into the limelight, their commentaries on accuracy and authenticity solicited. Steven Spielberg's *Lincoln* (2012) is only the most recent chapter in a long and continuing book, the substance of which turns on the history/historian/film relation.[4]

---

1   For comment on working-class historians and filmmaking see Walkowitz 1985 and Ramirez 1999. Steve Ross, whose early writing explored the history of labour in 19th-century Cincinnati, has produced two notable histories of film: Ross 1998; Ross 2011. Stephen Brier, Josh Brown and Roy Rosenzweig, mainstays of the collective *Who Built America?* project, pioneered in making a number of pedagogical films to accompany other aspects of their attempt to develop a historical appreciation of class formation in the United States. Note, for perhaps the most well-known example of an historian involved in the making of a feature film, Davis 1988.

2   Davis 2000; Rosenstone 1995.

3   Rosenstone 2012 covers much of this ground.

4   Davis 1987. For a relatively recent compilation that presents essays addressing 'history on film' see Hughes-Warrington 2009. Note as well Kelly Candaele, 'Film History: Columnists and Historians Assess Spielberg's *Lincoln*', *Los Angeles Review of Books*, 14 December 2012.

In my way of thinking – and I believe this relates to Marxism's appreciation of dialectics and the politics of representation in a cultural context of unmistakable capitalist hegemony – accuracy and authenticity within an artistic genre are never hard and fast articulations. They cannot be sculpted in the dead matter of ossified images that somehow convey, in forever frozen and seemingly one-dimensional portrayals, what happened in the past. In a medium meant to dramatise a past presented visually, a jarringly ahistorical and counter-factual image might well convey a critical truth in 'larger' ways than would a mechanical adherence to the strictly accurate. Metaphors, creatively developed, often illuminate authenticities that are being played with rather loosely, to excellent effect. Historians thus spend too much time, I think, anguishing over the representation of historical reality when, to the best of my knowledge, their own texts often find this sought-after end an elusive achievement. This does not mean that historical accuracy and authenticity can or even *should* be cavalierly discarded, their significance belittled as inconsequential. But neither should these touchstones of professional historical writing be reified within the entirely different project of cinematic production. More important is whether or not film makes us aware of connections and developments of central importance in history's making, cultivating insights not easily depicted in 'frames' constrained by time, place and available evidence. My experimentation with 'reel history' thus largely avoids the authenticity/historical accuracy hand-wringing that animates much historical commentary on film.

The first essay in this grouping of film commentaries grew out of my larger study of histories of the night as a venue in which to explore transgression and marginalisation, *Cultures of Darkness: Night Travels in the Histories of Transgression* (2000). 'Night in the Capitalist, Cold War City: Noir and the Cultural Politics of Darkness' used a cinematic fixation on cynicism, despair, defeat and disillusionment to foreground the deforming nature of the Cold War. It detailed one particular film's visual technique and jaded story-line to expose the social ills endemic to capitalism that it was the Cold War's objective to keep well hidden behind the dense veil of anti-Communism. That noir as a cinematic enterprise appeared and sustained its most accomplished examples in the 1940s and 1950s, during Hollywood's subordination to McCarthyism, is, I suggest, no accident. When the possibility of socially critical filmmaking was staunched, as it largely was in that period, critique was driven underground. Blacklisted director Jules Dassin, targeted by the Federal Bureau of Investigation and named as a supposed Communist before the House Un-American Activities Committee, went into exile in London, where he filmed the noir classic *Night and the City* in 1950. As I suggest in the commentary below, this film in particular, and noir as a genre/stylistic orientation in general, proved an accommodating reservoir for subtle but nonetheless subversive representations of the sordid underside of capitalist social relations, in which alienation permeated every pore of the body politic. The point is not so much an image's historical 'truth' as the capacity to suggest and draw out relevant meanings through symbolism.

The problem is more acute, of course, when film actually addresses, as part of its purpose, a specific historical period. This is very much an issue in *Gangs of New York* (2002). Unlike most historians, however, I am not particularly troubled by historical 'inaccuracy' in Martin Scorsese's much-maligned epic of nativism, racism, boss politics and the second American Revolution, more commonly known as the Civil War. Most critical, historically informed commentary on Scorsese's loose adaptation of Herbert Ashbury's informal account of a mid-19th-century New York 'underworld' cannot seem to get past the film's 'howlers': instances of accuracy incautiously thrown to the winds of irrelevance or incongruities blatantly defiant of authentic depictions of a 'real' history, embedded in actual time and identifiable place. When I first saw the film, I was instead excited by what I understood to be the significance of an intensified sense of representation, in which an incompletely and often wrongly represented 'moment' in historical development was presented in ways that brought into heightened relief large processes of class and state formation. In a United States where history is often used to sanitise power's fierce conquests, so often scratched into the flesh of subordination, the bloody history of New York's Five Points district was brought alive in ways that revealed the historical hurt of class, race and ethnicity and the ways in which these sites of oppression and exploitation were constructed through and alongside the making of the state. Scorsese may not be a revolutionary leftist and *Gangs of New York* is most emphatically not a Marxist 'text', but this representation of history can be read in materialist ways and appreciated for its revelations.

The final statement in this section is of a slightly different kind. *Searching for Sugar Man* (2012) received about as much critical acclaim as it is possible for a documentary made about a poor working-class Mexican American, directed by a novice filmmaker from Scandinavia who discovered 'the story' while backpacking through South Africa, to achieve. Winning an Oscar, as this cinematic study of the man known as Rodriguez managed to do, is about as good as it gets. When I first saw the movie it simply took command of me; in the theatre it brought tears to my eyes, and in the weeks that followed my seeing the film I could not get its narrative out of my head. I went looking for whatever I could find to historicise and contextualise it; I listened to Rodriguez's music and sought out texts of his lyrics. I began to think about Detroit's Mexicantown, upon which I had stumbled accidently years before, in new ways. Before I knew what hit me I had a manuscript in hand and had soon sent off different drafts to editors at left-wing magazines like *Canadian Dimension* and *Against the Current,* which published shorter and longer versions early in 2013. What appears below is the fullest and most elaborate variant of a journalistic homage to what Rodriguez represents: the diversity and decency, humility and honour, solidarity and sociability, principle and politics of an individual working-class subject who nonetheless tells us something about labouring people as a whole and the art that, in some circumstances, can become their lives.

CHAPTER 4

Night in the Capitalist, Cold War City:
Noir and the Cultural Politics of Darkness*

The Cold War reaches across the international history of the 20th century, a disfigurement that leaves a frozen burn scorching the politics and culture of diverse moments, scarring east and west in ways different but reciprocal. More than a brief interlude associated with the post-World War II campaigns of Senator Joseph McCarthy, the anti-Communism central to politics in the 20th century is a pivotal practice of containment that begins with the making of the first revolutionary workers' state in the Soviet Union in 1917 and continues well after the implosion of actually existing socialism at the end of the 1980s.[1] The ugliness of this two-sided Cold War conditioned and pressured Stalinist atrocity as well as the evils of disingenuous democratic display. The Russian purge show trials of the late 1930s[2] had their seemingly benign counterpart in the House Un-American Activities Committee (HUAC) meetings, where the dubious practice of naming names turned the United States into an informer society in which people traded the honour of political convictions for the material securities of status and positions.[3]

Bodies thus litter the political landscape. The extermination of the entire human apparatus of original Bolshevism in the degeneration of Stalinised Soviet life, not to mention the vast death march of induced famine in the countryside and the gulag of political and cultural repression, wrote *finis* to the liberatory hopes many associated with workers' revolution and the accomplishments of 1917. What followed in the United States was of course less chillingly

---

* 'Night in the Capitalist, Cold War City: Noir and the Cultural Politics of Darkness', *Left History*, 5 (1997), 57–76.

1 This position, in which the Cold War is extended back in time as well as perhaps forward into the future, seems to me congruent with positions William Appleman Williams adopted. See, for example, W.A. Williams 1962; Buhle and Rice-Maximin 1995. On McCarthy see Oshinsky 1983; R. Fried 1990.

2 See, for instance, Preliminary Commission of Inquiry into the Charges Made against Trotsky in the Moscow Trials, 1937.

3 This process is explored in the case of the Hollywood blacklist in Navasky 1980 and McGilligan and Buhle 1997, as well as in the more wide-ranging statement Ceplair and Englund 1983; for a particular figure, see Cole 1981. Note as well Belfrage 1994.

terroristic, but the visible tip of an iceberg of denunciation with deadly consequences that reached from the Rosenbergs to lesser-known figures such as E.H. Norman, the sensitive Canadian scholar of Japanese feudalism and career diplomat, who finally committed suicide in Cairo after being hounded by McCarthyism's watchdogs for almost a decade.[4] In the process few areas of cultural life remained untouched; as thousands were blacklisted from government circles, teaching jobs, journalist posts, Hollywood and the arts community,[5] the Cold War at its mid-century zenith exercised a pernicious impact on avant-garde movements from abstract expressionism to modern jazz.[6]

This article takes one such cultural form, noir, as a representational medium articulating a cultural politics of darkness and locates it within Cold War America. Drawing out the night as both a time and a place within which noir's narratives were ideally situated as well as a usefully symbolic metaphor in noir's oppositional scripts of estrangement and alienation, this essay attempts a broad introduction to the genre, albeit one situated at the intersection of discrete aspects of style and social content. It then closes with a particular reading of one classic noir text, the Jules Dassin-directed film *Night and the City* (1950), concluding with a brief acknowledgement of the different politico-aesthetics of contemporary, late capitalist noir productions.

Noir, both fiction and film, is one of those quintessentially modernist American cultural developments whose essence has proven, for generations of critics, notoriously difficult to locate with definitional precision.[7] As Raymond Borde and Etienne Chaumeton suggested in their original assessment of film noir, *Panorama du film noir américain* (1955), it was the darkness at the heart of this new genre that lent it a certain coherence, one that coincided, interestingly, with a set of techniques, from off-centred 'shots' and eerie lighting to filming on night location, many of which can be located in a materialised stylistics of wartime production over-determined by budget constraints that limited the small producers as well as affecting the large studios. Noir is thus defined foremost in

---

4   On the Rosenbergs see the old statement Wexley 1955, and the more acclimated Radosh and
    Milton 1984. E.H. Norman's case remains controversial. See Lyon 1991, pp. 219–59; Barros 1986;
    Bowen 1986.
5   Note Caute 1979; Scher 1992.
6   Consider Kofsky 1970, pp. 109–22; Guilbault 1983. For a general cultural history of the Cold
    War see Engelhardt 1995, while the context of the cultural front Michael Denning deploys in
    The Cultural Front: The Laboring of American Culture in the Twentieth Century (Denning 1996)
    provides a sense of the 'progressive' opposition's immediate historical background.
7   On problems of definition and the range of writings, especially related to film noir, see Silver
    1996, pp. 3–15.

content, but also in a congruent aesthetics, as disorientation. A fundamental break with literary and cinematic convention in which well-understood moral reference points had long been universally presented as statements of inherently timeless social values such as good, beauty and honour, noir's core was its refusal to reproduce the parables of propriety. Instead, noir introduced the destabilisation of ambivalence and the challenging referent of reversal: good and evil were conjoined to the point of being indistinguishable; classical heroes and heroines were displaced by protagonists mired in the depths of depravity; animating narratives of chaos and confusion were motivations presented in their most base and disturbing light. Stylistically juxtaposing the bizarre and fantastic with a relentless sequence of 'realist' snapshots, moreover, noir created an atmosphere of the ultra-normal periodically ruptured by the weird, the violent and the disturbing, often shot 'close-up' or framed tightly, lending it the tenor, again, of an off-putting imbalance, claustrophobic in its containments. Audiences thus experienced noir, especially in its cinematic variants, as anguish and insecurity, a genre of apprehension.[8]

The background to this complex emergence of noir's forms, which included its prose as well as Hollywood variants, is thus multi-faceted. Recent feminist commentary has often addressed noir as something of a male gaze, a fantasy of repression in which the desires and determinations of independent women are subordinated and brought back into the familialist fold of nurturing conventions. Such an interpretation certainly has resonance with historical circumstances, especially in the United States, where the fluidity of gender relations was quite pronounced in the decades preceding noir's evolving place in popular culture. From the post-World War I 1920s to the economically pressured malaise of the Great Depression and into the maelstrom of the 1940s, sexuality and male-female relations shifted gears dramatically, conditioning a volatility in gender relations that no doubt fed into the possibility that one dimension of anxiety addressed by noir would inevitably be the sustaining of male authority. There is no doubt much to this reading, although there is contention within critical feminist circles about the dissidence of a noir genre that congealed desire and destruction in ways that often eroded patriarchy's codes and conformities.[9]

If gender scripted noir's moment of emergence, so too did class. A part of the genre's origins lay in the depressingly stark 1930s realisation that even the seem-

8 I have drawn on the useful abbreviated statement in Borde and Chaumeton 1996, pp. 17–25.
9 See Place 1978, p. 50, on female repression and male power, and the extended engagement with this position in Cowie 1993, pp. 121–66.

ingly protected middle classes now faced the distorting prospects of economic insecurity, downward mobility, and the consequent psychological turmoil. It was the translation of the experience of socio-economic unease into the dark artistic conventions of the 1940s that allowed for noir's aesthetic purchase on an ambiguous generation that witnessed the capacity of boom to reverse itself into bust, sounding the death knell of complacent security and proclaiming an age of alienation. In Edward Hopper's oils, this representational engagement with estrangement found a uniquely American expression in which the shadowed virtual photo-realism of the archetypally noirish *Nighthawks* (1942) drew on themes the artist had explored earlier, pushing his 1920s articulations of anomie in more unambiguously alienated directions. The images of automats, drug stores and burlesque houses Hopper crafted in the late 1920s gave way to post-1940 productions of office scenes, often shadowed in the night.[10] In these paintings, Hopper cast the commerce of the day in the noirish juxtaposition of work time's supposed end, achieving an effect not unlike *Glengarry Glen Ross* (1992), the David Mamet play and James Foley-directed film in which darkness provides a context for capitalism's seamiest competitive manipulations and psychological damage to expose themselves. Hopper's *Summer Evening* (1947) typifies noir's rough-edged destiny of despair, the lighted porch framed by the night providing a venue pregnant with sensuality, conspiracy and a hard-boiled cynicism drifting inevitably towards an end of no good.[11]

This hybrid representational evolution can be located in the lead-up to and subsequent shadows of the Cold War.[12] Noir as a genre was born in the subterfuges of the 'popular front', where the programmatic suppression of revolutionary intention through integration into the mainstreams of bourgeois order orchestrated a politics of accommodation always ostensibly turning on clandestine articulations of oppositional theory and practice.[13] Left-leaning Hollywood auteurs made the most of this 'cultural front' and gravitated to the

---

10   For other comment on noir and the office see Jameson 1993, pp. 33–56.

11   Hopper's works, and biographical and analytic perspectives, are found in Levin 1980a, 1980b, pp. 123–7, and 1995; Lyons and Weinberg 1995; Schmied 1995; Doss 1983, pp. 14–36.

12   On contextualisation, see Higham and Greenberg 1968 and Polan 1986.

13   It goes without saying, then, that I reject the uncritical readings of the 'popular front' that have captivated much of the political and cultural historiography of this period, as evident in Denning 1996 and Isserman 1982. For an alternative reading more in line with my views, see Goldfield 1985, pp. 315–58.

ambivalences of noir instinctually, seeing in it 'a shrewdly oblique strategy for an otherwise subversive realism'.[14] A case in point was the quintessential 'popular front' writer Vera Caspary, whose route from Jewish middle-class Chicago to Hollywood took her through two-and-a-half years in the Communist Party in New York and Connecticut and involvement in the whirl-wind activism of the 'cultural front' of the 1940s. In her autobiography, *The Secrets of Grown-Ups* (1979), Caspary recalled engaging with the politics of the Anti-Nazi League, the American League Against War and Fascism, and the League of American Writers. She taught writing classes in order to earn money to bring refugee authors to America. 'For the Left', she remembered,

> these were fruitful years ... Almost every night there were fund-raising parties, benefits and concerts. There was a steady influx of new people coming to work in the studios – actors, writers, directors from New York, refugees from Europe.

Caspary's thriller *Laura* (1942) became a noir classic, albeit one, under Otto Preminger's direction, that exemplified the subordination of the femme fatale to the male voice-over and reduced women's experience to a superficial surface resistant to analysis, unlike Caspary's text.[15] In the period of the 'popular front', then, noir attracted dissident authors and film makers, and was even to a certain extent crafted by them: in its oblique capacities to scaffold a critique of capitalism on the disintegrating rungs of conventional moral authority, noir was a voice raised against the sanctimony of the socio-economic context from within its particular confinements. This was not *Marxist, pace* Michael Denning's appreciation of the 'cultural front', as much as it was comfortably in alignment with the ambivalences of the Communist Party's relationship with capitalism and the American state.

The disintegrating political certainties of the 1940s, in which the nation's moral core was a unified opposition to fascism, found themselves cut adrift in the realignments of post-World War II anti-Communism. With the 'popular front' dismantled and the posture of reaction hardening dangerously day by day, it was even more impossible to make cinema Marxist at mid-century. But noir's formalistic darkness continued to allow the depiction of capitalism's unsavoury undercurrents, spinning out the moral tales of an underground city

---

14   Mike Davis 1992, p. 41.
15   On Caspary see Denning 1996, pp. 144–5, 228; Caspary 1979. For a feminist critique of *Laura*, see Hollinger 1996, pp. 247–50.

where the productions of honest toil always lose out to the quick fixes of corruption and speculative vice, where the déclassé rich and the gangster predator
rule an economy of easy money and its purchase on the good life.[16] In noir, the
attractions of the night always supersede those of the day and, when given the
choice, noir anti-heroes inevitably choose betrayals and thefts, even murder,
over honest toil and hard labour. That they cannot win at capitalism's game
is what no doubt made noir an attractive vehicle for Hollywood's progressives, amongst them the writers John Huston and Malvin Wald and the directors
George E. Diskant and Jules Dassin.[17] This message of doomed defeat also had
its attractions in the Cold War climate of the reactionary 1950s, where the com-
pensations of the hard-boiled style renegotiated masculinity in an epoch of
proletarian defeat and domestication, both at the point of production and in
the ideological arena.[18]

   In its most successful cinematic expressions, noir negotiated these shifting
political contours in a unique fusion of heavy-handed German expressionism,
orchestrated by expatriate directors such as Fritz Lang,[19] Otto Preminger,[20]
Billy Wilder, Anatole Litvak, and Max Steiner, along with the hard-boiled American prose stylistics of Dashiell Hammett,[21] the 1941 Humphrey Bogart-Mary
Astor production of whose novel *The Maltese Falcon* (1930) marks the generally accepted debut of film noir.[22] On California's Sunshine Coast, where heavy
industry was weaker than in other geographic sectors, where old money was
judged in decades, not centuries, where rural America was physically quite
close but socially so phenomenally distant and where the hustling boosterism of Hollywood lent the economic climate a fantasy-like hyper-reality that
seemed not all that far removed from the actualities of a political economy
always on the verge of running away from itself, the potential for cultural and

---

16   Note, for background, the discussions in Ruth 1996; Warshow 1962, pp. 83–8; Grella 1968,
     pp. 186–98.

17   Biskind 1976, pp. 218–22.

18   See the readings provided by Worpole 1983; Mandel 1984; Madden 1968; and, albeit in less
     overt political terms, Krutnik 1991. For a recent gay reading of film noir, see the fascinating
     set of arguments in Corber 1997, pp. 23–104.

19   See Appel Jr 1974, pp. 12–17.

20   Lippe 1996, pp. 161–76.

21   On Hammett see Nolan 1983; D. Johnson 1983; Edenbaum 1968, pp. 80–103.

22   For commentary on the German contribution to noir and the hard-boiled style, see
     Schrader 1996, pp. 55–6. On *The Maltese Falcon*, see Malin 1968, pp. 104–9. An introduction
     to crime fiction, which structured some of the aesthetics of noir, is found in J. Palmer 1978
     and 1991.

political fermentation was, as Mike Davis has suggested, truly bizarre.[23] 'It is traumatic for an individual to lose a set of beliefs', writes the film noir critic Carl Richardson, whose exploration of the impact of the 1930s suggests that '[f]or a world-wide coterie of intellectuals and artists, it is a dark, frustrating process. It is a film noir on a large scale'.[24]

From out of the depths of the Great Depression came a series of real-life blows, their artistic renditions on the page beginning with James M. Cain's *The Postman Always Rings Twice* (1934),[25] Horace McCoy's *They Shoot Horses, Don't They?* (1935),[26] and Nathanael West's *The Day of the Locusts* (1939), stories of descent, debilitation, debauchery and despair that seemed to replicate a part of the argument of an unsettling analysis by Lewis Corey (Louis Fraina) in *Crisis of the Middle Class* (1935). Captured artistically in Philip Evergood's painting *Dance Marathon* (1934), this 'proletarian grotesque', in the words of Michael Denning, pushed images of play into the representational realm of its opposite, 'the dance marathon' becoming 'an allegory of an American capitalism in which endless, repetitive amusement and entertainment is oppressive, consuming the dreams of its youth', whose lives are squandered in economic depression, turning the pleasures of pastimes such as dance into the most routinised 'wage labor'.[27] In conjunction with Raymond Chandler's reconstruction of the world of the Los Angeles rich, eyeballed by the tough-guy private dick Phillip Marlowe and always tarnished by a moral darkness that could be opened up to the light only by the vernacular of the people, such texts turned the page towards noir's urban futilities.[28] Two years before he died, Chandler wrote to his London solicitor, 'I have lived my life on the edge of nothing'.[29]

If the origins of this accommodation lay in the economic malaise of the 1930s, the final reconciliation was one of a seemingly psychological realpolitik in which people recognised what was possible in the give and take of capitalism's ensemble of power and adapted to this rather than challenging it,

---

23   As an introduction to noir and Los Angeles, see the breath-taking argument in Mike Davis
     1992, pp. 36–46.
24   Richardson 1992, p. 183.
25   On the importance of Cain, see Oates 1968, pp. 110–28.
26   See Sturak 1968, pp. 137–62.
27   Denning 1996, p. 183.
28   On Chandler, see Jameson 1993, pp. 33–56; Ruhm 1968, pp. 171–85; Pfeil 1995, pp. 105–66.
     For statements on noir and urbanism, see Reid and Walker 1993, pp. 57–96; Christopher
     1997.
29   McShane 1976, p. 1.

with particular psychic costs.[30] The astute Afro-Caribbean Marxist C.L.R. James grasped the dualism of this cultural negotiation, appreciating its subtle subversions as well as its incarcerating incorporations. Noir institutionalised traditionalist values of individualism, and James located the attraction of the genre in the rugged American need to stand alone. The heroic fatalism of noir's protagonists was an almost universal self-reliance, apart from all structures of constituted authority and most emphatically distanced from law and propriety: 'He had to be an ordinary guy – *one who went out and did the job himself*'. In the context of closed frontiers and obvious barriers to the mythic dreams of American acquisitive individualism, undeniable in the post-Depression epoch of capitalism's powerful monopolistic grasp on material power, noir sustained 'a sense of active living, and in the bloodshed, the violence, the freedom from restraint to allow pent-up feelings free play', James discerned a possible release of 'the bitterness, hate, fear, and sadism' which he saw simmering below the discontented surface of social relations.[31] But if James saw, in this narrative of cultural appropriation and understanding, the potential of resistance, there was much to overcome to mobilise its possibilities, not the least of noir's cultivations being the construction of a dark imagery that, in its predictable postures, erases the living realities of day-to-day oppression in the distorted shadows of night's always unfulfilled dreams, sliding inevitably into the sinister hole of nightmarish fears from which the only exit appears a fantasy of forgetfulness.[32]

Noir's exploration of such themes often took on purely economic dimensions, albeit in ways that could blur into sexual pathologies, where the spent currency of erotic fulfilment generally had a crassly materialistic character. To be sure, the possibility of diversity was always present in noir's unfolding dramas. In Chester Himes's *If He Hollers Let Him Go* (1945), for instance, Hollywood's racism found a bitter chronicler, one that would be born again in the soft-pedaling 1980s and 1990s with Walter Mosley's Easy Rawlins mysteries *Devil in a Blue Dress, A Red Death* and *White Butterfly*, but this racial commentary was a rare intervention in the white plots of noir's acquisitive individualism.[33] Nevertheless, regardless of the route to noir's endnote, its cul-de-sac conclusion was universally marked by its darkened realism.

---

30   For a rather benign view, see Thomas 1992, pp. 71–87.

31   James 1993, pp. 121, 127, quoted in Corber 1997, pp. 27–8.

32   See the discussion of L.A. noir in Klein 1997, pp. 73–93.

33   Comment on Himes, whose other work focussed on Harlem, can be found in Diawara 1993, pp. 261–78; Pfeil 1990, pp. 64–8; Denning 1996, pp. 221, 227–8, 252, 257, 447–9. See, as well, Himes 1976. Note the argument in Lott 1996, pp. 81–101.

Chandler noted in 1950, the Cold War breaking out all around him, 'We still have dreams, but we know that most of them will come to nothing. And we also most fortunately know that it really doesn't matter'. With the Hollywood Ten battling the blacklist, Chandler could declare, 'This is not an age of reason or tolerance, but in Hollywood you don't learn to be a hero. You learn to be expedient – or you get to hell out'.[34] There wasn't much, after all, beyond the big sleep:

> What did it matter where you lay once you were dead? In a dirty sump or in a marble tower on top of a high hill? You were dead, you were sleeping the big sleep, you were not bothered by things like that.[35]

The message, again, would reappear in the twisted reversals of the staccato-like prose and sparse aesthetics of the Los Angeles novels of James Ellroy, a nightmare-induced 1980s/early-1990s noir quartet – *The Black Dahlia* (1987), *The Big Nowhere* (1988), *L.A. Confidential* (1990) and *White Jazz* (1993) – that had its origins in the author's mother's unresolved murder.[36]

Noir proved such a reservoir for the avant-garde aspirations of the 1940s and 1950s precisely because it seemed the perfect accommodation: one that embraced alienation, tried to overcome it, reproduced the evil it aimed to transcend and returned to the ever-troubling heart of darkness at the core of human existence. The contradictory impulse of the genre nurtured a profound moral ambivalence, a conspiracy of silencing anguish conscious in its intention to produce emotional insecurity: noir was nothing less, in the words of its original interpreters, than *'that state of tension instilled in the spectator when the psychological reference points are removed. The aim of film noir was to create a specific alienation'.*[37] One of the great character actors of film noir, Elisha Cook Jr, whose credits included 13 major motion pictures, starting with *The Maltese Falcon* and continuing through *Phantom Lady* (1944), *The Big Sleep* (1946), *Born to Kill* (1947), *The Killing* (1956) and *Baby Face Nelson* (1957), grasped this intuitively when he described his roles: 'I played rats, pimps, informers, hopheads, and communists',[38] a veritable catalogue listing of undesirables. Noir typecast, not the admirable hero, but the fall-guy anti-hero.

---

34   Durham 1963, pp. 76–7.
35   Chandler 1976, pp. 215–6.
36   See Ellroy 1997.
37   Borde and Chaumeton 1996, p. 25. Emphasis in original.
38   Cook quoted in Christopher 1997, pp. 49–50.

This dark moral reversal was as much an articulation of form as it was of substance. Moods, rather than plots, dominate noir, and as a cinematic genre noir was built around frustrations and fears, claustrophobias and psychic chaos, an anxiety-ridden context of paranoia all too often embedded in a troubling experience of defeat. Film noir's human centrepieces were constructions of lonely obsessions, narrowed to the point of suffocating those who cannot effectively wrestle their own demons into the backgrounds where they belong, allowing 'healthy' perspectives of human relationships and purposes to come into the foreground. Against idealised conceptions of families, communities and commitments, noir presented a dark, foreboding culture of shocking individualism, an endlessly alienated pursuit of illusory material gratifications that short-circuited the American dream, pushing it in the direction of a nightmare always on the verge of imploding. In the plot lines of noir everything good is permeated with the polluting evils of greed and lust, excesses of the estranged self that manage to corrupt human vulnerability and force it towards its ugliest poles of (dis)attraction. Stylistic devices, from close-ups of anguished faces to distorted lighting, mirror reflections, silhouetted figures, haunting flashbacks, outlandish camera angles, shadowed walls and twisted profiles, contribute to the making of skewed perspectives that are the formal presentation of a message of something seriously awry in the human condition.[39] All of this had its material origins in both the scarcities and social perspectives of World War II, which constricted the possibilities of shooting, lighting and editing, as well as highlighting the presence of evil's threat to humanity.[40]

Above all else, noir elevated the night to a dark moment of human estrangement, the time and place of unstable environment in which unattainable strivings produce the undoing of men and women, their every act 'shot' in orchestrated 'night-on-night' scenes that broke with cinematic tradition to present the oppositional possibilities of day and night. In *The Night Has a Thousand Eyes* (1947), Edward G. Robinson, a tormented psychic with the power to predict death, lives beneath the oppression of the stars, which fatally oversee his adventures. 'I had become a reverse zombie, the world was dead and I was living', Robinson explains.[41] Visual motifs thus translate into existential comment as the dark boundaries of existence constrict inward in a tightening knot of noir's capacity to effect a material transfiguration, in which the physicality of

---

39   See the discussion in Lipsitz 1994, pp. 279–302, and the introduction to Telotte 1989, pp. 1–39.

40   See Krutnik 1991, p. 21.

41   Silver and Ward 1979, p. 204.

a *scene* becomes the tortured *content* of a soul.[42] 'The streets were dark with something more than night', Robinson declares in *The Woman in the Window* (1945), while Mark Stevens proclaims in *The Dark Corner* (1946), 'I'm backed up in a dark corner and I don't know who's hitting me'. In both scenes the spatial and shadowed context of enclosure move, in conjunction with dialogue and the cinematic process of framing, from one of place to one of psyche, not unlike the HUAC settings in which the bright light of anti-Communism shone illuminatingly through speeches of pathetic recantation. After having resisted the McCarthyite witch-hunt for two years, for instance, Lee J. Cobb found himself penniless and out of work, his wife institutionalised as an alcoholic. He finally broke, testified before HUAC and informed on his colleagues by naming 20 individuals as 'known' communists and identifying others as left-wingers within the Actors' Equity Association. Now able to secure employment, Cobb suffered a massive coronary (his hospital bills were covered by Frank Sinatra) before landing the entirely appropriate role of the compliant Johnny Friendly in *On the Waterfront* (1954). Cobb's final statement to HUAC was a pusillanimously pitched justification of his sad denouement, in which he thanked the modern-day Inquisition for allowing him 'the privilege of setting the record straight ... further strengthening ... our Government and its efforts at home and abroad'.[43] Film noir at least spared its audience such pathetic blandishments. All that the noir anti-hero could generally accomplish, against such powerful transfiguration, was a temporary stay of personal solitude, a quiet, desperate retreat from the confusion that relentlessly sinks optimism in the rough waves of impending darkness, a final futile statement or gesture.[44] Cobb would have done better to have settled for as minimalist much.

To isolate a classic film noir presentation analytically is perhaps an impossibility, so diverse were the Hollywood offerings in this genre. Between *The Maltese Falcon* (1941) and Orson Welles's *Touch of Evil* (1958), literally hundreds of noir films were made encompassing a range of formalised types, from the socially critical commentary of *The Naked City* (1948) and *Nightmare Alley* (1947) through the gangster films *The Racket* (1951) and *The Asphalt Jungle* (1950) to the generalised noir theme of fatalism and demoralisation attendant on greed and the adventure of quests for pathological acquisitions, be they material, psychological or sexual. In the latter category can be placed many of

---

42   For another reading of space, see Copjec 1993, pp. 167–98.
43   For Cobb see Navasky 1980, pp. 268–73.
44   Consider the statements on styles and motifs in noir films in Place and Peterson 1996 and Porfirio 1996.

the private-eye adaptations of classic Hammett and Chandler fiction, as well
as Humphrey Bogart films such as *High Sierra* (1941), *Key Largo* (1948), *Dead
Reckoning* (1947) and *In a Lonely Place* (1950). Ironically enough, the least successful variants of noir were those consciously right-wing statements, such as
the dour melodrama *Ride the Pink Horse* (1947), and explicit Cold War productions that attempted to actually frontally address anti-Communism. Films
such as *I Was a Communist for the F.B.I.* (1951) pale in comparison, aesthetically
and intellectually, to the materialised eroticisation of estrangement evident in
Double Indemnity (1944), *The Postman Always Rings Twice* (1946) or *Clash by
Night* (1952). Yet as the blacklisted director-in-exile Jules Dassin's *Night and the
City* (1950), perhaps one of the classic noir statements, reveals, the imagery and
representational force of noir were never all that far removed from the Cold
War's stifling presence.[45]

Dassin was one of the premier Hollywood noir directors. Between 1941 and
1946 he directed eight shorts and features, including *Nazi Agent* (1942) and
the light comedy *The Affairs of Martha* (1942), in which a servant authors a
scandalous book about her employers. Dassin's creative genius burst forth in
1947–8, however, with three critically acclaimed credits, *Brute Force*, *Thieves'
Highway* and *The Naked City*, some of which drew the ire of the FBI. While the
latter had the stark presentation of a docudrama, the former two films marked
Dassin as one of Hollywood's more socially conscious artists, unrelenting in his
condemnation of the meaninglessness and everyday violence of routinised life,
a champion of the mythic, proletarian conflict ubiquitous in the maelstrom of
bourgeois order. When his noir counterpart, imprisoned Ukrainian-Canadian
Edward Dmytryk of the infamous 'Hollywood Ten', sought the favour of HUAC
and 'purged' himself before the Committee by identifying Dassin as a supposed
Communist, the latter, against whom there was little tangible 'evidence' save for
Dmytryk's self-interested testimony, found himself persecuted and blacklisted.
Dmytryk, the only member of the Hollywood Ten to recant in this way, went
on to direct *The Sniper* (1952), a thinly veiled defence of political repression
that elided deviance and dissidence in justifying incarcerating sex offenders
in mental hospitals (it was the time of Frances Farmer, after all)[46] and the

---

45   For guides to noir film see the abbreviated and much criticised statement, Durgnat 1996,
      pp. 37–52, and the more extensive compendium presented in Silver and Ward 1979.
      Snapshot depictions of particular films appear in Gifford 1988.
46   Frances Farmer was a left actress who worked with the Group Theatre in the 1930s and had
      modest success in Hollywood before being incarcerated in a mental asylum in the 1940s.
      For a fictional account see DeMarco 1982; her life is memorialised in the 1982 film *Frances*,
      starring Jessica Lange.

highly-acclaimed *The Caine Mutiny* (1954), which carried the authoritarian message that even incompetent leaders deserve the regard of those serving under them, whose allegiance must be total and unwavering.[47] Rather than dignify HUAC and its project, Dassin left the United States and set himself up in England. After being out of work for five years, his first film in exile was *Night and the City*, a cinematic tour through the themes of noir shot against a background of darkest London, a Dickensian underworld of con men, hustlers, petty thieves, street urchins, dance-hall girls, beggars and bookies, a labyrinth of stairwells, bridges, construction sites, hideaways, constricted spaces and parodied dangers.[48]

Inhabiting this terrain of the street and its foggy and smoky alleyways, through which he is most always on the run, is the American expatriate on the proverbial make, Harry Fabian, played by the noir icon Richard Widmark. Fabian is forever in search of his rightful score, a man on the perpetual edge, for whom his long-suffering, golden-hearted girlfriend, Mary Bristol, is a ready source of petty cash. But as Harry works himself into the limelight of 'being somebody', of actually 'having it all', the stakes are raised to the point where nobody, certainly not Mary, can pull Harry out of his fated demise. Harry, described as 'an artist without an art' by a romantic rival whose genuine decency (and somewhat homosexualised persona) eliminates him from Mary's slightest consideration, succumbs in the end to a betrayal of art, paying the ultimate price. Cynically befriending Gregorius, the innocent if patriarchal figurehead of European Greco-Roman wrestling and the aged, disenchanted father of the unsavoury, immigrant criminal 'boss' of London's emerging post-war commercialised wrestling scene, the ruthlessly powerful Kristo, Harry Fabian uses his capacities as a con man to hustle his way into potentially rivalling the underworld emperor, angering in the process his nightclub-owner employer, the obese Philip Nosseross. Nosseross's faithless wife Helen barters her husband's fetishistic and pathetic love in a crudely symbiotic sexualised/materialised hit on Harry meant to secure her a difficult-to-obtain liquor licence. For a while, Harry's capacity to con virtually everyone around him appears to be paying dividends. With Gregorius in his corner, his ventures bankrolled by Nosseross and his ploys playing out, Fabian's name is about to head the marquee of

47 See Lipsitz 1994, p. 291.

48 Dassin was indeed a Communist, albeit one rather loosely affiliated with the Party. On Dassin, see McGilligan and Buhle 1997, esp. pp. 199–224. This collection of interviews with blacklisted Hollywood figures also contains extensive reference to the much-despised Dmytryk.

London wrestling's biggest coup, an epic, theatrical battle between classical, artistic Greco-Roman wrestling and the psychopathology of 'the fight game' as a presentation of freaks, epitomised in the personage of Kristo's star performer, the sub-human 'Strangler'.

Yet Harry's bonanza, unfolding as it seems to be, eventually unravels as his con predictably oversteps itself and his markers are called in by those, such as Nosseross and Kristo, who hold the decisively powerful cards. In the end Harry is reduced to what he has always been, a man on the run. (He complains in his last hour that he has forever been running, from welfare agents, his father, the police, while Mary warned him at the beginning of the film that he had to stop running someday if he ever wanted to be 'normal', to stop sweating.) Harry is an exile in his own adopted city (not unlike Dassin himself), a figure with a price on his head that few of his fellow hustlers can resist (again, not unlike Dassin in the world of Hollywood's HUAC). London becomes a literal city of the damned, its night scenes ones of Harry scrambling over war-bombed rubble, seeking futile refuge against the damp-darkened walls of the Thames or in the refuse of London's wharf rats. With the bridge aswarm with Kristo's ready soldiers, Harry faces a dark dawn as a man whose time has finally run out. Without a word of politics, Dassin creates a commentary on the world of the Cold War, in which exile, frustration and defeat at the hands of powerful forces of evil dogs those 'who just want to be somebody', a line of pathos uttered by Fabian that predated Marlon Brando's famous *On the Waterfront* statement by three years.

Visually the film is a condemnation of the cynicism and despair of the corruptions of the post-war capitalist marketplace. In Beggar's Lane, where one of Harry's cronies outfits the commercial panhandlers with false limbs and other props that make them a more viable conduit for cash, the pit-like darkness captures capitalism's incarceration of the working class, while the seediness of exchange relations offers a stark metaphor for the crass hucksterism of metropolitan capital. In the subterranean nightclub lair of the Silver Fox, an aptly named den of wily duplicity, a grotesque Nosseross strokes his cash like a caricature of the grasping, bloated exploiter. His life is confined to the office from which he looks appropriately down upon the nocturnal theatre where he crassly bilks a male clientele that makes itself a ready sucker for every costly pseudo-sexual come-on. The underground emperor, Kristo, flanked by his lawyer and bodyguard, is the only figure who looms over London's skyline, marking his time and eventually exacting his revenge, a living embodiment of the principle that not only does crime pay, it ultimately calls all of the shots. In the background, the smaller predators circle the ever-present human prey.

Money rules this universe of greed and corruption, a signifier of worth that appears always out of nowhere, emerging from transactions behind the scenes, manufactured from wheelings and dealings always bargained falsely, money that passes hands in thick elastic-wrapped packages, money that is stroked sensually by those devoid of human eroticism, money that talks the language of empty promise but can never actually buy anything of worth. Between a man and his money, one of the characters soliloquises, nothing can come. Harry's obsessional pursuit of this money and the supposed fame it will secure him is the tragic flaw in a life of anguished movement that spirals Harry through his inevitable free-fall into a final, friendless hell. Mary tells him in the end that he could have done anything: with brains, ambition and hard work Harry is a heroic figure, but his lack of art ensures that he will always pursue 'the wrong things'.

In the London night Harry Fabian is eventually reduced to just such a 'wrong thing': everything is for sale as a car speeds through the enclosed blocks of his increasingly claustrophobic world, announcing to all and sundry the thousand-pound price on his head. The man who had managed to 'get it all' has also signed his own death warrant by pushing the game of self-realisation too far. The rules of class place and social station, bent to the point of snapping by those at the top of the small social pyramid of London's night-street subculture, are only so flexible. For the Harry Fabians they provide just enough give to rebound back in death. Harry at least goes to this end with some grace, doing what he can to secure Kristo's blood money for his lover Mary who, alone in the London of the night, stands by the man who has offered her only the cold comfort of his own insatiable ambitions and a willingness to do virtually anything to realise them.[49]

Night and the City is thus an on-going social commentary on the labyrinth of post-war capitalism and its Cold War politics of repressive containment, a challenging exploration all the more effective precisely because it seems far removed from the subject of its caustic critique. Symbolised at its highest level in Dassin's film as commercially promoted wrestling, capitalism is insightfully constructed as a staged event, a noir preface to post-modern theory's grasp of the critical importance of spectacle in a decaying order in which the marketing of images outpaces the production of goods, of which there is no sign whatever in the rotting darkness of *Night and the City*, where everything for sale is a recycled subterfuge, a crafted fraud.

---

49 Commentary on *Night and the City* appears in G. Erickson 1996, pp. 203–7; Christopher 1997, pp. 75–84.

Roland Barthes's understanding of Parisian wrestling in roughly the same period suggests the significance of this spectacle and its relationship to noir as a genre. 'The virtue of all-in wrestling is that it is the spectacle of excess', states Barthes in his opening analytic line; indeed, noir and its Cold War subjects are also about excess. Wrestling, like noir, 'abandons itself to the primary virtue of the spectacle, which is to abolish all motives and all consequences', a process the Cold War codified. Noir anti-heroes are not unlike Barthes's wrestlers, nor are they all that different to those who purged themselves before HUAC: '[T]he function of the wrestler is not to win; it is to go exactly through the motions which are expected of him ... a man who is down is exaggeratedly so, and completely fills the eyes of the spectators with the intolerable spectacle of his own powerlessness'. This can be marketed and sold as spectacle precisely because the genuineness of its content is beside the point: 'What the public wants is the image of passion, not passion itself', an axiom applicable to the Silver Fox nightclub. It is a staged sensuality that, in all of its darkly designed disingenuousness, poisons the capacity for passion between Nosseross (or No Eros), and his calculatingly cold wife Helen. Noir and wrestling elevate the 'bastard' to the standard of humanity, as perhaps does capitalism. To visualise such a 'bastard' aesthetically is noir's contribution, a culture of darkness entirely congruent with post-war capitalism's politics of Cold War night. 'Some fights', comments Barthes, 'among the most successful kind, are crowned by a final charivari, a sort of unrestrained fantasia where the rules, the laws of the genre, the referee's censuring and the limits of the ring are abolished, swept away by a triumphant disorder ... [a] return to the orgy of evil which alone makes good wrestling'.[50] Noir's final frames could hardly be better described, nor capitalism's trajectory more aptly characterised.

What Mike Davis calls the 'transformational grammar'[51] of noir was thus capable of sustaining an acute artistic paradox within the constricting socio-political climate of the Cold War; noir's oppositional success was to play within conventional boundaries, but caricature those boundaries mercilessly. Not only did noir, as Davis suggests, shift the language of charming boosterism and optimistic ambition away from its veneer of social niceties and into the dark recesses of its sinister counterparts of greed and the materially induced manip-

---

50   Wrestling as spectacle and its relationship to noir are touched on briefly in Christopher 1996, pp. 81–3; I have drawn on the particular analysis in Barthes 1983, pp. 15–25, from which all quotes in the above paragraph are drawn. For a more general statement on spectacle, see Debord 1990.

51   Mike Davis 1992, p. 38.

ulations (and worse) of hucksterism, it managed to represent themes literally outlawed in the moment of the Cold War freeze on social commentary. Anti-Communism had so suppressed cinematic depictions of working-class life that noir's unsubtle exploitation of this equally unsubtle exercise of censorship merely followed the trajectory of exclusion by exaggerating the inversion of powerlessness, creating a dark reservoir of humanity whose marginality pushed past that of an organised proletariat into the shadowy isolations of rootless 'society', where cab drivers, dance-hall girls, war veterans, boxers, private detectives and criminals symbolise the 'have nots' stripped even of the collectivity of wage-earning jobs and the associational authorities of unions, communities and political activities. As capitalism was reified in the post-World War II years as a saviour of humankind, the acquisitive individualism of the marketplace was darkened in noir's depiction of 'bosses' as emperors of the underworld, czars of their particularly disreputable enterprises of the night: the clubs, bars, rings and cul-de-sacs where cash always changes hands in the most sordid of ways. If race, a pivotal social divide in post-war America, was also exorcised by the Cold War demons as too contentiously hot a political issue to handle without yet again introducing the potential of dissidence, noir's pressured whiteness managed to racialise otherness in the contorted savagery of a set of dangerously powerful freaks and geeks,[52] usually used crassly by powerfully evil figures who can be undone by the simple humanity of their cretinous but ultimately innocent dupes.

Even in noir's unashamedly misogynistic presentation of the inner tensions of gendered greed, the mere presence of the femme fatale was potentially powerfully subversive of sexual stereotyping, not only because she was a persistent frustration of male desire but because she defied a patriarchal culture's limiting subordinations of female place and tightening definitions of womanly need.[53] As Janey Place has suggested, noir women usually disrupt the conventional narrative in the disorienting presentation of an unrepressed female sexuality, often combined with rapacious materialism – a rare cinematic articulation of women's strengths in the realms of eros and accumulation.[54] The only winner in *Night and the City* is the old hag of the Silver Fox nightclub, shunned by beauty but rewarded by the nightclub-owner beast, who wills her his property in a final act of revenge directed against his unfaithful and contemptuously repulsed wife.

---

52   Note the discussion in Shapiro 1968, pp. 218–23.
53   See, for instance, R.B. Palmer 1994, pp. 139–66; Hollinger 1996, pp. 243–58.
54   Place 1978, pp. 35–54.

Noir thus rewrote the script of Cold War culture. If its darkness submerged themes of social protest in the long night of alienation, noir refused to collapse the entirety of critical representation's repertoire into the soft, fleshy mono-tones of prettified propagandising for an 'American way of life'. Films such as Nicholas Ray's *They Live by Night* (1947) battled the censors' demands to down-play social criticism, eliminate reference to war profiteering, and tone down depictions of post-war affluence as propelled by consumer hucksters such as used car dealers, who were the thieves of a new, crudely acquisitive social order.[55] Noir's elevation of the night and the searches for self-realisation that unfolded within its darkness offered coded counterpoints to the jaded and jaundiced conventions of the time, centred in the mythologies of idealised fam-ilies and communities. Noir presented an introspective, always fatally flawed flight from such conformist confinement, an escape pushed by scarred back-grounds and unwholesome needs but one at least cognisant of human suffering and abuse and incapable of papering over the larger social ills that it was the Cold War's ultimate purpose to deny and obfuscate.

This open-ended set of noir possibilities has proven particularly durable and, after a momentary decline in the context of a mid- to late-1950s Hollywood demand for a more prettified pontification of the bourgeoisie's many virtues, noir has proven a rare modernist genre that manages to both keep a prolet-arian kernel and the anti-Communist background of its formative moment alive, as in Gordon DeMarco's Trotskyist-leaning 1980s detective Riley Kovachs, who battles Stalinist union corruption, racism and McCarthyism.[56] The genre assimilated other stylistics, to be sure, but it cloned its spectacular rebirth in the 1970s and 1980s, where the neo-noir productions *Chinatown* (1974), *Taxi Driver* (1976) and *Blue Velvet* (1987) were but a cinematic preface to an onslaught of resurgent noir in the 1990s,[57] extending from the big screen to the televised popularity of noirish series such as *Miami Vice* and *Homicide*. These had been preceded by such late 1950s television productions as *Peter Gunn*, perhaps the most mass-directed introduction of the subtle subversions of jazz to a white mainstream audience.[58]

---

55   Lipsitz 1994, pp. 296–7.

56   See the DeMarco trilogy: *October Heat* (1979); *The Canvas Prison* (1982); and *Frisco Blues* (1985).

57   Among many possible commentaries, note Pfeil 1993, pp. 227–60; Jameson 1991, pp. 19–20, 279–96; Gallafent 1992; Grist 1992.

58   See, for instance, Butler 1996, pp. 289–306; Ursini 1996, pp. 275–87.

Ideally suited to the rebirth of the 'savage art' of the now-depoliticised anarcho-communist populist Jim Thompson, whose dark explorations of the underworld of the 1930s and 1940s produced some of the most volatile fiction of the noir genre (moving well past Chandler and Hammett), the cinematic reconfiguration of noir under late capitalism commenced with two 1990 Thompson remakes, *The Grifters* and *After Dark, My Sweet*.[59] Soon followed by the innovations of Quentin Tarantino and others, most of 1990s neo-noir had a decidedly destructive conception of the 'family values' that had been pressured into the politics of mainstream culture at the time: *Reservoir Dogs* (1992); *Red Rock West* (1992); *Pulp Fiction* (1994); *The Last Seduction* (1994).[60] Throughout this explosion of dark cinema, the gendered nature of greed, always present in traditional noir's inability to transcend a bifurcation of woman into evil, predatory temptress or saintly, victimised adornment, flows easily into late-20th-century constructions of masculine womanhood, every bit as capable of seizing whatever main chance presents itself as debased manhood.[61]

With noir's rebirth in the late 20th century, however, its production was less pressured by the political containments of the 1940s and 1950s and its sexualised possibility expanded considerably from the tighter censorship restrictions of earlier decades, when it was governed by Will Hays, the prudish Production Code Administration, and the Catholic Church's Legion of Decency.[62] Transgressive sexuality, from the sub-themes of incest that figure forcefully in *Chinatown* and *The Grifters* to the bending content of homosexuality in *The Last Seduction*, fuses with the overarching theme of noir: money and its disfiguring capacities. If there is a 'hard-boiled' equivalent to Chandler and Hammett in the 1980s and 1990s, where the proliferation of assembly-line 'mystery' writers such as James Lee Burke, Lawrence Block, and Sue Grafton have bleached noir of much of its darkness, smoothing its rough edges and filing down the genre's open antagonisms, it is Andrew Vachss, whose private detective, Burke, is an eroticised avenger, a product of child abuse and the ugliness of the state reformatory system. A crusader untroubled by the moralities of Marlowe or Sam Spade, Burke is a mercenary of the night, a depoliticised defender of innocent children, the strong, silent type gone outlaw. His turf is the city of dark-

---

59   See Polito 1995.

60   Note Porfirio 1979; T. Erickson 1996, pp. 307–30.

61   Among the important, and differing, statements on women and noir, see Hollinger 1996,
      pp. 243–60; Cowie 1993, pp. 121–66; R.B. Palmer 1994, pp. 139–68; and the essays in Kaplan
      1978.

62   On this background, see Black 1994.

ness, the night markets where predators prowl for victims and where the rough justice of noir can still manage a late-20th-century scaffolding, albeit one crafted somewhat differently than traditional noir's recognisable politics of representation.[63]

This *fin-de-siècle* re-scripting of noir's nature, in which the Cold War is displaced, leaves the contemporary 1990s genre twisting in the winds of a peculiar 'end of history' culturalist climate, where nihilism, chaos and sensationalism blow with gusto.[64] But the subtle craft of noir's original imagery has, in the process, been jettisoned, yet another casualty of the truly 'big sleep' of capitalism's current ascendancy.

---

63   Andrew Vachss's writings include *Flood* (1985); *Strega* (1987); *Blue Belle* (1988); *Hard Candy* (1989); *Blossom* (1990); *Sacrifice* (1991); *Shella* (1993); *Born Bad* (1994a); *Down in the Zero* (1994b); *Batman: The Ultimate Evil* (1995b); *Footsteps of the Hawk* (1995c); *False Allegations* (1996); and *Another Chance to Get It Right: A Children's Book for Adults* (1995a). For commentary see Gary Dretzka, 'Disturbed Avenger: Seeking Evil with Andrew Vachss's Urban Vigilante', *Chicago Tribune*, 11 June 1989, and Paul Mann, 'A heart and a fist', *Saturday Review* in *Vancouver Sun*, 1 June 1991.

64   Obviously I do not agree with the ultimatist ideological posturing of Fukuyama's understanding that the implosion of the Soviet Union in 1989 resolved the global confrontation of communism and capitalism in the latter's rightful and unambiguous favour, thus homogenising the future of politics in an 'end of history'. The crisis of capitalist restoration in the once-Soviet Union, unfolding with terrifying rapidity over the course of the 1990s, confirms the banality of any 'end of history' posturing. Nevertheless, the cultural impact of this process is singularly important, especially in the capitalist West, as the evolution of noir suggests. For the original Fukuyama statement, see Fukuyama 1989, pp. 3–18, and the more complex elaborations in Fukuyama 1992. Significant readings of the problems posed in Fukuyama include McCarney 1992, pp. 37–54, and Anderson 1992b, pp. 279–375.

CHAPTER 5

The Hands That Built America: A Class-Politics Appreciation of Martin Scorsese's *Gangs of New York**

> What is your money-making now? What can it do now?
> What is your respectability now?
> Where are your theology, tuition, society, traditions, statute-books now?
> Where are your jibes of being now?
> Where are your cavils about the Soul now?
>
> WALT WHITMAN, 'Song of the Broad-Axe'[1]

∴

The mean streets of New York have seldom been meaner.[2] Blood does not just run in them, it gallops, spilled by blades and bludgeons that slice and crack the bodies of the past in a violence that is at once ritualised and reverential. Martin Scorsese's *Gangs of New York*, a $120 million epic inspired by Herbert Asbury's 1928 'informal history' *The Gangs of New York*,[3] commences with a fictitious 1846 gang battle in Paradise Square, heart of the infamous Five Points district of lower Manhattan, pitting Bill 'The Butcher' Cutting and his Protestant 'Know-Nothing' nativists against the Irish Catholic immigrant forces of Priest Vallon and the Dead Rabbits.

---

* 'The Hands that Built America: A Class-Politics Appreciation of Martin Scorcese's *The Gangs of New York*', *Historical Materialism*, 11 (2003), 317–45.

1 Whitman 1993, p. 160.

2 This paper was first presented to Toronto's Marxist Institute in February 2003, and the author is grateful to the audience for its critical comment.

3 Asbury 1928.

Historical Hurt: 'The Blood Stays on the Blade'

This opening scene of gore and mayhem, in which the white snow is soon stained various shades of red and pink, sets the cinematic stage, with the victorious Butcher withdrawing his knife from Vallon's chest, affording an opportunity for the close-up gush of spurting blood, a kind of Scorsese 'money shot'. 'Ears and noses are the trophies of the day', proclaims Cutting to the triumphant nativist ranks as the defeated Dead Rabbits stand oddly subdued, the entire combative lot looking, many commentators have remarked, as if they stepped off a set cast midway between *Braveheart* and *Mad Max*, the weaponry eerily reminiscent of some working-class street-warfare equivalent of the gynaecological instruments of *Dead Ringers*.[4] Yet this surreal gladiatorial imagery is introduced by a scene of seeming incongruity, marked by consummate gentleness. A supposedly celibate priest tutors his motherless son about life's harshness and the need to keep this always in mind. As he prepares with a meticulous toilet for the impending battle, Vallon shaves while his young boy, Amsterdam, watches in the shadows. A father's hand passes a blood-stained straight razor to his son, who starts to wipe the red residue on the bottom of his jacket. 'No son, never', admonishes the priest, who continues with caring guidance: 'The blood stays on the blade ... Someday you'll understand'.[5]

This insistence that the historical blood stays on the blade is Scorsese's under-appreciated accomplishment, a metaphor of history's hurt that is suggestively extended into a range of complex realms associated with United States class and state formation. To be sure, the odd mainstream critic does indeed gesture towards this fundamental historicisation. Jami Bernard of the *New York Daily News* ends her review, 'Scorsese and the Age of Violence', with a brief, if historically misguided and somewhat pejorative, allusion to what she claims is *Gangs of New York*'s large truth, 'that today's melting pot is yesterday's witches' brew'. More insightful, because it offers at least a few words of elaboration upon such a rhetorical one-liner, is A.O. Scott's *New York Times* 'To Feel a City Seethe'. Scott appreciates Scorsese's ambition, the creation of 'a narrative of historical change' constructed 'from the ground up'. Moreover, Scott grasps the uniqueness of this presentation: 'There is very little in the history of American cinema to prepare us for the version of American history Mr. Scorsese presents here. It is not the usual triumphalist story of moral progress and enlightenment, but

---

4   See the depiction of weaponry in Scorsese 2002, p. 146.

5   For exact dialogue, I rely on Scorsese 2002. All quotes from dialogue in the film are from this source unless otherwise stipulated.

rather a blood-soaked revenger's tale, in which the modern world arrives in the form of a line of soldiers firing into a crowd'.[6]

But such gestures towards the reciprocities of past and present hardly abound in the reviews, most of which are incarcerated within the pageantry of specific personas: Daniel Day-Lewis's riveting role as the Butcher, the rage level appropriate to the theatrical rendition supposedly primed by Day-Lewis blasting his eardrums non-stop with Eminem; Cameron Diaz's miscast beautification of a 'bludget', the female pickpocket, Jenny Everdeane; and the rather unfortunate Leonardo DiCaprio, the film's 'star' and narrator, Amsterdam Vallon, who finds himself ironically out-classed and over-shadowed by the rough-hewn Day-Lewis and his mesmerising performance. While most critics swoon over the stunning Five Points set, constructed on the grounds of the Cinecittà studios in Rome and supervised by Dante Ferretti, one reviewer noted with irritation that the 'fetish for authenticity' – bought and properly paid for in the hiring of various consultants who advised actors, crew and director on such essentials as Chinese opera, butchering, hand-lettered signs and mid-19th-century fighting techniques – got in the way of the drama.[7]

Not surprisingly, however, historians and socialists (and New York journalism's historically minded), first out of the gate with their comments, have found the film's *lack* of authenticity a disappointment, a point made most tellingly in Joshua Brown's thoughtful *London Review of Books* piece 'The Bloody Sixth' and, in a journalistic equivalent, Pete Hamill's *Daily News* review, 'Trampling City's History'. As J. Hoberman complains succinctly, Scorsese's film is 'a hothouse historical fantasy inspired by the already fantastic demimonde chronicles' of Asbury, the result a reading of 'the present back into history' that 'reimagines the past to suit itself ... a lavish folly'. No *Sexy Beast* this, Hoberman dubs *Gangs* a very rough beast indeed, one 'saddled with abundant backstory'. If history is not, à la Henry Ford, necessarily bunk, Scorsese stands condemned by some as turning it into little more than that.[8]

---

6 Jami Bernard, 'Scorsese & the Age of Violence', *New York Daily News*, 20 December 2002; A.O. Scott, 'To Feel a City Seethe', *New York Times*, 20 December 2002.

7 Kenneth Turan, 'Murder, Revenge, Rage ... and Apathy', *Los Angeles Times*, 20 December 2002.

8 Joshua Brown, 'The Bloody Sixth', *London Review of Books*, 23 January 2003; Pete Hamill, 'Trampling City's History', *New York Daily News*, 14 December 2002; J. Hoberman, 'Vice City', *Village Voice*, 18–24 December 2002; Tyler Anbinder and Jay Cocks, 'Is *Gangs of New York* Historically Accurate?', *Gotham Gazette*, 23 December 2002. Two decided hostile socialist reviews are Lee Sustar, 'A Whitewash of Epic Proportions', *Socialist Worker* (US), 10 January 2003, and Walsh 2003a. An intriguing set of comments from the historian James M. McPherson which concentrates on the Draft Riots, the $300 commutation fee and the alliance of New York's

Scorsese: An Unconscious Brecht in an Unconscious Age

For the most part, I approach the film differently. If, as Fredric Jameson has argued, the one 'trans-historical' imperative of all Marxist, dialectical thought is the demand to 'always historicise!', it must be recognised that in cultural production, not unlike the actual research and writing of history, the issue of authenticity can never be reduced to the merely factual. Yet there *is* a difference separating historical from artistic productions, and the disciplines of dependency on evidence are obviously more rigorous within the writing of history than they can, or perhaps should, be in the making of historical film. As Jameson suggests, within the projects of theory and cultural criticism, a developing 'metacommentary' focusses less on 'the text itself than the interpretations through which we attempt to confront and appropriate it'. Jameson thus makes the case in *The Political Unconscious* for a specific aesthetics of presentation, the narrative form, alongside an understanding of interpretation's primacy:

> These divergent and unequal bodies of work are here interrogated and evaluated from the perspective of the specific critical and interpretive task of the present volume, namely to restructure the problematics of ideology, of the unconscious and desire, of representation, of history, and of cultural production, around the all-informing process of *narrative*, which I take to be (here using the shorthand of philosophical idealism) the central function or instance of the human mind ... I happen to feel that no interpretation can be effectively disqualified on its own terms by a simple enumeration of inaccuracies or omissions, or by a list of unanswered questions. Interpretation is not an isolated act, but takes place within a Homeric battlefield, on which a host of interpretive options are either openly or implicitly in conflict. If the positivistic conception of philological accuracy be the only alternative, then I would much prefer to endorse the current provocative celebration of strong misreadings over weak ones.[9]

In short, art, unlike the writing of history, which combines a conceptual imagination with a rigorous and disciplined recourse to actualities of evidence and event, thrives first and foremost through its creative licence. That licence suc-

---

poor whites and Democratic Party/mercantile élite supporters of the racist plantocracy is found in Walsh 2003b.
9   Jameson 1981, pp. 9, 13.

ceeds, for Marxists at least, if it historicises experience in ways that illuminate truths that are often obscured over time, and that have remained hidden from engagement precisely because large connections and continuities in histor- ical process have been seemingly fractured by change, the tyranny of present- mindedness (which severs our lives from those of earlier generations) and the necessary but unfortunate limitations of painstaking scholarly reconstructions that often get the empirical detail of various trees right only to lose sight of the broad expanse of the forests of the *longue durée*.

Scorsese, I will suggest, has managed to do what few historians and even fewer filmmakers can legitimately claim as accomplishment. In compressing mid-19th-century history, he develops a narrative that leads inexorably towards some of the major socio-political dilemmas of a revolutionary encounter with the making of modern American class society. Something of an unconscious Bertolt Brecht of our times, Scorsese's cast of *Threepenny Opera* characters has, in the past, included child prostitutes, delusional taxi drivers, made guys, punch-drunk boxers, dirty cops and other assorted and sordid urban hustlers. It is not surprising that he is enthralled by the gangs of an earlier epoch. Like Brecht, as Terry Eagleton has noted, Scorsese starts not from the 'good old things' so prevalent in what we might designate Hollywood's capacity to nos- talgise the past but from the 'bad new ones' of our own unfortunate historical moment.[10] His major films, from *Mean Streets* through *Taxi Driver* and *Raging Bull* to *GoodFellas*, have never managed to step out of the confines of an almost obsessional fixation on the violence of the present; although these films have made strong statements, they have always proven politically enclosed in ways that the historicised *Gangs of New York* is not.[11] As a consequence, Robert De Niro's drift into pathology in *Taxi Driver*, while powerfully evocative as a rep- resentation of social crisis in the 'post'-1960s decade of the 1970s, never manages to shake loose of a fundamentally alienated individuality. When Travis Bickle stands defiant before a full-length mirror asking 'Are you talking to me?', his tone increasingly one of menacing belligerence, Scorsese is not necessarily able to draw us into this one-way conversation. Indeed, we want no part of it. But in Amsterdam's voice-over commentaries in *Gangs of New York* or in the Butcher's racist soliloquies, it is impossible not to engage with the politicised meanings of collective historical process, however unsettling they may be. If Scorsese's film thus stands very much as one director's urban myth creation, it nevertheless works on the large, often Brueghel-like cinematic canvas, precisely because its

---

10   Eagleton 1981, p. 6.
11   Two helpful overviews are Kelly 1980 and Connelly 1991.

art of representation intersects with historical developments in insightful and stimulating ways. The film *does* talk to us as Marxists, I would maintain, if only we can get past the tyrannical fetishisation of 'factuality' to glimpse the wider worlds of class and state formation as they were made in the mid-19th century and as that making lived on, in various ways, over the course of the next 150 years.

Historical Authenticity and Film

Historians have of late commented much on film, and their judgements often turn on various 'truth tests'. In a way, this is oddly out of step with contemporary discussion of historiography and historical method, given that in certain avant-garde historical circles 'truth' itself, and the possibility of achieving it in any authorial narrative of the past, are generally regarded with scepticism. So, too, have historians questioned the ways in which evidence itself is constructed, asking of seemingly routinely generated sources such as the census how they came to be and what their relationship was to evolving structures of power and the not-inconsiderable authority of 'archives of knowledge'. Imagine asking of Foucault's histories of sexuality or of the meanings of prison discipline if they are, in actuality, 'true', or arguing forcefully for the ultimate 'truth' of a newspaper account or a case file: I can hear the peals of jaundiced laughter from the high pews of contemporary theory's sophisticates. Why do we expect the transparency of truth and a discipline of balance in historical filmmaking, at the same time that we often let others who work in much closer proximity to archives, evidence and the layered sedimentation of historical experience so easily off the hook?

Natalie Zemon Davis discusses authenticity in ways characteristic of historians' demands of film, and no one, perhaps, has more experience than Davis in actually working through the creation of an historical film, her role in *The Return of Martin Guerre* being somewhat exceptional. Moreover, Davis grapples sensitively with the ways in which the creations of film and historical writing differ, but are also grounded in specific common concerns.[12] She cites two reasons historical films go off track. First, she is critical, for example, of Hollywood's underestimation of film audiences and the almost ubiquitous suggestion that mainstream cinema distorts the past the better to make it palpable to audiences suffocating in their present-mindedness. Steven Spielberg's *Amistad*, for

---

12   See, among other statements, Benson 1983, pp. 55–8.

instance, was said to have pandered to what he imagined to be contemporary film-goers' need to have the past relate simply and clearly to modern experience, a reductionism that Davis rightly deplores.[13] But second, more relevantly for any discussion of *Gangs of New York*, Davis also singles out a habit of cinematic production that demonstrates 'too cavalier an attitude toward the evidence about lives and attitudes in the past'.[14]

This is a tall-order, double-barrelled critique, for most historians would, if answering honestly, accent how humble we should be with respect to making films that can be appreciated within their historical settings, just as they would underscore how complex are the issues involved in claiming certainty about knowledge of attitudes in the past. Davis then hooks on to such deeply difficult issues an injunction that '[w]e must respect that evidence, accepting it as given, and let the imagination work from there'. The phrase that evidence must be accepted 'as given' necessarily gives one cause to pause, but granting Davis the benefit of certain doubts, it is apparent that, for her, making films and making histories, save perhaps for the pride of place reserved for dramatisation in cinematic productions, are similar creative projects. Yet I am not so convinced that film should operate by the same rules as those we have elaborated for historical texts, especially given that some historians clearly do not recognise the rules of evidence to which Davis alludes (although I would agree with what I take to be Davis's main point, that evidence should be grappled with seriously, something that is ironically too often lost sight of in the textualism of our times). Davis moves on to even more narrowly confining ledges:

> If ... we still decide to depart from the evidence – say in creating a composite character or changing a time frame – then it should be in the spirit of the evidence and plausible, not misleading. Exceptionally, a historical film might move significantly away from the evidence out of playfulness or an experiment with counter-factuality, but then the audience should be let in on the game and not be given the impression of a 'true story'.

Counter-factuality aside, for surely no director is concerned with arguments about historical method circa 1972, Davis's position, for all its attractiveness, constructs the problem of authenticity in rather narrow ways, precisely because

13   N.Z. Davis 2000, p. 131, drawing on Perry 1998, p. 100.
14   N.Z. Davis 2000, p. 130.

it locates an historical film's 'truth testing' within the parameters of affirmation of ascertainable 'facts': the nature of costumes, the location and character consistencies of specific historical individuals, the sequence of events. What is the meaning of a filmmaker's adherence to 'the spirit of the evidence'? How are we to ascertain if a direction taken is plausible, rather than misleading? Surely these caveats are centrally about *interpretation* and where the possibilities of history's *meanings* lie. These are large, often contentious, matters, not easily reducible to ways of presenting history so as to convince readers and viewers of its authenticity. We may know, with some certainty, what Civil War soldiers wore, but are we so easily in agreement about what the historical meaning of the Civil War indeed was?[15] How, if issues of authenticity are broached in this way, extending beyond the questions we can answer decisively into arenas where conflicting historical opinion certainly exists, are we to ascertain just how audiences might 'be let in on the game' and the explanation of creative licence professed? It is a question easier asked than answered, unless one reverts to the most banal of significations.[16] Would we really want Ken Russell's *The Devils*, a film that speaks to the almost timeless themes of power, hypocrisy and evil's corruptions as much as it does to medieval witchcraft and its suppression by established authorities of church and state, to fly warning flags

15   I happen to agree with the general argument about the significance and meaning of the Civil War propounded by radicals since the time of Marx, and running through the writings of W.E.B. Du Bois and into the best modern historical writing, such as that of James M. McPherson. This stresses the revolutionary character of the confrontation. That said, there remain questions even within Marxist analysis. For instance, precisely because the victory of bourgeois forces in the Civil War was inevitable, given the timing of the conflict and the historically situated development of the productive forces, the *class* meanings of the Civil War are still open to different analytical accents. McPherson's tilt on the $300 commutation fee, for instance, is apparently to downplay its material significance on the grounds that there were ways around paying and that the state, at various levels, orchestrated loopholes. Yet McPherson recognises the fee's symbolic importance as a visible reminder of inequality (albeit too lightly in my judgment). This, and other evidence, conditions McPherson's argument that making too much of the draft and adhering to the claim that the Civil War was a rich man's war but a poor man's fight overstates the significance of draftees (who comprised only 74,000 of the million men Lincoln called for and got to fight for the North). This may be true enough, but the *class* symbolism of the $300 exemption fee was a powerful factor in mobilising working-class resentments. See Walsh 2003b.

16   Ironically, some historians found Davis's involvement in *The Return of Martin Guerre* problematic in this very area. See, for instance, Finlay 1988. Note the further statements of N.Z. Davis 1987 and 1988.

concerning historical 'authenticity' in the face of its viewers? Is this not also underestimating an audience's capacity to make discriminating judgments?

Taken in this light, Davis's injunctions, as sensible as they appear on the surface, tend to bypass what I would consider historical film's most significant emancipatory potential, the capacity to make the past speak to our present without boiling it down to digestible 'authenticities'. Larger relational truths that, in Marxist terms, are central motifs in the making of the modern world will tend to get lost in the shuffle to produce realities of everyday life and chronological validities and comprehensiveness. Highly complex and historically developed processes such as class and state formation or the problematic character of collective solidarities criss-crossed with fragmentations of race, gender and national identity, all of which are pivotal in understanding why revolution has both been an absolute imperative for humanity *and* an undertaking that has almost universally failed, are inevitably obscured in this constricted appreciation of historicisation.

What must be acknowledged is that the imperatives of social history's evolution may well take us in this narrow direction of reproducing authentic detail regardless of larger issues of interpretation and meaning. Social historians once imagined their project as one of liberating historical research and its dramas from the limitations of an ideological consensual historiography. Their agenda was, it could be suggested, a radical provisioning of pasts locked into specific paradigms. 'Histories from below' and studies of subaltern groups, as well as attention to resistance and scrutiny of theories associated with Marx and other radical Enlightenment thinkers, all spoke in a 1960s idiom of challenge that was rooted in the desire to turn the interpretive tables and stand 'history' on its proverbial head. But social history has moved off this ground and, along with the new cultural history, has located new subject matters and new theoretical frameworks. It is now coloured by new perspectives, few of which embrace revolution as a desired end. Social histories have developed in ways distanced from the working class and its collective struggles and have recently accented subjectivity, liberal order consensus and varied accommodations and adaptations. As insightful as studies orchestrated by such concerns are, they are differentiated from the radical understandings of a useable past that animated social history's beginnings. Whereas the general strike or the riotous confrontation figured as central subjects two and three decades ago, we now have studies of tourism, royal pageantry and the debutante ball.

This is not unrelated to how historians approach the issue of historical film and authenticity. As social historians have increasingly valorised subjectivity over collectivity and immersed themselves in the spectacle and the micro-experience, insisting on the equally politicised weight of realms perhaps once

understood as somewhat removed from the directly political, our conceptualisation of the dimensions of the political has expanded and, it might be suggested, inevitably suffered dilution. In the process we may reify detail over
political engagement. Many historians relate to film, I think, out of this new
and somewhat politically problematic context. Thus, contemporary comment
on film and history that strikes too literalist a note on authenticity may invariably be limiting film's possibilities just as social history has become, over the
last decade, increasingly distanced from its 1960s origins in a political project
of remaking the social order, constraining its engagement with a transformative project. Marxists demand more of film (and of history), because more is
at stake than 'art for art's sake' (although by this I do not suggest some blunt
demand that all art merely serve class-struggle ends or that we must see some
kind of Stalinist socialist realism as the only 'true' political aesthetic), more at
stake than 'historical authenticity for authenticity's sake'.[17]

Filmmakers, it needs to be pointed out, do not see any of this as a problem. They understand, for the most part, that they are not putting historical
fact on film. Their purpose is rarely one of making histories visually true, but
of presenting histories that relate to the intersections of past and present. To
stop the histories of the past at any given 'moment' and expect filmmakers
to both get detail *and* continuity right is not only asking a lot, it may be
demanding that they gut any potential politics in the name of 'authenticity'.
John Sayles, criticised by historians for playing fast and loose with the 'facts'
of *Matewan*'s past, getting details of mining experience wrong,[18] offered the
rejoinder that he deliberately reconfigured the historical terrain the better to
convey through an atypical event, the Matewan massacre, a larger representative history.[19] In a sense, the issue is even more elastic than Sayles's defence,
because it could well be the case that a 'historical' film would collapse historical experience into a particular periodisation doing actual violence to a
specific time frame, but use a kind of narrative to do grander justice to historical trends and experiences. Historians who do not have such licence need
to ask themselves what can be wrong with such a representational strategy,
given the paucity of historical consciousness that exists in our times.[20] The

17   Ramirez 1999.
18   Brier 1988; Dubofsky 1990; and the more sympathetic discussion of *Matewan* and historical
      criticism in Newsinger 1995.
19   Mico 1995, pp. 13, 11–28; Sayles 1987.
20   With respect to *Gangs of New York*, it needs to be recognised that those making the film
      were not unaware that they were violating the 'authentic' record of the past, inasmuch as

slight, we as historians must recognise, is less on movie-goers in the 21st century than it is on ourselves as 'practitioners' and 'dues-payers' of a particular
guild.

Gangs of New York and the Detail of (Non-)Authenticity

What is wrong with Scorsese's *Gangs of New York*? The list is long, starting with
the pivotal place of gangs and race riots.

The Dead Rabbits-Bowery Boy Riot took place on 4 July 1857 and had no
connection to the traumatic events of the Draft Riots of 1863, in which no
naval bombardment of the Five Points district ever took place. Indeed, the Five
Points, although it was the site of rioting, was hardly the epicentre of the Draft
Riots outbreak, which probably left approximately 120 dead: the concentrated
fighting was uptown in streets in the 20s and 30s, strongholds of the Republican
Party. While Scorsese's historical consultant, Luc Sante, declares with certainty
that 'the core of the participants [in the Draft Riots] unquestionably came from
the Five Points', more scrupulous research has established that only two of the
hundreds of rioters arrested could be established to have been residents of the
infamous Sixth Ward. But the anti-black pogrom in the Five Points was nevertheless virulent, and interested Democratic Party attempts to depict the 'Bloody
Sixth' as free of riotous taint in 1863 were little more than cover-ups. Mobs of
hundreds of Irish attacked African-American workplaces, bars employing black
waiters, the New York African Society for Mutual Relief and shanties, boarding houses and tenements in which blacks resided, many of them on Baxter
Street. Buildings were torched (although not the Five Points Mission), blacks
were beaten in the streets and rough musickings were the nightly norm. Three
days of violence convinced most African Americans in the Five Points that
'their only safety is in flight'. This capped 40 years of insecurity for blacks in
the Sixth Ward. In the 1820s, the African-American population of the district
had been roughly 15 percent of those living in the congested slum (twice the
norm throughout New York City). But many blacks left the Five Points after a
series of anti-abolitionist riots and confrontations in the 1830s and 1840s; the
1863 debacle drove the final African-American population of the Five Points
into retreat, where it settled in safer havens such as Long Island. Once home

---

they were cognisant of how they were blurring chronology and event into a congealed
presentation of a fiction that was nevertheless rooted in a general historicisation. See
Scorsese 2002; Anbinder 2002.

to over 1,000 blacks, the Five Points, which claimed a black population of just under 400 in 1863, recorded only 132 'coloured' residents in the 1870 census.[21]

Despite this obvious openness to racism, a nativist leader such as Bill Cutting would never have set himself up in the Five Points, let alone come to have ruled the rookeries of the rough fare – demographic, commercial and cultural – that intersected the old Anthony, Orange and Cross Streets, for the dominant immigrant population was Irish Catholic. A Know-Nothing like Butcher Bill had no base in the Five Points: in an 1856 presidential election, the Democratic candidate polled an overwhelming majority of 574 votes, outdistancing his Republican and nativist rivals who managed between them to secure a meagre 25 ballots. Indeed, Cutting's actual inspiration, the real-life Bill 'The Butcher' Poole, memorialised in Asbury's *The Gangs of New York*, plied his trade, his Know-Nothingism and his legendary prowess in the bar-room brawl on what is now Christopher Street and the West Village piers, rather than in the Sixth Ward itself. Shot in the heart by Irish gang leader John Morrissey in a Broadway saloon on a bitter cold 1855 night, Poole clung to life for two weeks before dying. His last words, 'Good-bye boys, I die a true American', were destined to be appropriated as the rallying cry of nativist forces, who gathered 5,000 strong to march the 'Butcher's' body through New York's streets in a declaration of martyrdom.[22]

As James M. McPherson has suggested, Scorsese's understanding of this Democratic Party hegemony, especially the pivotal role of its anti-Civil-War wing and its ties to New York City's mercantile élite, which sealed a pro-Southern plantocracy alliance of the richest and poorest (decidedly *not* the skilled, organised working-class) segments of the North's metropolitan capital, is scant indeed. The film does far too little in exploring the ugly politics of this Democratic Party faction, bypassing such figures as Mayor Fernando Wood of the Mozart Hall group, who called for New York to secede from the Union in 1861. Wood and his fellow pro-Confederacy 'Copperheads' utilised their power and their control of sections of the press (Wood's brother Benjamin was a long-time editor of the *New York Daily News*, the largest circulation daily in the United States at the time) to fan the flames of racist animosity. They used a recent history of blacks being driven from the New York docks as strikebreakers in June of 1863, as well as a tense economic climate in which rising rents, higher food prices and a rash of trade-union organising signalled, in the

---

21   Joshua Brown, 'The Bloody Sixth', *London Review of Books*, 23 January 2003; Anbinder 2002, pp. 314–18; Sante 1991, p. 353. On the Draft Riots the two major modern statements are Bernstein 1990 and A. Cook 1974.

22   Asbury 1928, pp. 81–100.

words of *Fincher's Trade Review*, 'The Upheaving Masses in Motion!' to exacerbate fears amongst workers that hordes of freed slaves were about to invade Northern cities such as New York and overrun job markets long designated the 'property' of 'white labour'. In adding insult to injury, according to the 'Copperheads', the Northern white working class was being asked to fight a war that was destined to lead to its economic and social ruination.[23]

Beyond these lapses in authenticity and problems of adequate coverage of the lay of the contemporary political land in *Gangs of New York* lies a plethora of what some historians will designate 'howlers'. The cavernous underground tunnels in which Amsterdam retreats to have Jenny lick his wounds, replete with its background of stone ledges lined with skulls, could not have existed in the Five Points, whose marshy subsoil defies such a labyrinth. Scorsese's depiction of the New York City Chinese in the early 1860s is perhaps seemingly the most egregious pushing of the authenticity envelope: constructed as pig-tailed and inscrutable but commercially adept enough to entice the nativists to celebrate at their Mott Street Sparrow's Chinese Pagoda, in which acrobats bounce off the floor and caged prostitutes are suspended from the ceiling and auctioned off by none other than P.T. Barnum, the Chinese hate the Butcher and have a silent agreement with Amsterdam. In actuality, the Asian population in or adjacent to the Five Points in 1863 was tiny to the point of being inconsequential; Chinese immigration to New York City did not begin in earnest until after completion of the transcontinental railroad in 1869. Just as Chinatown would be an actual creation post-dating the period in which *Gangs of New York* is set, so too would be the authority of a central figure in the film, William 'Boss' Tweed of Tammany Hall. In the time period in which Amsterdam pursues his revenge of his father's killing at the hands of Bill Cutting, Tweed was indeed climbing the ladder, but his ring would not control New York until later in the 1860s and 1870s. Nor would Barnum's American Museum burn in 1863, during the Draft Riots, but in 1868, or would public hangings, the last of which happened in 1835, be a part of the political theatre of the early 1860s.

Finally, although no reviewer (historian or film critic) to my knowledge has mentioned this, there is scant evidence, if any, that cross-dressing or what we now call transgender women, those to whom Cutting refers as 'she-hes', would have frequented the Five Points with such confidence that they would walk the streets openly and cause barely a ripple of notice in public dances put on by proselytising Protestants. To be sure, the Bowery border of the Five Points was an early promenade of all manner of sexually open and transgressive char-

---

23   Walsh 2003a and 2003b; Montgomery 1967, pp. 102–7.

acters and the Sixth Ward was infamous as a centre of commercialised vice, but even George Chauncey's diligent searches have found no reference to the Five Points' fairies (in his terminology, drawing on a language of description from a later period). The closest we can come to locating such a presence any-where near the Sixth Ward is the late 1870s Armory Hall dance pavilion at the corner of Hester and Elizabeth Streets, where an Irish sex and entertainment entrepreneur, Billy McGlory, hired half a dozen men who powdered and rouged themselves, sometimes dressing in feminine attire, to entertain high rollers and big spenders with a risqué sexual 'circus' in the curtained privacy of solitary booths. McGlory was a graduate of the Five Points and bare-knuckled it in the 1850s with the Forty Thieves and Chichesters, but his Armory Hall was a night haunt and its offerings hardly the norm of daylight hours.[24]

More serious because it is more sinister, as Joshua Brown has suggested, is Scorsese's residual assimilation of Asbury's reproduction and sensational-ising of 19th-century missionary slum literature, epitomised by Matthew Hale Smith's *Sunshine and Shadow in New York* (1868), in which the Five Points is con-structed as a degraded netherworld of vice and violence, an anarchistic orgy of brutality and criminality coincident with the arrival of the immigrant Irish.[25] 'A culture of poverty' in which the belligerence of the 'underclass' is accen-ted, suggests Brown, excuses the nativism that animated Asbury and paints the gangs and the Five Points district itself in bold, 'larger-than-life' strokes that distort the history of oppression within which the immigrant Irish worked and suffered. As Happy Jack, a one-time Dead Rabbit turned 'crusher' cop, escorts a sight-seeing crew of uptown ladies and gentlemen through the Five Points, he waxes eloquent on the Irish arriving in America: 'Ah, but only shattered dreams await them. Pauperism and dereliction. Drunkenness and depravity. Molestation and murder, kind sirs and ladies'. Evangelicals flit through the film, deploring the God-forsaken vice, misery and squalor of the Sixth Ward. 'They said it was the worst slum in the world', Amsterdam narrates. 'To us it was home'. In Scorsese's construction, the gangs are the families of the Five Points. But

---

24   The above paragraphs draw upon Joshua Brown, 'The Bloody Sixth', *London Review of Books*, 23 January 2003; Pete Hamill, 'Trampling City's History', *New York Daily News*, 14 December 2002; Callow 1966; Connable and Silberfarb 1967, pp. 138–72; Mandelbaum 1990; Beck 1898, pp. 11–12; Ernst 1965, p. 45; Kuo Wei Tchen 1990, pp. 16–63; Werner 1926; Chauncey 1994, p. 37; Asbury 1928, pp. 186–9.

25   Joshua Brown, 'The Bloody Sixth', *London Review of Books*, 23 January 2003; M.H. Smith 1868; Ladies of the Mission 1854. Anbinder 2002, pp. 14–37, outlines the literature on the Five Points 'culture of poverty', in what he calls the 'Five Points of the mind'.

archaeological evidence unearthed in the early 1990s with the construction of a new court house in an old neighbourhood of what was once the Bloody Sixth, tells a different tale. Some 850,000 artefacts were uncovered and, while the job of dating precisely these remnants of the past was never done, they do suggest a varied socio-economic life considerably at odds with the Asbury-Scorsese myth-making. The assortment of buttons, needles, fabrics, medicine bottles, combs, hairbrushes and crockery dug out of the bowels of an old Sixth Ward block hints at the robust presence of home work and family routines that have unfortunately been over-shadowed by the extravagant depiction of 'the dark side' all too prominent in 19th-century accounts of the Five Points, upon which both Asbury and Scorsese have drawn uncritically.[26]

Born of resistance to the impersonal cash nexus of the wage relation and the 'market revolution', gangs were marked with the mechanic accents of dishevelled trades and rough labours resistant to the encroachments of capitalism. This new market-driven productive order increasingly brought under its sway the relations of master and man in various tanneries, distilleries, slaughterhouses, modest manufactories (producing looking glasses, umbrellas, shoes), tobacco works, furniture-producing sheds, building sites and artisanal trades, reconfiguring public works projects and the docks of the transatlantic trade as well. This process of accelerating socio-economic change also demanded class subordination in the wider non-work worlds of politics and culture. The gangs, in their recalcitrance, were complemented by other arenas of youthful masculine associational life, including fire companies, local militias and target and sporting clubs.

All of this was played out not only in the mayhem of the so-called 'ancient laws of combat' so extolled by Scorsese in his depiction of the almost constitutionalist courts of conflict participated in by various gangs – Shirt Tails, Plug Uglies, Daybreak Boys, Chichesters, American Guards, Little Forty Thieves, Roach Guards, Native Americans, Bowery Boys – but also through the film's protagonists, the Butcher and the Vallons (father and son). It left its mark on and was influenced by the emerging radical, and often German-led, trade-union movement, a point stressed by one of the few explicitly socialist reviews of *Gangs of New York* that suggests something positive in Scorsese's contribution, Mike Davis's 'The Bloody Streets of New York'. Davis feels that Scorsese gets the squalor and oppression of the Five Points right, differentiating him from other historians. But he fixes his sights on what Scorsese (and indeed almost every other reviewer) has missed, for New York's mid-century immigra-

26   Walsh 2003a.

tion stream was not merely fed by tributaries of starving, cholera-ridden, job- and freedom-seeking Irish.

As late as 1860, New York's major Old World population, its 203,000 Irish immigrants, was rivalled seriously in terms of the newly arrived only by some 118,000 Germans. Broadly speaking, these Germans had been forged in differ- ent circumstances than those of the destitute Irish, the failed revolutionary impulses of 1848 being of paramount importance. Yet there were some within the Irish diaspora, such as radical Fenians, who connected with German rad- icalism (as well as with the smaller enclaves of Scottish Jacobins and Eng- lish Chartists), especially in New York's Lower East Side Kleindeutschland, a 400-city-block area adjacent to the Five Points, encompassing the city's Tenth, Eleventh, Thirteenth and Seventeenth Wards. There, German socialists and communists toiled for wages and struggled to build a workers' movement that united ethnicities and trades. Roughly 15 percent of New York's population in these years was German-born, and thoughts of the red promise of 1848 and its barricades still permeated a consciousness of producer rights, labour- capital conflict and social justice. This heritage reached forward from the nas- cent beginnings of labour radicalism in the 1850s into struggles for the shorter working day in the 1860s and 1870s, culminating in the massive successes of the New York City Knights of Labor, which contained subterranean cells of anarcho-communist influence in a secret order within the order known as the Home Club. The Henry George mayoralty campaign of 1886, a mobilisation that came dangerously close to securing power for the working class in the country's major metropolitan centre, was perhaps the culmination of this 19th- century politics of class struggle, which achieved the 1880s designation 'The Great Upheaval'.

Despite overlapping connections amongst the differentiated working-class constituencies of this at times generalised upsurge, the day labourers and sweated workers of the Irish Five Points travelled Scorsese's meanest streets, and their historical experience was never quite that of the artisanal proletari- anisation and radicalism associated with German New York. Irish gang lives and fire-company raucousness pegged them as 'traditionalists' in their polit- ically unconscious resistance. In 1863, they rioted against the draft and its $300 exemption for the 'socially superior'; they resented the rich, but they killed their poor black brothers and sisters. Amongst German radicals, such 'traditionalist' hostilities to established bourgeois power were scorned, and as Irish and nativist gangs battled throughout the 1850s, knocking heads and eventually exchanging primitive pistol fire in the crooked alleyways off the Bowery, European immigrant rebels embraced abolitionism, variants of anti- capitalism, co-operation and trade unionism. During the depression of 1857,

THE HANDS THAT BUILT AMERICA

as the Dead Rabbits honed their weapons, German radicals combined with Irish and native-born American labour figures to beat back the rising tide of unemployment. When the Draft Riots erupted in 1863, many dissident Germans repudiated the deadly formalisation of class privilege the exemption fee embodied, just as they condemned the vicious attacks on black Americans as a tragic division of the ranks of the powerless. But the radicals could not keep the anti-black, largely Irish Catholic mob in check and were soon swept off the streets as the ugliness of the moment brushed class solidarities aside in the name of an incendiary racist revenge.[27]

With this much wrong and missing from Scorsese's film, what can be right and powerfully suggestive about it? In a word, quite a bit.

Class Politics and the Janus Vision of a Fragmented Working Class

The message of Scorsese's film is not so much that America was made in its bloody streets, as so many critics claim with interpretive certainty and ease. Rather, *Gangs of New York* is suggestive of a more two-sided historical exchange. At the core of Scorsese's representation is, to be sure, the impulse 'from below', the place of the rough culture of masculine muscle and the street authority of head-knocking violence and intimidation. As the Butcher puts it, with characteristic brutality:

> The spectacle of fearsome acts. Someone steals from me, I cut off his hands. He offends me, I cut out his tongue. He rises against me, I cut off his head and stick it on a pike. Hold it high in the streets so all can see. That's what preserves the order of things.

But what is apparent in the film is that this plebeian power is never entirely removed from relations of reciprocity with other structures of order, in which the terrorism of established (and often quite 'polite') authority is more masked.

---

27   The above paragraphs draw on Mike Davis 2003, which contrasts markedly with other left commentary in Lee Sustar, 'A Whitewash of Epic Proportions', *Socialist Worker* (US), 10 January 2003, and the even more vehement antagonism in Walsh 2003a. See, for background on labour organisation and German radicalism, Wilentz 1984b; Schneider 1994; Levine 1986; Wittke 1952; Binder and Reimers 1995, pp. 59–92. For discussions of working-class typologies relevant to this period which include discussion of 'traditionalism' see Dawley and Faler 1976; Laurie 1980, pp. 53–66. On the Knights of Labor and the Home Club see Weir 2000, pp. 23–46.

In this sense, the violence of Scorsese's mean streets is in reality more integrated with the institutions of class domination than most critics seem to grasp. The gangs exist in symbiotic relationship with other spheres: the police; the law; the political boss; agencies of discipline to which youth can be submitted for 'an education'; the state. If this is not historically 'true', in all of the particular evidential detail, it is nevertheless true in a larger relational sense, and Scorsese is thus able to sustain analytical insights through his film that are in some ways beyond what historians can 'prove' with recourse to the archives. Moreover, *Gangs of New York* conveys with panache a contest between one sector of the plebeian poor, with its backward-looking feudalistic understandings of American 'loyalty', and its class nemesis, a forward-marching bourgeoisie that would fashion its power and authority in production and exchange as well as out of the enticing carrot of 'democracy' and welfare provisioning, backed by the violent stick of the state's repressive terror.

For all of Bill Cutting's 'ownership' of the Five Points, it is an oddly feudal vas-salage that is his due: 'But in all the Five Points there's nothin' that runs, walks, or cocks his toes up don't belong to Bill the Butcher', Johnny tells Amsterdam as they walk through the streets of the Bloody Old Sixth. Tribute and loyalty are the gang leader's due, his régime less one of accumulation than rightful obeis-ance, driven not so much by the relentless need, logic and laws of capitalist development but by a purposeful resistance to winds of change:

> Everything you see belongs to me, to one degree or another. The beggars and newsboys and quick thieves here in Paradise. The sailor dives and gin mills and blind tigers on the waterfront. The anglers and amusers, the she-hes and chinks. Everybody owes, and everybody pays. Because that's how you stand up against the rising of the tide.

This is, first and foremost, an *ideological* stand, one made against inevitable historical defeat. As Tweed reminds the Butcher in a public encounter, 'You're a great one for fighting, Bill, I know, but you can't fight forever'. 'I can go down doing it', replies Cutting. 'And you will', is the Boss's curt reply. Scorsese seldom lets us pass through those Paradise Alley/Five Points streets in which Amster-dam is tutored on the lord's tithes, without confronting a looming sign, 'Money Lent', symbolic of the new relations of the cash nexus that are everywhere trans-forming the meanings of everyday life for the plebeian masses and their rude seigneurial overlords. The film never allows us to forget that the gang leader's proprietary right is fragile, precisely because it is in a state of transition. Defiant of capital and the state, the 'muscle' that the Butcher commands is clearly on its last legs in 1863, and Boss Tweed reminds the Butcher of this hard reality in

THE HANDS THAT BUILT AMERICA

words both deferential and demanding. Tweed pleads with Cutting to curb his excesses in the name of a larger prize of shared spoils:

> Bill, I can't get a day's work done for all the good citizens coming in here to fret me about crime in the Points. Some, I'm horrified to say, have gone so far as to accuse Tammany of connivance with this so-called rampant criminality. What am I to do? I can't have this. Something has to be done.

The Butcher, who knows well that Tweed controls the police, is able to at first shrug the problem off with an offering of a public hanging to appease the malcontented and the expectation that, in the end, since the state and its armed force appear to him a malleable tool of specific interests, the politicians ought to be able to get 'the crushers', or cops, to do whatever is needed. Tweed is aghast at the crudity of the suggestion: 'The police? Oh, Jesus, no. Jesus, no. The appearance of the law must be upheld. Especially while it's being broken'.

For a time, the old street power and the new machine politics of an emerging capitalist state work in tandem. But, in the end, the alliance must crack, for the Butcher knows only raw power and its threat of fearsome acts:

> Mulberry Street and Worth. Cross and Orange and Little Water. Each of the Five Points is a finger, and when I close my hand the whole territory is a fist. I can turn it against you.

Tweed, emblematic of the capitalist project of hegemony, has a wider vision, in which 'progress' pays:

> But we're talking about different things, Bill. I'm talking about civic duty. Responsibilities we owe to the people. Schools and hospitals, sewers and utilities; street construction, repairs and sweeping. Business licences, saloon licences, carting licenses ... streetcars, ferries, rubbish disposal. There's a power of money to be made in this city, Bill. With your help, the people can be made to understand that all of these things are best kept within what I like to call the Tammany family. Which is why I'm talking about an alliance between our two great organizations.

Just as the declining powers of feudal Europe bartered for a time their fading longevity, placating an emerging bourgeoisie, Cutting and Tweed dance their mutual material attraction through much of Scorsese's film. But ultimately the Butcher's ragged honour, soiled to its violent core by his commitment to an ideology of nativist and racist entitlement cloaked in the convenient garb of patriotic 'Americanism', is incapable of being as pliant as Tweed, whose instincts, like those of capital, are to turn every profit, whatever the 'price' and with whomever will enhance the prospects of this happening. Eventually, Bill will no longer play. He wants no part of anything that will

> befoul his [father's] legacy by givin' this country over to them what's had no hand in the fighting for it? Why? Because they come off a boat, crawling with lice and beggin' you for soup?

Cutting believes in history, however distorted his sense of the past; for him, the blood truly does stay on the blade. Tweed, Henry Ford-esque in his willingness to massage the historical past into whatever suits the accumulative appetites of the present, informs Bill, 'You're turning your back on our future'. 'Not our future', replies the Butcher. By the end of the film, the Butcher's absolutist Five Points 'state' and the rising bourgeoisie of the capitalist nation are mortal enemies. Tweed bemoans the outcome, 'You don't know what you've done to yourself'. Cutting is, ironically, the more eloquent:

> You think lightning strikes when you talk, Mr. Tweed, but I can't hardly hear you ... I know your works. You are neither cold nor hot. So because you are lukewarm, and are neither cold nor hot, I will spew you out of my mouth. You can build your filthy world without me ... Come down to the Points again and you'll be dispatched by mine own hand. Now go back to your celebration and let me eat in peace, I've paid you fair.

The film ends for the Butcher as it began, but with the mythical gang leader on the opposite end of the knife. 'It's fair', Cutting might well have remembered himself saying. 'A touch indelicate, but fair'.

But Tweed's victory, a metaphor for capital's capacity to vanquish the 'ancient' powers of its plebeian challengers, is not possible without new pacts with sectors of the subaltern classes. In Amsterdam and the revived Irish-immigrant Dead Rabbits, Tweed finds a forceful alliance, one that seals his victory with the glue of incorporation, the rising youth gang leader bartering for political representation and grasping the potential power of the Luxemburgist mass uprising:

> There's more of us coming off these ships every day. I heard fifteen thousand Irish a week. And we're afraid of the Natives? Get all of us together and we ain't got a gang, we got an army. Then all you need is a spark. Something to wake us all up.

THE HANDS THAT BUILT AMERICA

As the Draft Riots provide that first spark, ignited in the resentments of the poor against the rich and their capacity to buy the continued lives of their sons with a few hundred dollars, Scorsese suggests through Amsterdam's groping towards class consciousness the coming conflagration that pits labour irrevocably against capital:

> From all over the city they came. Ironworkers, factory boys, day laborers, school teachers, street cleaners ... Irish, American, Polish, German, anyone who never cared about slavery or the Union – whole or sundered ... The Earth was shaking now, but we was the only ones who didn't know it.

And because they do not know it, because the Earth's shaking takes place with workers handicapped in their state of unconsciousness, the waking up does not happen.

The first cries of the Draft Riots in the film are screams of class rage: 'Nobody goes to work today. They shut the factories down'. Outraged yells of 'the hell with your damned draft!' are punctuated by images of rioters ripping the doors of a mansion open, smashing exquisite vases and splintering a billiards table. The symbolism of such acts is unmistakable: 'Let's smash the bastards to hell!' Material meanings are posed with blunt determination: 'Hey! There's a three-hundred-dollar man. Get him!' But all of this quickly gives way to a sorry descent into racist vendetta. As a woman in the crowd yells, 'Come on, lads! Kill the nigger bastards! String them up!', the Draft Riots move rapidly out of their articulation of class resentments and into sickening scenes of lynching, beating and burning alive scapegoated African Americans, a hideous carnage of white rage. The Natives and the Dead Rabbits square off. Class struggle is overwhelmed by intra-class warfare: white against black; white against the not-quite-white-enough.

The ultimate victor is the newly consolidated state, with its special bodies of armed men subduing its unconscious proletarian challenge (ordered by the feudal gangs) as a prefatory volley to its subjugation of the seigneurial slave régime. Capital wrought its vengeance against the first deformed working-class insurrection that struggled to unfold in New York's streets in 1863, just as it would crush the regionalised power of a counter-posed 'order' premised on unfree labour. Thousands of federal troops, many of them working-class Irish New Yorkers, slashed into and fired upon crowds of their mothers and sisters, uncles and cousins. The New York streets succumbed, as would Savannah plantations. Scores of the poor dropped in the bloody streets of New York metropolitan industrialisation, just as poor whites would fall throughout the slave South. The corpse of Northern, urban class struggle was riddled with the bullets and bayonets of a state that was about to extend its colonisation and conquest of a way of life incompatible with the ever-widening ethos of the market revolution and its demanding extensions of the reach of accumulation and exploitation. As one of the Scottish actors, playing the Irish but nativist McGloin, comments, in summing up his sense of what the film is about:

> [P]olitics is an extension of war by other means. Looking at the period in which the film takes place, the tension between these two outlooks seems to be present, because there's a brutal, intense warfare happening between the gangs. But this tribalism is ultimately superseded when the big guns come. Who's got the big guns? The state. And the way the film covers that enormous scope is wonderful.[28]

What *Gangs of New York* depicts, through its historically inaccurate congealing of the Dead Rabbits-Native American gang warfare with the Draft Riots, is the larger historical accuracy of capital's simultaneous subjugation of the challenges of the plebeian street and the Southern plantocracy. This came about through the power of the capitalist state at the same time as it was a formative moment in the consolidation of that state.

Had Scorsese's film made only this elementary point, it would have made a significant contribution. The Draft Riots were indeed the climax of an age and, if the gangs were but a part of that historical moment, rather than its defining feature, they were nevertheless an articulation of critical components of class formation. The 'muscle' of the mean, plebeian streets and the politics of provisioning that Boss Tweed and Tammany Hall came to epitomise were a Faustian bargain in the complex relations of industrial-capitalist America's formative years. A good part of the rough and smooth hands that came together in an 'alliance' of the 1850s and 1860s ended with the Civil War and the consolidation of United States capital and its servile state. 'Democracy' was born as the gang-ordered 'electioneering by riot' gave way to the more orchestrated ordering of votes by political machines, which bought the public purse with soup and jobs and secured their hegemony with the disembodied 'votes' of the poor. What Tweed bemoaned in the Draft Riots was *not*, of course, the racist wall of fire that now separated black and white workers, nor the deaths of so many on both sides of the colour line. 'We're burying a lot of votes down here tonight', he moans, for in America, votes, like time, are money. Amsterdam is left the last, sad word, the voice of class unconsciousness:

---

28   Gary Lewis in Scorsese 2002, p. 95.

How many New Yorkers died that week we never knew. We thought there wouldn't be no country left by the end of it. And that no matter how much blood they spilt to build the city up again, and keep on building, for the rest of time, it would again be like no one even knew that we was ever here.

Having won the ear of the political boss on the basis of his 'traditionalist' street muscle, the young Vallon barters effectively within capitalism's metaphorical network of the state's brokerage politics. He cajoles Boss Tweed, wins Monk away from the limiting loyalties of self and strength, putting him on the hustings and giving voice to 'democratic' possibility, in the end securing the election of a sheriff who threatens the Butcher more than he does the evolving machinery of hegemonic urban politics. Yet, for all of Amsterdam's pulling of the wires of modern state-building somewhat successfully 'from below', he ultimately finds himself and his class on the short end of power's historical stick.

This suggests that historians have perhaps been of late too quick to revere 'republicanism's' rhetoric of egalitarianism while ignoring Alan Dawley's old suggestion that, in the United States, electoral politics 'was the main safety valve of working-class discontent', the ballot box a coffin of class consciousness.[29] But something lived on in this coffin. It produced a 20th-century New York that would simultaneously sustain a social-democratic polity and racial inequality, a vibrant and militant working class and widening gaps between rich and poor, episodic instances of labour-capital conflict and political administrations and histories of corruption and cynicism.[30] As Amsterdam would have said: 'It's a funny feeling being took under the wing of a dragon. It's warmer than you think'.[31] The Dead Rabbits, both their 'muscle' and their negotiations, were gone, but they could hardly be forgotten.

---

29 Dawley 1976.

30 J.B. Freeman 2000.

31 Amsterdam's comment takes us, I would argue, in different, indeed more fruitful directions than those posed by Walsh's rejection of what he considers Scorsese's misanthropy. Walsh wants to merely *reject* the backward ideology of racism and 'mindless violence' that he sees as the central animating forces in Scorsese's 'street-level' 'reactionary and anti-intellectual distortion of history'. Walsh cites the 1840s and 1850s as a Renaissance period in which the influence of Hawthorne, Poe, Melville, Emerson, Thoreau, Longfellow, Dickinson, Whitman and Stowe was paramount. I do not dispute the significance of this 'high' culture and its accomplishments, but question the validity of divorcing it entirely from 'lower' forms of thought and cultural practice, as is surely indicated by the case of Whitman. Moreover, it is necessary to understand the class *inflections* of problematic historical processes rather than simply rejecting them as wrong and inadequate. See Walsh 2003a.

Class and Race: A Relation of Proximity

Race and understandings of Americanism and whiteness are obviously central to both contemporary historiography and Scorsese's *Gangs of New York*.[32] Many critics will no doubt find the chaotic congealments of the film suspicious. How can Bill Cutting, a nativist anti-Irish bigot, walk side-by-side with Irish Catholics such as McGloin or cultivate a young Irish protégé, Amsterdam? Could the Dead Rabbits, an Irish Catholic street gang, have harboured blacks? The particularities of a detailed factuality are perhaps, however, less important that the suggestiveness of Scorsese's depiction of what Five Points life was like racially.

There is no mistaking the interracial and cross-ethnic character of the Sixth Ward; as in many similar urban districts of the United States at mid-century, racial and ethnic mixing was a norm that co-existed with varied levels of racism which cut themselves into the fabric of everyday life. This process was, however, a double-edged sword. On the one hand, as Fanny Kemble noted in her *Journal of a Residence on a Georgia Plantation* (1863), the more Irish and African-American people were lumped together, the greater the hostility between them. On the other, as was apparent in New York and Boston, 'mixed' marriages often involved poor black men and poor Irish women. The Five Points was a cauldron of this 'race mixing', its dance halls, cock pits, hotels of assignation, sexualised streets, grog shops and raucous theatres a venue for liaisons and cultural crossovers. Frederick Douglass regarded the Bloody Old Sixth as little more than a receptacle for 'the filthy scum of white society', but there is no doubt that blacks and whites mixed on more equal terms in its dark alleyways, squalid tenements and biracial bagnios than in uptown salons, where relations between blacks and whites turned largely on the necessity of African Americans serving their plutocratic masters. It was, not surprisingly, in the notorious Five Points that an 1844 dance contest pitted the Irish 'Master', John Diamond, against the black 'Juba', William Henry Lane.[33]

Scorsese materialises this black-white relation and, although historians are prone to downplay crass economism in our understandings of class and race, the Butcher's nativism and racism are constant reminders of just how critical the hierarchy of racialised wages was in the making of class. As Bill surveys the

---

32   On whiteness studies, both their richness and suggestiveness as well as some problems
      of the field's handling of evidence, see Arnesen 2001, with replies by James Barrett, David
      Brody, Barbara J. Fields, Eric Foner, Victoria C. Hattam and Adolph Reed Jr and a rejoinder
      by Arnesen.
33   See Ignatiev 1995, especially pp. 41–2.

Irish descending from the ships in the harbour onto the streets of republican citizenry he snorts,

> I don't see no Americans. I see trespassers. Paddies who'll do a job for a nickel what a nigger does for a dime and a white man used to get a quarter for – then moan about it when you treat them like niggers.

Professing his preference to shoot 'each and every one of them before they set foot on American soil', Cutting acknowledges that he does not have the guns. It is as if Scorsese is forced to acknowledge that, in some instances, mere firepower cannot do the job. And so black and white, Irish and 'Native', come together, their lives in the Five Points ones that find themselves invariably cheek by jowl. More could have been done with this in *Gangs of New York*, of course, and the few African Americans who appear in the film are under-developed as characters and as a racial presence.[34] They are almost always at a distance until they are the object of racist assault and killing during the Draft Riots, when the threat of blacks rampaging through the workplaces and neighbourhoods of white immigrant New York (not unlike Barnum's elephant,

---

34   This could also be said about the representation of the Chinese in Lower Manhattan in the 1860s, which, as indicated earlier, is historically inaccurate. The question that needs asking about Scorsese's representation of the Chinese is not unlike a host of other histor-ically problematic 'imaginings' in the film that can be interrogated. But the larger analytic issue is whether or not this creative historical licence distorts the large narrative picture of United States history or, rather, whether it contributes, through its particular use of repres-entation, to wider understandings. For instance, did Scorsese succumb to the Orientalist constructedness of Asian peoples, their cultures and ways of life encased in the mysteri-ousness of 'the Other'? Or, rather, was he placing them, however historically out of time, in the large historicised proximities of white-Asian relations, recognising nevertheless that Asian-white relations were different from black-white relations inasmuch as the com-mon dialogues and overlapping histories (in terms of work and sociability) that animated African-American, white ethnic, and native-born working people in the mid- to late 19th century were much less in play for whites and Asians? There is no doubt that, in present-ing Amsterdam as the sole humane link among whites, blacks and Asians, Scorsese's film relies on Hollywood-esque conceptions of 'the heroic' protagonist stepping outside of his-tory, and for this he can be criticised. But whether he has lapsed into the racist imagery of 'the inscrutable Chinese' or attempted to locate Chinese-white relations in plebeian Man-hattan as rather more complicated by social distance than other race relations is, to my mind, somewhat open to question. On Orientalism and the social construction of Asian otherness see Said 1979, which of course deals with the Muslim 'Orient' but is applicable to the conception and social construction of other Asian societies, including China.

the emblematic African 'beast', loose in the streets of urban civilisation) is seemingly realised with sudden viciousness. Nevertheless, there are hints in Scorsese's film of the symbiosis of black-white relations and of the ways in which this reciprocity conditioned the nature of racism.

This is conveyed visually in a striking brothel scene. A black prostitute is draped over Amsterdam's slumbering shoulder as Jenny dresses the Butcher's wounds across the table. White and black, Irish Catholic and nativist, are, in this view, literally touching. As an Irish fiddler plays, an African American entertains the crowd with the energetic tap dance that was one of the Five Points' cultural inventions. Bill's analytical oratory takes us somewhere interpretively important:

> Look at that. What is that? Rhythms of the Dark Continent tapped down and thrown into an Irish stew, and out comes an American mess. A jig doing a jig.[35]

This passage of racist commentary is perhaps as insightful as many recent writings on whiteness and United States racism precisely because it conveys the proximities within which working-class racism was made. Unlike other 19th-century racisms, born of empire's conquests of civilisations of colour, working-class racism in the United States was forged not at a distance but in the hearts and minds of closeness, one part of which was competition, another being commingling, co-existence and cultural blending. Out of this would come the vehement denial of dependencies often articulated in intensities which explain both the violence and the deeply sexualised nature of American racism. This is precisely why the fomented racism of the Draft Riots' immediate context was one part economic (the threat of job loss) and one part sexual, in which grotesque caricatures of 'miscegenation balls' ran in the Copperhead press, depicting Lincoln and other prominent Republicans dancing with caricatured African-American women. Along with jobs, black men were widely presented as on the move to steal white men's wives and sisters. Bill's brief comment on the 'race mixing' of 1860s plebeian culture thus takes us into 20th-century class and race relations, where Northern black-white sex districts, the evolution of blues and jazz, the hideous history of the lynch mob and the sexualisation of racist legal attacks like that on the Scottsboro Boys come together.[36]

---

35   The script in Scorsese 2002, p. 210, is not the same as the actual language of the film. I have relied here on my own notes.
36   See, for only a suggestion of the scope of all of this, Mumford 1997; B. Palmer 2000a; Carter

Masculinising Class and the Gendered Obliteration of Women

The one area where there is little to defend in *Gangs of New York* relates to women. It is simply not possible to say much positive about Scorsese's film in this regard. In focussing, in typical Hollywood style, on the flamboyant attract-iveness of Jenny, who marches through the film as first a tough-minded, relent-lessly cynical and staunchly independent pickpocket, a former object of Bill's honourable but inevitably compromised attractions and then, second, as Ams-terdam's unconditional lover who, third, returns to her stubborn sensibilities of a personal agenda, Scorsese constructs women as the adornments of men. They are merely appendages to the gangs, either used up and discarded (Hellcat Maggie) or forced, ultimately, to break ranks in futile escape. Jenny, to be sure, does have one of the more powerfully representative gestures of historiograph-ical critique in the film. She traces her route to California with a hand on a map, her finger outlining the journey to the freedoms of the West, not through the continent but around land masses, the ocean-going route moving south along the eastern seaboard, continuing down the coast of South America and around Cape Horn, and then back up the continents to San Francisco. This pilgrim-age will of course be thwarted, and Jenny's dreams end, as many did, badly. But could there be a more decisive repudiation of Frederick Jackson Turner's long-influential 'frontier thesis', in which the lure of land and the West was said to be a safety value that siphoned off class discontents and explained the quiescence of United States labour?[37]

It cannot be said, of course, that Scorsese is blind to gender. This and many of his other films present a gendered reading of their subject, for masculinity is central to all of Scorsese's plot lines and is most emphatically a dominant structure in *Gangs of New York*. Indeed, it is too dominant, because in its over-zealous depiction of the gangs it manages to one-sidedly write out of the history too much, including the presence of women and, with the ironic origin of the film in Amsterdam's childhood memory of his father's murder at the Butcher's hand, children. It is almost as if Scorsese has followed a radical feminist plot line in which the violent power of patriarchy is unleashed in all-encompassing ways that obliterate the agency, indeed, often the very presence, of women and the young.

To be sure, the Five Points was no haven for infants, adolescents or women. While *Gangs of New York* is notably negligent in developing women as charac-

<hr />

1969.

37   On the Turner thesis, see Billington 1966.

ters and as a force in the Five Points adequately, it perhaps makes the necessarily brutal point with stark suggestiveness: family life and the possibilities
for women and children in the Bloody Old Sixth of the 1850s and 1860s were
culturally claustrophobic and socially catastrophic. As Carol Groneman Pernicone's unpublished dissertation reveals, death was a predator stalking family
life relentlessly: one out of every three children in the Five Points died before
the age of five, which registers in the film with the brief allusion to Jenny's stillborn child. With Irish male labourers equally likely to succumb to the dangers
of work in the manual and construction trades, women were left the small pick-
ings of the sweated trades or the travails of the street, such as selling hot corn:

> Hot Corn! Hot Corn!
> Here's your lily white hot corn.
> All you that's got money –
> Poor me that's got none –
> Come buy my lily hot corn.[38]

But such penny capitalism of the alleyways and squalid squares could easily
shade over into the bartering of sexual treating that was a benign version of
the occupation if not of choice then of necessity of many Five Points women:
prostitution.[39]

The Hands That Built America

If Scorsese misses obvious opportunities to represent women and blacks more
fully, he is also immune to the daily labours that sustained life in all of mid-19th-
century America, even in the Five Points. There is almost no engagement with
the trades and occupations that dotted the landscape of the life of the Sixth
Ward and within which gang formation was materially embedded. Perhaps
the sole exception is the portrayal of the Butcher's technique, but this merely
proves the rule of Scorsese's disinterest in actual labour, for the Butcher's butchering has almost nothing to do with meat as a commodity. Indeed, the only
'cuts' that are dispensed are given as a gift to an old 'mother' by the lordly, benevolent Bill. Rather, carcasses are flesh useful for demonstrating the particular

---

38   Asbury 1928, p. 8.
39   On women's sweated work, prostitution and other aspects of female experience in New
      York in the first half of the 19th century see Stansell 1986; Pernicone 1973.

knife thrusts that will result in wounds or kills. The dilapidated businesses of the Five Points, in which cigars, chairs and combs were made, the dirty tasks of slaughtering animals, tanning hides and brewing drink undertaken or the back-breaking labours of those casually employed on the docks or as teamsters, hod carriers and the like sweated out, are not even a shadowy presence in the film. Money is made through theft and the quick score of raking in bets on prize fights. The streets and alleys are scenes for standing, scoring and squaring off in combat. 'Work', conceived as wage labour, is non-existent. This is, to be sure, a further shortcoming, but given that the film is concerned not so much with the extraction of surplus value and the production of goods and services as it is with the ensemble of relations at the core of class politics and its relation to state formation, this strikes me as a shortcoming that can be lived with. *Gangs of New York* is about the *exchange* relations of class politics in a nascent capitalist order rather than the productive relations of a capitalist economy.

Scorsese is nevertheless unambiguous and adamant that his film *is* about the hands that built America, inasmuch as the machinery of politics, republican order and democratic 'governance' are reflections of capitalist enterprise and its class relations and creations of that layered materiality. Indeed, the symbolism of hands is everywhere throughout the film, from its opening to its close, and the parade of panoramic, historical shots of the built New York skylines are flashed at the viewer with U2's 'The Hands That Built America' rounding out the film's musical score. If, unlike Brecht, Scorsese is unconcerned with the actual erection of towers, the hauling of stone and the forging of materials, *Gangs of New York* never loses sight of the varied hands that held knives and brickbats, that passed the stained blade from generation to generation, that bloodied rivals, that stuffed ballot boxes, that lynched blacks *and* clasped possibilities of class and racial solidarity – such hands being the often invisible counterparts to the sinewy arms and calloused fingers of waged labour. In the contradictory wrestling that is the essence of modern history, these were indeed the plurality of hands that built, unevenly and often brutally and tragically, a United States of America in which class power was seldom far from the surface of relations which so many have bathed in obfuscation. Scorsese, whatever his flaws, is to be applauded for presenting us with a different and more insightful visualisation.

It perhaps cultivates awarenesses that take us beyond the spaces Scorsese himself inhabits to new ground like that envisioned by Walt Whitman, who penned lines of verse at roughly the same time the Dead Rabbits and the Bowery Boys were clashing in 1857. That 'dreadful fight' left much blood on many blades, with 12 dead and 37 injured. Whitman had the capacity to see differently:

> I see those who in any land have died for the good cause,
> The seed is spare, nevertheless the crop shall never run out,
> (Mind you O foreign kings, O priests, the crop shall never run out.)
>
> I see the blood wash'd entirely away from the axe,
> Both blade and helve are clean,
> They spirit no more the blood of European nobles, they clasp no more
>   the necks of queens.
>
> I see the headsman withdrawn and become useless,
> I see the scaffold untrodden and mouldy, I see no longer any axe upon it,
> I see the mighty and friendly emblem of the power of my own race, the
>   newest, largest race.[40]

---

40   Whitman 1993, pp. 161–2.

CHAPTER 6

Sugar Man's Sweet Kiss: The Artist Formerly, and Now Again, Known as Rodriguez*

'Imaginations Working Overtime'

Imagine a shy man dressed in black, guitar slung over his shoulder, walking the meanest streets of one of the meanest cities in the United States. Imagine this man making his way to a waterside bar of questionable repute. Let us, for accuracy's sake, call it 'The Sewer'. He performs for a pittance, his audience a routinised, if motley, crew of down-on-their-luck, up-on-their-illusions, out-with-conventionality types. They sit in crumpled shirts, spinning tall tales and 'drinking the detergents/that cannot remove their hurts'.[1]

Imagine this man, hailed by a select few as a poet of the people, a prophet in unpropitious times, singing of what he has lived:

> The inner city birthed me
> The local pusher nursed me
> Cousins make it in the street
> They marry every trick they meet.

Imagine this man, his wallet picked by his handlers (perhaps unbeknownst to him), growing troubled as his heart becomes little more than 'a crooked hotel full of rumours':

> A dime, a dollar, they're all the same
> When a man comes to bust your game
> The turnkey comes, his face a grin
> Locks the cell, I'm in again.

---

* 'A Life Beyond Imagination: The Artist Formerly, and Again, Known as Rodriguez', *Against the Current*, 162 (2013), 31–35, 44. Published here in an adapted form as 'Sugar Man's Sweet Kiss: The Artist Formerly, and Now Again, Known as Rodriguez'.
1 All lyrics in this chapter are from the *Searching for Sugar Man* soundtrack (2012, Sony Legacy), and *Cold Fact* (2008, Light in the Attic Records). Quotes are from the film *Searching for Sugar Man* (2012, Sony Pictures).

Then imagine a night like any other, as 'the local diddy-bop pimp comes in'.
He slides, limp-postured, into the crowd,

> Next to a girl that has never been chased
> The bartender wipes a smile off his face
> The delegates cross the floor,
> Curtsy and promenade through the doors.
> And slowly the evening begins.

Yet again, this man puts on a show, his back to barstools and tavern tables
slimy with spilled beer, littered with soggy coasters and ashtrays piled high with
the discards of the day. Amidst the dull din of countless unrelated and often
incoherent conversations, his eyes shielded by trademark ebony sunglasses,
this man's soft voice slices seamlessly through the smoke and mirrors and haze
of just another eleven-PM gig:

> Yeah, every night it's the same old thing
> Getting high, getting drunk, getting horny
> At the Inn-Between, again.

Having completed what he regarded as his final soliloquy, this man then supposedly raises a gun to his head, pulls the lethal trigger, and ends it all. Or,
arguably even more grotesquely, calmly drenches himself with gasoline, lights
a match, holds it to his shirt cuff, and burns to death on what has passed for his
stage.

> But thanks for your time,
> Then you can thank me for mine,
> And after that, forget it.

Imagine, as memory of this man fades in his homeland and even his neighbourhood ('So I set sail in a teardrop and escaped beneath the doorsill'), the
bar where he died long torn down, that he becomes, astonishingly, a figure
of legend halfway around the world. In a place where he had never walked,
myths of his dramatic demise circulate freely, wildly innocent of any connection to his truths. The man's bootlegged music echoes in the ears of
youthful rebels, his haunting lyrics seared into the consciousness of a generation. 'We made love to your music', says an apostle in awe, 'we made war
to your music'. Imagine this man being able to converse with this kind of
reverence, to look back on such an unbelievable turn of events, asking

himself, 'how many times can you wake up in this comic book and plant flowers?'

This man was not an imagining. He actually lived, born in 1942, ostensibly on Michigan Avenue, a few blocks from the centre of downtown Detroit and what was then the city's most impressive skyscraper, the 430-foot-tall One Woodward Avenue:

> Born in the troubled city
> In Rock and Roll, USA
> In the shadow of the tallest building
> I vowed I would break away.

Sixto Diaz Rodriguez, sometimes called Jesús Rodriguez or confused with him (apparently a brother), aka Rod Riguez, was the sixth son of a hard-luck first-generation Mexican-American family. Rodriguez never managed to succeed in his bid to get free of Detroit. He is now destined, in part because of an unusually evocative documentary, *Searching for Sugar Man* (2012, directed by Swedish filmmaker Malik Bendjelloul), to be forever known simply as Rodriguez. He is bigger than the imaginings.

History's Hand

If you are heading to downtown Detroit via Windsor and the Ambassador Bridge, and you are prone to make a wrong turn, as I am, you could easily find yourself lost in the Motor City's southwest (the designation is both geographically and symbolically apt). This happened to me a few years ago. Pulling off the Fisher Freeway I was astounded to find myself in a small world I had no idea existed. Signs proclaiming *Mercado* and *Taverno* abounded; there were taco vans dispensing dinners, colourful murals splashed across brick walls (some of them with decidedly class-struggle content), and old factory buildings announcing their products to be tortillas, not tires.

Detroit's Mexicantown has its origins in the 1940s. Migrants made their way north to the vegetable fields that traverse south-western Ontario and southern Michigan as early as the 1910s. Soon they were working in the sprawling auto plants of the Ford Motor Company, which by the end of the 1920s had become the largest employer of Mexican labour in the Midwest. Establishing residences in Detroit, this wave of immigrants settled in Corktown, an old Irish Catholic enclave dating to the 1850s. Gradually, they spread throughout the city's south-west, concentrated along a corridor that came to be known as La Bagley.

Before the onslaught of the Great Depression, in which racist attacks on Mexican workers intensified in the climate of constricting economic opportunity and job losses that conditioned deportation mobilisations, 15,000 people sometimes called Chicanos considered Detroit home. By the mid-1930s, however, the enforcement of an exodus engineered under the designation 'repatriation' wrote *finis* to a good deal of the robust inner-city Latino life that had been developing throughout sections of south-west Detroit. The number of Mexicans living in the city dropped to a mere 1,200.

The defence industry 'boom' of the early 1940s and a post-World War II revival of Michigan's sugar-beet industry combined to reboot the migration of Mexicans to Detroit. As of 1943, four to six thousand Mexicans had crowded into an increasingly concentrated Detroit district, many of them living amidst the kinship networks long established in the Bagley/Vernor Street-bounded familiarities of Detroit's Spanish-speaking enclave. As wartime labour needs relaxed, however, the possibility of unionised jobs in the high-paying Fordist assembly-line sector was constricting. Government orchestrated *bracero* programmes were required to keep Mexican migrant streams flowing. There was little inducement for a Mexican-American population to set down roots when available wages came largely from seasonal field-work sustained by state programmes that defined harvesting labour as 'temporary'. La Bagley was a locale of resettlement and revival that struggled against the odds. Given a boost by a 1960s jump in migration and sliced in half by freeway expansion, Detroit's Mexican residential neighbourhood cohered in what would, in a 1980s promotional designation, be dubbed Mexicantown. In this process of social colonisation, previous immigrant institutions, like the Lithuanian Hall, were appropriated and became Unidos Hall.

Mexicantown began to flourish in the 1990s, with the generalised revival of migration to the United States from Mexico and Central and South America. Detroit was something of an anomaly in what Mike Davis has called 'magical urbanism', the modern Latino reinvention of America. By 2000, Detroit exhibited 'the most threadbare private-sector economy of any major central city' in the United States and bucked a national trend which saw Spanish-surnamed people achieve unprecedented influence in most of the country's metropolitan centres.[2] That said, even the de-industrialising Motor City was not immune from the phenomenal impact of migrations from the south, Mexico in particular: as the overall population of the city plummeted, tens of thousands of Latinos came to Detroit, revitalising a long-standing Mexican-American com-

---

2   Mike Davis 1999, p. 3.

munity to the point that Mexicantown's Spanish-speaking population grew by leaps and bounds over the course of the 1990s, expanding 70 percent to just under 50,000.

Rodriguez's parents were part of the initial 1920s wave of migration to Michigan, having come north to work in the auto plants. They would help establish the first vigorous, visibly Mexican-American neighbourhoods along and adjacent to Bagley Street. They adapted to American society in ways slightly different than would be the norm in California, Texas, and other conduits of the demographic drift from south to north. Racism against Mexican Americans was undeniable, of course, but it was, especially for early newcomers, less bellicose in places like Detroit and Chicago than it was in San Diego, San Antonio, or Phoenix. Lighter-skinned Mexican people experienced something of a reprieve; they might appear as but another segment of the already highly diverse immigrant, Catholic working class. The epithet 'wetback' was no doubt spit out at Mexican migrants to the United States in all regions of the country, but the vitriol behind such a derogatory slur, in certain times past, was more intense the closer one was to the Rio Grande. Even today, as racist attack on Latinos in Detroit escalates, the situation is different than it is in the broader South-west. In 2005 the Michigan Border Patrol arrested 1,800 'illegals'. The comparable figure in San Diego was an astounding 120,000.

'Good Only for Pick and Shovel'

A Spanish Jazz-Age pop tune, 'El Enganchado' or 'The Hooked One', bemoaned the extent to which Mexican workers at Chicago's Inland Steel were moulded into proletarians in the 1920s:

> I came under contract from Morelia
> To earn dollars was my dream ...
> But here they say I'm a camel
> And good only for pick and shovel.

This lament of degradation was deepened by a sense that, for the second generation of Mexican Americans, the mills of the assimilation gods were grinding slowly but surely:

> Many Mexicans don't care to speak
> The language their mothers taught them
> And go about saying they are Spanish

> And denying their country's flag ...
> My kids speak perfect English
> And have no use for Spanish,
> They call me 'fadder' ...
> And are crazy about the Charleston.

'I am tired of all this nonsense', sang the Inland Steel Mexican worker. 'I'm going back to Michoacán'.[3]

Rodriguez grew up in this wolverine-state snarl of coerced proletarianisation and generational acculturation. It was anything but easy. His mother died when Rodriguez was only three. Unable, on his own, to care for a large family properly, his father placed young Sixto in an orphanage. By this time the number of Mexican Americans in Detroit was shrinking. Immigration restrictions were tightening and access to auto-industry jobs, more open two decades earlier, was largely blocked. Detroit's migrants from Mexico carried the all-too-visible marks of the resulting stranglehold of class degradation on their collective body. They did the roughest and worst-remunerated labour, a good deal of it without the protections and securities of the newly established mass-production trade unions. Assimilation came with a price tag marked 'super-exploitation'. It is astounding, in the mainstream journalistic comment on Rodriguez generated by *Searching for Sugar Man*, to see repeated references to his Mexican-American background as 'middle class' or 'lower middle class'. It is as though labouring life has been excised from a sanitised, ethnically cleansed 'American dream'.

The Charleston was no longer in fashion by the time Rodriguez was ready to do his particular dance, but he garnered a sense of Mexican melodies and rhythms from his father. He was also drawn, in the 1950s, to the fast pace of Canadian-American country singer Hank Snow. A decade later he had come to regard Mick Jagger as 'king'. Taking up the guitar at age 16 (he claims it changed his life), Rodriguez's music evolved over the course of the 1960s. It was a blend of Bob Dylan, Leonard Cohen, and Donovan, with a whiff of the protest folk of Dave Van Ronk and a touch of psychedelic San Francisco thrown into the mix, anticipating Tom Waits at times. But the sound, as well as the substance, was uniquely Rodriguez. He produced a single on an obscure label in 1967, followed by two albums with the short-lived Sussex Records, owned by future Motown mogul Clarence Avant: *Cold Fact* (1970) and *Coming from Reality* (1971).

---

3   Quoted in Gutman 1976, pp. 8–9.

Rodriguez's Radicalism

The 1960s clearly formed Rodriguez, not only musically but politically. 'When I was writing those songs', he told one journalist, referring to his albums of the early 1970s, 'it seemed like a revolution was coming in America. Young men were burning their draft cards, the cities were ablaze with anger'. This was the moment of 1967 through 1969.

In Detroit, this 1960s conjures up images of rebellion in the streets, riotous clashes between a vindictive and racist police force and the city's poor, and working-class mobilisations of challenge, the vanguard of protest being African-American youth. The last three years of the decade were ones of momentous upheaval. A 1967 conflagration was marked by 43 dead, 7,200 arrested, 80 percent black; 2,500 stores looted and burned out; and upwards of $80 million in property damage. Wildcat strikes of black and Polish workers erupted in 1968 at the infamously unsafe Dodge Main factory complex. A year later the League of Revolutionary Black Workers was formed.

Across America antagonism to constituted authority was endemic, with mobilisations against the Vietnam War resulting in hundreds of thousands marching in the streets, chanting slogans of searing repudiation. Demands for change were loud and long. Many of them came from Students for a Democratic Society (SDS). To the extent that SDS can be regarded as a surrogate for the student revolt of these years, it was born and died a stone's throw away from Detroit. Launched from the Ann Arbor campus of the University of Michigan in 1960, SDS penned its manifesto, the Port Huron Statement (1962), in Detroit's upstate backyard. When SDS imploded in 1968 and 1969, its death notice was delivered at the Weathermen faction's Flint War Council, a mere 60 miles of freeway from the Motor City.

This was the 1968 meal of militancy on which Rodriguez clearly dined. He also had aesthetic predecessors. The early Dylan of 'Masters of War' (1963) and Barry Maguire's apocalyptic version of 'Eve of Destruction' (1965) are self-acknowledged influences on Rodriguez:

> I wonder about the tears in children's eyes
> And I wonder about the soldier that dies
> I wonder will this hatred ever end
> I wonder and worry, my friend
> I wonder, I wonder wonder, don't you?

But it is the unmistakable condemnation of the entire edifice of capitalist political economy that is the razor's edge of Rodriguez, most cutting in 'This Is Not a Song, It's an Outburst: Or, the Establishment Blues':

The mayor hides the crime rate
Council woman hesitates
Public gets irate but forget the vote date ...

Garbage ain't collected, women ain't protected
Politicians using people they've been abusing
The mafia's getting bigger, like pollution in the river
And you tell me that this is where it's at.

Woke up this morning with an ache in my head
Splashed on my clothes as I spilled out of bed
Opened the window to listen to the news
But all I heard was the Establishment's blues.

Rodriguez is never far from the fundamental dispossession that marks him not just as Mexican American but as a worker. In 'Cause', for instance, he opens with class resentment: 'Cause I lost my job two weeks before Christmas/and I talked to Jesus at the Sewer'. Rodriguez then closes with acknowledgement of the psychic costs of racialised oppression, but this is in fact a rare reference in his overall oeuvre: 'Cause I see my people trying to drown the sun/in weekends of whiskey sours'.

Rodriguez fused this anti-capitalist sensibility, in which class place was pre-eminent, with recognition of the youthful rebelliousness of the 1960s. He assailed patriarchal authority and the sterile promise of the suburbs, revelling in the countercultural possibilities of the moment. 'Inner City Blues' admonishes parents to loosen their restrictive grip on the young:

Met a girl from Dearborn, early six o'clock this morn
A cold fact
Asked about her bag, suburbia's such a drag
Won't go back
'Cos Papa don't allow no new ideas here
And now he sees the news, but the picture's not too clear.

'I Wonder' gestured to a generation emerging out of the confines of sexual repression and double-standards, recognising new-found freedoms: 'I wonder how many times you've had sex/I wonder do you know who'll be next'.

In what has become his signature piece, 'Sugar Man', Rodriguez provides an intriguingly challenging commentary on drugs:

Sugar man, won't you hurry
'Cause I'm tired of these scenes
For a blue coin won't you bring back
All those colors to my dreams
Silver magic ships you carry
Jumpers, coke, sweet Mary Jane.

This acknowledged drugs' attractions. But it did so by recognising, as well, what drugs stifled: 'Sugar man you're the answer/that makes my questions disappear'. Questions, of course, were fundamental to Rodriguez and his purpose. He was not unaware of the ways in which 'turning on/tuning out' could benefit – economically and politically – the most retrograde social forces, feeding the appetite of apathy:

While the mafia provides your drugs,
Your government will provide the shrugs,
And your National Guard will supply the slugs,
So they all sit satisfied.

Rodriguez Busy being Born is Sadly Dying: The Dark Side of the Early 1970s Moon

Rodriguez not only failed to make it big, he did not even make it small. The albums died. The claim is that Rodriguez never received a penny in royalties. Sussex Records dropped him from its failing label. Few in the United States, including some musicians who contributed to the studio-makings of his recordings, remembered him when asked directly about his music. To be sure, there were those who championed his talents and recalled his promise, but they were discordant notes in a chorus of amnesia. What explains this?

Rodriguez's premature artistic death was no doubt accelerated by a musical industry less interested in his radical and often complicating message than the medium of his money-making capacity. Certainly he was the victim of the commonplace practices of the recording industry at the time. These placed naïve artists at the mercy of the many voracious sharks who bilked musicians shamelessly. Eerily enough, Rodriguez foresaw all of this in what is arguably his artistic masterpiece, 'Crucify Your Mind':

Was it a huntsman or a player
That made you pay the cost

That now assumes relaxed positions
And prostitutes your loss?

His lyrics perhaps spoke directly to those who would, over the years, rationalise
acts of unconscionable self-interest:

So con, convince your mirror
As you've always done before
Giving substance to shadows
Giving substance ever more.

If Rodriguez was capable of pointing an accusatory finger, he did not exempt
himself from responsibilities in what would be his musical unmaking:

Were you tortured by your own thirst
In those pleasures that you seek
That made you Tom the curious
That makes you James the weak?

Always a mysterious figure at best, Rodriguez was clearly a loner, reticent to
demand rights and entitlements from those who seemed to be helping him. He
was likely content to be creating and recording his songs, rather than attending
scrupulously to contracts and charting careful career moves.

More importantly, neither black nor white in a Detroit music scene ordered
by these racial binaries, Rodriguez had no support networks to call upon in
the protection of his interests. He was the prototype of an outsider. This was a
product of how class and race intersected in this particular historical moment
and also in this specific place, the Detroit of Bob Seger-type working-class rock-
ers and African-American Motown. Rodriguez, simply put, lacked the resources
to contend adequately with the well-heeled hucksters on whom he necessarily
depended and with whom he met and conducted what passed for 'business' in
seedy bars or on the corners of dimly lit streets.

As a Mexican American, then, Rodriguez was invariably socially constructed
as an 'easy mark' by those more than willing to write him off in all manner of
racist and class-based ways. Quick money was obviously there to be effortlessly
had. There were those willing and able to do a grab and run. Rodriguez, reliant
on his own meagre devices, would be left standing still.

But there was more to Rodriguez's failure to crack the big time than this. His
music was too much, too late by a few years. Even before the socially explosive
happenings of 1967 and 1968, Dylan, an astute weather-cock if ever there was

one, had already consciously discarded much of his protest voice (which always masked outrage in the kind of ambiguities Rodriguez never relied on), clinging tenaciously, and adroitly, to his commercial capacities. Apparently you *did* need a Weatherman to know which way the wind blows, especially when a hard rain was gonna fall. It was an era where everything was moving *so fast.* Uncompromising in both his politics and his tone, Rodriguez was forged in the crucible of 1968's certainties of wrongs, and even if he often shied away from clear statements on rights, he pointed unerringly in their direction. As a receptive 1960s waned, Rodriguez's stock necessarily nose-dived; a more sceptical and reticent 1970s unravelled the tight knots of a previous youthful political intransigence.

The countercultural alternative, meanwhile, was spiralling downward, the tragic 1969 Rolling Stones Altamont Speedway concert an orgy of violence and chaotic lack of judgment culminating in death and demoralisation. As a metaphor, Altamont seemed to spell the sad end of the 'Woodstock nation', with its message of 'peace and love'. Over the course of 1969 and 1970 musical figures such as the Rolling Stones' Brian Jones, Alan Wilson of Canned Heat, Jimi Hendrix, Janis Joplin and the Doors' Jim Morrison all died in circumstances in which drug overdoses were either confirmed or suspected. Too many 'bad trips' shred the promise of alternative, leaving the counterculture in nihilistic tatters. Disco was around the corner.

Rodriguez provided an anthem to this denouement, but poised as it was on the cusp of recognition of drugs' attractions and acknowledgement of the fundamental illusion of such 'magic ships', it was not exactly welcomed by either countercultural rebels or the law-and-order brigade:

> Sugar man met a false friend
> On a lonely dusty road
> Lost my heart when I found it
> It had turned to dead black coal.

As the utopianism of the counterculture soured, emptying it of so much radical content, what was often left was little more than a vacuous individualism. Rodriguez exposed the inadequacies of this trajectory, on political and personal levels, in 'Street Boy':

> There's one last word then I'll conclude
> Before you pick up and put on your attitude
> Bet you'll never find or ever meet
> Any street boy who's ever beat the streets.

The countercultural dilemma would perhaps have been enough to sink Rodriguez. His insistence on hanging his anti-capitalist, pro-working-class lyrics on a hook that was an uncomfortable fit for so many may well have sealed his fate. Neither the far left (with its emerging Maoist, Trotskyist and socialist-feminist politics) nor the surviving Old Left, trapped aesthetically in the limitations of the radical folk-song paradigm, were drawn to Rodriguez in the 1970s:

> And there's the militant with his store-bought soul
> There's someone here who's almost a virgin I've been told
> And there's Linda glass-made who speaks of the past
> Who genuflects, salutes, signs the cross and stands at half-mast.

Rodriguez seemed to have run his short and seemingly reversing course. Indeed, for the next three decades – throughout much of the 1970s, 1980s and 1990s – he was largely confined to the pick-and-shovel brigade of the dispossessed. To be sure, *Searching for Sugar Man*, exercising some dramatic licence, fails to acknowledge that Rodriguez did take some time off as a wage worker to tour in Australia and New Zealand with the band Midnight Oil, but this does not (in spite of some cynical reviews) detract from the main points that should be taken from the film.

The Multi-Racial, Multi-Ethnic Working Class

As *Searching for Sugar Man* makes all too clear, Rodriguez lived a hard, labouring life over the course of these years of seeming obscurity. He worked for a time during the 1970s in the most taxing of jobs at the decrepit hub of Chrysler's Motor City empire, Dodge Main, but the antiquated 67-acre factory on the Detroit-Hamtramck border was eventually closed. He also served a stint in the Eldon Avenue Gear and Axle plant, notorious for its dangerous work conditions. Both of these awful and alienating production purgatories were nurseries of working-class uprisings, sites that spawned the League of Revolutionary Black Workers. They gave rise to defiant acts of sabotage and other creative kinds of 'counter-planning on the shop floor' chronicled in Bill Watson's famous article in *Radical America* (1971).

Rodriguez ended up in demolition work, inhaling dust and absorbing grime, back-breaking toil on the lowest rung of the non-unionised construction industry. This was the kind of work that no one, in a Detroit not quite yet decimated by the later collapse of the auto industry, wanted. As Rodriguez told one interviewer, he wasn't part of any glitzy 'rock and roll' Detroit scene: he was strictly 'blue collar'. But unlike those who cannot quite fathom that wage labour is not necessarily either a waste or a tragic descent into oblivion, Rodriguez insists that just because his years of tough, dirty work in Detroit seemed to make him invisible, he was never lost. 'I knew exactly where I was', he states knowingly. He even stood for municipal office repeatedly, as a candidate for both mayor and city councilman. This effort at electoral intervention proved futile, however: on one ballot he received less than 150 votes, and the official-dom managed to misspell his name.

Rodriguez's three daughters, who figure prominently (and clearly lovingly) in *Searching for Sugar Man*, are adamant that their father's life is indeed rich in many ways, but this has nothing to do with acquisitive individualism. Rather, Rodriguez's ultimate resource, and the obvious foundation of his calm content-ment, is the unshakeable conviction that he has always been on the side of the poor, that his roots are in the working class, and that his values have been formed by this experience.

The working class that Rodriguez embraces and symbolises looks rather dif-ferent in *Searching for Sugar Man* than conventional wisdom suggests. Against the grain of popular culture stereotypes, as well as learned depictions prom-inent in much contemporary critical theory, for instance, this class is not frac-tured and fragmented by racial and ethnic division. Instead it is a multi-racial, multi-ethnic formation. Mexicantown is now 50 percent Latino, 25 percent African American, 20 percent white, and 5 percent Arab. In a Detroit where political power municipally often appears to be in the hands of peoples of col-our, those with Spanish surnames are something of a bridge between black and white constituencies; tensions evident in other locales where Latino-Black con-frontation is rife seem rather subdued.

Rodriguez's wife, the mother of his daughters, is of European and Native American ancestry. (Most of Detroit's Native American people live in Mexican-town). This makes Rodriguez's children white, Aboriginal and Mexican or, to put it differently, quintessentially 'American'. Rodriguez has spoken movingly about his respect for the richness of Native American cultures. As he exited the music scene in 1974 he spent a summer living and travelling with Aboriginal people. Rodriguez helped organise pow-wows throughout Michigan, including at Wayne State University, where he was studying philosophy. Rodriguez also ventured into Canada, where he spent time at Grand Bend near the Kettle and Stoney Point First Nations lands, site of the 1995 occupation of Ipperwash Pro-vincial Park that culminated in the Ontario Provincial Police murder of Dudley George.

Those expecting to see a white ethnic working class seething with racial prejudice, then, will find little confirmation in *Searching for Sugar Man*. This is not to deny that examples of working-class racism are not commonplace and deplorably vicious. Detroit has its share of this sad pollution of working-class collectivity. But Rodriguez's experience complicates our understandings of class, forcing appreciation of the ways that in particular settings a multi-ethnic, multi-racial working class has negotiated a sense of itself as something other than divided irreconcilably by diverse 'identities'.

Two of Rodriguez's white co-workers talk of their relationship with him, their astonishment that he is a musician of mythical stature in other parts of the world and their regard for his work and for his fundamental humanity. Not only are they articulate and proud of their friendship with Rodriguez, their running commentary on his good fortune is generous and genuine, often sophisticated in its reflections, always happy and sometimes quite hilarious. *Searching for Sugar Man* provides, in passing, rare glimpses of specific working-class 'types': the gregarious workplace conversationalist, the kind of guy who punctuates the nine-to-five grind with a touch of the stand-up comedian and the auto-didactic proletarian philosopher, reminding us that paths taken are choices always straining against convention. There is no hint of jealousy or antagonism or petty carping in any of this, let alone racial chauvinism. Instead, what is conveyed is a sense of class comradeship, of respect for a fellow worker, of heartfelt joy at his good fortune, however late arriving. This multi-racial, multi-ethnic working-class élan, visible in so many Detroit watering holes at shift changes and on Friday nights, is a welcome reminder that not all workers conform to Archie Bunker-like caricatures.

Globalisation from the Bottom Up

How do we know all of this? The answer to this question takes us into realms of discovery and recovery that illuminate subterranean currents of globalisation, a kind of cultural process of combined and uneven development leading towards the making of *Searching for Sugar Man*.

Rodriguez's *Cold Fact* found its way to South Africa in the early 1970s. The isolations and repressive containments of the apartheid regime boomeranged culturally, nurturing already existing strains of rebelliousness amongst white youth *and* making it possible for an underground mythology to envelop an artist whom no one knew and who had dropped off the radar screen of the international music scene. Precisely because albums like *Cold Fact* were banned from the heavily censored public airways (the film shows a South African government employee in the archives of 'avoid stamped' material handling a record in which deep scratches have been made in the lead 'Sugar Man' track, making it impossible to play the song), Rodriguez became a cult figure. He personified sex, drugs and rock and roll, with an unmistakable oppositional undercurrent. As a Mexican American he occupied uniquely accessible ground in the racially charged atmosphere of a South Africa where conflict seemed invariably ordered along a black-white axis.

To his disaffected audiences in Cape Town, Johannesburg, Pretoria, Durban, and other centres where apartheid seemed to have less and less purchase on the political sensibilities of the young, Rodriguez served as a surrogate for the challenge of a different socio-cultural/political order. He was as important as Elvis had been in the late 1950s, the Beatles in the 1960s or Neil Young in the 1970s. Difficult though it may be to appreciate, Rodriguez's reputation as a songwriter in South Africa climbed to almost unimaginable heights. He was compared favourably to Bob Dylan and to Simon and Garfunkel. According to some, Rodriguez was 'bigger than the Rolling Stones'. *Cold Fact* had as much of a South African impact as *Abbey Road* or *Exile on Main Street* did in the rest of the English-speaking world.

Rodriguez's aura soared all the more because nothing was known of him and little, apparently, could be discovered that cast light on his doings, even his whereabouts. It was thought that he must be dead or in jail. Then the stories circulated of how this had happened, all involving increasingly wild speculation about his self-destructive farewell, drugs, criminal behaviour and the like. 'Imaginations', in Rodriguez's words, were 'working overtime'.

Consider having grown up on a diet of songs like 'Street Fighting Man', 'Jumping Jack Flash' and 'Sympathy for the Devil' and not knowing, or being able to find out, who the Rolling Stones were or what became of them. The mystique would have been overpowering. Ignorance wasn't bliss, but it kept the songs alive – more so, perhaps, than if Rodriguez had been an open book, capable of being read in the marketplace of cultural productions. Rodriguez was never made familiar, and the strange could not truly die.

Post-1970 South African anti-apartheid white youth kept buying his music, and someone was making lots of money. *Searching for Sugar Man* provides no adequate explanations of what happened to the piles of Kruggerrands that accumulated on the basis of sales of Rodriguez's albums, which were certainly in the hundreds of thousands. Most of this commercial bonanza may well have related to bootlegged or pirated variants of Rodriguez's music. Nonetheless, in the early to mid-1970s, some of these sales undoubtedly involved Sussex releases marketed through supposedly legitimate channels. During this period Sussex was bought by A&M Records, at the time one of the largest, independent record companies in the world, if not *the* largest, and it is unfathomable that this enterprise did not profit from Rodriguez's popularity in South Africa.

Meanwhile, the dedicated throngs who bought Rodriguez albums and listened to them intently aged. The songs seemed hard-wired into their sense of themselves, a 'soundtrack to their lives'. There were those who had tattoos of the *Cold Fact* album cover sketched into their upper arms.

Eventually, in the late 1980s and into the 1990s, a journalist, Craig Bartholomew, and an ex-soldier, jewellery-store owner and hard-core Rodriguez fan, Stephen 'Sugar Man' Segerman, combined forces. They had been pursuing parallel interests in the Rodriguez mythology for years, but united to launch a methodical South African attempt to track down the phantom singer-songwriter. Lyrics were searched for clues, leading them, via Dearborn, to suspicions of a Detroit connection. A website was launched, complete with a milk-carton cartoon drawing of a 'lost' Rodriguez. It constituted nothing less than a search party on a quest to find out what had happened to the illusive and inspirational creator of *Cold Fact*.

In the age of the Internet, it was perhaps inevitable that someone would connect with someone who knew Rodriguez, who was reclusive, had no inclinations to be plugged into computers and preferred to live without a phone. His daughter Eva was of a different generation and contrary habits. One day, through workplace connections, she was directed to Segerman and Bartholomew's website, designated 'The Great Rodriguez Hunt'. Incredulous at her father's influence in far-away South Africa and shocked by the sensational stories of his suicidal end, she left an email response that ultimately put Rodriguez in touch with Stephen Segerman.

This then led to a series of hugely successful concerts in South Africa in March 1998, memorialised in a TV documentary aired in July 2001 entitled 'Dead Men Don't Tour'. *Searching for Sugar Man* provides incredibly moving footage of these concerts, in which the awe in which Rodriguez is held by his fans is written on the faces of men and women who cannot quite believe that they are seeing in the flesh someone they had long lived with as legend. The crowds ecstatic, their icon was gracious. 'Thanks for keeping me alive', Rodriguez bowed in closing. Rodriguez was resurrected. Light in the Attic Records re-released his albums, starting in 2008, paying him royalties on sales for the first time in his life.

Adding to this world-beat mix, the *Searching for Sugar Man* film came about because Swedish director Bendjelloul decided to go on a six-month global backpacking walk-about in search of the story to end all stories, one into which he could sink his cinematic teeth. The myth complex surrounding Rodriguez in South Africa seemed too good to be true, a 'fairy tale' already scripted. He spent four years of his life on the film, scrounging funding where he could, financing production, in part, by self-sacrifice. In conjunction with the

Bartholomew-Segerman detective hunt and the Light in the Attic promotions, *Searching for Sugar Man* has finally made Rodriguez widely known outside of South Africa and Australia, where he also has a long-standing and committed following.

Unlike so much celebrity in our times, however, the artist formerly and now again known as Rodriguez manages to say little and get a lot of recognition. Concert performances are promoted, sold out and celebrated; rave reviews are now the norm; and Rodriguez has appeared on David Letterman's programme and comparable high-visibility venues. Rodriguez is not unlike one of his own anonymous characters, the 'man with his chin in his hand/Who knows more than he'll ever understand', paid homage to in 'A Most Disgusting Song'. It is all a refreshing rejoinder to the self-promotional narcissistic cultivation of banality central to our cultural times.

Sugar Man's Sweet Kiss

Rodriguez has taken all of this in his peculiarly lanky and awkward stride. He is over 70 years of age, failing in health and somewhat frail, but he is buoyant in spirit and anything but embittered. 'I'm a lucky man', he tells one interviewer. Complaints about not receiving financial compensation for the sales of his albums never cross his lips. He is grateful for what he does have, rather than resentful of what he has never received. Convincingly Zen in his humility, modest and quietly self-assured, Rodriguez is impossible not to admire.

A man of few spoken words, Rodriguez lets his songs be his critical voice. After all, he answered his exploiters in 'Like Janis':

> And you measure for wealth by the things you can hold
> And you measure for love by the sweet things you're told
> And you live in the past or a dream that you're in
> And your selfishness is your cardinal sin.

And reminded them, in 'Crucify Your Mind', of the persistence that characterises those who will settle for nothing less than a full accounting of the many crimes against the poor:

> Soon you know I'll leave you
> And I'll never look behind
> 'Cause I was born for the purpose
> That crucifies your mind.

When asked about the Rip Van Winkle-like nature of his story, Rodriguez replies, obviously bemused: 'Yes, I suppose it does have a magical twist to it. But I was never asleep'. He is content to know that as a 'musical political' he is doing what he can to address inequality, poverty and the governance and greed of the rich. With an intuitive sense of hegemony, he distrusts 'current truths', appreciating where, how and why so many of them are fashioned. It is surprisingly refreshing that Rodriguez's songs seem almost timeless, but then the deep reservoir of working-class experience on which he draws is characterised by fundamental continuities. 'The issues are as urgent today as when I first wrote those songs', Rodriguez insists.

We need so much that we do not have in the struggle against a decayed capitalism. A great deal has yet to be built. It is crucial to use all that the resources of our past can rally to our cause. Even metaphors are of an inestimable service, which is what a poet like Rodriguez provides: 'This system's gonna fall soon, to an angry young tune/And that's a concrete cold fact'.

Rodriguez offers no blueprints of how to organise resistance, as he would be the first to acknowledge. But he does reveal to us the dream of what can be, largely by framing this necessarily imaginative construction within grittily realist revelations that expose the utter unacceptability of what is.

'Cause the sweetest kiss I ever got is the one I've never tasted', Rodriguez sings. *Searching for Sugar Man* gives anyone interested in social justice and a better world a precious gift, a very sweet, lingering kiss, one whose taste will last.

Historiography: The Revolutionary Left

..

Introduction to Part 3

There is no great surprise in a working-class historian turning to the study of the revolutionary left. Most historians of the workers' movement have a sense of the importance of dissidents in the trade unions, and of activists who have struggled to realise Marx's vision of the proletariat as a transcendent class, the architect of a new world order. To study the working class and its history is to be constantly bumping into a wide variety of labourists, anarchists, communists and socialists, and even within such general designations there are contentious separations of position.

My own contribution to the historiography of the revolutionary left is premised on this sense of differentiation. In August 1857, Charles Darwin wrote to his friend J.D. Hooker that 'It is good to have hair-splitters and lumpers', adding, for clarification, 'Those who make many species are the "splitters", and those who make few are the "lumpers"'.[1] More than a century later, Jack Hexter, in a critique of the method of the pre-eminent Marxist historian of 17th-century England, Christopher Hill, suggested, somewhat disingenuously, that the key divide within historiography was not between right and left but between the lumpers and the splitters. Hexter deplored Hill's lumpish, ostensibly indiscriminate use of sources, claiming that it allowed the historical materialist to subordinate important differences to his overall distorted understanding of 17th-century dissent. 'Splitting', Hexter insisted, was the better strategy for historical research. It accentuated the particular, suggesting the importance of nuance and subtlety within experiences of the past that were seldom easily reduced to commonplace, and usually formulaic, generalities.[2]

Of course, we are not required to choose in an absolute sense. There are times, as indicated in Volume I of *Marxism and Historical Practice*, where the inclination to lump can produce illuminating and necessary statements of historical trends. So, too, are there times when splitting is a crucially important project, for it is sometimes necessary to differentiate even in the face of pressures to congeal.

The historiography of the revolutionary left is one field of study where an unhealthy and unhelpful tendency – strongest on the right, but with expression

---

1 Darwin 1888, p. 105. See also Darwin 2009.

2 Hexter and Hill crossed swords as a result of Hexter's article "The Burden of Proof," *Times Literary Supplement*, 24 October 1975, with Hill's "Reply to Hexter" and Hexter's rejoinder appearing in subsequent November issues of the TLS. For a reasoned and more distanced response to Hexter, see W.G. Palmer 1979.

on the left as well – to lump all manner of dissident thought into one common container has had evident effect on historical analysis. This takes the form of reducing the history of the revolutionary left to its most dominant tendency, the Soviet Union-affiliated Communist Party, with its particular variant of communism[3] structured by the Stalinist trajectory of the Communist International from the mid- to late 1920s onwards. Other variants of revolutionary leftist politics get short shrift, most especially that particular current known as the Left Opposition, which is associated with the critique of 'the revolution betrayed' and Leon Trotsky. Even within this specific political formation there would be important 'splits' worth recognising, drawing attention to their reasons for forming new political tendencies and accentuating specific developments that the revolutionary left addressed in different ways.

The first essay in this grouping of writings reflects my sense that the historiography of American communism demanded an infusion of differentiation. At the time of its writing, in 2003, historians of the Communist Party in the United States were largely divided into two hostile camps. On one side of an interpretive divide stood a contingent of political scientists and historians who adhered to the interpretive framework first espoused by Theodore Draper, whose major texts *The Roots of American Communism* (1957) and *American Communism and Soviet Russia* (1960) elaborated a liberal Cold War-influenced anti-communism that stressed, ultimately, the extent to which communism in the United States was a foreign import, a 'made-in-Moscow' politics that was always alien to American conditions. On entirely opposite analytic ground were those, largely coming out of the New Left of the 1960s or influenced by the sensibilities of this epoch and the generation of radical historians it nurtured, who instead adhered to a view that communism in the United States had been embraced and promoted by home-grown dissidents. They struggled in a particular context in ways entirely congruent with that setting and, whilst they were certainly aligned with the Soviet Union, these United States communists were never entirely subordinated to it. Their struggles against racism and in opposition to all manner of oppressions and the exploitative essence of capitalism could not be boiled down to the pre-packaged priorities of a distant Communist International.

As I suggest in 'Rethinking the Historiography of American Communism', this historiographic impasse had long stalemated. Draper-esque histories tended to be unduly dismissive of communism's appeal and influence, just as

---

3 Throughout these pieces, I will use 'communist' to indicate the general orientation and 'Communist' to indicate the ideology specifically associated with the Comintern.

New Left narratives bypassed the confines within which communism existed in its United States variants. Neither 'side', which I argued were really mirror-images of one another, addressed Stalinism with much in the way of sophistication, and both orientations wasted few words in their counter-posed narratives for explaining or addressing Trotskyism's meaning. 'Rethinking the Historiography of American Communism' thus demands a more complicating reading of the revolutionary left, even suggesting that the field's pioneering researcher, Theodore Draper, can be in some ways 'split', emphasising the ways in which different writings from different periods occupy analytic ground that highlights subtle but significant interpretive changes.

To demand this kind of revisionist refinement of a field highly charged with ideological baggage is necessarily to open the floodgates of misinterpretation and misrepresentation. Thus Randi Storch, a New Left-influenced historian of Chicago Communism in the Third Period, uses my 'Rethinking' essay to lump me with Theodore Draper and his supporters, claiming that I am part of a contingent that removes 'Communists from their neighborhoods, workplaces, and networks in order to show, with condescension and disdain, that Communists in the United States acted as Soviet puppets'. So distorting is the historiographic impasse of writing on American Communism that Storch misreads my statement that '[o]nly if we are capable of seeing Stalinism's degenerations, and how they registered in the transformation of Soviet politics and the role of the Comintern over the 1920s, can we appreciate what was the foundational premise of the American revolutionary left' to mean that I agree with Draper, even when I was clearly suggesting something quite the opposite. Storch argues this wrong-headed position even though, in the paragraph following that statement I write of the genuine exchange of revolutionary perspective that characterised the first stages of the relationship between American revolutionaries and their Leninist supporters and advocates within the world's first workers' government. My position, that early relations amongst communists in the United States and Bolsheviks in the Soviet Union and its Comintern were healthy and productive and differed dramatically from later Stalinist practices characterised by 'crude dictation' and 'unassailable directives', is hardly confirmation of Draper's ultimate claims that communism was first, last, and always a creation of Moscow. Yet Storch is able to reduce me to an appendage of Draper's 'forgone conclusion'.[4] From the other side of the historiographic impasse, John Earl Haynes, associated with what might now be called the 'Draper School', finds that my 'Rethinking' essay 'is directed at Theodore

---

4   Storch 2007, pp. 3, 232–3.

Draper', an interpretive choice with which he disagrees vehemently.[5] Once an opposition is ensconced in the historiography, creating a third way of seeing through the stalemate is obviously no easy task, especially when the interpretive work demands acknowledging what is both suggestive *and* limiting in both counter-posed positions.

No doubt this is complicated further by the extent to which the lumpish designation of Trotskyism, while capturing much in the way of alternative, is also bedevilled by differentiation. In the two reflections that close out this section on the historiography of the revolutionary left, I address the histories of two figures in the conflicted politics of Trotskyism. 'Harry Frankel' was the Socialist Workers Party pseudonym of Harry Braverman, a name well known to American labour historians because of the publication of his influential study, *Labor and Monopoly Capital: The Degradation of Work in the Twentieth Century* (1974), by the distinguished socialist press Monthly Review. Braverman was part of the emergence of Trotskyism in the United States, indicative of how Stalinism could be rejected by some of the best and the brightest gravitating to revolutionary politics. But he was also a reminder of how those schooled in the kinds of revolutionary refusals that allowed no truck with capitalism's enticements, Stalinist subterfuge or social-democratic blandishments could well prove contentious comrades. Perhaps no figure in the history of late-20th-century Trotskyism struggled more valiantly to keep the movement from fragmenting under the pressures of the kinds of internal conflicts which the history of Braverman, in and out of the Socialist Workers Party, illuminated than Ernest Mandel. He is addressed in this historiographic grouping through a review essay that takes as its point of departure Jan Willem Stutje's important biography, *Ernest Mandel: A Rebel's Dream* (2009).

---

5   Haynes 2003, p. 185.

CHAPTER 7

Rethinking the Historiography of United States Communism: Questioning American Radicalism*

We ask questions of radicalism in the United States. Many on the left and amongst historians researching and writing about its past are driven by high expectations and preconceived notions of what such radicalism should look like. Our queries reflect this: Why is there no socialism in America? Why are workers in the world's most advanced capitalist nation not 'class conscious'? Why has no 'third party' of labouring people emerged to challenge the established political formations of money, privilege and business power? Such interrogation is by no means altogether wrong-headed, although some would prefer to jettison it entirely. Yet these and other related questions continue to exercise considerable interest, and periodically spark debate and efforts to reformulate and redefine analytic agendas for the study of American labour radicals, their diversity, ideas and practical activities.[1] Socialism, syndicalism, anarchism and communism have been minority traditions in US life, just as they often are in other national cultures and political economies. The revolutionary left is, and always has been, a vanguard of minorities. But minorities often make history, if seldom in ways that prove to be exactly as they pleased.

Life in a minority is not, however, an isolated, or inevitably isolating, experience. In the late 19th and early 20th centuries the US gave rise to a significant left, rooted in what many felt was a transition from the Old World to a New Order. Populists, anarchists, Christian socialists, early feminists, bohemian intellectuals, trade unionists, immigrant Marxists, exiles from failed European revolutions, Wobblies, co-operators and countless other stripes of radical rubbed shoulders in metropolitan centres, in the towns of middle America and in frontier settings, all of which sustained varied institutional and cultural spaces in which the sociability and politics of the left were generated and

---

* 'Rethinking the Historiography of United States Communism', *American Communist History*, 2 (2003), 139–73.

1 Among many studies that might be cited: Sombart 1976, a reprint of the original 1906 German publication; Laslett and Lipset 1974; Wilentz 1984a, pp. 1–24; Foner 1984, pp. 57–80; Kirk 2000, pp. 1–26.

regenerated over time. It was a heady time for those who thought themselves revolutionaries, although it would not be without its dangers, most evident in the wave of repression that engulfed radicalism in the period from 1917 to 1921. Many on the US left emerged from the turmoil of these post-World War I years convinced that the newly established Soviet workers' state was a revolutionary breakthrough of unparalleled significance and that a Communist Party was precisely what was needed in America.[2]

Joseph Freeman, whose *An American Testament* (1936) was praised by Theodore Draper as 'one of the few Communist human documents worth preserving' and by Max Eastman as the 'best and most engaging book written by an American communist',[3] vividly recalls the developing radical politics of the US in the early 20th century. He captures a sense of its disruptive, destabilising impact on all aspects of life:

> Socialism was an aspect of the American scene long before the war, and I felt its impact in my daily experience. But it was so sharp a break with the prevailing order, that you had to adjust yourself to it at every point of your existence ... [Y]ou were caught in the conflict between the old world and the new, and felt you had to choose between them ... The American generation of which I am a member had neither the catastrophe of capitalist economy in this country, nor the rise of fascism in western Europe, nor the astounding successes of the Soviet Union to guide its choices. Its development was consequently confused and painful ... For we were compelled to be conscious of every step when we grappled with unprecedented problems raised by the war, the October Revolution, the American class struggle, the melancholy capitals of postwar Europe, the frank and free life of Greenwich Village, the rise of the Communist Party in this country, the critical relations between art and society, the transformation of love, marriage, and the family.

Writing between 1934 and 1936, Freeman, like most radicals who gravitated to the revolutionary left in the period associated with World War I and the Russian Revolution, came to regard the Communist Party of the United States (CP), for a time at least, as the place where the struggle for the new radical order was to be carried out to best effect: 'Every day brings a living testament to the nobility and

---

2 As an introduction only, see Weinstein 1969; Stansell 2000; Dawley 1994, pp. 139–294; Draper 1957.

3 Draper 1957, p. 129; Eastman 1964, p. 604.

heroism of the vast majority of men and women in [the] movement, whether they are fighting for liberty on the barricades of Barcelona, building socialism in the Soviet Union, distributing strike leaflets south of the Mason and Dixon line or repelling the encroachments of Japanese imperialism in China'. Freeman, an editor of the Communist magazine *New Masses* and a teacher at the CP Workers' School when he penned these words, wrote compellingly of the idealism that mobilised the revolutionary left in the 1920s and 1930s. He was drawn particularly to the inspiration of the Party ranks, 'selfless, incorruptible'. From them he learned, and for them and for himself, he worked: 'To abolish poverty, ignorance, war, the exploitation of class by class, the oppression of man by man'. Freeman saw in socialism 'the utmost imaginable freedom for the mass of humanity', and he lived for the realisation of this glorious end.[4]

Freeman's passionate Communist commitment was not to survive the 1930s Red Decade of economic depression and social upheaval, which had done so much to steel his anti-capitalist convictions and dedication to socialist humanity. His *American Testament* was insufficiently critical of Leon Trotsky, whom the American cultural radical had witnessed first-hand in one of the last Comintern debates of the 1920s. As a consequence, Freeman was, in his word, 'excommunicated' – Moscow demanded that he self-censor his own publication by barring mention or advertisement of it in *New Masses*, call off a promotional speaking tour and cancel a large order for the book placed by the Workers' Bookshop. That accomplished, the seemingly well-ensconced 'captain of cultural activities' of the Party sufficiently humbled, the Comintern then insisted that Freeman's CP affiliation be terminated. The ex-Communist's next novel, *Never Call Retreat* (1943), sounded the inspirational cry of on-going struggle with a predictable awkwardness, but Freeman's loud voice of radicalism was essentially quieted.[5]

Another American Communist, James P. Cannon, would be harder to sideline and impossible to silence. He had been drummed out of the CP a decade before Freeman was given his walking papers, expelled for embracing Trotsky's views late in 1928. Cannon never relinquished his attachment to the original Workers Party, later renamed the Workers (Communist) Party (and, a few years after, subsequent to Cannon's expulsion, the Communist Party USA). Like Freeman, Cannon expressed considerable regard for the 'thousands of courageous and devoted revolutionists willing to make sacrifices and take risks for the movement'. Long after he himself had broken with this party, Cannon saw

---

4   Freeman 1936, pp. vii–viii, x, 667–8.
5   Eastman 1964; Bloom 1992, pp. 71–110.

those won to its struggles through their sincere desire to create a better socialist world as victims, a radical generation motivated by the best of intentions but misguided by a leadership that he characterised as squandering and Stalinist. Reflecting on the labour upheavals of the 1930s from the disillusioning height of the Cold War, Cannon wrote in 1951:

> The chief victim of Stalinism in this country was the magnificent left-wing movement, which rose up on the yeast of the economic crisis in the early Thirties and eventually took form in the cio through a series of veritable labor uprisings. Such a movement, instinctively aimed against American capitalism, ... [was] ready for the most radical solutions. The Stalinists, who appeared to represent the Russian Revolution and the Soviet Union, almost automatically gained the dominating position in the movement ... The story of what happened to these young militants; what was done to them, how their faith was abused and their confidence betrayed by the cynical American agents of the Kremlin gang – that is just about the most tragic story in the long history of the American labor movement. The best young militants with independent minds, who wanted to think and learn and act consistently according to principle, were ruthlessly expelled. Others were cowed into silence and acquiescence, befuddled into the sadly mistaken belief that by all the lies and treachery they were somehow or other serving a good cause.[6]

---

6 Cannon 1972a, pp. 13–14; Cannon 1973c, pp. 294–7. On Cannon, see Cannon 1992; Barnes et al. 1976. Of leading figures in the Workers (Communist) Party in the United States in the 1920s, Cannon rivalled key figures C.E. Ruthenberg (who died in 1927), Jay Lovestone, and William Z. Foster. No other leaders were as significant. Note Klehr 1978, pp. 110–11, which presents tables that rank Party leaders with respect to their years served on the Central Committee and other committees. Because Cannon was only in the Party from 1921 to 1928, he does not rank among the top 24 leaders for the entire period 1921–61. But if Cannon's time in the Party is taken into consideration, his rank is first, with only J. Louis Engdahl and Jay Lovestone of comparable stature. Engdahl, however significant, was never an independent force within the Central Committee, owing his allegiance to the Ruthenberg-Lovestone faction, which also secured his editorship of the *Daily Worker* and later posts of significance. If the pre-1921 underground years could be accounted for in such a committee tabulation, it is likely the case that Ruthenberg and Cannon would rank very near the top. Draper had particularly high regard for Cannon's capacity to recall the details of Communist history in the 1920s, stating that his memory on events in the early history of the American revolutionary left was far superior to others he interviewed. See Draper 1973, pp. 9–12.

How radicals like Cannon and Freeman came to embrace Communism, and how that Communism repudiated so much of itself in the 1920s, are subjects worthy of reconsideration. Such a treatment of the origins of the American revolutionary left necessarily concerns itself with another question historians have often wrestled with: whether or not US Communism was a *genuine* expression of American radicalism.

In assessing the historiography of Communism in the United States with an eye to such questions,[7] I begin where many others have perhaps not wanted to go. The history of America's revolutionary left, in its origins and in the uneasy formative years of Communism's US birth, cannot be understood, I suggest, without attention to the ways in which it was transformed by Stalinism in the 1920s. Moreover, the varied historiographies that chart developments, accent particulars and lay interpretive stress on specific parts of the left experience in America are also understandable only if we begin to grapple openly with Stalinism's forceful historical presence. As the words and experiences of Cannon and Freeman would suggest, Stalinism matters in what happened to 20th-century American radicalism.[8]

---

7 Because of these questions, I focus selectively on the historiography of Communism; this essay does not purport to survey the field in its entirety. Its concern is largely with the original foundational studies of the 1920s by Theodore Draper, tangentially with the institutional/political school of 'traditionalist' liberal anti-Communism associated with Harvey E. Klehr and John Earl Haynes and, perhaps most decisively, with the New Left-inspired histories that commenced, in part, as a response to published Communist memoirs of the 1970s and 1980s. For these reasons I accent the significance of the 1920s, as a decade of Stalinisation, and address works that tend to concentrate on the 1930s and 1940s. This slights older, and useful, social-democratic accounts, including Oneal and Werner 1947 and Howe and Coser 1957. It also bypasses the eight non-Draper volumes in the Clinton Rossiter-edited 'Communism in American Life' series commissioned by the Fund for the Republic in the late 1950s, as well as earlier scholarly accounts, among them the sociological and survey-based studies Lasswell and Blumenstock 1939; Almond 1954. Important 'confessional' literature is also not considered, the prime example of which is undoubtedly Gitlow 1940, nor do I address early works of recollection from former Communists or those on the margins of the CP, such as Beal 1937. For one recent survey of the field, see Haynes 2000, pp. 76–115, which contains a statement on the Fund for the Republic books, pp. 77–80.

8 A useful documentary collection is A. Fried 1997.

Stalinism: What's in a Name?

As a short-hand term, 'Stalinism' is not so much a personalised denunciation as it is a designation of political defeat. The aspirations and expansive potential of revolutionary Communism were suffocated in bureaucratisation, compromise of political principle, abandonment of theoretical and programmatic consistency, a waning commitment to socialism and its spread throughout the world, and a narrowing of agendas to the most defensive and mundane. 'Stalinism' was, of course, guided in part by the subjective agenda of the individual Trotsky would come to conclude was capable of proclaiming, 'I am Society'. But Stalinism was also determined to some extent by objective historical conditions and developments detrimental to sustaining the revolutionary cause, much of which took place in situations once-removed from Stalin's direct influence. These included the revolutionary Soviet State's 'backwardness', with its history of czarist autocracy and the class dominance of the peasantry; World War I's immense drain on the resources of the Russian/Soviet social formation and the subsequent containment of the first workers' state by a hostile grouping of powerful capitalist nations, all of which continued to oppose what Lenin and the Bolsheviks stood for well after the end of hostilities in 1918; the crucible of civil war, in which the practice of governance in the world's first socialist state was inevitably hardened over the course of the 1917–21 years, as many Bolsheviks faced the necessity of institutionalising an apparatus of repression, centred in the Cheka, in order to preserve the revolution and its advances; the failure of the socialist revolution in Europe, on which the healthy continuity of the Russian Revolution depended, first in 1919 and then in 1923; and a series of misplayed hands at the table of Russian revolutionary politics, all of which consolidated Stalin's power, weakened and marginalised his potential opponents and, ultimately, culminated in the decimation of the Leninist party that had registered such gains in 1917 and the immediate post-Revolution years.[9]

The practical consequence of these inhibitions and steps backward inside and outside the Soviet Union was formidable. Within the degenerating revolutionary Soviet society, the ruthless elevation of Joseph Stalin produced an autocratic state eventually governed by terror. Stalin ordered the first Bolshevik shot in 1923, and between 1927 and 1940 he orchestrated the trial, exile or execution of virtually the entire revolutionary leadership. Beyond the boundaries of

---

9 The Trotsky quote is from Trotsky 1941, p. 421. For a succinct interpretive introduction to Stalinism's historical emergence and meaning, see Nove 1975.

'socialism in one country' a series of defeats and international misadventures, beginning with the routing of the Chinese Revolution in 1926 and reaching through the debacles of fascism's rise to power in Germany and the blood-letting of the Spanish Civil War in the 1930s, haunted the revolutionary communist conscience in decades that might well have witnessed pivotal political advances and radical successes.

This dismal record of opportunities wasted was eventually blunted with the Stalinist brokering of a reconfigured Europe in the aftermath of World War II, establishing a buffer zone of 'socialist' economies in Eastern and Central Europe as the price the capitalist world was willing to pay for the monumental losses the Soviets sustained in helping to 'liberate' Europe from Hitler's awful designs. But such Iron Curtain socialism was born deformed, as were the post-colonial regimes of national liberation, such as Cuba and Vietnam, which ended up taking both material aid and political inspiration from the Soviet Union.[10]

From possibly as early as 1926, then, and certainly from the late 1920s and 1930s on, the forces of the international left faced not only the resolute opposition of global capital and its considerable power, vested in nation-states and their militaries as well as the widening material and ideological reach of hegemonic capitalist markets and cultures, but also the constraining defeatism of leaderships, structures of power and political orientations committed, in their Stalinism, to anything but world revolution. Specific communist parties paid dearly in the process, as evidenced in Isaac Deutscher's and Pincus Minc's recollections of the sacrifice and destruction of the Polish Communist Party (KPP) which, in 1938, was 'dissolved' by Comintern dictate. The KPP, born of the Russian Revolution, was ultimately destroyed by its degeneration: its leaders' heads were delivered on a platter to fascist terror, its mass base squandered with cynical abandon.[11] This is not, of course, to say that varied struggles and campaigns conducted within Stalinised Communist parties, the Communist International and other venues where the disciplined apparatus of a Leninist vanguard exercised an impact, throughout Europe, Asia, Latin America and Africa, were without their significant, often heroic sacrifices and important victories.[12]

---

10   See, for instance, Löwy 1981.

11   Deutscher 1984, pp. 91–127; Minc 2002.

12   As an introduction only see the collection of essays in Deutscher 1984; Trotsky 1937; Trotsky 1941; Mandel 1968; Weissman 2001; Drachkovitch 1966, pp. 159–224; Fischer 1948; Claudin 1975; Carr 1982; Eley 2002, pp. 139–64, 249–60.

American Communism: Histories of Ambivalence and Accomplishment

In the US, from Harlem to southern sharecropping plots,[13] within the communities of arts and letters associated with writers' congresses and left-wing theatre troupes[14] and in the Abraham Lincoln Brigade mobilised to fight in the Spanish Civil War and through peace and anti-war movements,[15] as well as amongst housewives' organisations,[16] labour-defence bodies, industrial unions and unemployed protests,[17] Communists fought for much that was honourable and achieved not a little that was necessary and humane. If one realm of special oppression, women's subordination, has been regarded as 'the question seldom asked'[18] on the American Communist left, there is still no denying that women in the ranks of the revolutionary Party promoted progressive, feminist causes and struck important blows not only for female emancipation but for women's public involvement in political struggle.[19] It is striking how much US history in the 20th century that is associated with eradicating racism is inextricably entwined with the Communist Party, whatever its programmatic and

---

13 See, for instance, Naison 1983; Kelley 1990; Rosengarten 1974; Painter 1979.

14 Much is written on Communists and the arts; the original Fund for the Republic statement, Aaron 1959, was particularly strong. But note the recent extensive overview in Denning 1996. On African Americans and culture, see Kelley 1994, pp. 103–22; Horne 1993, pp. 199–237. Alan M. Wald, whose writing has consistently addressed issues of culture within a framework sensitive to race, class, and gender, offers an overview: Wald 1993, pp. 281–305. Other accounts include Bloom 1992; L. Schwartz 1980; L. Browder 1998.

15 The Abraham Lincoln Brigade, a Communist battalion of Americans fighting on the republican side during the Spanish Civil War, is the subject of much writing, including Landis 1967; J. Yates 1989; and Kelley 1994, pp. 123–58.

16 See, for instance, Gosse 1991, pp. 110–41; Dixler 1974, pp. 127–95.

17 Again, the writing that touches down on such mobilisations is extensive, but see, for examples, Keeran 1980; Levenstein 1981; Cochran 1977; Rosswurm 1992; Rosenzweig 1976, pp. 37–62; Carter 1971.

18 Baxandall 1993, pp. 141–62, raises a number of issues that are further addressed and extended in emphasis on 'the personal' in Brown and Faue 2000, pp. 9–45; Brown 1999, pp. 537–70; Dixler 1974. See, as well, Shaffer 1979, pp. 73–118.

19 In the case of US Communism consider Inman 1941. Early Communist feminists included Clara Zetkin (Germany), Alexandra Kollontai (Russia), and Dora Montefiore (Britain). For this international history of women and Communism, see E. Foner 1984; C. Porter 1980; Hunt 2001, pp. 29–50.

practical lapses.[20] Internationalism, too, was undoubtedly fostered by Communist parties and their members.[21]

But the histories of these 'just' accomplishments were paralleled by an early bureaucratisation, political retreat and ultimate reversal of revolutionary programmes that gradually, from the mid- to late 1920s, stifled Communist commitment in varied subordinations, leaving the gleam of a socially transformative idealism tarnished and souring the principles of socialism in the mouths of many of its most ardent advocates. This unease has been reproduced in the writing on American Communism. When we look to why this has indeed been the case, answers invariably converge on the important, if problematic, role of Stalinism, a historical and political process that has received a dearth of interpretive commentary in writing on the US left.[22]

The Tension-Ridden Communist Memoir

Communist memoirs, often written in years when Stalin's atrocities and the debasements of Soviet-style socialism were difficult not to acknowledge, are permeated with the tensions of this fundamental unease. 'We lived in the center of the world's first successful socialist revolution', wrote Peggy Dennis, adding that the complexities of that allegiance were 'pre-digested for us and reduced into Stalin's edict that the achievements were "to the glory of the Party" and "behind our difficulties are concealed our enemies"'. As Dennis noted, in this atmosphere it was 'difficult to understand' the 'unquestioning beliefs' that guided most Communists.[23]

---

20   For an early overview, see Record 1951. A major autobiography, Haywood 1978, conveys something of the sweep of Communist and African-American experience. Intellectual histories of merit include Cruse 1964 and Robinson 1983. A recent study of significance is Solomon 1998. On the relational significance of the Communist Party, black Americans, and the development of the United States, see Goldfield 1985, pp. 315–56, which places stress on the importance of Communist work among black Americans in the programmatically skewed 'Third Period'. For a documentary collection detailing these years, see P. Foner and Shapiro 1991.

21   See Postgate 1920; Lorwin 1929; Silverman 1999.

22   Possibly the one area where Stalinism is addressed most frontally is in the cultural realm, where the studies of literary radicalism undertaken by Alan M. Ward have persistently engaged with the meaning of Stalinism and anti-Stalinism. See, for instance, Wald 1978; 1983; 1987; 1992; 1994.

23   Dennis 1977, pp. 70–1.

Indeed, many accounts of life in the CPUSA convey an almost otherworldly defensiveness, evident in George Charney's 'explanation' of how, upon becoming a Communist, he ceased to exercise the critical capacities that had in fact brought him into the movement: '[I]t was not long after I joined the party that I came to accept each doctrine promulgated by the party as an "article of faith", never to be questioned. Somehow, somewhere, the element of faith extricated itself from its scientific embodiment to dominate our outlook and ultimately prove our undoing'.[24]

The black Bolshevik Harry Haywood perhaps exemplified the staying power of this problematic continuity of belief over actuality. In the 1970s he was still able to proclaim: 'Those today who use the term "Stalinist" as an epithet evade the real question: that is, were Stalin and the Central Committee correct? I believe history has proven that they were correct'.[25] Lacking unease, some clearly lacked perspective.

One of California's leading Communist women, Dorothy Healey, suggested that the rank and file often knew so little about 'theoretical' issues which related directly to Stalinisation because they were overwhelmed by activist commitments: '[T]he great majority of Communists, maybe 60 to 70 percent of the Party, never got around to reading much of Marx or Lenin. The Trotskyists were so good at theoretical debates because they had more time to read'.[26] No doubt there were Trotskyists who would challenge the notion that they had spare hours to pore over the fine print of Marxist doctrine because they spent less of their days and nights on picket lines, in demonstrations and building various mobilisations.

In striking contrast to Healey, Steve Nelson claims that as a young rank-and-file Communist in the 1920s, he followed Party polemics and theoretical discussions on 'socialism in one country' versus 'permanent revolution' zealously and was convinced that Stalin had the better case. Nelson's claims seem to have benefitted from hindsight's capacity to rationalise past behaviour. The actual record of debate and discussion amongst US Communists in the period from 1924 to 1928, and the availability of documents and substantive exchanges of views, especially concerning Trotskyist positions, is quite limited. Indeed, Nelson contradictorily asserts that he 'didn't really give the Trotskyist point of view serious consideration until [he] left the Party' in the aftermath of the

---

24   Charney 1968, p. 29.
25   Haywood 1978, p. 184. For another black Communist's views of 'never rais[ing] questions prematurely', see Painter 1979, especially p. 25.
26   Healey and Isserman 1990, p. 29.

1956 Khrushchev revelations and the Soviet repression of workers' uprisings in Poland and Hungary. It was then that he faced most acutely the confusions and unease that his commitment to the Communist cause engendered in the shock atmosphere of the mid- to late 1950s.[27]

Al Richmond, a mere high-school youth of 15 when he joined the Young Communist League in 1928, was 'bewildered and fascinated by the factional debate' of that time and confessed an essential 'unpreparedness for coping with theoretical concepts in dispute ... I succumbed to a common failing: attributing profundity to something simply because you cannot understand it'. Not knowing what the arguments were about, Richmond took the path of least resistance: siding with the majority. 'It is the easier way out', Richmond wrote, 'and you have the handy rationale of the democratic premise that the greater wisdom is more likely to reside in the greater number'.[28] Such thinking would, of course, have justified a politics of accommodation, if extended out of the CP and into wider circles of society. Recollections from the Third Period (1929–34) and Popular Front agitations of the 1930s and 1940s – such as those of John Gates, whose imprisonment under the Smith Act caused him to rethink his allegiance and leave the CP in 1956 – sometimes recall with specific pain the costs that were exacted amongst Communists who, if they had it to do all over again, would, they claim, refuse certain Party codes of political conduct in which dissidents on the revolutionary left who declined to bend the knee to Stalinist dictate were written out of the workers' movement.[29]

---

27   Nelson, Barrett, and Ruck 1981, pp. 48–9, 386–7.
28   Richmond 1973, pp. 71–2.
29   See, for instance, the comments of Herbert Benjamin, who occupied a prominent position in the Communist Party in Philadelphia and was an activist in the unemployed agitations of the 1930s, on the treatment of James Cannon in Herbert Benjamin, 'Outline of Unpublished Manuscript: A History of the Unemployed Movement and Its Struggles During the Great Depression', pp. 70–1, 107–12, 150–2, 213–14, deposited in Columbia Oral History Project, Columbia University, New York, NY. Both Dorothy Healey and John Gates recalled with shame the Communist Party's failure to come to the defence of Trotskyists attacked and imprisoned during the 1940s in the first Smith Act prosecutions. Gates would be jailed under the same act a few years later. See Healey and Isserman 1990, pp. 114–15; Gates 1958, p. 127.

Receiving the Oral Record: The New Left and the Ironic Attractions of History

Most of the Communist 'oral histories' that were published in the post-1956 years are thus documents of a certain political ambivalence or, more rarely, a blinkered commitment to positions long entrenched and equally long discredited.[30] They reflect the life course of a generation that came to political maturity in the late 1920s or 1930s and remained committed to anti-capitalist/pro-Communist ideals through the traumas of the 1950s and, often, beyond. Their audience was, at least in part, a later generation of scholars that emerged in the shadows of the New Left, for whom the Communist past was an often uneasy fit with commitments and sensibilities rife with ambivalence. On the one hand, many New Leftists had been either 'red-diaper babies', their family lives and childhood/adolescent years reflective of a close connection to US Communism, or influenced by figures with a past link to the Old (often non-CP) Left.[31]

On the other, the New Left consciously constructed itself as something of a mirror image of the CP. Uncomfortable with all bureaucracy, consciously hostile to the very notion of an all-authoritative 'vanguard' and unencumbered with much of the baggage associated with defending the Soviet Union, New Leftists schooled themselves in the movement atmosphere of anti-war, civil rights and early feminist agitations, separating their thought and action, in many ways, from the legacies of Lenin, Trotsky and Stalin, if not of Marx. This willed to the New Left-influenced historians of the 1970s a conflicted radicalism and, with the failure of the oppositional momentum of the 1960s to sustain itself, ensured that the scholarly rebirth of American Communism's assessment would be characterised not only by deep commitments and passions but by specific limitations.

An initial irony of this revival of interest in the CP amongst New Left-influenced historians was that the typical Communist memoir which began to

---

30 My own experience on working through an oral biography of a Communist suggests that only those who actually broke with the Communist Party over political differences were capable of articulating a forthright recollection of what happened historically. But this did not necessarily ensure that Stalinism's meaning would be addressed. See B. Palmer 1988a.

31 See Kaplan and Shapiro 1998; P. Buhle 1990; Isserman 1987; Gordon 1976, pp. 11–66. For another perspective on growing up Communist, see Kimmage 1996. It is critical to note that I am referring to the US New Left, a different phenomenon than the British New Left which preceded it and which had a much different relationship to the international Communist movement. See, for a brief introduction to the relevant political scene in Britain, Widgery 1976.

appear in the 1970s and 1980s was quickly championed as a 'distinctively American' voice of revolutionary authenticity.[32] Historians embedded in the context of the 1960s, one part of which was a heady search for an oppositional politics untainted with the problematic lapses of Stalinism, would, oddly enough, return to the experience of Stalinism 'in one country' as a wellspring for radicalism's American revival. That they were able to do so, it might be suggested, was precisely because the New Left in the US, for all its strengths, never wrestled adequately with issues that were central to the Communist milieu in the 1920s, when the ideology of Stalinism (its programmatic wheels greased by a powerful bureaucratic apparatus) triumphed over Trotsky's Left Opposition and its advocacy of 'permanent revolution'.[33]

One part of this avoidance of specific issues of theory and programmatic direction was historiographic. With the turn to a social history of rank-and-file experience characteristic of the intellectual climate of the 1970s,[34] questions of leadership and of ideas assumed, initially at least, an almost inconsequential status. New Left-influenced studies carved out appreciations of Communist history that highlighted discrete experiences and particular locales, and in so doing added immeasurably to the scholarship of the revolutionary left.[35] Secondary cadre, on whom could never be placed the blame of decision-making and the responsibility for the direction of politics, but who were the recipients of an understandable reverence due to their 'lives in the struggle', were often fêted, their remembrances of activist pasts especially attractive to New Left historians and writers drawn to those who had taken life's meaning to be defined by unyielding opposition to oppression.[36]

---

32   See the argument in Rosenzweig 1983, especially pp. 32–3.

33   Aside from the Rosenzweig article cited above, see, among other statements, Gerstle 1984, pp. 559–66; P. Buhle 1981, pp. 38–45; Walzer 1983, pp. 259–67; Isserman 1985, pp. 538–45. A historiographical exception is Goldfield 1985, pp. 315–56.

34   As Paul Berman and Paul Buhle have noted, the 1960s was arguably a decade whose radicalism was associated with social history, as the novel was linked to the bohemian radicalism of the 1910s or literary criticism associated with the proletarian currents of the 1930s. See Paul Berman, 'The World of the Radical Historian', *Village Voice*, 18 March 1981, cited in Buhle 1990, p. 2.

35   Naison 1983 is a particularly well-researched and significant book. Less successful is Lyons 1982.

36   This was certainly the tenor of Vivian Gornick's consciously personalised, popularising and uncritical account, premised on a series of oral histories, in Gornick 1977. More useful, and more understandable given its focus on individuals associated with Hollywood, is McGilligan and Buhle 1997.

As Geoff Eley has suggested with respect to this historiographic trend: 'The pull towards social history can sometimes diminish the significance of formal communist affiliations, leading in extreme cases (mainly in the literature of the CPUSA) to a history of communism with the Communism left out'.[37] When ideas were somewhat later taken seriously, as in Paul Buhle's creative account *Marxism in the United States: Remapping the History of the American Left* (1987), Communism's Comintern programme was seldom highlighted and the depiction of the formative years of the CP tilted noticeably towards the cultural and distanced itself from the political.[38] But paralleling this historiographic initiative was a politics that consciously strove to promote American Communism as an indigenous radicalism that grew in the social soil of the US during the 1930s and 1940s and influenced the wider political environment.

A Palatable Periodisation and Popular-Frontism

These were also times when Stalinism was most palatable to Americans who were either out of work, intent on supporting mass-production unionism or at war with a declared enemy of the Soviet Union, fascist Germany. 'Home-grown' Communists struggled to improve the lot of the American people, and were often in the forefront of democratic initiatives, opposing racism, favouring trade unionism and standing firm in the war effort.[39] As a consequence, outside of small contingents of the anti-Stalinist left[40] and placing aside the few years of the Hitler-Stalin pact (when state repression of Communists and vigilante-like popular hostility did indeed run high), the Communist Party had a relatively easy ride through the political culture of the late 1930s and early to mid-1940s.

In its American guise, Stalinism's agenda understated the need for socio-economic transformation. Whether this deflected the combative demands of workers is something of an open question, but there is no doubt that in 'making the political turn' to Popular-Frontism and Browder's equation of Communism with 20th-century Americanism, Stalinism within the US conditioned specific

---

37   Eley 1986, p. 92. See, as well, Samuel 1985, pp. 3–53; 1986, pp. 63–133; 1987, pp. 52–91.

38   Buhle 1991. Comparing Buhle to Macintyre 1980 is instructive because it poses a contrast between historiographies of ideas that are ordered by political as opposed to cultural concerns.

39   For a brief introduction, see the discussion in Lichtenstein 2001, pp. 33, 45–6, 77–8, and the strained case of the CP as a cutting edge of American freedom presented in Eric Foner's laudatory appraisal of the Popular Front in E. Foner 1999, pp. 210–18.

40   See Wald 1987, especially pp. 101–98; Kutulas 1995.

accommodations, especially in the years between 1941 and 1945. Browder would later recall with boastful pride that the CP in the later 1930s and 1940s

> moved out of its extreme left sectarianism ... toward the broadest united front tactics of reformism for strictly limited immediate gains. It delegated its revolutionary socialist goals to the ritual of the chapel and Sundays on the pattern followed by the Christian Church. On weekdays it became the most single-minded practical reformist party that America ever produced.

In Browder's admittedly self-serving judgment, the Communist Party of this period 'buttressed the Roosevelt New Deal and postponed revolutionary prospects immediately'. Max Shachtman agreed: 'The CP announced that socialism was not at all the goal, or even the issue in American politics; indeed, that the demand for socialism stood in the way of real progress'. The Party 'became at first a tacit and then an open supporter of the Democratic party and the New Deal as the arena for a new political alignment for the country'.

One side of this was reformist commitment to a 'progressive' bourgeois politics in which the rise of industrial unionism and the emergence of the welfare state loomed large domestically, and this accent figures prominently in the classical Popular Front history of the later 1930s. But this cannot be divorced from the Stalinised Comintern's appreciation, given the disastrous consequences of Third Period sectarianism in making Hitler's rise to power in Germany much easier, that national domestic 'fronts' cultivating close ties with bourgeois democratic governments in the West would garner the Soviet state much-needed support in its battle to beat back fascism.

This dawned on Stalin and other Comintern leaders strikingly in the post-1941 years, necessity being something of a mother of 'programmatic' invention, the sordid non-aggression alliance of Russia and Germany implemented in 1939 proving predictably short-lived. Domestic politics pursued by various national Communist sections, including that of the United States, were thus cut from the same cloth as Communist International policies. Indeed, the pattern had been set in the 'socialist fatherland' at the Seventh Congress of the Communist International (1935) in Moscow, which codified the new People's Front policy that all Communist Parties functioning under its leadership take as their guiding slogan the need to wage 'the fight for peace and for the defence of the USSR'.

This broad approach to unity aligned class forces traditionally understood to be irreconcilable, even to the point of positing umbrella-like *national* coalitions under which class struggle was internationally subsumed in the interests of turning back the fascist threat to the Communist fatherland:

The concentration of forces against the chief instigators of war at any given moment (at the present time Fascist Germany ...) constitutes *the most important* tactical task of the Communist parties ... [T]he mutual relations between the Soviet Union and the capitalist countries have *entered a new phase* ... [making necessary] cooperation in the cause of the preservation of peace with the small states to whom war represents a special danger, as well as with *those governments which at the present moment are interested in the preservation of peace.*[41]

Whether the Popular Front was conceived in Moscow, Paris, or some other metropolitan centre is far less significant than that it would never have been implemented had it not suited to a tee the needs of the political programme of 'socialism in one country'. Such a politics garnered something akin to mass support in America in the early to mid-1940s precisely because it had so little revolutionary content and meshed well with the mainstream needs of US foreign and domestic policy.[42] It could even justify the repression of other revolutionary leftists, for whom capitalist jail sentences were rationalised if such dissidents were judged insufficiently committed to the 'patriotic cause'. Thus Earl Browder, the leading US Communist of the early to mid-1940s and a figure not without a high profile in international circles of the left, penned a 24-page typescript, 'The Fifth Column Role of the Trotskyites in the United States', which would be used in the prosecution of James P. Cannon and other Minneapolis-based members of the Socialist Workers Party (SWP) under the Smith Act (a 1941 conviction was upheld in a 1943 appeal). The Communist *Daily Worker* castigated Cannon and the SWP as little better than 'the Nazis who camouflage their Party under the false name, National Socialist Workers Party'.[43]

Maurice Isserman's *Which Side Were You On? The American Communist Party during the Second World War* (1982) is perhaps the single text that captures best this political trajectory, attempting to revive somewhat the fortunes of that

41   The above paragraphs draw on quotes from E. Browder 1938; 1967, pp. 237, 246, quoted in part in Le Blanc n.d.; Shachtman 1967, p. 33; Claudin 1975, pp. 182–7. Eley 2002, pp. 261–98, presents an overview of developments in Europe in the 1930s and 1940s.

42   Consider, for instance, Eric Hobsbawm's account of the Popular Front and, especially, his admiration for Franklin D. Roosevelt in Hobsbawm 2002, pp. 322–3, 388, as well as the extraordinarily perceptive review by Perry Anderson, 'The Age of EJH', *London Review of Books*, 3 October 2002.

43   Jaffe 1975, pp. 50–2.

champion of acclimatising United States national identity and the politics of Communism, Earl Browder. Here was a figure who popularised Jefferson rather than Lenin, a leader on the left whose fortunes rose and fell with the Popular Front and American involvement in World War II. But in resurrecting Browder and the Popular Front, Isserman rationalises subduing the revolutionary content of US Communism, precisely because that had been Browder's role during the 1930s and 1940s. Stalinism had some necessity to don small fig leaves of revolutionary intent, the better to keep alive the illusion that it retained a commitment to world revolution. This meant that, in the aftermath of World War II, Browder was quickly displaced to the ranks of disillusioned ex-Communists and crank commentators on political economy.[44] So, too, would capitalism move on to more aggressive ground in its crystallising Cold War opposition to a Communism that was now constructed not as a wartime ally but as a demonic evil intent on conquering the 'free world'.

The political accommodations evident in Isserman's attraction to Browder and the Communist experience in wartime are at work as well in Michael Denning's exhaustive accounting of the 'cultural front'. In this reading, the Popular Front, a programmatic dictate/direction of the Communist International, is reconfigured as a left-progressive 'culturalism'. Denning sees the Popular Front as vastly more significant than a Comintern policy, baptising it with the sanctified Gramscian nomenclature of a 'historic bloc', a social movement composed of non-Communist socialists and independent leftists working with CP members, 'a broad and tenuous left-wing alliance of fractions of the subaltern classes' that encompassed Frank Sinatra and Louis Armstrong as well as Paul Robeson. '[T]he rank-and-file of the Popular Front were the fellow travelers, the large periphery', asserts Denning, and 'the periphery was in many cases the center, the "fellow travelers" *were* the Popular Front'. Eschewing what he regards as an antiquated fixation on *the* Party, Denning focusses not on politics but on prose and poetry, visual and theatrical productions and varied genres. He offers an encyclopaedic view of 'progressive' culture in the 1930s and 1940s, sweeping across ballads and cartoons, ghetto pastorals and jazz. As a project of cultural recovery Denning's work is a *tour de force*, albeit one lacking in some necessary discrimination. But as an analytic contribution to the history of the left, *The Cultural Front* is conceptually flawed in its refusal to recognise that Stalinism did indeed matter, not only in the gestation of the Popular Front but through its cultural manifestations as well.

---

44   Isserman 1982; Jaffe 1975; Starobin 1972. See also Ottanelli 1991; Ryan 1997.

Denning inevitably assimilates and congeals when there is a need to separate with discernment. C.L.R. James, in the 1938 publication *The Black Jacobins*, cannot easily be moulded to the same politics or aesthetics as Herbert Aptheker's *American Negro Slave Revolts*. Nor can the art and mobilising commitment of the International Labor Defense (ILD) organisation's work on the campaign to free Sacco and Vanzetti from 1925 to 1927 be discussed in the same way as that body's meaning in the defence of the Scottsboro Boys in the early 1930s. If James accounts for the ways in which the struggle for emancipation – 'national and racial' – intersected with a politics of the world-historic 1790s transformations that linked revolutions in France and Haiti, Aptheker's empirical accounting of slave uprisings, for all its strengths, makes few such connections.[45] And while ILD work in the mid-1920s was premised on genuine commitment to united-front struggles in which all segments of the left could march under their separate understandings of what constituted oppositional politics, the better to strike together on single-issue campaigns in which the freedom of political prisoners was at stake, by the early 1930s this kind of non-sectarian activity was all too rare, and seldom was it initiated by the CP.

The most famous ILD work in the early 1930s, associated with a relatively successful defence campaign geared to save nine African-American Alabama youths from being railroaded to the electric chair on groundless charges of raping two white women, is highly complicated. An ultra-left swing in Comintern policy in the Third Period was paralleled in the CPUSA's commitment to the fight for racial equality, including its embrace of the nationalist 'Black Belt Nation' thesis. This posited the right of national self-determination for American blacks in a specific cotton-producing region of the Deep South, a programmatic departure from both a Marxist materialist analysis of social relations in the US and a politics of class struggle that would have bound black and white labour together as a leading force in the creation of a proletarian state.[46]

Yet, there is no denying the unflinching nature of the CP's anti-racist work in the early 1930s; its characteristic Third Period sectarianism and willingness to espouse ultra-left positions were, ironically, a critical ladder on which could

---

45 Consider the discussion in Genovese 1979.

46 The following paragraphs on Scottsboro, the ILD, and the Communist Party draw on the brief discussions in Carter 1969, pp. 64–9, 251, 330–1; Kelley 1990, pp. 78–91, with the entire book containing commentary on the wider struggles of the CP and African Americans in Alabama; Naison 1983; and for a sensitive account balancing Third Period problems and possibilities vis-à-vis work with African Americans, Goldfield 1985, especially pp. 328–30. For a useful commentary on Kelley's important work see Wald 1994, pp. 171–7. A recent state study of the Third Period is Cherny 2002, pp. 5–42.

be scaffolded an audacious and genuinely revolutionary ascent into mass activity amongst American blacks. This registered in significant gains in organising Southern workers, particularly sharecroppers, whose unionisation was a potential lever in prying apart the tight grip exercised by racism, debt peonage and the open shop throughout the American South. So few were alternative anti-racist voices in the South, and so timid (and at times rabidly anti-Communist) were organisations such as the National Association for the Advancement of Colored People (NAACP), that the CP stepped very much into a void in its open espousal of racial equality and aggressive defence of blacks victimised by racist courts. As the case of the Scottsboro Boys showed clearly, rape charges were a tried-and-true method of publicly showcasing white power, the inviolable sanctity of a defence of white womanhood assailed by African-American 'animal sensuality' being the standard by which ultimate race rule was often paraded before the public and blacks terrorised into submission.

In the case of the ILD defence of the Scottsboro defendants, then, it is ultimately impossible to separate the extent to which the militancy of the CP raised the voice of African-American protest in the South and won over black support from the extent to which its ultra-left sectarianism isolated Communists and possibly kept the movement to free victims such as the Scottsboro Boys shackled to an unnecessarily rigid and inflexible agenda. Certainly the CP adopted a sectarian stand towards the NAACP, leading one liberal to ask how it was possible to build a common struggle to free victimised African Americans when Communists were quick to castigate those not in their ranks as guilty of '"treason", alliance with the Ku Klux Klan, "lyncher boss" tactics and anything else they see fit'. Communists so dominated events like the 1933 'March on Washington', spearheaded by *Amsterdam News* publisher, William Davis (who found himself quickly shunted to the side-lines by the ILD machine), that some African-American activists thought the Party was 'polishing up the electric chair' for the Scottsboro Boys, so blatant were the calls to link the defence mobilisation to the overall programme of the Communist Party.

The ILD responded with a blanket condemnation of all segments of the 'traitorous middle class', from Harlem ministers to the Socialist Party, accusing a wide array of individuals, black newspapers and political organisations of everything from 'Hitlerism to petty larceny'. Nevertheless, that said, there is no denying the important and militantly uncompromising steps forward the ILD took in the early 1930s, evidence of which is presented tellingly in Robin D.G. Kelley's stimulating study of Alabama Communists and Mark Naison's discussion of developments in Harlem. Yet it must also be remembered what happened when the Comintern 'line' shifted in mid-decade: organised black sharecroppers found their unions liquidated by the CP in 1936, and there were troubling ramifications within the ILD as well. With the proclamation of the Popular Front, the ILD lurched from its ultra-left sectarian stand to an abstentionist capitulation, willing to hand the Scottsboro mobilisation over to any and all comers. Now welcoming formerly designated 'social fascists' with open arms, indeed withdrawing deeper and deeper into a background surprisingly devoid of left politics so that others could lead, the Communists of the ILD abandoned any pretence of an independent Communist defence built through a united front with all others committed to freedom for such victims of racist repression. Predictably, having faced the contemptuous political assaults of CPers for a number of years, many in the defence milieu were having none of it. As a consequence, much invaluable Communist work with black Americans was discarded, as years of paced inactivity left the activism of the early 1930s little more than a distant memory. Whatever the difficulties Communists working in the ILD confronted in the 1920s, nothing approaching this twisted political experience of the 1930s took place. To lump such dissimilar developments on the left together is possible only *if* the powerful politic of Stalinisation is ignored.[47]

At the Point of Embattled Historiographic Production: The Meanings of Theodore Draper

A further irony in the historiography of American Communism is that the New Left historians were, in their original engagement with memoir and their further development of specific slices of CP history, almost always bumping up against the ghost of other memoir and scholarship. But that bumping would be of a particular kind. The central figure was Theodore Draper, who joined the Communist student movement in the 1930s but left this milieu after he thought through the full implications of the 1939 Hitler-Stalin pact. Thereafter, as with many ex-Communists who witnessed the revolutionary left as a 'God that failed',[48] Draper experienced something of a political transformation. His anti-Communism, however, was 'liberal' rather than 'reactionary', let alone 'neoconservative'. Over the course of the 1960s through the 1980s, Draper remained critical of much of US foreign policy in ways that differentiated him from the likes of Norman Podhoretz, Midge Decter, and Sidney Hook.

---

47   Denning 1996, especially pp. 4–13.
48   See Crossman 1949; Deutscher 1984, pp. 49–59.

Draper's obvious strengths as a historian were that he knew the CP well and had an eye for detail as well as a keen sense of archival preservation, gathering sources diligently and compiling extensive dossiers of communications and interviews with as many of the major figures in the formative years of US Communism as would engage with him. The former Communist eventually produced two impressive volumes, researched and written over the course of the mid- to late 1950s, that addressed the founding years of US Communism in the 1920s. They are distinguished by their careful scholarship as well as their relentless interpretive insistence that American Communism, like all post-1921 Communist experience, was a 'made in Moscow' affair.[49]

Draper proved a convenient target for the 'new' histories of US Communism that emerged in the 1980s. His perspective flew directly in the faces of those who placed the accent on social histories of rank-and-file particularity, emphasised the indigenous roots and Americanised character of Communism or asserted some kind of blend of international influence and national experience.[50] Few were the book prefaces or historiographic articles in the New Left revival of American Communism's significance that did not dissent from Draper's characterisations of the CP and its meaning. That Draper refused to lie down and politically die and that he had, by the 1980s, access to the pages of some rather significant literary venues, such as the liberal-establishment *New York Review of Books*, ensured that a debate over the interpretation of American Communism unfolded with vehemence.[51]

---

49   Draper 1957; 1960.

50   Draper's equivalent in Great Britain, perhaps, would be Pelling 1958. Recent revisionist historiography on the British CP rejects Pelling's stress on the Party's subordination to Moscow and argues, albeit not from a social history/rank-and-file perspective, that the British Party was a master of its own fate. For an example of this scholarship see Thorpe 2000, and for a critical response see McIlroy and Campbell 2002b, pp. 147–87; McIlroy and Campbell 2002a, pp. 535–69.

51   See, for example, Isserman 1982, pp. vii–viii; Isserman 1985; Rosenzweig 1983, pp. 32–3; Gerstle 1984, pp. 559–66; Walzer 1983, pp. 259–67. Draper responded to the New Left-influenced histories in a two-part essay originally published in the *New York Review of Books* and later consolidated as an afterword to the 1986 re-publication of his *American Communism and Soviet Russia* (Draper 1986, pp. 445–82). See Theodore Draper, 'American Communism Revisited', *New York Review of Books*, 9 May 1985; 'Popular Front Revisited', *New York Review of Books*, 30 May 1985. Subsequent issues of the *NYRB* (15 August 1985 and 26 September 1985) contained a series of letter exchanges that pitted Draper against almost all of the New Left-influenced combatants. Note as well Sean Wilentz, 'Red Herrings Revisited: Theodore Draper Blows His Cool', *Voice Literary Supplement*, June 1986. A

Draper rapidly became the key figure in a school of Communist studies labelled 'political' or 'institutional', a pioneer who inspired advocates in a revived 1970s 'traditionalist' anti-Communist cohort of writers headed by Harvey Klehr and John Earl Haynes.[52] Klehr and Haynes were as out of favour with the New Left-influenced historians as Draper was, but, like their detractors, they usually took as their subject discrete periods or aspects of Communist studies that post-dated Draper's attentiveness to the origins of US Bolshevism. When, in a 1992 overview jointly authored by Klehr and Haynes, *The American Communist Movement: Storming Heaven Itself*, the duo ranged broadly (if rather brusquely) over 70 years of Communist history, Draper utilised the back cover of the book to declare that it would tell readers 'as much as we are likely to know or care to know' about the tortured development of the CP.

Haynes, in particular, continued the useful bibliographic initiatives that flowed from the original Fund for the Republic-financed 'Communist problem' series, edited by Clinton Rossiter, that spawned Draper's volumes.[53] In the 1990s aftermath of the Cold War, Klehr, Haynes and others found further ammunition for their cause in the opening of the Soviet archives, which proved a boon for books on spies and the 'secret world' of that age-old shibboleth, 'Moscow gold', or the Comintern's financing of revolutionary activity, all of which merely confirmed the notion of Soviet 'dominance'.[54]

As the New Left waned and the political climate turned decisively to the right in the 1980s and 1990s, some 1960s scholars shifted sides and lined up more directly with the growing ranks of academic anti-Communism. Early bail-outs included Ronald Radosh, whose growing conviction of the guilt of the Rosenbergs moved him directly into the anti-Communism of the Klehr-Haynes camp.[55] More subtle, because they refused somewhat the binary oppositions and cloistered positionings of blunt Communist/anti-Communist designations, were the responses of New Left-inspired historians such as Maurice Isserman and Sean Wilentz, who were now far more willing to entertain the prospect that not all in the anti-Communist tradition was to be written out

further instalment appeared in Theodore Draper, 'The Life of the Party', *New York Review of Books*, 13 January 1994.

52   Among their earlier writings see Klehr 1978; 1984; Klehr and Haynes 1992; Haynes 1984.
53   Fund for the Republic, Inc. 1955; Haynes 1987.
54   See especially Klehr and Radosh 1996; Haynes 1996; Klehr, Haynes, and Firsov 1995; Klehr, Haynes, and Anderson 1998; Klehr and Haynes 1999; Ryan 2002, pp. 125–42. Of course the 'spy' phenomenon cut both ways. See, for instance, Leab 2000.
55   See Radosh and Milton 1984.

of a left-liberal coalition that increasingly wanted less and less to do with the belated discoveries of Stalinism's tainted past.[56]

As much as the Cold War was at least militarily over, it thus continued amongst historians of American communism, where attachments to and repudiations of the Old Left remained strong as the 20th century closed. But the war had been de-escalated to a skirmish. Most commentators on the Communist past, whether they aligned themselves with the Communists (in part) or against them (in whole), had been drawn closer together by contemporary political events. Few New Leftists were as staunch in their willingness to embrace US Communism in the 1990s as they had been in the 1970s, while the once-beleaguered 'traditionalists', following in Draper's footsteps but glossing over the 1920s period which their mentor had cultivated so closely, seemed buoyed by new evidence and a reconfigured political climate in which Communism's reduction to an anachronism allowed longer-standing hostilities to the revolutionary project an increasingly free rein.[57]

At issue was a deep historiographic irony in which Draper and the original New Left-inspired historians (now fragmenting into varied positions) shared a certain reverse reciprocity vis-à-vis their understandings of Stalinism. For the American New Left, Stalinism was, for the most part, the association of Communism and Comintern domination of American radicalism that their histories of locale, particularity, secondary cadre and Browderesque Popular-Frontism were at pains to deny. As such, these New Left historians engaged with Stalinism, ironically, by not engaging with it: they simply reversed Draper's construction of 'Communism = Moscow domination' by declaring that 'American Communism = genuine, native-born radicalism'. If they were able to recognise, as some indeed did abstractly, that the Communist Party of the United States was inevitably a blend of national and international developments, they looked incompletely at Comintern influences and, perhaps most importantly, they skipped almost entirely over the actual period of Stalinism's development by largely ignoring the 1920s and concentrating their research on the 1930s and 1940s of the Popular Front and World War II.[58] Its gaze narrowly national, the

56   Maurice Isserman, 'Notes from the Underground', *Nation*, 12 June 1995; 'Guess What – They Really Were Spies', *Foreword*, 29 January 1999; 'They Led Two Lives', *New York Times Book Review*, 9 May 1999; Sean Wilentz, 'Seeing Red', *New York Times Book Review*, 21 January 1996.

57   Note the discussion in Haynes 2000, pp. 76–115.

58   Ottanelli 1991 seems to fit this pattern. It stresses (pp. 3–4) the need to balance rank-and-file-oriented histories of US Communism with appreciation of Comintern influences, crediting Draper with some insights and acknowledging the importance of social-history

American New Left largely averted its eyes from the show trials, repression and terror of Stalin's USSR in the same period that it saw Communism mobilise the masses in a democratic US.[59] This ensured that the New Left in the US missed not only the meaning of Stalinism but the kernel of substantive research and a misnamed, bluntly formulated 'truth' that lay at the heart of Draper's problematic histories.[60]

The Three Drapers

This is evident in Draper's *development*, which few New Left-influenced social historians and none of Draper's so-called institutional followers address. In the

---

findings. But the resulting book is very much premised on avoiding the significance of Stalinism, and this is possible because Ottanelli misunderstands developments of the 1920s. In spite of characterising the decade according to a periodisation drawn from James P. Cannon's understandings of the these years (outlined in Cannon 1973a, pp. 16–19), Ottanelli misses Cannon's grasp of the relationship of factionalism and Stalinisation within the linked histories of the Communist International and the US Party. Ottanelli thus skims the surface of the 1920s and claims, 'By 1930 the factionalism that had caused havoc in the Party throughout most of its short existence had ended. The Party was united around a new leadership which was to head it for the next fifteen years ... The new decade presented Communists with new challenges and opportunities which, having put factional strife behind them, they felt ready to seize' (pp. 9, 15–16). Klehr 1978, p. 89, captures the significance of the end of factionalism more correctly and succinctly: 'The Stalinisation of the CPUSA was complete, and organized opposition to the party leadership ceased'.

59   As an introduction only, see Weissman 2001; Phelps 1997, especially pp. 140–233; Wald 1987, pp. 128–63; 1978, pp. 61–75; Preliminary Commission of Inquiry into the Charges Made Against Trotsky in the Moscow Trials 1937; Preliminary Commission of Inquiry into the Charges Made Against Trotsky in the Moscow Trials 1938; Glotzer 1989, pp. 235–81.

60   Perhaps the clearest example of this emerges in a text that, because of its focus on McCarthyism and the 1950s, falls largely outside of my discussion of mainstream Communist historiography, with its emphasis on the 1930s and 1940s. Schrecker 1998 contains a justifiable attack on the McCarthyite witch-hunt that nevertheless manages to evade discussing Stalinism by congealing *all* elements of the highly differentiated anti-Stalinist left and assimilating them to a generalised 'intelligence service' for McCarthyism's repressive anti-Communist network. That elements of what had been an anti-Stalinist left in the 1930s moved decidedly to the right (Lovestone is perhaps the best example) and by the 1950s had made common cause with 'official anti-Communism', including the CIA and the State Department, is undeniable. But to claim that *all* on the anti-Stalinist left had such a trajectory is intellectually and political irresponsible. See Schrecker 1998, pp. xii, 75–6, 81, and the criticism of Schrecker in Jacobson 2000. Note, for the Lovestoneite 'right opposition', R. Alexander 1981; T. Morgan 1999.

interpretive canon of Communist historiography, *the* central strand of which can be dated from Draper's foundational contribution to the Fund for the Republic studies of the 1950s, there are in actuality three historically situated Drapers. Following his break from the politics of the organised left, Draper, for all his anti-Communism, shifted gears historiographically, working through his two volumes in the mid- to late 1950s, seemingly in ways that ground down some of his original sensibilities, a process that became louder with his response to New Left history and commentary on Communist memoirs in the 1980s and 1990s.

First was the historian's Draper, a commentator who, whatever his anti-Communism tilt, could be counted on to scrutinise and present evidence. Draper's first volume, *The Roots of American Communism* (1957), commenced with statements of analytic direction that many New Left-influenced historians (not to mention others) could well have, or should have, accepted. Draper concluded his introduction to this initial study of the origins of the American revolutionary left with the improbable (in hindsight), if unchallengeably balanced, claim that '[e]ven in the days of Lenin,' the period dealt with in this book, 'Communism was not merely what happened in Russia; it was just as much what was happening in the United States'. He ended his account of the early 1920s grappling with the seed of a degeneration he could not name – Stalinism: 'For Moscow in 1923 was just entering on a period of fierce and ugly fratricidal struggle to determine the succession to Lenin's leadership in Russia. This struggle poisoned the life of the Comintern and seeped into the bloodstream of every Communist party in the world'. Precisely because Draper's anti-Communism was, at the time of his writing *The Roots of American Communism*, already sufficiently entrenched, the ex-Communist could not address the possibility that Communism per se was not the original problem in this poison, but that the poison was a transformation of the Soviet revolutionary process over the course of the 1920s, a Stalinisation that reversed the very meaning of revolution not only in Russia but around the world. Unable to accept that a Stalinism he could neither conceptualise as distinct from Leninist Communism nor address substantively on such terms of differentiation was *not* simply a more universal politics of timeless 'Moscow domination', Draper saw inevitability where historical contingency should have appeared.

This was the second Draper, the historian blinkered by an ideological shortsightedness that incapacitated him. He read the contests of 1923, when Comintern bureaucratisation and Stalinist machination were in their nascent beginnings, in an exaggerated way, and he projected them both backward in time and forward into the mid- to late 1920s, a period he was embarking on reconstructing in what would later appear as *American Communism and Soviet Russia*

(1960). The result was a distortingly dismissive, almost biologically determinative understanding of revolutionary internationalism as pure and simple Communist dictation:

> The first change of line was every other change of line in embryo. A rhythmic rotation from Communist sectarianism to Americanized opportunism was set in motion at the outset and has been going on ever since. The periodic rediscovery of 'Americanization' by the American Communists has only superficially represented a more independent policy; it has been in reality merely another type of American response to a Russian stimulus. A Russian initiative has always effectively begun and ended it.

Draper's ideological antagonism to Communism thus overwhelmed his scholarly insights. *The Roots of American Communism* ended on a note of premature judgment that would nevertheless capture a part of the future trajectory of the Comintern's relations with US Communism:

> Something crucially important did happen to this movement in its infancy. It was transformed from a new expression of American radicalism to the American appendage of a Russian revolutionary power. Nothing else so important ever happened to it again.

Draper might well have reread the first two sentences of his book: 'It is possible to say many true things about the American Communist movement and yet not the whole truth. It is possible to be right about a part and yet wrong about the whole'. A judicious reading of *The Roots of American Communism* would suggest that Draper was in fact more right than wrong and that he had many true things to say about the uneasy birth of American Communism, but that, ultimately, he succumbed to his own ideological blind spots and proved incapable of seeing the interpretive possibilities that an analysis of Stalinisation would have provided, opting instead for an overly deterministic assertion of Communism's inevitable reduction to Russian domination of the forces of world revolution, the American revolutionary left amongst them. The first and second Drapers thus struggled with one another in the publications of these two original Fund for the Republic volumes.[61]

The second Draper would of course win out. Stalin figured barely at all in *The Roots of American Communism*, understandably so given his less-than-central

---

61   The above paragraphs quote from Draper 1957, pp. 3, 10, 394–5.

role in Russian revolutionary developments in the years 1917 to 1922, which formed the core of Draper's study. But in Draper's sequel, *American Communism and Soviet Russia*, it was inevitable that Lenin's successor would enter more prominently onto the stage of Comintern politics and their meaning for the US revolutionary left. Yet because Draper had concluded that Moscow's domination of American and other Communist parties was an inherent feature of the Communist International, there proved no great need to analyse the nature of Stalinism, which, as a term used in this second of Draper's volumes, is more of a description of the wielding of Communist power than an analytic lever used to pry open an interpretation of revolutionary degeneration.

Moreover, in *American Communism and Soviet Russia*, Draper tends increasingly towards a reductionist view of US Communism, highlighting factionalism in a disembodied way and understating the extent to which such factional struggle involved critical questions of programmatic direction, some of which related directly to mass struggles in the United States and all of which figured in whether or not American Communism would reach out to a wider constituency. For Draper, the meaning of American Communism was now settled, decisively and forever: '[N]othing and no one could alter the fact that the American Communist Party had become an instrument of the Russian Communist Party ... American Communism would continue above all to serve the interests of Soviet Russia'. This was not so much a product of Stalinist degeneration for Draper as it was a political *essence*:

> Whatever has changed from time to time, one thing has never changed: the relation of American Communism to Soviet Russia. This relation has expressed itself in different ways, sometimes glaring and strident, sometimes masked and muted. But it has always been the determining factor, the essential element.[62]

It was precisely for this reason, Draper's predetermined judgment that Communism was an organically flawed project destined to reproduce time and time again a subordination of American to Russian interests, that some Communists who lived through the struggles of the 1920s rejected Draper's account. They recognised its strengths, but insisted that its weakness was a failure to grasp that there was more to US Communism's uneasy formative years than Draper's 'cocksure interpretations and summary judgments' implied. Even ex-Communists with a profound – and rightward-leaning – aversion to Stalin-

62   Draper 1960, pp. 5, 440.

ism, prone to accept implicitly Draper's interpretive stamping of Comintern-American relations with a 'Made in Moscow' finality, recalled the early to mid-1920s differently.

Bertram Wolfe, for instance, suggested that prior to 1926, young US Communists, though inspired by the success of Lenin's Bolsheviks, had 'no thought of becoming a mere adjunct and agency of the Russian Communist Party'. Instructions from Moscow were never perceived as cast in authoritarian stone, but as 'helpful suggestions, often exciting ones, and as successful examples to imitate, after adapting them to American conditions'. Improvising from day to day, Wolfe insisted, was the way in which the revolutionary left in the US worked. 'Ours was an interesting game', Wolfe claimed; quoting Draper himself, he posited that the 'rules had not yet been invented'. The Workers (Communist) Party that Wolfe and others were building was thus being shaped according to the will and commitment of American revolutionaries, albeit often in ways that struggled to 'overcome those who wished to shape it according to their European traditions and loyalties', many of whom, of course, were displaced, emigrant Marxists who found themselves uncomfortably living in the present United States, when their thoughts and perspectives were rooted in an 'alien' past. 'It was still a time when nothing had taken permanent shape in our movement', Wolfe argued.

Jay Lovestone echoed such views in his insistence that the Russian revolutionary leaders treated early American Communists 'as equals, with equal respect ... They were big men, and because they were big men they did not act in little or small ways'. If Russian influence was 'decisive' and veneration of the Comintern leaders undeniable, Lovestone was adamant that Lenin, Zinoviev, Trotsky and Radek never advocated or nurtured this. When Max Eastman later questioned Trotsky brusquely about the Comintern's inclination to offer directives to American revolutionaries rather than treating 'potential leaders of the world revolution' as independent thinkers, Trotsky's somewhat nonchalant response undoubtedly reflected his recognition that, as Zinoviev's bureaucratism gave way to Stalinisation and US Communist leaders sidestepped issues raised by the early Left Opposition, the question of national autonomy cut two ways: 'In general', Trotsky replied to Eastman, 'we treat each of them according to what he deserves.'[63]

---

63   See Cannon 1973a, pp. 311–33. I read Cannon's reviews of the two volumes, originally published separately, as being far more drawn to *The Roots of American Communism*, where Cannon's praise is effusive, than to *American Communism and Soviet Russia*, where Cannon more vociferously tackles Draper's problematic argument that American Commun-

For Draper, then, the notion that a Russian Bolshevik cadre, experienced in having made a revolution and dedicated to seeing that revolution spread around the world, might have something to contribute to American Communism was, in the aftermath of his departure from the Communist movement, anathema. Draper, his understanding of world Communism squeezed into the narrow confines of antagonism by the experience of Stalinism on the left *and* the Cold War pressures of the 1950s on the right, could only interpret the origins of the American revolutionary left with a telescoped hostility. He came to see narrowly, into a tunnel that began and ended with Moscow domination. Draper thus proved unable to draw a necessary distinction between advice and guidance from a Comintern healthy in its commitment to world revolution – developed through consultation and genuine regard for the advancement of the revolutionary forces in the West, as existed in the dialogue between US Communists and their Soviet comrades in the early years of the 1920s – and a Comintern drifting into bureaucratisation by 1925. This mid-1920s change, accelerating in the latter half of the decade, ensured that the Comintern succumbed to the machinations and manoeuvres characteristic of a Stalinisation that made a mockery of revolutionary internationalism, caring only for the entrenched power of a new caste of Soviet officialdom and materially propping up socialism's degeneration into a planned economy in one country.

When a former Communist such as Steve Nelson, who developed from a youthful rank-and-file figure in the CP in the 1920s to a major influence in the

---

ism's 'original sin' of attaching itself to the Russian Revolution 'led it inexorably, from one calamity to another, and to eventual defeat and disgrace' (Cannon 1973a, p. 329). Although Cannon never drew a distinction between Draper's two volumes, it is implicit in the differences in tone and substantive critique that characterise the two separate reviews. This is merited, I would suggest, because there is a shift in Draper's tone and substantive argument between the two volumes. Moreover, it is surely not accidental that Draper, in the face of New Left histories, historiographic articles and Communist memoirs of the 1970s and 1980s, republished his more aggressively critical and hostile volume, *American Communism and Soviet Russia* (reprinted 1986), as a riposte to a historiography 'soft' on Bolshevism. He did not reprint *The Roots of American Communism*, a book that could rightly have been seen as more sympathetic to Communism, until much later, when the post-1989 historical tide had turned. For other former Communists' critiques of Draper, see Herbert Benjamin, 'Outline of Unpublished Manuscript: A History of the Unemployed Movement and Its Struggles During the Great Depression', p. 108, deposited in Columbia Oral History Project, Columbia University, New York, NY; and Earl Browder, quoted in Isserman 1982, p. ix; Browder to Draper, 16 March 1959, Series III, Box 18, Browder Papers. Wolfe is quoted in Wolfe 1981, p. 229; Lovestone in Le Blanc n.d., citing Lovestone 1939–40; and Trotsky in Eastman 1964, pp. 348–9.

Party's New York leadership in the 1940s and 1950s, sidestepped the issue of American Communism's degeneration by referring to Communist 'discipline' as perhaps making CP members 'more vulnerable to Stalinism' (as if, over the course of the 1930s and 1940s, Stalinism was not an established foundation of Party life and politics), Draper saw more than red. This was the birth of the third Draper, the liberal Cold War warrior 'gone ballistic'. As historical writings in the 1980s increasingly castigated earlier accounts for their depiction of the CP as 'a monolithic totalitarian organisation whose history reflected the shifts and turns in the Comintern line', instead positing the need for histories of US Communism as 'an authentic expression of American radicalism', Draper moved into a crankier articulation of his hostility to the Communist Party and its meaning. If his critical engagement with so-called 'new' histories of Communism did indeed strike appropriately at many vulnerabilities, over time Draper grew more and more likely to slip into attacks that, in their demand that Stalinist foibles and much worse be resolutely identified, often lapsed into complacent acquiescence with respect to the unsavoriness of the Cold War right, all too evident in the 1950s. His barbs were now flung as much at the New Left as at the Old. Something had been sacrificed as the first Draper gave way to the third.[64]

---

64   Nelson, Barrett and Ruck 1981, p. 246. The problem with Nelson's formulation of issues
      of Communist discipline and their relation to Stalinism is not so much conceptual as
      historical. Lenin's development of Party discipline and the emergence of a 'machinery' of
      Bolshevism in the pre-Revolution and immediate post-1917 years undoubtedly presented
      opportunities for Stalin to seize that 'machinery' and change its meaning by severing the
      Party from its historic relation to revolutionary ideas. In this sense, as Trotsky noted, Stalin
      was in part a creation of the Bolshevik 'machine', which in turn came to be taken over by
      an individual who personified its negation. To pose the issue of the revolutionary Party
      and its degeneration in this way in the Soviet Union of 1921–26 is one thing, but to suggest
      that this interpretation is easily transferable to the experience of US Communism in the
      1930s ignores the extent to which the Soviet Party, the Comintern *and* the US Communist
      Party had already succumbed to Stalinisation by this late date. See Trotsky 1941, p. xv. Note,
      on Draper and the New Left, Walzer 1983, pp. 259–60, 266; Gerstle 1984, pp. 561, 563–4.
      Draper's broadside rejoinder, a two-part *NYRB* essay, is republished in the 1986 edition of
      American Communism and Soviet Russia, pp. 445–82. Draper's later attack on Eric Foner's
      The Story of American Freedom, 'Freedom and Its Discontents', *New York Review of Books*,
      23 September 1999, may have been prompted by some legitimate concerns, but it seemed
      shrill given the limited treatment Foner afforded the Popular Front (pp. 210–18), and it
      exposed how Draper was now capable of overreaching himself in rejecting all arguments
      that claimed the need for a critical engagement with the deficiencies evident in American
      democracy. This led Draper to whitewash the role of Sidney Hook and the American

Making the Communist Biographical Turn: Stalinism Sidestepped

Scholarship addressing US Communism in the 1990s has relied very much on Draper's original contribution. Much of this work, where it has not drawn somewhat mechanically from Draper's 'Soviet domination' argument, as in the writing of the Klehr-Haynes 'traditionalist' cohort with its fixation on the 'secret' and 'Soviet' worlds of US Communism as revealed in newly released Moscow documents,[65] has taken individual Communists of long-standing significance in the American movement as its subject.

Close examinations of the 'making' of Communists, their origins in specific kinds of class struggles and attractions to the ideas, disciplines and potential of a revolutionary party linked to the first successful proletarian state, illuminate the experience of Communism with a sense of development and detail that is often lacking in more general studies. Such disciplined, archival-based biographical study, reaching well beyond 'memoir', is relatively new within Communist historiography and is beginning to register both internationally and within the United States.[66] This is especially evident in what are undoubtedly the best recent contributions to American Communist studies, sophisticated

---

Committee for Cultural Freedom in the ugliness of 1950s anti-Communism. See Jacobson 2000.

65   The central texts here are Klehr, Haynes and Firsov 1995 and Klehr, Haynes and Anderson 1998.

66   McIlroy, Morgan and Campbell (2001) commence with the statement that 'Communist historiography has in the main been impoverished by its disregard of biography' (p. 5). Kevin Morgan's opening chapter (2001, pp. 9–28) makes a case for biography's contribution, and subsequent chapters provide glimpses of biographical potential. In Canada the first truly sophisticated biographical treatment appeared only recently: D. Frank 1999. On the lack of biography in international Communist historiography, note especially Anderson, 'Communist Party History', in Samuel 1981, pp. 150–6; and the essays in Hobsbawm 1973, 3–54. In the *Bibliography on the Communist Problem in the United States* (Fund for the Republic, Inc. 1955), the entry on biography constituted slightly more than one page in a 474-page text. Other bibliographies, such as Seidman 1969, are not organised in such a way as to access biographical material. Haynes 1987 repeats entries throughout various sections, but, even allowing for this exaggeration in the biographical realm, contains a total of 50 pages out of 321 that relate in the loosest way to biographical writing. Extremely useful are recent compilations such as Buhle, Buhle and Georgakas 1992. For a psychological discussion that refuses a crude anti-humanism and posits the need for a scientific Marxist humanism in which the accent on forms of individuality and a theory of the individual could well be developed to sustain a biographical approach to the origins of the revolutionary left, see Seve 1978.

biographies of the syndicalist-turned-Communist William Z. Foster by Edward P. Johanningsmeier and James R. Barrett. Each text, moreover, addresses seriously the formative decade of American communism, the 1920s, Foster's history necessitating a return to this critical period upon which Draper concentrated but which few New Left histories probed. These histories now stand as the most accomplished accounts of the origins of the American revolutionary left. Yet it would be fair to say that neither places Stalinism at its analytic core, although it is difficult not to see what they regard as the tragic dimensions of Foster's revolutionary life as in some senses framed by the political defeat that Stalinism designates. This takes us, inevitably, into an appreciation of the international meaning and making of Communism and the particularities of its expressions in the United States.

Both books literally begin with Draper. (Johanningsmeier acknowledges Draper's volumes as the most thorough and insightful of all Party histories; Barrett quotes Draper on the first page of his study). Foster, whose impressive early years as a labour organiser encompassed pre-Communist mass-production union drives in the meat-packing and steel industries, joined the Workers (Communist) Party late in 1921, although his membership was kept under wraps for some time. One of Bolshevism's most celebrated 'trade-union' catches, Foster was a committed revolutionary, and in his legendary exploits in the mining districts or amongst needle-trade workers he exhibited the kinds of courage, tenacity and commitment that earned him the respect, even reverence, of militants in countless US workplaces, where enclaves of radicalism survived throughout the deadening political climate of the mid- to late 1920s.

Yet for all of this, Foster was destined to be battered from political pillar to proverbial post in the Stalinist factional machinations that dominated his first decade in the Communist movement. The experience, coupled with constant harassment by the forces of US anti-Communism, a gruelling early 1930s presidential campaign and, possibly, the frustration of his vain ambitions, brought Foster to a debilitating 1932 nervous breakdown that side-lined him for three years. It no doubt accommodated the once-defiant revolutionary to whatever the thoroughly Stalinised Comintern had in store for him, the feisty mass leader reduced to an unseemly supplicant, waiting on Moscow's decisions to haul him out of the shadows and place him, once again, in the forefront of revolutionary agitation.[67] Stalinism, as the defeat of proletarian internationalism, is central

---

67   Johanningsmeier 1994; Barrett 1999. The advances of these texts over a past treatment of Foster written by his secretary and research assistant over the course of the 1950s are monumental. See Zipster 1981.

to this Fosterian tragedy. Johanningsmeier and Barrett chart a sure interpretive course towards just this kind of analysis, although neither author addresses Stalinism frontally and they diverge in their understandings of what is at stake in grasping Foster's, and Communism's, failures.

Johanningsmeier concludes his assessment of Foster on a highly subjective note, suggesting that 'it was finally his voiceless rage that formed the inviolable core of his identity ... because his anger always survived the test of his scepticism'. Alienated always, Foster was capable of holding 'many convictions ... their multifariousness and the ease with which he embraced, abandoned, or renounced them ... defin[ing] his career for most observers'. This ostensibly pragmatic outlook, which christened Foster with the nickname 'Zig-Zag' in some non-Stalinist left circles, was for Johanningsmeier 'adaptive, experimental, and innovative' at its best, an 'aggressive modernism' that marked Foster as 'a truly American radical', albeit one who, ironically and tragically, never quite came to understand himself as 'fully the product of the society he so despised'.[68]

Foster's failures thus lay within his complex and cross-purposed subjective identity. On one level this is a truism, inasmuch as all individuals choose specific life and political courses, but on another it bypasses *political* explanation, inasmuch as it thoroughly marginalises the very Stalinism that conditioned the jettisoning of Marxist principle and programme in varied and oscillating adaptations, opportunisms and underminings of principle. The culmination of these would be the repudiation of revolution's ultimate project and, in the case of figures such as Foster, a bartering of revolutionary possibility for the security of a lesser, personally aggrandising 'place' in a movement that claimed to be something other than what it was. To be sure, that process of exchange was not without its individual costs, ironies and tragedies, but it could not have happened outside of the larger structure of subordinating political defeat which was evident in Stalinism's consolidation throughout the latter half of the 1920s and which then proved the sad continuity within which Foster lived out his remaining decades as a compromised revolutionary.

Barrett reaches for a more political reading of the tragedy of American radicalism; ironically, it is one that he comes to by blending the counter-posed views of Draper and the New Left. Insistent that the lessons to be learned from Foster's life are not those of radicalism's inevitable defeat, but the 'importance of rooting ... politics in everyday life, in the political and cultural traditions of our own society, and in the democratic aspirations of our own society',

---

68   Johanningsmeier 1994, pp. 353–4.

Barrett speaks in the language of the New Left. But in acknowledging that Foster himself was a product of the US industrial and political environment, a revolutionary who assimilated the lessons of American conditions, Barrett also confronts the extent to which Foster adapted his organisational strategies and capacities to lead effectively to Comintern influences, bending his will and his creative class impulses to those of the Party. On this terrain, Barrett crosses over to Draper's turf, his vocabulary becoming one of 'Soviet domination'. The tragedy of Foster, in Barrett's presentation, is that he could not sustain his American-born revolutionary talents and dedication without sacrificing them before the altar of Party exigencies, which were determined in the Soviet Union. 'The Communist prescription', for Barrett, failed 'the vision of a more just and democratic American society' that had originally animated Foster and that must, according to Barrett, continue to be the foundation of efforts to create our history anew.[69]

This attractively argued assessment of Foster and the US Communist experience appeals to the radicalisms of our time because it raises a series of critical questions. How are revolutionary experiences situated in what Eric J. Hobsbawm has referred to as the universal experience of Communist Party formation, the marriage of 'a national left and the October Revolution'? This was a union, according to the British Marxist historian, which in earlier times, such as the pivotal 1920s, proved to be one of both love and convenience, precisely because 1917 was still very much a galvanising, inspirational force on the left and was widely perceived as an authoritative centre of revolutionary accomplishment.[70]

How does this historical actuality mesh with democratic aspirations struggling to be fulfilled in the stark face of capitalist hegemony's capacity to mask autocracy in the ideology of 'equal opportunity', the counter to which many militants have believed, and continue to claim up to this day, is a disciplined collectivism? Foster is himself an excellent case study of an American radical who came to believe fervently that political solutions to these and other dilemmas were nowhere to be found if not through the defeat of capitalism, which, surely, has never been going to relinquish itself without a fight. What all of this boils down to, bluntly put, is a basic question: Is there now, and has there ever been, a necessity for a Communist Party? Foster came to answer in the affirmative, but because the experience of American Communism was an uneasy affair from its inception, his history is a troubled one, as indeed is the development of

---

69   J. Barrett 1999, pp. 273–7. See, as well, J. Barrett 1994, pp. 197–203.
70   Hobsbawm 1973, p. 3.

any figure of importance in the history of the revolutionary ranks in that most inhospitable of climates for the political left, the United States.

To probe that uneasiness in its formative period, the 1920s, it is necessary to return to the origins of the American revolutionary left, to trace the tributaries of diverse origins that fed this swift river of early anti-capitalist sentiment and militant practice and to explore the current that eventually drove it forward and, ultimately, diverted its direction, the relationship of the Comintern and American Bolshevism. Was Communist internationalism, as Draper always insisted, increasingly so in his more truculent later writing, inherently incompatible with an indigenous American revolutionary left? Barrett suggests as much, but he does so by sidestepping the possibility that 'Communist prescription' had, in a larger international tragedy, been turned into its opposite by the degenerating politics of 1920s Stalinisation, a defeat it is possible to reverse in our time only by beginning with the need to address its constitution and meaning historically.[71]

71   A similar theme of tragedy is trumpeted in Ryan 1997. Ryan cautions historians to utilise the term *Stalinist* with considerable care, as if the very concept of Stalinism was somehow suspect (p. 2). This echoes arguments made in K. Morgan 2001, which posits the existence of a post-Stalinist left. I am unconvinced by this kind of argument, which was in some ways refuted by E.P. Thompson in *The Poverty of Theory and Other Essays* (Thompson 1978c), pp. 328–31. Works such as Ryan's, capable of evading Stalinist terror on the grounds that it did not happen in Browder's America, indicate that Stalinism within the Communist International and various national Communist Parties can be glossed over rather easily. Browder's elevation to a position of leadership is nevertheless unintelligible in the absence of Stalinisation, one part of which was juggling Party factions in foreign sections in order to destabilise leading cadre so that a sustained challenge to the Comintern's oscillating programme, orchestrated by a commitment to secure Stalin and the politics of 'socialism in one country' dominance, could never arise. The failure to grapple with this Stalinism mars Ryan's treatment of Browder, as well as the discussion of another major Communist figure of the 1920s, Jay Lovestone. Ted Morgan, *A Covert Life: Jay Lovestone – Communist, Anti-Communist, and Spymaster* (T. Morgan 1999), is perhaps the most disappointing of recent biographies from the standpoint of sophistication of Communist scholarship. Isaac Deutscher addressed the issue of post-Stalinism far more convincingly than Morgan, who largely seems to want to drop contemporary reference to the phenomenon. Deutscher wrote in 1953, reflecting on Stalin's death and the 'moral climate' of a post-Stalin Russia: 'As society's guardian Stalin exercised control so tyrannically that he deprived his ward of any intrinsic political identity. In time Soviet society grew tired of the harness of Stalinism and was anxious to throw it off; but it had also grown so accustomed to the harness that it could take no step without it'. See Deutscher 1953, especially pp. 95–6; and also 1969a.

A central concern of Communist scholarship in the United States, the fixation on 'foreign domination', can thus only be addressed substantively when the historical significance of Stalinisation is appreciated. This issue has vexed writing on the American revolutionary left for decades, no less so now than in the 1950s. Only if we are capable of seeing Stalinism's degenerations, how they registered in the transformation of Soviet politics and the role of the Comintern over the course of the 1920s can we appreciate the foundational premise of the American revolutionary left. Figures such as James Cannon invested their revolutionary lives of sacrifice in the genuine, and not misguided, belief that a healthy and victorious proletarian state and the arm it created to sustain revolution abroad, the Communist International, could well advise national sections of the Communist movement in various matters.

But crude dictation and unassailable directives were not generally the mode of political interchange in this original give and take amongst revolutionaries. Influence and rational argument through instruction, justified by experience and willingly acceded to by foreign Communists who looked to the Russian revolutionaries for guidance, can by no means be comparable to the bureaucratised and, later, thoroughly Stalinised practices of the Comintern, in which 'orders' were conveyed from Moscow to various Communist Parties around the world. At issue was not so much the formal separation of Communist discussion, debate and decision, often arrived at in Moscow in the early years of the revolutionary Comintern, and the method of ultimate Stalinist authority typical of the post-1928 years, but the *programmatic* divide that ran through a politics of revolution, in which the content of that politics was forever changed as Stalinism hardened the arteries of the beating heart of proletarian revolution.

This shifts our concerns, recasting issues of national domination and refocussing our attention on Communism's potential, thwarted by Stalinism, to build revolutionary internationalism. Few national sections of the Comintern have experienced 'tragedy' more pointedly than the Polish KPP, and fewer still have found sorrier, if passionate, refuge in nationalist mythologies. Yet as Deutscher concluded in his 1958 discussion of this unfortunate history, revolutionary Marxism can never find comfort in a programme of parochial national self-determination:

> Poland ... absorbed from the Russian Revolution its shadows as well as its lights and took over from it, together with the blessings of a progressive upheaval in social relationships, the curse of bureaucratic terror and the Stalin cult ... History so far has not always been a good and sensible teacher. The lessons in internationalism which it attempted to teach

the Polish masses were singularly involved, badly thought out, and ineffective. During almost every one of these 'lessons', history mocked and
insulted Poland's national dignity and, in the first place, the dignity and
independence of the Polish revolutionary movement. Is it surprising then,
that the 'pupil' has not been very receptive, and, trying to escape the peculiar 'teacher', has sought refuge in the jungle of our nationalist legends?
The Polish masses will understand that the bonds which unite their destiny with that of the Russian and other revolutions are indissoluble, but
only after they have recovered from the blows and shocks inflicted on
them in the past, and when they feel that nothing can ever again threaten
their independence and national dignity. Marxists, however, must rise
above the shocks and the traumas from which the masses suffer; and they
must even now be deeply and thoroughly aware of the common destiny
of Poland and other nations advancing towards socialism. Marxists have
no right to nourish themselves, nor to feed others, on the spiritual diet
of stale and warmed-up myths and legends. Socialism does not aim at the
perpetuation of the nation state; its aim is international society. It is based
not on national self-centredness and self-sufficiency, but on international
division of labour and co-operation. This almost forgotten truth is the very
ABC of Marxism ... [W]hat is at stake this time is the 'organic integration'
of Poland into international socialism, not her incorporation into a Russian Empire.[72]

These words, with their reference to the indissoluble bonds of revolution, are
more difficult to appreciate in 2003 than they were in 1958. Our attention is
not now fixed on dissident Communist uprisings in Eastern Europe. Rather,
what looms before us is the final, decisive 1989 defeat of the Soviet Revolution,
a world-historic event as earth-shattering in its consequences as that of its
predecessor, the Bolshevik seizure of state power in 1917.

It is this final 'death' of a Communism long ago stifled and suffocated by
Stalinism that has dominated international relations in our times, establishing
a new Russian regime of capitalist restoration feeding brutally off the primitive accumulations of past socialist attainment and unleashing a threatening
period of global destabilisation and imperialist aggression, the catastrophic
implications of which have yet to run their final destructive course. Yet such a
defeat, however telling its blows, must not be allowed, intellectually or politically, to condition defeatism. Against the events of our time, anything but

---

72   Deutscher 1984, pp. 126–7.

propitious for socialists and socialism, it is critical to re-establish the parameters of possibility in which a new and just world can be, first, envisioned, and second, made.

A small blow can be struck in resurrecting the history of the revolutionary left, wherein lie, often obscured and buried under the debris of previous misinterpretations, the programmatic orientations that direct the more substantial and mandatory interventions and struggles of political activity.[73] In this undertaking, the revolutionary internationalism that Deutscher championed 45 years ago is as necessary and obvious a strategic direction for the left now as it was then. This organic Communist integration, whereby national 'self-determination' in the sphere of revolutionary politics is constructed within a healthy dialogue amongst international sections united on a principled programmatic basis, constitutes a globalisation of the left in which the rebirth of a Communist International is of fundamental importance. For all the roadblocks barring easy entry to this end, it remains the surest route through and past what many historians of US Communism designate the 'tragedies' of American radicalism.

---

73   See, for example, the recent collection of documents associated with a struggle for programmatic clarity within the early Trotskyist movement in the United States: Prometheus Research Library 2002.

CHAPTER 8

Before Braverman: Harry Frankel and the American Workers' Movement*

What was so great about Harry Braverman? The question, obviously rhetorical, elicits a predictable response in academic circles, where the author of *Labor and Monopoly Capital* (1974) is deservedly praised for a text that christened the emerging field of labour process studies.[1] Braverman's book was rigorous in its conceptualisations, sufficiently abstract to present an argument that reached beyond particularities into generalised, universal experience and historical and empirical enough to sustain an analysis meant to be received across disciplinary boundaries. Moreover, it bridged the academic and activist worlds of left scholarship and practice, a breeze of fresh interpretive air that reinvigorated intellectual sensibilities and revived the study of the work process in fields such as history, sociology, economics, political science and human geography. One of the 50 or so most important studies produced in the third quarter of the 20th century, *Labor and Monopoly Capital* earned its author a remarkable reputation that, sadly, he never lived to enjoy.[2]

Authors of great books, having scored the music which rings in the collective ear of generations of readers, inevitably face a cacophony of criticism, some very good, some quite indifferent and some irritatingly bad. Braverman soon faced an avalanche of revisionist study, much of which was written to displace his analysis by showing that somewhere, somehow, some group's historical engagement with the work process stepped outside the general boundaries developed in *Labor and Monopoly Capital*. In the end, such studies remain, for the most part, mere footnotes to the edifice of labour process studies, the foundation of which has been, for almost a quarter-century, Braverman's book. Written by the director of a small, independent left press, Monthly Review, an author with next to no university training and no disciplinary, scholastic axe to grind, consciously scaffolded on an argument that generalised capitalist experience in order to better sustain the perspectives needed to build a socialist

---

* 'Before Braverman: Harry Frankel and the American Workers' Movement', *Monthly Review*, 50 (1999), 33–46.

1 Braverman 1974.

2 Brief comment on Braverman can be found in Wald 1987, p. 298, and Breitman 1976, p. 12.

society, *Labor and Monopoly Capital* was, and remains, a deep irony. As a powerfully influential academic text that made its mark on tens of thousands of students and instructors, Braverman's book made an intellectual splash and has remained an important study used in many classrooms and read widely outside the university. Yet it would almost certainly have been rejected by any university press to which it was submitted in the early 1970s.

My task is thus a modest one, rooted in humility and respect for who Harry Braverman was and what he accomplished. I cannot lecture anyone on any theme that even gestures towards the pretence of going 'beyond Braverman'. I have no inclination of suggesting some deep structure of interpretive reciprocity, in which exercises in textuality will bring Braverman into line with the fashionable 'critical theory' icons of our time. My purpose is much more mundane – embarrassingly so, since it is not particularly theoretical at all, but is, rather, unashamedly political. I want to address what was great about Harry Braverman. And to do that I offer only a sketch of a life 'before Braverman', commenting on a man some will know as Harry Frankel.

Harry Braverman, like so many of his generation, came to radicalism in the Great Depression. 'Socialism and Marxism were in the air', he recalled 40 years later. 'Capitalism was putting on a pretty bad performance'.[3] Born in 1920, the son of a shoemaker, he aspired to a college education but the pinch of hard times and the pressures on the family economy forced his father to terminate his enrolment in Brooklyn College after one brief year. As Irving Howe and a host of others have suggested, the New York public-college scene was perhaps the nation's most fertile seedbed of radical ideas in the 1930s,[4] but Braverman ended up in a particular current of the oppositional stream. His choice was to be a minority within a minority, and he aligned himself not with the Popular-Frontist Communist Party but with the Young People's Socialist League (YPSL).[5]

The 'Yipsels' were a rare phenomenon: associated with the Socialist Party, they were nevertheless an almost autonomous entity, much more than the youth wing of the older, established party apparatus. Having gone through a series of radicalisations and reorganisations, including voting to join the Communist movement in 1919, the Yipsels were in particular motion in the mid- to late 1930s. Led by the iconoclast agitational firebrand Albert Weisbord in the early 1920s, the YPSL lost its leader to the CP and its political moorings

---

3 Quoted in Barnes et al. 1976, pp. 203–4.
4 Howe 1982, pp. 61–89.
5 On the Yipsels see Buhle 1982b, pp. 875–7; Howe 1985, pp. 49–86; Drucker 1994, 68–105.

in the populist-progressive presidential bid of Robert La Follette. After 1924 it was virtually moribund. But with the revival of the Socialist Party in the 1932 electoral bid of Norman Thomas, the YPSL re-emerged as a vital, youthful player in socialist politics, throwing its growing membership ranks behind movements of the unemployed and supporting the growth of militancy and organisation in the labour movement.

The greater New York area was the centre of YPSL's strength as several thousand radical youth galvanised the Socialist Party, pushing the entrenched, often foreign-born leadership, dubbed 'the Old Guard', back into the fray. There they faced off against their Communist counterparts who, by 1935, had gravitated from the ultra-left sectarianism of the Third Period (1929–35) to the 'Communism is 20th-century Americanism' of Browder's Popular Front.[6] It was the Yipsels, known as Norman Thomas's 'Militants', who most vociferously challenged the politics of Stalinism's sordid compromises with bourgeois power in this period, just as it was they who stood firm for socialist internationalism in their defence of a revolutionary perspective on the Spanish Civil War and their uncompromising support for labour's upsurge (evident not only in the 1934 strikes in Toledo, Minneapolis and San Francisco,[7] but also in the struggle to build the Congress of Industrial Organizations, or CIO). In their refusal to paper over Stalinist deformations in the Soviet Union, most evident in the Dewey hearings exonerating Trotsky (held in Mexico, but much debated in New York and elsewhere in 1937), the Yipsels also maintained revolutionary principle in the face of much opposition.[8] In such a climate it was not surprising that the YPSL was a major recruiting ground for the small but dedicated band of Trotskyists (headed by James Cannon, Max Shachtman and Martin Abern) who led a disciplined contingent of Left Oppositionists into a fusion with A.J. Muste's American Workers Party and then charted entry into the Socialist Party. The left-leaning Yipsels found themselves ostracised from their own organisation and were denied credentials at the 1937 Socialist Party convention. Soon after, many would gravitate to the first Trotskyist party in the United States, the Socialist Workers Party (SWP), whose founding convention was held in 1938.

As a mere teenager, Harry Braverman was one of the Yipsels won to Trotskyism in this period. To support himself and his politics, he apprenticed at

6   For a sample of perspectives see Klehr 1984; Isserman 1982; Howe and Coser 1962; Goldfield 1985.
7   Brief discussions are in Preis 1964, pp. 19–33; Cannon 1973c, pp. 75–126.
8   Phelps 1997, esp. pp. 140–97; Morrow 1974; P. Frank 1979.

the Brooklyn Naval Yards from 1937 to 1941, where he learned the coppersmith's trade and branched out to become a steel-fabricating layout man, an occupation he would master to the point that he was soon supervising a team of 18 to 20 workers refitting the asbestos-covered pipes of docked ships (a critical contributing factor in his premature death). It was in this period that he solidified his relationship with his wife Miriam, also a Trotskyist in the SWP. Drafted by the army in 1944, Harry was sent to Cheyenne, Wyoming, where he transferred his skills to locomotive piping. With the end of World War II hostilities (Miriam having been posted to Akron by the SWP), the Bravermans finally set up a common household in Youngstown, Ohio. There they lived from 1946 to 1951, developing close ties to a talented contingent of Midwestern proletarian activists, among them Bert Cochran and Jules Geller; parenting a son; and fending off the red-baiting hounding of the FBI, which managed to have Harry fired from his job at Republic Steel but failed in similar efforts at the Pollack blast-furnace operations.

Braverman was thus, by the mid-1940s, a steeled dissident communist, formed at the intersection of the Great Depression's debilitating poverty and the material context of working-class deprivation in America, Trotskyism's oppositional challenge to both capitalist exploitation and Stalinism's political deformations,[9] and a deep training in the skilled trades of the most advanced sectors of the monopolistic workplace. As a committed communist, moreover, Braverman had already experienced the prelude to McCarthyism. Eighteen of the SWP's leaders were imprisoned late in the war, the first victims of the notorious Smith Act, which made it a crime of treason to publish and proclaim the ideas of Marx, Engels, Lenin or Trotsky. Like so many of his comrades who, in their routine waged labour and political involvement, might amass an FBI file of three thousand pages or more, Braverman experienced first-hand the intrusively threatening anti-communism of the state. This was the parentage of Harry Frankel, the party name Braverman adopted upon joining the SWP.

The Trotskyist milieu that shaped Frankel was a unique political formation. Unlike the politics of Stalinism, where slavish adherence to Comintern dictate and blind obedience to the favoured leadership of the movement were hallmarks of Communist Party practice, the Trotskyism of the Socialist Workers Party meant on-going debate and discussion over tactics and strategy within the newly formed Fourth International, within which the American section was

---

9   For an informed recent account of the Trotskyist-Stalinist relation, see M.E.G. Smith 1996–
     7.

a source of strength and material resources. Frankel, after a brief two-and-a-half years in the movement, faced the critically important faction fight of 1939 and 1940. James Burnham and Max Shachtman led an assault on the fundamental Trotskyist defence of the Soviet Union. Unlike most of the Yipsel New York youth, who followed Shachtman out of the SWP and into the Workers' Party, Frankel stuck with the SWP leadership and party head, James P. Cannon.[10] He would later remember Cannon, after many years of political separation, as a principled defender of what the Soviet Union had once been and a native voice of the historic significance of the Russian Revolution and its central importance for the US working class. Frankel was soon elected to the New York-based National Committee of the Party and became embroiled in controversies associated with how the SWP had handled the repression of the Second World War years, aligning with George Novack, George Clarke and Morris Stein in a 1942 questioning of Cannon, Albert Goldman and others in the national leadership.[11]

The 'young Harry', as he was affectionately known in the inner circles of the party, was nevertheless a stanch SWP loyalist, assailing 'renegades' such as Lewis Corey and denouncing party enemies like Shachtman as 'a petty-bourgeois counterfeit' in a blunt, rather sanctimonious review that earned him the condemnation of James T. Farrell and the praise of the jailed Cannon. Cannon held Frankel up as a pillar of Marxist polemical engagement, his article an example of the 'critical and independent thinking which we recommend to all

---

10   For introductions to this defining factional struggle see, from the SWP side, Trotsky 1973; Cannon 1972b. From the Workers' Party perspective see Drucker 1994, pp. 106–84; Bubis 1985.

11   For this period, see Cannon 1970 and 1975. Readers confused by the swirl of party-formation acronyms can be guided by the following: The Communist League of America (Opposition) was the first Trotskyist grouping in the United States, known as the CLA or Left Opposition. The CLA fused with the American Workers Party (AWP), led by A.J. Muste, in 1934, forming the Workers Party of the United States (WPUS). This short-lived organisation dissolved when it entered the Socialist Party of America, led by Norman Thomas, in 1936. The Trotskyists in the SP constituted a left wing which was expelled in 1937, and most of the YPSL contingent aligned with this group, which went on, under the leadership of Cannon and Shachtman, to found the Socialist Workers Party (SWP) in 1938. Over the course of 1939 and 1940, Shachtman, in the context of the outbreak of World War II, developed a position on the nature of the USSR which was different to that of the SWP and led a split which culminated in the founding of the Workers' Party (WP). Most of the YPSL left the SWP, becoming part of the Shachtman-led WP. This history of party formation was, in many ways, central to the political formation of Braverman/Frankel, who remained within the SWP.

comrades, especially the youth ... we appreciate the *tone* of the article. That is the *right* way to write about renegades and charlatans'.[12]

One of Frankel's close allies in the Yipsels had warned Harry that to side with Cannon in the 1939–40 faction fight would seal his political fate: he would never be much more than a 'wheelhorse' to the 'Irish politician' who ran the SWP.[13] Frankel rejected this assessment, but undoubtedly there were those in the dissident communist movement of the 1940s who saw Harry as merely one more Cannonite hack. As another faction fight brewed in the mid-1940s, coming to a head with the exit of the Goldman-Morrow group from the SWP, questions of Marxist philosophical method (dialectical materialism), the nature of the Soviet workers' state and the relationship of a home-grown American Bolshevik organisation to both Stalinism and Shachtman's Workers' Party blurred into a growing minority critique of the SWP as a cult organisation, top-heavy in its bureaucratised isolation from the currents of world politics and the possibilities of mass socialist work in the United States.[14]

If Frankel, now immersed in the daily politics of his Youngstown work as well as being a valued element of the proletarianised Midwestern wing of the SWP, remained somewhat outside the fray in the Goldman-Morrow battle, which was centred in New York and Chicago, there were subtle signs that he was finding the climate of what he would later refer to benevolently as 'small group politics in the American socialist movement' constrainingly sectarian.[15] His writings for the party theoretical press moved, in this period, away from scathing, personally directed polemics towards broad-ranging, *historically* scaffolded analyses of the class foundations of late 18th- and early 19th-century American society. The Marxist bite in Frankel's public presentations remained, evident in his conclusion to a challenging analysis of the Jacksonian era:

> If Jacksonianism has any 'modern significance' it is this: only by allying themselves with an economically predominant class on the road to power can the urban and agrarian petty-bourgeois masses break the capitalist chains that bind them. That modern class, which is the gravedigger of capitalism, is the proletariat. Marxists will work to build the power of

---

12   See Harry Frankel, 'The Renegades: Lewis Corey', *Fourth International*, January 1943; and 'A Defamer of Marxism', *Fourth International*, May 1944; Wald 1978, pp. 126–7; Cannon 1973b, pp. 141–4.
13   Barnes 1976, p. 205.
14   For Cannon's writings on this period, see Cannon 1977.
15   Barnes 1976, p. 206.

this class and to gain for it allies from other classes. We leave empty-headed liberals to celebrate the reactionary subservience of the popular movement to the slaveholding class a century ago, as they celebrated the subservience to the capitalist-Roosevelt demagogy more recently.[16]

Frankel's concerns thus moved, over the course of the 1940s, away from denunciations of party opponents to sophisticated, challenging interpretations of the materialist conception of American history, in which he situated his accounts polemically in terms of the existing historiography, from Frederick Jackson Turner through Charles Beard to Richard Hoftstadter. His movement in this direction was facilitated by the immensely invigorating and intellectually challenging programme of Marxist study offered periodically to promising comrades in the SWP's Trotsky School. This party-funded opportunity enabled select figures, of whom Frankel was one, to study philosophy and history in a disciplined six-month daily course of interrogation, in which the methods and development of the revolutionary movement and US class formation were principal subjects of concern. In the process of this interpretive engagement, and in the increasingly closed climate of McCarthyite America, Frankel's politics shifted gears; he began to question the nature of the SWP and its leadership, especially his political mentor, James Cannon.

By the late 1940s, with the Cold War enveloping the politics of permanent revolution from many quarters, Cannon and the SWP found it difficult to maintain the prospects of an American revolution and sustain their international prominence in the world Trotskyist movement. One part of this was perhaps Cannon's early deference to European theorists such as Ernest Mandel, with whom he often clashed tactically but who seemed more adept at charting the increasingly convoluted conceptual waters of Eastern Europe's post-Second World War 'Baltic Sea' of deformed-workers-state buffer zones, from Yugoslavia to Poland; Mandel and others were also more obviously at home in the theoretically charged atmosphere of the traditional European revolutionary left. But another part of the difficult context of the late 1940s was the pressured push, in times of acute reaction, away from the revolutionary politics of principle which Frankel had found so attractive in Cannon. As

---

16   Harry Frankel, 'Three Concepts of Jacksonianism', *Fourth International*, March 1946. Other Frankel *Fourth International* articles preceding this account include 'Class Forces in the American Revolution', *Fourth International*, March 1946; 'How the Constitution was Written', *Fourth International*, April 1946; and 'The Jackson Period in American History', *Fourth International*, December 1946.

the 'American century' closed in around US revolutionaries, one wall pressing in the intensely coercive containments of a rabid anti-communism and
the other squeezing Marxist commitment with the promise of affluence and
the pacification of an increasingly bureaucratised trade-union movement, the
broad left appeared trapped in its own shrinking space. Small wonder that
the SWP experienced international pressure to align with supposedly like-
minded adherents of fragments of Trotskyism's programme, and that there was
even a concerted effort to construct an alliance with the beleaguered Stalinist
milieu.

Cannon's leadership in the SWP faced a series of challenges as the brilliantly
eclectic Caribbean Marxist C.L.R. James and Trotsky's former secretary Raya
Dunayevskaya forged the Johnson-Forest tendency and moved in and out of the
SWP over the course of the late 1940s and early 1950s. They brought with them
their politics of 'third campism' in which the Soviet Union was depicted as 'state
capitalist', a hair-splitting differentiation that separated itself from Shachtman's
perspective of Soviet 'bureaucratic collectivism'.[17] A symbolic blow was struck
when Trotsky's widow, Natalia Sedova, abandoned orthodox Trotskyist positions and embraced Shachtman and the Workers' Party.

On the international scene, new waves of revisionist accommodation were
being charted by the enigmatic Michel Pablo, an exotic figure of international
intrigue who would face imprisonment by Dutch authorities in the 1960s before
finding a home as a political adviser to Ahmed Ben Bella, leader of the Algerian
National Liberation Front and eventual head of the post-colonial northern
African state. In a nutshell, Pablo's early-1950s position boiled down to an
acknowledgement that, for generations to come, the key forces in the contest
for world socialism would inevitably be the revived capitalism of the post-war
world and the Stalinist formations of mid-century. All that was possible for the
small forces of the Fourth International was to lend what little weight they had
to the long centuries of 'degenerate workers' states' that might lay in the future,
pressuring Stalinism and neo-colonialist mobilisations towards some kind of
rapprochement with revolutionary politics.[18]

---

17 Johnson-Forest, 'State Capitalism and World Revolution', SWP Internal Bulletin No. 4, September 1950; Shachtman 1962.

18 A collection of documents that provides a perspective on this context is Slaughter 1974.
Note, as well, 'Against Pabloist Revisionism', Fourth International, September–October
1953; Socialist Workers Party, 'The 12th Plenum of the IEC', International Information
Bulletin, January 1953, which contains Pablo's 'Report on the Evolution of the World
Situation since the Third World Congress'.

In the United States this new configuration of politics emerged most clearly in a complex bloc of SWP oppositionists headed by Bert Cochran. A talented figure who bridged the proletarian and theoretical wings of the party, Cochran's writings (under the pseudonym E.R. Frank) were a mainstay of the *Fourth International*'s coverage of events in Europe. His long-standing trade-union work in the auto sectors of Michigan and Ohio made him a pivotal player in the SWP's industrial politics.[19] By 1952, Cochran had lined up with George Clarke, Mike Bartell and Harry Frankel to push within the National Committee of the SWP for a re-orientation of the Trotskyist party's relationship with the Stalinist milieu, as well as a broad reconsideration of Trotskyism's approach to trade-union and mass work. As factions hardened, the debate within the SWP grew more acrimonious, coming to a head at a May 1953 plenum. Much was at stake in what was undoubtedly a complicated political situation, exacerbated by the worsening fortunes of an American revolutionary organisation enmeshed in the ugly coercions of McCarthyism. For Cannon and others nothing less than the survival of the Trotskyist party was at stake, while for Cochran and Frankel the issue was one of bureaucratised cliques and Stalinophobia,[20] forces that insulated an ossified politics from any possibility of contact with the larger radical milieu or the masses of potentially militant workers.

The language of debate was rancorous and often personalised; if Frankel contributed some of the most penetrating political commentary, he also gave as good as he got in vituperative dismissal. Jean Tussey, an unaligned Ohio-based SWP activist, recalls pressing members of the Cochran group on what was wrong with the Party's programme and orientation. All she could get was the repeated exclamation, 'Cannon is a son of a bitch!' The Cochran-Frankel minority lost the political fight at the May plenum, a supposed truce (on Bolshevik principles of democratic centralism and minority representation) was worked out and it appeared, for a brief moment, that some possibility of reconciliation within the SWP factionalism was possible. Within months, however, the pact was breaking down, and eventually Cochran, Frankel and others, having disloyally refused party assignments and boycotted a major SWP function, the 25th anniversary celebration of the Trotskyist newspaper *The Militant*, instead

---

19   On Cochran see E.R. Frank (Cochran) Papers, Tamiment Library, New York University, New York.

20   The Cochran-Frankel position found the SWP approach to Stalinism's victimisation during the McCarthy period inadequate. For the official SWP approach, see Socialist Workers Party, 'The Capitalist Witch-Hunt and How to Fight It: Resolution of the SWP National Committee, February 1950', *Education for Socialists*, July 1968.

organising a counter-meeting, split from the SWP. The rhetorical bombast of
the parting of ways exceeded anything that had developed out of past schisms,
splits and factional suspensions.[21]

In the aftermath of the rupture, Harry Frankel lived on for a time. Cochran
and Frankel founded the Socialist Union of America; their first propaganda
organ was *The Educator*, a mimeographed sheet whose title was borrowed
from the 1930s publication of the Mechanics Educational Society of America,
a forerunner of the United Auto Workers with which Cochran had worked in
his early auto-industry organising days. Frankel penned an initial article on
sectarianism and splinter groups in the Trotskyist milieu, but within a year he
had passed from the scene as a figure in the American workers' movement.

Harry Braverman re-emerged as the co-editor, with Cochran, of the *American Socialist* and leading spokesman of what purported to be a new politics of
socialist clarity, in which the cancer of sectarianism would be excised from the
left. Braverman and Cochran proposed to spread socialist propaganda that was
comprehensible and liberated from jargon and ossified orthodoxies, strengthening ties to the union and progressive movements, the better to lay the foundations for the future birth of a socialist Marxist party. In a 1954 speech, 'Setting
a New Course', Braverman pilloried the SWP as an isolated sect, trapped in fulfilling the obligatory 'moral action undertaken as a push-button response to
an immutable law'. Trotskyist theory, he suggested, had died in 1940, failing to
move beyond its hardened formulae. Like all sectarians, Braverman argued, the
SWP did not want to learn from the masses, merging with the struggles and
experiences of the working class, but to swallow them.

Cochran and Braverman proposed that their socialist group and its paper
would be different, precisely because they offered no programme and no agitational agenda. Their publications would be guided by the interest in particular subjects that existed beyond their ranks; they would not purport to

---

21   See Slaughter 1974; Cannon 1953; Bryan D. Palmer, interview with Jean Tussey, Cleveland,
      14 May 1995; Wald 1987, pp. 298–300. A proliferation of position papers and internal party
      documents and correspondence outlines various positions. See, for instance, James P. Cannon Papers, State Historical Society of Wisconsin, Madison, Boxes 48, 49 and 50; Socialist
      Workers Party Records 1928–55, State Historical Society of Wisconsin, Madison, Microfilm Reels 6, 7, 18 and 19; Mike Bartell, 'The New York Local – Reports and Tasks', *Internal
      Bulletin*, February 1953; and 'The Struggle in the New York Local,' *Internal Bulletin*, February 1953; Lou S., 'Opponent Work Report', *Internal Bulletin*, No. 5 NY Local Pre-Convention
      Discussion, 18 March 1953; Joyce Cowley, 'Remarks Made on Floor of Downtown Branch
      Meeting – January 29', *Internal Bulletin*, No. 5 NY Local Pre-Convention Discussion, 21
      March 1953; Hansen and Frankel Exchange, *Internal Bulletin*, February 1953.

have answers, but simply provide readers with a perch from which they could develop perspective and gain information. 'All of our material, with occasional necessary exceptions', Braverman proclaimed, 'tries to indicate a course of action, but we aren't agitating anybody, because we don't see anybody around who is interested in being agitated or ready for it'. This was a long way from the 'young Harry' of the early 1940s and the veritable antithesis of the Leninist-Trotskyist approach that had animated the Frankel of the Socialist Workers Party.[22]

Ironically, if predictably, this experiment in non-agitational agitation came to a relatively abrupt end, with Braverman eventually reaching the conclusion that Cochran's Walter Lippman-like politics of eclectic propaganda were actually losing sight of anything resembling a socialist purpose. The two participated in a Cochran-edited Monthly Review publication, *American Labor in Mid-Passage* (1959), which no doubt moved Braverman closer towards Paul Sweezy and Leo Huberman, paving the way towards his eventual affiliation with the press that would publish *Labor and Monopoly Capital*.[23] But *American Socialist* ceased publication after a five-year run, well before the upheavals of the 1960s it had, in some senses, been awaiting.

Braverman's *Labor and Monopoly Capitalism* was, at this point, some 14 years from publication. But it would be written by a man of socialist conviction and learned cultured sensibility, a socialist who knew the price the American working class had paid for its labours in the factories of capitalist accumulation and who understood what it meant to give one's life to the struggle for social transformation. Before Braverman, there had been the 'young Harry', the Frankel of Marxist perspective and party discipline. Revolutionaries, unlike conservatives, honour the ideas and ideals of their early years. Harry Frankel was, like so many others of his youthful Depression-decade generation, the best that the American working class had ever produced. He was one of those 1930s radicals, moreover, whom Stalinism could not capture and then squander. Against the raw exploitation of capitalism's marketplace, in the face of the repressive incursions of the state and in opposition to the blandishments of acquisitive individualism or the road of Stalinist disillusionment, the young Frankel chose the life of the dissident communist. His training in a period of political ferment

22   Copies of *The Educator* containing Frankel/Braverman articles are in the E.R. Frank (Cochran) Papers, Tamiment Library, New York University, New York. See especially Harry Frankel, 'The Marcy and Vern Groups', *The Educator*, December 1953; Harry Braverman, 'Setting a New Course', *The Educator*, June 1954.
23   See Braverman 1959, pp. 99–112.

made him what he was; as a Yipsel 'Militant' and Trotskyist recruit of rare conviction, he carried the values and vision of his formative years forward into his mid-life period of intellectual labour. He educated himself, with the help of other Marxists and their struggling party, to be an educator and gave to his class the best years and the cherished enthusiasm of his youth. Later, we would be fortunate indeed that Braverman would bestow on us the gift of *Labor and Monopoly Capital*, a book written out of the passions and workplace and political practice of the younger Harry Frankel.

What we really need in the 1990s, however, is what Frankel/Braverman could not will into existence: the reproduction of his generation of working-class communists, a contingent of young proletarian revolutionaries dedicated to the pursuit of socialism. Men and women like these knew, as so many in our times do not, that '[t]hose who cannot defend old positions will never conquer new ones'.[24] They knew – their lives a constant contest to create a way forward out of capitalist barbarism – that the degradation of labour was the protracted undoing of humanity, but they grasped as well that in the contradictions of this process lay history's only hope. Braverman wrote the central passage of *Labor and Monopoly Capital*, but it was Harry Frankel who kept its insights foremost in the Monthly Review author's mind:

> The apparent acclimatization of the worker to the new modes of production grows out of the destruction of all other ways of living, the striking of wage bargains that permit a certain enlargement of the customary bounds of subsistence for the working class, the weaving of the net of modern capitalist life that finally makes all other modes of living impossible. But beneath this apparent habituation, the hostility of workers to the degenerated forms of work which are forced upon them continues as a subterranean stream that makes its way to the surface when employment conditions permit, or when the capitalist drive for a greater intensity of labor oversteps the bounds of physical and mental capacity. It renews itself in new generations, expresses itself in the unbounded cynicism and revulsion which large numbers of workers feel about their work and comes to the fore repeatedly as a social issue demanding solution.[25]

This is, to be sure, an old set of ideas, a constellation of Marxist thought that some have, in the unparalleled confluence of arrogance and complacency that

24   Trotsky 1973, p. 178.
25   Braverman 1974, p. 151.

often masquerades as 'critical theory' in the years post-dating Braverman's text, constructed as an antiquarian attachment, risible in its sympathies and sensitivity. Scholastic hyperbole notwithstanding, such apparently laughable thought is the premise of a politics of social transformation; however many new positions we may be justifiably exhorted to embrace, none are achievable if the old positions of the young Harry Frankel are not defended and deepened.

CHAPTER 9

The Personal, the Political, and Permanent Revolution: Ernest Mandel and the Conflicted Legacies of Trotskyism*

Biographies of revolutionary Marxists should not be written by the faint of heart. The difficulties are daunting. Which revolutionary tradition is to be given pride of place? Of many Marxisms, which will be extolled, which exposed? What balance will be struck between the personal and the political? This dilemma cannot be avoided by those who rightly place analytic weight on the public life of organisations and causes and yet understand, as well, how private experience affects not only the individual but the movements, ideas and developments he or she has influenced. Social history's accent on the particular and its elaboration of context, political biography's attention to structures, institutions and debates central to an individual's life and intellectual history's close examination of central ideas and the complexities of their refinement present a trilogy of challenges for any historian who aspires to write the life of someone who was both *in* history and dedicated to *making* history. As Jan Willem Stutje's *Ernest Mandel: A Rebel's Dream Deferred* (2009) shows, Ernest Mandel was just such a someone, an exceedingly important and troublingly complex figure.

Mandel's Making: Fascism and the Fourth International

Benefitting from a cosmopolitan childhood, Mandel, born in Antwerp of Polish parents in 1923, nonetheless grew up with fascism. Relatives died in Auschwitz. His parents and brother escaped the Gestapo; living underground in Brussels, Mandel was arrested by the German secret police during a routine check of identity papers in 1942. At this point an active Trotskyist, young Mandel's revolutionary politics had been nurtured in the home, his father drawn to anti-Stalinist radicalism by the Moscow trials and the Spanish Civil War. Ernest

---

*   'The Personal, the Political, and Permanent Revolution: Ernest Mandel and the Conflicted Legacies of Trotskyism', *International Review of Social History*, 55 (2010), 117–32.

was further inspired by Abraham Léon, a moving force in the small circle of Belgium's communist Left Opposition.

As a Jew and a revolutionary, Mandel's eventual capture by the Nazis was perhaps inevitable, yet he never relinquished the certainty that fascism would be defeated. His first arrest ended in Mandel breaking free from his captors: it was his father's ability to pay a ransom of 100,000 francs to corrupt police officials that almost certainly paved the way for his son's escape. Mandel used his freedom to good effect, building Trotskyism in tandem with the Resistance. Clandestine work took him across the Belgian border into France. There he first crossed paths with a Greek revolutionary known as Pablo whose later history would intersect decisively with Mandel's. In 1944, while engaged in the dangerously heroic act of leafleting German soldiers occupying Belgium, Mandel was again arrested and sentenced to two-and-a-half years of forced labour. Deported to Germany, he was bounced from one work camp to another. Mandel made a daring bid for his freedom, succeeding for a day, but was almost immediately recaptured. Cultivating political relations with some of those guarding him, Mandel discovered that many of his wardens were former German Social Democrats whose commitment to the Nazis was weak. Though he was fortunate to survive, Mandel suffered greatly. Emaciated and plagued by a number of serious health problems, he spent the winter of 1944 and 1945 at Camp Nieder-Roden, cutting reeds on frozen lakes before being hospitalised. At the end of March 1945, with the US Armed Forces overrunning Germany, Mandel's ordeal finally came to an end.

In the post-war period, Mandel dedicated himself to building and sustaining the Fourth International (FI), established by Trotsky in 1938, which aimed to draw together the global forces of Marxists who opposed both capitalism and Stalinism. Operating at first under conditions of illegality, the FI was subject to attack from its Soviet and Maoist opponents; its advocates ran the gauntlet of repression from one capitalist state to another. Important and contentious issues of principle divided the young movement. The 1950s saw the Fourth International fractured, with the significant American section (the SWP) aligned with others opposing the leadership of Mandel and Michel Raptis/Pablo. In 1953, Mandel and Pablo led what became known as the International Secretariat of the Fourth International (ISFI), while their opponents headed the International Committee of the Fourth International (ICFI). Many of the forces advocating Trotskyism reunited in 1963, as Mandel and Joseph Hansen of the SWP co-authored a programmatic statement on the dynamics of world revolution that staked out common ground on the nature and meaning of the Cuban Revolution and how to approach revolutionary struggle in colonial and Stalinist settings. When Pablo departed the now-renamed United Secretariat of the Fourth International (USec/USFI) in 1965, ending his long and tumultuous tenure in the Fourth International, Mandel was positioned to become world Trotskyism's principal spokesman.

With the upsurge of radicalism associated with 1968, the United Secretariat grew. One part of this enhanced prestige was that, under Mandel's leadership, the USec saw the potential of the Vietnamese struggle against imperialism and the role this would play in galvanising a generalised radicalisation of youth. Mandel's ties to charismatic dissidents, like the German student leader Rudi Dutschke, solidified in common struggles. Never far from the global political fray, Mandel and the USFI subsequently championed and/or had roles to play in the so-called Iranian Revolution of 1978 and 1979, which saw the royal regime of the Shah toppled, replaced by an Islamic Republic headed by the Ayatollah Khomeini; Poland's early-1980s *solidarność*; and the Brazilian Workers' Party of the 1980s and 1990s, which brought together trade unionists, intellectuals and dissidents, eventually catapulting Luiz Inácio Lula da Silva into the presidency. Mandel exhausted himself in his efforts on behalf of the International and died in 1995, his last years a whirlwind of activity that unfolded as the aging Marxist neglected his health.

Complementing his primary political work at the organisational centres of global Trotskyism was Mandel's contribution to Marxist theory, a corpus of texts that oscillated productively between synthesis and polemic. Among the library of books which Mandel authored (including a social history of the crime novel) were his two-volume treatise *Marxist Economic Theory* (1962), an intervention into the debate surrounding the concept of 'alienation' in Marx, *The Formation of the Economic Thought of Karl Marx* (1967) and a trilogy of highly influential works addressing capitalist crisis and the rise and fall of the welfare state as the long boom of post-war expansion ground to a halt in the mid-1970s: *Late Capitalism* (1972); *The Second Slump: A Marxist Analysis of Recession in the Seventies* (1978) and *Long Waves of Capitalist Development* (1980). Widely translated, Mandel's prodigious writing was imaginative and influential. It earned him lectureships and eventually an academic appointment at the Free University of Brussels. The professorship did not come easily: having published more than ten books, consolidating an enviable reputation as a stimulating and compelling lecturer, there were still those amongst the species *academicus supercilious* who thought Mandel's credentials (specifically the lack of a doctorate) wanting.

There was a more serious backlash. As the invitations to speak to left audiences proliferated from the 1960s on, the paranoia of the security state's counter-intelligence (an apt designation) officialdom went into overdrive. Mandel was banned, at various times, from entering the United States, France,

West Germany, Switzerland and Australia. Yet he soldiered on, producing books and articles with a military discipline, battling what he conceived as 'sectarianism' within the ranks of the Trotskyists and continuing to identify himself with the authority of the original Fourth International.

It was no easy row to hoe. As Jan Willem Stutje's engagement with and assessment of Mandel shows, the warhorse of the fractured Fourth International carried baggage he had accumulated as a victim/survivor of the Shoah. Much of Mandel's willingness to vacillate and compromise in order not to sever relations with comrades he valued but knew to be pursuing a wrong course, Stutje implies, can be explained by this history. A revolutionary whose leadership of a 'section' was subordinate to his figurehead status as a spokesman for all 'parties', Mandel needed, desperately so, to keep the forces of world Trotskyism together. Just as he was the archetypal 'non-Jewish Jew', so too, as a revolutionary internationalist, did he travel the planet without a truly effective visa, however much his Belgium roots mattered to him.

A deep divide seemed to separate Mandel the public advocate of revolutionary hope from Mandel the man, be he son, husband or friend. Having been wrenched from his family during the displacements of World War II, isolated in the incarcerations of work camps and prisons, not knowing the fate of loved ones, Mandel survived only to face the premature death of his father. For much of the rest of his life he lived with a mother whom he cherished, but who was clearly overbearing. He had no capacity to deal with children, whose boisterousness unsettled his routines. Responsibilities in personal relations he rarely acknowledged, and emotion was something Mandel no doubt saw as a burden borne by the irrational. His first marriage to Gisela Scholtz had tragic undertones. Scholtz not only had to contend with his mother, but struggled to be recognised as Mandel's equal within the leadership of world Trotskyism. This ultimately drove her deeper into a depression that had been lingering since late adolescence. There were happy times for Gisela and Ernest, but the last years of their marriage, from the late 1970s into the early 1980s, were sad. Painkillers and anti-depressants kept Scholtz going, but she felt abandoned by her husband, trapped in a bleak existence. In 1982 she died at the age of 47. Shortly thereafter Mandel met and married Anne Sprimont, finding love and happiness in a relationship with a younger, cultured woman who had little background in the politics of the left and no desire to move into Mandel's public space.

As this all-too-brief gloss on Mandel's extraordinary and complex history suggests, three strands weave themselves through this ambitious biography. The personal, the political and the published work form components of *Ernest Mandel: A Rebel's Dream Deferred*. Stutje is sympathetic to Mandel, declaring at the outset that his book is 'an exercise in critical admiration', an exploration of 'a Flemish revolutionary Marxist with whose ideas I feel a close affinity'.[1] For all Stutje's proclamations that he subjects Mandel to critical scrutiny, however, it is at precisely those levels where one would expect criticism to register decisively – political programme and principles – that he lets Mandel rather easily off the hook. It is, ironically, in the realm of personal relations where he finds Mandel most decidedly wanting, subjecting his relationships with women and friends to critical commentary. Stutje's book opens pages of Mandel's life that were to some extent closed to all but those who knew him intimately. Yet it turns too rapidly over pages of the history of Trotskyist principles and bypasses ideas that framed Mandel's long list of publications.

Tariq Ali, in a rather self-serving and politically complacent foreword to this Verso edition of the English translation of Stutje's original 2007 study (in which he insists, in effect, that Trotskyism, with its 'interminable polemics' and 'arid and unrewarding' routine, was never much more than a utopian 'road to nowhere'), quotes Yeats: 'The intellect of man is forced to choose/Perfection of the life, or of the work'. He notes that, for Mandel, 'it was always the latter'.[2] This perhaps bifurcates too neatly. Mandel lived for the work of revolution. These labours, and the promise of revolution's end, were in his view life's ultimate sustenance, the only force that could ensure survival. Stutje, who understands Mandel's position, offers us his subject's life and work with a different emphasis, one that places the accent of interpretation less on the political and more on the personal. If this does not falsely separate, it tends to skew.

The Personal as Substitute for the Political

To say this is not to disparage the importance of what Stutje has attempted. As an author, Stutje had enviable access to important and revealing correspondence between Mandel and his wives, family members, colleagues and comrades, as well as insights gleaned from interviewing those who worked closely with Mandel in all kinds of capacities. This is a great strength of his treatment of Mandel. The social can both explain and contextualise the political and make it come to life. But sometimes the personal is *not* overtly political. There are times when explanations of public, political developments are ill-served by recourse to explanations that rely on assessments of individual psychology or determin-

---

1   Stutje 2009, p. xv.
2   Ali 2009, pp. xi–xiii.

istic readings of personal characteristics. This is especially the case when such analysis is formed on the basis of evidence that is incomplete or open to conflicting interpretation, premised on conjecture.

Stutje seems to have fallen prey to a tendency of our depressingly subjective era to substitute the personal for the political. He relies on rather thin tissues of inference to read into Mandel's politics the *structure* of an over-determined personality, one that he associates with an historical cohort that 'divided life into public and private spheres'. Mandel attained maturity in his politics and writing, but he supposedly could not transcend childhood 'in emotional life'; his personal 'development ... stalled on the way to adulthood'. Insisting that 'the political always took priority over the personal', Mandel showed 'more concern for humanity than for himself or those around him' and found 'the need to change society ample justification for remaining blind to the soul'. All of this ostensibly explains why Mandel, according to Stutje, consistently deluded himself that he could protect and retain his International followers by avoiding divisive confrontations over matters of political principle. He preferred not the clarity of open and decisive political debate and programmatic reconfiguration, but the politics of mobilisation and the press to move on to the next item of the agenda. 'This impatient, adolescent attitude helped [Mandel] keep aloof from key problems – from realities – that were too unruly for analysis and prognosis', writes Stutje.[3]

There are myriad problems with this kind of explanatory direction. First and foremost, it throws in the political towel. If realities are indeed too chaotic and out of control to be analysed and acted on rationally, revolutionary politics is doomed, a position Mandel would surely have attacked with all of his being. Second, in attributing to Mandel a certain personality, Stutje is suggesting much more than his evidence will allow. Furthermore, the 'personality structure' that Stutje has sketched would apply to almost any revolutionary born before 1930, virtually all of whom would have willingly conceded that public, political life took precedence over the private realm and that humanity's needs trumped those of the individual. Leading figures on the revolutionary left understood well that friendships were often put to the test in the cauldron of debate and difference over principles. Not all of them saw solutions in temporising. Third, and perhaps most decisively, this critical accent on the personal becomes in Stutje's book a substitute for the necessary development of a substantial account of the politics and ideas that animated both Mandel's leadership of a formidable wing of the Trotskyist movement and his writing. With the

---

3   Stutje 2009, pp. 201–3.

personal becoming both an explanation for the political and the primary arena where criticism of Mandel is developed, the requisite scrutiny of Mandel's political life which most readers of this book will want is often lacking. When we contemplate what Stutje is suggesting about Mandel's 'blindness to the soul', we might stop to ask where this kind of 'analysis' leads. Do those uncommitted to large causes necessarily appreciate more sensitively the spiritual and immortal nature of humankind?

Stutje's tendency to miss the mark in his speculations about personal character is evident in a comparison he makes between Trotsky and Mandel, suggesting that neither figure was able to stand firm in his principles and ideas when faced with battles that he thought would isolate him. Trotsky may indeed have made errors of concession in the 1920s, when he faced the difficult task of assessing how best to preserve the world's first revolutionary workers' state, but this can hardly be taken as a measure of either his personality or his political trajectory. When Trotsky did indeed come to appreciate that no appeasement was possible in the case of the Stalinisation of the Communist International, he rose to the occasion and led a principled fight for the programme of world revolution, opposing the parochialisms and worse of a programme of socialism in one country. Against the slanders and violent intimidations of Stalinism, which culminated in his murder, the condescending dismissals of an increasingly pragmatic and politically enervated social democracy and the ideological and material might of the 'free world colossus', Trotsky stayed this principled, and testing, course. It is hardly appropriate to conclude, as does Stutje, that Trotsky, like Mandel, 'found it difficult to fight unhesitatingly, if need be alone, for what he believed was right'.[4]

As a structuring feature of *Ernest Mandel: A Rebel's Dream Deferred*, recourse to the personal traverses and truncates the text. It frames almost every key moment in Mandel's political leadership of international Trotskyism. This may seem an odd criticism to level at a biography. The point is not that the personal is unimportant and irrelevant, but rather that it must not overwhelm the political, serving in its constant references, allusions and speculations as a substitute for the detailed analytical accounting of political orientation that Mandel himself would have acknowledged was decisive in the lives of all revolutionaries. It is necessary, then, to reread Mandel in order to retrieve a fuller understanding of the politics that structured his life.

---

4   Stutje 2009, p. 202. This reiterates a view first put forward in Deutscher 1964, p. 498.

Rereading Mandel: The Retrieval of the Political

Mandel's post-World War II political work in Belgium saw him playing a leading role in orchestrating a Trotskyist entry into the Socialist Party. He edited and wrote for left-wing newspapers such as *La Gauche* and *Le Peuple*. Mass strikes like the 1960–1 conflict saw public-sector unions and Walloon coal miners and steelworkers lead a concerted charge against government cutbacks and retrenchment in pivotal economic sectors. This provided a test of Mandel's political mettle. Stutje recounts how Mandel had a falling out with the militant but mercurial trade-union leader André Renard in 1959, when Renard put the brakes on a miners' general strike that Mandel had been championing in the pages of *La Gauche*. 'He is and remains at base a left-centrist', Mandel fumed.[5] Mandel and Renard found themselves facing one another again in the 1960–1 upheaval, heralded throughout Europe as the 'strike of the century', but in effect Mandel was subordinated to Renard's ultimate authority in particular and the constraints of the Socialist Party hierarchy in general. Neither could be misconstrued as revolutionary. Stutje presents Mandel as the unadulterated voice of revolutionary class struggle, but in effect *La Gauche*, with Mandel at its helm, vacillated. Repudiations of the coalition government and calls for workers to power were subtly reconfigured *if* certain conditions could be met. 'All participation in government must be ruled out, unless ...'[6] Mandel called for a massive mobilisation of protest, a march on Brussels, in January 1961, only to draw back in the face of Renard's opposition two weeks later. Well poised to offer a critique of the trade-union bureaucracy's strategic refusal to confront the state, collapsing the struggle into pressuring federalist solutions that would secure concessions serving the socio-economic interests of Wallonia, Mandel abdicated and, even retrospectively, failed to make clear what had sealed the fate of the Belgian upheaval of 1960–1.[7]

Much of this was predictable for those who had been keeping a keen political eye on Mandel and Trotsky's original Fourth International. Indeed, that body no longer existed as a united entity in 1960. It had separated at the programmatic seams. The rupture was occasioned by Pablo's insistence in the early 1950s that a new conjuncture in the global politics of the revolutionary left had arrived. He initiated talk of the objective opposition to capitalism and imperialism that Stalinism was leading, even to the point of establishing seemingly

---

5 Stutje 2009, p. 75.
6 Stutje 2009, p. 76.
7 See Mandel 1963, pp. 5–31.

revolutionary regimes. The post-war reconfiguration of Europe, the Chinese
Revolution and anti-colonial struggles in Algeria and Vietnam redrew the map
of socialist possibility, according to Pablo. The survival of regimes that were
either objectively Stalinist or supported and sustained by Stalinism could, in
his view, last for a century and more. This necessitated that the Fourth International re-evaluate its orientation. It was enough to make old-guard Trotskyists,
like France's Pierre Broué, shiver.

In the apocalyptic cauldron of an anticipated Third World War, more threatening than ever with the proliferation of nuclear weaponry, Pablo argued that
standing alone as Trotskyists was futile. The task was to align with and merge
into whatever oppositional force offered the greatest likelihood of effectively
challenging and displacing capitalist hegemony. Too often the line between
outright advocacy of those resisting imperialism or challenging capitalism, on
the one hand, and principled critical support and defence that never relinquished the entirely necessary exposure of programmatic weakness and capitulation, on the other, was crossed. In Pablo's post-1953 International Secretariat
of the Fourth International, within which Mandel functioned as something of
a loyal critical conscience, the Trotskyist commitment to organising the working class for its revolutionary self-emancipation found substitutes in various
adaptations: to peasant-based, Stalinist-led, anti-colonialist mobilisations in
the Third World and, depending on the circumstances, tailing after Stalinist
or social-democratic parties in the capitalist West, even liquidating Trotskyism
in 'deep entries' into such political formations.

The contested politics of this decisive turn have remained central to debates
amongst the world Trotskyist movement to this day. Yet Stutje's book passes
over the rupture very lightly, brushing it off as the product of strong leadership
personalities clashing in 'mutual jealousy'. It presents the Trotskyist milieu as a
set of incestuous battlegrounds on which 'tight moralistic communities' rallied
around all-powerful figures who demanded 'devotion and imitation'.[8] Explaining political development and debate in this way colours Stutje's account of the
world Mandel inhabited.

Too little is made, for instance, of Mandel's specific political role in the
pivotal period of the early 1950s. What is available in Stutje's account is often
open to challenge. Pablo's ideas, for instance, galvanised an immediate opposition, concentrated in the French section of the Fourth International. It was
soon arbitrarily suspended by Pablo, who was nothing if not decisively and
aggressively authoritarian in dealing with opponents. Mandel had no taste

8   Stutje 2009, p. 102.

for repudiating Pablo directly, but early in 1951 he authored a document that came to be known as the 'Ten Theses' on Stalinism. Stutje interprets Mandel's theses as 'a limited acceptance of Pablo's analysis', one that 'dimmed the rather rosy light Pablo had shone on the Soviet bureaucracy'.[9] In actuality, Mandel's manifesto could just as easily be considered a rejection of Pablo's positions, advocating as it did that the Fourth International stay true to its 'fundamental task: to create new revolutionary parties'. Certainly the French section thought Mandel was on board with its positions, calling on him to defend his own principles and hold firm to the political ideas of revolutionary Trotskyism. He did not. In capitulating to Pablo, Mandel, according to Stutje, preferred 'to serve unity rather than get his own way'.[10] The tragedy of this apparently selfless politic was evident in the years to come. By the end of the 1950s Mandel and others who joined him in failing to fight for principled Trotskyist positions within the Fourth International at the beginning of the decade had come to the conclusion that Pablo 'doesn't lead, he brutalizes'.[11] Had Mandel aligned early with the French-section dissidents of the FI and rallied to their standard James Cannon and the SWP and others in the International, the history of Trotskyism and possibly the history of radicalism in the 1960s and beyond might well have looked very different. Mandel opted for another course.

Stutje too often presents those who opposed Mandel, Pablo and Pierre Frank, the other major Fourth International figure who aligned with them in 1953, as caricatured straw men, easily knocked down for their unwholesome personal characteristics. An example is the leader of one of the Fourth International's largest sections, Cannon, whom Stutje portrays as an autocrat concerned only with preserving his own organisational power. To be sure, the Socialist Workers Party's separation from the Pablo-Mandel Fourth International, undertaken with a British contingent led by Gerry Healy and the Argentinian followers of Hugo Bessano (Nahuel Moreno), was late in coming; Cannon, especially, failed to rise forcefully to the necessity of opposing Pablo quickly and unambiguously. Stutje explains Cannon's cavalier response to Pablo's early 1950s reversal of Trotskyist politics as self-interested parochialism. It was only when an eruption of factional 'Pabloism' within the United States section of the FI threatened Cannon's personal power that the SWP deigned to act.

---

9   Stutje 2009, p. 100.
10   Stutje 2009, p. 297.
11   Stutje 2009, p. 113.

There is something to this, but Stutje misses much in coming to this conclusion. There were all kinds of reasons why Cannon and the SWP were slow off
the mark in opposing Pabloism which relate to the particular circumstances
of American Trotskyism. These would necessarily include the jailing of Cannon and other Trotskyists in the mid-1940s, an act of state repression that
understandably left the revolutionary organisation struggling to regroup in the
late 1940s and early 1950s. Cannon was, as the undisputed leader of the SWP,
approaching retirement, and somewhat reluctant to take up yet another factional struggle, especially one that depended on international resolution. There
was, moreover, the ugliness of McCarthyism to deal with.

Stutje also gets some basic information wrong. Rather than engage with
what Mandel and Cannon thought the political issues in the 1953 differentiation entailed, Stutje settles for a garbled and inadequate assessment, one
that relies on mis-readings of specific documents. He disapprovingly cites a
Cannon article that appeared in the SWP's theoretical journal, *Fourth International: A Marxist Quarterly*, entitled 'Trotsky or Deutscher?', presenting Cannon's views as 'a commentary on *The Prophet Armed*, the first volume of the
Polish-British historian Isaac Deutscher's monumental biography of Trotsky'.
Particularly galling for Stutje was Cannon's position that 'Deutscher's belief in
the possibility of reforming Stalinism was heresy'.[12] In a footnote, Stutje further
notes that the SWP newspaper, the *Militant*, published 'an abridged version of
the same witch-hunting review' by George Breitman.[13]

This is all quite wrong. Cannon's article, subtitled 'On the New Revisionism
and Its Theoretical Source', never mentions Deutscher's *The Prophet Armed*. It
cannot, even at a casual glance, be confused with a review of the first volume
of Deutscher's Trotsky trilogy. Rather, it was a discussion of Deutscher's role
in reformulating Trotsky's positions on Stalinism. First evident in Deutscher's
1949 biography of Stalin, Cannon saw these problematic positions developing further in Deutscher's *Russia – What Next?* (also published as *Russia After
Stalin*), a 1953 book that Cannon regarded as opposed to Trotsky's perspective precisely because it predicted that there would be a gradual evolution of
the Soviet regime after Stalin's death, leading to the restoration of socialist
democracy. Deutscher's views here were undeniably related to the developing
politics of Pabloism. Deutscher argued, somewhat disingenuously, that what
was happening in the Soviet Union after Stalin's death was precisely the 'limited political revolution' against Stalinism which Trotsky had advocated in the

---

12   Stutje 2009, p. 103.
13   Stutje 2009, p. 299.

1930s. That Deutscher bastardised Trotsky's position, insisting that only reform decreed from above could overcome Stalinism by forestalling upheaval from below, was indeed telling insofar as it actually reversed Trotsky's understanding of what was required to right the Soviet road.[14] Not surprisingly, Cannon raised these and other issues.

Stutje can speak of 'heresy' and of a 'witch-hunt', but unless one believes that Trotskyist organisations should bury all hatchets, including those thrown directly at their programmatic heads, this all seems a little off the mark. So too does presenting Breitman as 'a thin silent man' given to taking orders from Cannon. Breitman's long assessment of *The Prophet Armed* (a six-part extended review) was hardly an 'abridged version' of anything, let alone Cannon's article. It provided a sustained, if polemical, discussion of a book entirely different than the Deutscher study against which Cannon bent his pen. Breitman, while more often than not in agreement with Cannon, can hardly be reduced to his national chairman's cipher-like mouthpiece.

If the original divide in the Fourth International is thus given short (and overly personalised) shrift in *Ernest Mandel: A Rebel's Dream Deferred*, it must also be noted how often Stutje sidesteps later political developments in like manner. There is much useful material, for instance, on the nature of the Pablo-Mandel International Secretariat's support for the Algerian National Liberation Front in the 1950s and early 1960s, and Stutje's revelations about what went on under Pablo's leadership are illuminating. But there is never a political accounting of the original politics of change and what they entailed for Trotskyism. As the rise of the Argentinian soccer player, Juan Posadas, revealed, the trajectory of the International Secretariat in the late 1950s and early 1960s contained more than a little that revolutionaries should have been questioning. Posadas was apparently a fine organiser and certainly a charismatic figure, but he also descended into being a cultist capable of truly fantastic flights of 'theoretical' fancy, much of which had the consequence of downgrading the significance of the working class in the advanced capitalist political economies.

Mandel responded by holding firm to the importance of the proletariat, inching back towards a rapprochement with the American SWP. This was eventually engineered, ironically, because the break with Pabloism that Cannon and others orchestrated belatedly in 1953 had given way, a decade later, to accommodations centred on the Cuban Revolution, a draft statement on this being drawn up by the SWP's Joseph Hansen and Mandel. This reunification gave birth to what became known as the United Secretariat of the Fourth International

---

14   See Deutscher 1969b, especially pp. 96, 164.

(USec). Even when Mandel had reconstructed the FI, aligning in leadership with Pierre Frank and Livio Maitan, and thus displacing Pablo, the programmatic shift that had been associated with the latter had indeed sunk deep, long-standing roots.

At this point, the SWP disappears from Stutje's narrative. Much is consequently missed, including an opportunity to highlight different aspects of Mandel's story. Between 1969 and 1974, for instance, Hansen (who had served as Trotsky's secretary in Mexico) and other SWP leaders initiated a Leninist-Trotskyist tendency within the United Secretariat, questioned (albeit all too gingerly) Mandel's growing enthusiasm for the perspective of continental guerrilla warfare in Latin America. This view, which had little in common with orthodox Trotskyist understandings of building mass revolutionary movements led by the working class, was increasingly popular with young, New Left Europeans influenced by Ché Guevara. The older SWP leadership, still embedded in the traditions of labour struggle associated with Cannon, grasped something of the significance of what was at issue as Mandel and the USec seemed content to jettison fundamental principles of Trotskyism's approach to the organisation of revolutionary forces, but by this point too little was made of divergences from basic Trotskyist principles. By the 1980s, moreover, a new layer of younger SWP leaders, with Jack Barnes first amongst them, was calling the shots, and it opted for an entirely different approach than that Hansen and his SWP colleagues of the 1960s and early 1970s espoused. Many veteran comrades reared in Cannon's SWP continued to insist on the relevance of Trotskyist fundamentals and were expelled for their views. At stake was nothing less than the on-going relevance of the basic concept of permanent revolution, a founding premise of the FI stipulating, amongst other things, that socialist revolutions could be achieved in the developing colonised world, but only if they were led by the proletariat, as opposed to the peasantry or other cross-class forces. It was Mandel's turn to mount a defence of basic principles, which he did. But the SWP was manoeuvring to exit the United Secretariat, and it had broken its affiliation with Mandel by 1990. Distancing itself from its own revolutionary heritage, the SWP became little more than a Cuba support group.

There is, to be sure, fascinating personal detail in Stutje's account about Mandel's relations with Ché Guevara and the Cuban state in the 1960s. It is unfortunate that this intriguing material could not be *integrated* with an analysis of the centrality of the Cuban question for late-20th-century Trotskyism. As much as Mandel and others in the USFI clung to the rhetoric of Trotskyism in their opposition to the SWP's 1980s trajectory, their actual politics often reflected the same appetite to substitute a 'quick fix' for the protracted and difficult politics of building working-class revolutionary organisations that could lead socialist revolutions effectively. Indeed, the history of the Mandel-led USec from the 1960s into the 1990s includes a fairly long list of those for whom revolutionaries were recruited to illusion. Some, such as Guevara in Bolivia, Allende in Chile or Lula in Brazil were more easily rationalised than others, such as Khomeini in Iran. Stutje asks at one point in his discussion of Mandel's position on 'armed struggle' in the late 1960s and early 1970s whether political stands which seemed to take 'no account of reality' were 'a failure of leadership', but never really gives an answer.[15]

Stutje thus neglects the important ramifications of the eventual USec/SWP split. He concentrates instead on Mandel's hopes for a revolutionary breakthrough on the part of Poland's Solidarność. In an accounting that places the accent not so much on the absence of a revolutionary leadership in Poland as on Mandel's relations with Polish comrades and his misplaced optimism in the possibilities of the moment, Stutje perhaps exaggerates the importance of the Polish debacle for Mandel and of his role in the Solidarność upheaval. It was, however, a pivotal turning point, a dry run for the implosion of the Soviet order.

When it all came to naught for the forces of revolution and the heralded fall of the Soviet Union produced not movement to the left of workers' democracy but to the right of a possessive individualism that reinstituted markets, profit-taking and private ownership, Mandel had no answers. He had not seen the writing on the wall in Poland, where a workers' resistance to Stalinist bureaucracy had been disfigured by clerical nationalism and the guiding light of American capitalism. Nor could Mandel discern that, as the Berlin Wall fell and Gorbachev gave way to Yeltsin, the primitive accumulation of capitalist restoration would result in a truly barbaric gutting of what remained of the gains of the October Revolution. Stutje, acknowledging that Mandel 'did not succeed in grasping the nature of the world in which he'd reached old age', avoids confronting the extent to which what he designates Mandel's 'optimism' was itself a reflection of a political wavering on the fundamental Trotskyist principles he claimed to have espoused his entire life.[16]

Intellectual Productions

If Stutje skirts the political, so too does he often give Mandel's ideals, expressed in his many books and articles, a surprisingly wide berth. Those looking to

---

15   Stutje 2009, p. 187.
16   Stutje 2009, p. 260.

this biography for an intellectual history of Mandel's contributions to Marxist political economy may well feel short-changed.

Take the all-too-brief ten-page chapter on Mandel's two-volume *Marxist Economic Theory*, for instance. It describes the book in outline, but then concentrates on Mandel's personal connections with mentors and friends associated with its writing, especially Roman Rosdolsky, whose comradely response was nonetheless resolutely critical. The difficulties in publishing the study are recounted, the reviews are listed, some correspondence with friends is cited. There is more in a chapter called 'The Worlds of Politics and Scholarship', but not enough to temper the criticism that the book reduces Mandel's writing to descriptive phrases, rather than engaging with and elaborating upon it.

In abbreviated passages on Mandel's *Late Capitalism* and his writing on long wave theory, Stutje relies on correspondence in the Mandel archives to stress that a number of colleagues thought these texts inadequately developed and in need of a more coherent presentation. He draws upon published criticism in *New Left Review* and *Historical Materialism*, but what seems missing is an appreciation of the extent to which, in the 1970s, this work broke new and creative ground in suggesting how the long boom of post-World War II capitalist expansion set the stage on which the Keynesian welfare state emerged. Yet capitalism could never make itself immune from the endemic crises that invariably punctuate its regimes of accumulation and restructure the politics, ideology and culture of an epoch. Mandel's studies of late capitalism and long waves thus creatively set the stage for appreciations of the material context of class struggle from the 1970s to the present, providing Marxists with a rare political economy of oscillation that has proven useful in explaining the episodic nature of workers' uprisings. In addition, as the Marxist cultural critic Frederic Jameson suggested, drawing on Mandel, the ideological wellsprings of late capitalism have the capacity to revive obfuscations at the point where the material relations of class seem to demand a war of opposing interests, masking the necessity of class struggle in a proliferating pyrotechnics of aesthetic productions.

Stutje touches down on little of this. He suggests that as much as Mandel's writings in these spheres sparkled, they too often lapsed into mono-causal explanation (the rate of profit) or failed to 'yield the promised synthesis'.[17] He seems content to call into question Mandel's formulations as incapable of differentiating capitalist continuity and the breaks that separate specific periods of capitalist development. It is entirely possible, however, that no such

---

17   Stutje 2009, p. 140.

divide need be imposed on Mandel's framework, which is able to accommodate appreciation of the *essential* continuities of capitalist regimes of accumulation *and* the *particularities* of epochs governed by important and determinate changes. As his friend and critic Rosdolsky would suggest to Mandel, Marx's method was dialectical and able to grasp the nature of change within seeming stasis. The difficulty was, as Mandel's life's work revealed, knowing when and how to push the change struggling within capitalism's confines in directions of revolutionary transformation. This was the task of the Fourth International and its various post-1953 incarnations, but the realisation of this end was balanced precariously on the difficult subjective struggle to cultivate and develop a revolutionary leadership capable of intervening in the inevitable crises of capitalism. But what produced such crises? It would be useful to have an assessment of this question in light of Mandel's writing, one that addresses the material significance of the tendency of the rate of profit to fall and the impact of combined and uneven development during late capitalism's intensified global reach. One of Mandel's last books, *Trotsky as Alternative* (1992), provides an opportunity to develop such a discussion, but the study receives only a few lines of rather idiosyncratic comment in *A Rebel's Dream Deferred*.

The Balance Sheet

The biography of a Marxist like Mandel, who struggled all of his life to keep the possibility of revolutionary advance alive, is a tremendously difficult undertaking. Invariably, the biographer, who is drawn to his subject not out of some 'great man' understanding of historical process but in the belief that a specific individual can, if properly situated within his or her historical context, cast light on an era and the subject's areas of influence, brings together the private and the public. How these spheres are balanced well so that they *develop* understanding is a delicate art, one far more difficult than most social historians, many of whom disparage biography, allow.

The articulation of the social, a short-hand for private life, is indeed well developed in this book; sympathetic readers will rightly find much in Stutje's pages that presents Mandel in new ways, not all of them pleasant for political readers to grapple with. This is to the good. The book, as a consequence, has a substantive feel for Mandel as a person, which is one reason that some of the strongest parts of the book outline his early years, when relations with his father and his intrepid struggles against fascism provide a fascinating background to his later development. As Mandel becomes increasingly important in the history of late capitalism's communist Left Opposition, necessitating deep understanding of his ideas, the politics of the Fourth International and its post-1953 Secretariats which Mandel headed, however, much is passed over too casually and quickly. Stutje ends up masking what Mandel, in his own writing and mobilising efforts, also obscured: the ISFI/USec's substitutionist politic, a perpetually unravelling thread running through Mandel's political life from the 1950s to his death in 1995.[18]

Who cannot, on some levels, empathise with Stutje? It is difficult to see how he could have adequately dealt with Mandel's life, his writings and theoretical contribution *and* his politics in anything less than a multi-volume study. This is neither what publishers want nor what many in the reading public welcome.

It is nonetheless what Mandel deserves. It is what is needed. As critical as it is necessary to be about this formidable figure in the history of late capitalism's small but pivotally important army of dedicated, *conscious* gravediggers, there is no denying Mandel's immense contribution and courage, both of which were evident as early as the 1930s and 1940s, when the ideals of his youth moved him to acts of sacrifice and daring. As he matured, his contributions shifted gears and the nature of his intellectual work revived Marxist appreciation of the centrality of materialist economic theorising. Yet Mandel was much more than a man of words: he revered revolutionary possibility and was willing to bank much, too much, on insurrectionary impulse. He was exhilarated by struggle, whether on the urban barricades or in the jungle; he would not renounce those who were in the fight when so many others were not. This drew him to the New Left, but it compromised him time and time again. If Mandel never dichotomised the organisational imperatives of the revolutionary left and the analytic richness of Marxist thought, he was too willing to champion the rebel who had insufficient grounding in either. At times (too many times, some will proclaim loudly) this revolutionary giant had toes of clay. Nonetheless, he still stood tall amongst those who have kept the hopes of revolution alive in the inauspicious times of our epoch. His dream may have been deferred, but all of us who see similarly what might be if only the workers of the world could break their ever-entangled chains owe Mandel much. A respectful deference is Mandel's due, albeit in ways always critical and never yielding the primacy of the political.

---

18   Note the parody of Mandel and the USec in Ali 1990, pp. 214–16, which presents a Mandel-like figure advocating deep entry into the world's religious institutions, so that the Trotskyist vanguard could eventually 'occupy the Vatican', electing a Pope as well as securing positions as cardinals, ayatollahs and rabbis.

PART 4

Appreciations

∴

Introduction to Part 4

Two essays in the last section constituted attempts to come to grips with the significance of individuals in the history of the revolutionary left. This concluding collection of writings continues this endeavour, but does so in ways that place the accent less on the historiographical and more on the individual.

The discussions of Eric J. Hobsbawm that lead this concluding section were originally written as keynote addresses for a 2005 conference at the Instituto Nacional de Antropologia e Historia in Mexico City. This remarkable event, celebrating both the history of the Mexican Revolution and Hobsbawm's role in developing a set of historical sensibilities that have contributed to understanding both revolution and what he termed 'primitive rebels', nurtured an exciting and wide-ranging dialogue amongst historians, anthropologists and others. My discussion of Hobsbawm was consciously schizophrenic. On the one hand, I have always been drawn to Hobsbawm's immense Marxist erudition, the reach of his knowledge and the richness of his global approach. The strengths of this 'metropolitan Marxism' are undeniable, and it is not an overstatement to declare that Hobsbawm's capacity to synthesise the history of capitalism in the epoch reaching from the 17th century to our present has no equal. On the other hand, it is not possible for someone immersed in the traditions of the Left Opposition to see in Hobsbawm's evasion of specific political realities associated with Stalinism an entirely laudable historical practice. It was no accident that many historians associated with the Communist Party Historians' Group in the 1950s took their leave from the CP and its Stalinism in 1956, but Hobsbawm did not. By the end of the 1970s Hobsbawm was associated with a variety of questionable political judgments. At the point of 'actually existing socialism's' dissolution in the 1980s and into the beginning of the 1990s, Hobsbawm had bent his pen too often in ways that proclaimed 'the end of class', which had become a mantra in certain intellectual circles. There is no doubt that Hobsbawm helped feed the appetite of the Labour Party's social-democratic immolation. Not for nothing was he known as 'Neil Kinnock's favourite Marxist' at a time when Kinnock was doing his best to savage the Labour Party left, led by Tony Benn but encompassing a number of militants whose allegiance was less to any iconic figure than it was to 'class-struggle politics'. It was Hobsbawm's tragedy that he would lend his voice to the ultimate descent of Britain's party of parliamentary socialism, reduced by the 1980s and 1990s to a compromised shell of its former but always moderate origins, into Blairism. As much as I admired one Eric, whom I knew as a congenial individual and powerful Marxist intellect, I could never quite make my peace with the other Eric and his politics of capitulation, however 'reasonable' the rationales on offer.

If my appreciation of Hobsbawm was thus tempered and divided, I must confess to being less able to rein in my sentiments of regard and affection for the two individuals who are the subject of short statements closing this volume of writings. In ways as different as it is possible to imagine, James P. Cannon and Edward Palmer (E.P.) Thompson have tracked my own trajectory and its concern with Marxism and historical practice.

In the case of Cannon, I never met the man, yet I feel that I have spent more time with him than with most of the people who inhabit my circles of family and intimates. I once asked my friend James Barrett, who has published an important and stimulating biography of Cannon's contemporary William Z. Foster,[1] whether he actually liked Foster. He could not really answer – in part, I suspect, because Foster was not terribly easy to like. Cannon was somewhat different; although he was often reviled, he was, as I learned from talking to those who survived into the 1990s and were part of his inner circle, equally likely to be revered, even amongst those who laughingly pointed to his many foibles. Cannon has captivated my interest for decades, and one volume of my three-volume study has been published.[2] I cannot shake my liking of his indomitable revolutionary spirit, which he translated into a life-long struggle for social justice guided by his belief in Marxism and its meaning in the modern world. The short reflection on Cannon's life that appears here was commissioned for a collection of essays on radicalism in the United States, and stands as a shorthand statement of a legacy of struggle waged against a bank of stacked decks.

Thompson I did know, and found him impossible not to appreciate. It was not his Marxism that I admired, for E.P. Thompson's Marxism came and went. In this he differed markedly from Cannon. But Thompson's contribution to historical practice, in terms of articulating a sensibility about the past and conveying it in published works of explosive passion and unrivalled imaginative argument, were for my generation of materialist social historians a boundless well of stimulation and suggestion. We all drank the Thompson brew, perhaps sometimes with too much abandon. Once tasted, Edward was intoxicating, and the high did not diminish from knowing him personally. My own writing on Thompson began in the late 1970s, as I was coming to grips with being a historian and seeking to correct what I considered apolitical and wrongheaded understandings of Thompson's 'gentility' then current amongst certain

---

1   Barrett 1999.
2   B. Palmer 2007.

ill-informed historians in Canada.[3] Later, deeply affected by Edward's death, I sat down to write a 'short' obituary for *Labour/Le Travail*, which quickly turned into a two-part essay, over 100 pages in length, that was then republished by Verso in 1994.[4] As I stated in the introduction to that book, it was not a 'biography' – more of an homage. But I do not think, contrary to some commentary, that this constitutes hagiography. In the essay that closes this collection, commissioned for a volume commemorating the 50th anniversary of the publication of *The Making of the English Working Class*, I address Thompson's argumentativeness, his awkwardness and his penchant for paradox. It seems to be a fitting note on which to bring to an end a collection of my own writings on Marxism and historical practice.

---

3   B. Palmer 1981a.
4   B. Palmer 1994b.

CHAPTER 10

Hobsbawm's History: Metropolitan Marxism and Analytic Breadth*

'There's a freshman in King's who knows about everything', declared Cambridge's undergraduate weekly, *Granta*, on 7 June 1939. The precocious undergraduate profiled was, of course, Eric J. Hobsbawm, said to have 'at his fingertips the strangest details about the obscurest subjects and the names of all the authorities which he could bandy around with an easy familiarity'. He would wander into the English club and raise puzzling questions about Wordsworth; the French and German societies looked upon his casual digressions as profundities that 'might properly come only from God'. Historians he chastised as in need of 'adventure in the cultural arts'. But he managed to skip a lot of their lectures. A jazz enthusiast and a lover of literature, the student Eric could also be counted on, when the political chips were down, to stick to 'Lenin and Stalin'. Cambridge in the late 1930s was a unique nursery of the radical and the irreverent and, admittedly, the brief student note had been penned by a man, Pieter Keuneman, who was destined to spend much of his life as the general secretary of the Sri Lankan Communist Party. But Hobsbawm was clearly *sui generis*.[1]

This has perhaps been lost sight of in our recent attentions to the *collectivity* within which Hobsbawm emerged as a singular figure in contemporary historiography. We too easily lump together a strikingly productive, creative and politically engaged cohort of historians whose origins lay in the Communist Party of Great Britain and its Historians' Group, labelling them rather lumpishly *the* British Marxist historians.[2] Leaving aside the *political* differences within

---

* 'Marxismo Metropolitano y Amplitud Analitca en la historia de Hobsbawm', in *Los Historiadores y La Historia para el Sigo XXI: Homenaje a Eric J. Hobsbawm*, edited by Gumersindo Vera Hernandez and José Patoja (Mexico City: Escuela Nacional de Antropolígia e Historia, 2006), 145–58. Published here under the title 'Hobsbawm's History: Metropolitan Marxism and Analytic Breadth'.

1 The Keuneman article is reproduced in Samuel and Stedman Jones 1982a, pp. 366–8. On Keuneman, see Ferns 1983, pp. 101, 104; Hobsbawm 2002, pp. 112, 125.

2 Writing on the Historians' Group ranges from right to left. See Himmelfarb 1987, pp. 70–93; Hobsbawm 1978a, pp. 21–48; Kiernan 1984, pp. 7–10; B. Schwartz 1990, pp. 44–95; Parker 1997, pp. 33–58; Ashman 1998, pp. 145–60. There is of course an advantage in treating the British

this contingent, which surfaced in complicating ways in 1956,[3] there are significant divergences in how these historians practiced their craft evident in even the most cursory comparison, for instance, of Eric Hobsbawm, E.P. Thompson and Christopher Hill.

Hobsbawm's history generally exhibits a kind of metropolitan and synthetic vision most congenially developed out of printed sources accessible in major research libraries and amenable to being painted on a 'national', even international, canvas. This is most emphatically the case in his trilogy plus one (how many historians produce tetralogies?), a powerful overview that takes us from 1789 to the close of the 20th century.[4] But it is even the mark of titles such as *Primitive Rebels* and *Bandits* that would seem to be more specifically cast in the mould of social and cultural histories of particularity, even of his origins as a labour historian, where essays in *Labouring Men* rarely draw on archival researches.[5] Sustained in part by prodigious reading and a felicity with languages, as well as an eye always trained on the big picture of capitalist development and transformation and the sociological relations thrown up and constantly disrupted in its wake, Hobsbawm's metropolitan Marxist vision has focussed on generality and interpretation's widest of reaches.

E.P. Thompson, in contrast, was always a *provincial* English writer in the best sense of the word, producing histories that began with the specifics of evidence and the particularities of experience best culled from original probes into sources others had passed by or neglected to examine carefully and sensitively. Thompson, too, generalised, but unlike Hobsbawm, who was attracted to

---

Marxist historians as a collectivity, for it allows an immensely useful formulaic introduction to a body of generally congruent work. This is the value of Kaye 1984 and 1992.

3 For instance, the issue is more complex than that of E.P. Thompson and John Saville leading an exit from the British Communist Party and Hobsbawm remaining with the CP. While Christopher Hill made his departure along with Thompson, Saville and others, he harboured a lengthy difference with Thompson, whom he criticised posthumously for not having stayed in the Party and fought for its reform. See Christopher Hill, 'The Shock Tactician', *Times Higher Education Supplement*, 7 October 1994.

4 Hobsbawm 1962; 1975; 1987; 1994. A stimulating assessment of these volumes appears in Perry Anderson, 'Confronting Defeat', *London Review of Books*, 17 October 2002.

5 Hobsbawm 1959; 1969; 1964. In a 'Note on Selection and Sources' to his first book, a documentary collection, *Labour's Turning Point, 1880–1900* (1948), Hobsbawm commented that the extracts had been culled from 'pamphlets and leaflets; newspaper and periodical files, Socialist and non-Socialist; the important series of official and unofficial surveys and enquiries; and the mass of biographical and memoir literature'. Hobsbawm 1948, p. xxv. In short, original archival probes were not part of his method of collection.

'models',[6] he always accented a deeper sense of historical context, even to the point of pressing home peculiarities rather than universals, building on local texture and a fine-grained sensibility of layered complications.[7] West Riding sources, he acknowledged, coloured his account of the making of the English working class, for he had lived and worked in the district,[8] and wherever he travelled and lectured Thompson relished the prospect of visiting the local archive to unearth, in a disciplined way, the specific context he wanted to illuminate.[9] Indeed, it would be difficult to imagine two historians who were more instinctually different than Thompson and Hobsbawm, whose research and analytic methods parallel some rather sharp oppositions of personal character. As Hobsbawm noted in a 1995 obituary of Thompson, for the author of *The Making of the English Working Class*, '[b]ig cities, even those with Public Record Offices and British Libraries, were places to visit, not for living'.[10] Thompson's final publications, including his close and meticulous reconstruction of Blake's spiritual universe and his exploration of his father's connection to Rabindranath Tagore, depended on fresh archival discoveries and examination of previously unexplored evidence: in the one case of a cache of material relating to the religious influence on Blake of Emanuel Swedenborg and Ludwig Muggleton, and in the other of his forays into the Thompson family archives.[11]

Christopher Hill, as yet a third member of the Historians' Group, was still again another case. His scholarship, more narrowly focussed on the English Revolutions of 1640 and 1688, constructed his 17th-century studies on the basis of an encyclopaedic command of the extensive pamphlet productions of the period, especially those of his beloved Diggers and Levellers. Supplemented by deep appreciations of critical figures such as Cromwell and Milton, Hill came to dominate his field in a way that Hobsbawm and Thompson, in spite of their influence, never managed to achieve.[12] Not until the 'hard right' backlash of

---

6   On models and the contrasts between Hobsbawm and Thompson with respect to this and social anthropology, see Hobsbawm 1985, p. 71, and Thompson 1972, pp. 41–55; Thompson 1978b, pp. 247–66.

7   Thompson 1965, pp. 311–62.

8   Thompson 1963a, p. 13.

9   B. Palmer 2002, pp. 190–1.

10   Hobsbawm 1996, p. 532. In my judgment, Hobsbawm understates Thompson's commitment to archival research in this account.

11   See Thompson 1993c; Thompson 1993a.

12   Christopher Hill's published work is extensive, but note possibly his best and most influential study, Hill 1972b. See as well Hill 1972a; Hill 1984.

revisionism assailed all interpretations that posited the possibilities of class struggle influencing historical development in ways that might register in intelligible progress did Hill come under forceful attack in the 1970s and 1980s.[13]

Too much, to be sure, can be made of such methodological (not to mention personal and political) differences. But Thompson, certainly, was aware of their significance, as a somewhat critical short review of the work and career of George Rude revealed.[14] Moreover, they colour much of the relations of a crop of rugged individualists who have been assimilated to an almost canonical 'group' status. Whatever Hobsbawm shared with this collectivity, and this was not trivial, it is nevertheless the case that he stood out from the ranks in more ways than one.

Critically important in this constellation of difference was his metropolitan Marxist breadth of analysis, the range and reach of his reinterpretations. A survey of Hobsbawm's intellectual concerns and published texts find him as comfortable in commentary on the Marxist theory of pre-capitalist economic formations as he is in discussing (albeit in ways that can be criticised) the current state of labour and the left.[15] Historically his writings range across centuries and continents. Hobsbawm seems to know all 'ages' – of revolution, of capital, of empire, of our own interesting times – just as he addresses timeless and, of late, particularly timely topics, such as nationalism.[16] Exploring subjects that bear his own stamp of discovery – such as primitive rebels or tramping artisans – he is also capable of intervening in debates, like the standard-of-living controversy, and placing on them his particular Marxist interpretive accent.[17] A historian of his own analytic framework, historical materialism, Hobsbawm has provided informed commentary on the broad history of Marxism and its meaning,[18] just as he wades into troubled contemporary analytic waters buoyed by a wide understanding of the left, its past, its present and its future.[19] No one who came out of the British Communist Party Historians' Group commented so regularly on communist fortunes in countries other than the United

---

13 Anderson 1992a, pp. 284–5.
14 E.P. Thompson, 'Sold Like a Sheep for a Pound', review of George Rude, *Protest and Punishment*, *New Society*, 14 December 1978.
15 See, as examples only, Hobsbawm in Marx 1969; Hobsbawm 1981; 1989.
16 Hobsbawm 1990.
17 Hobsbawm 1959; 1964, esp. pp. 34–63, 64–157.
18 Hobsbawm 1968, pp. 37–56; 1971a, pp. 5–21; 1982b, pp. 327–44; 1982a, pp. 1–28.
19 Most controversial, perhaps, was Hobsbawm 1978b, pp. 121–38, which gave rise to a sharp feminist rejoinder, Alexander, Davin, and Hostettler 1979, pp. 174–82.

Kingdom, including Italy, Germany and France, or maintained an interest in non-communist movements of the revolutionary left, such as anarchism.[20] Whether in narrative histories rich in idiosyncratic insight or polemics now embedded in the historiography – such as his contribution to the debate over the crisis of the 17th century[21] – Hobsbawm has charged and recharged the batteries of historical practice with his special boost. In Perry Anderson's list of Hobsbawm's 'astonishing fusion of gifts' are: 'economy of synthesis; vividness of detail; global scope, yet acute sense of regional difference; polymathic fluency, equally at ease with crops and stock markets, nations and classes, statesmen and peasants, sciences and arts; breadth of sympathies for disparate social agents; powers of analytic narrative; and not least a style of remarkable clarity and energy, whose signature is a sudden bolt of metaphoric electricity across the even surface of cool pungent argument'.[22] Hobsbawm is obviously as uncommon a historian as the uncommon common people he has so often written about.[23]

This range and scope is of course the antithesis of academic scholasticism, in which careers and reputations rest on increasingly narrow ledges of partial knowledge.[24] Hobsbawm has never been interested in such restricted terrain, in spite of the fact that some of his early historical essays pioneered the examination of discrete subject areas, from custom, wages and workload to machine breakers and Methodism.[25] Rather, in what is the lost tradition of 19th-century Marxism, Hobsbawm has always gestured towards the expansive generalisation and, whatever the locale of his study, tried to grasp totality, never settling for the limited. Even when examining sectional interest – as in his treatment of the labour aristocracy, a preoccupation that links his path-breaking 1964 collection of essays, *Labouring Men*, to a companion volume published two decades later, *Workers: Worlds of Labor* – Hobsbawm insists on connecting the particular and specific to the general and broad-ranging trends of development and change.[26]

---

20   Note the number of essays on such topics in Hobsbawm 1973, and, for particular attractions to the Italian communist movement, Hobsbawm 1977b; 2002, pp. 346–61.

21   Hobsbawm 1954a, pp. 33–53; 1954b, 44–65, this two part article being reproduced in Hobsbawm 1967, pp. 5–62; 1960, pp. 97–112.

22   Perry Anderson, 'Confronting Defeat', *London Review of Books*, 17 October 2002.

23   Hobsbawm 1998.

24   Hobsbawm 1971b, pp. 20–45.

25   Hobsbawm 1964, pp. 5–33, 344–70. Note the commentary in Hobsbawm 1985, pp. 63–74, as well as the early documentary collection *Labour's Turning Point* (1948).

26   Essays on the labour aristocracy appear in Hobsbawm 1964, pp. 272–315 and in Hobsbawm 1984, pp. 214–72.

In doing so he cultivates knowledges esoteric and theoretical as well as subjects well off the beaten path. What Marxist historian's repertoire includes equally sophisticated treatments of the gangster, the guerrilla and Gramsci?[27] And who combines this with the artistry of cultural criticism, Hobsbawm having cultivated, under the pseudonym Francis Newton, the reputation of an accomplished connoisseur and published commentator on jazz?[28]

It is the audacity of this project that overwhelms. Hobsbawm has the intellectual *chutzpah* to create fields, as with his stimulating provocations to explore the invention of tradition.[29] He is also willing to fly in the face of traditions he finds less than exemplary, evident in his brave 1982 address to the Irish Labour History Society, 'What is the Workers' Country?', in which he queried the extent to which it is in the interests of labouring people to embrace nationalism.[30]

In the sense that Hobsbawm's metropolitan Marxist vision allows him to peer into quiet corners of neglect and sweep boldly across the macro-histories of large-scale development, he is the living embodiment of the revolutionary reach for totalising interpretation that characterised the founders of historical materialism, Marx and Engels, and that has always informed historical writing in the best of this tradition. This results in certain difficulties for those who wish to pigeon-hole or to imitate.

Hobsbawm, for instance, is impossible to categorise easily. When Richard Johnson insisted on creating a catalogue-type listing of oppositional texts in the Marxist tradition of historical research, pitting the culturalist against the structuralist, Hobsbawm stood virtually alone in his bifurcation. Johnson placed some of the essays in *Labouring Men* in the culturalist column, along with *Primitive Rebels*, but clearly acknowledged the more structuralist bent of other writings.[31] There is no Hobsbawm 'school' of historical practice,[32] although widespread allusion to a Thompsonian sensibility is evident in historical writ-

---

27 Hobsbawm 1955, pp. 243–56; 1970, pp. 51–62; 1973, pp. 163–97; 'The Great Gramsci', *New York Review of Books*, 4 April 1974; Hobsbawm 1977a, pp. 205–13.

28 Originally published under the Newton imprimatur in 1959, note Hobsbawm 1993; Coe 1983, pp. 149–58; Hobsbawm 1998, pp. 236–94.

29 Hobsbawm 1983a, pp. 1–14; 1983b, pp. 263–308.

30 Hobsbawm 1984, 49–65.

31 Johnson 1979, p. 60.

32 Note the brief opening comment in Genovese 1984, p. 13. Indeed, as Anderson comments, his synthetic histories have received 'less discussion than they deserve ... This is partly a matter of the scale of their performance, which virtually defies any all-round view of them'. Perry Anderson, 'Confronting Defeat', *London Review of Books*, 17 October 2002.

ing. Hill has left his interpretive edge cutting deeply into the understanding of the 17th century, but Hobsbawm's history has been too grandiose in its analytic breadth to register so decisively or to be mimicked in dissertations or drawn together in commentaries by other academics. Of all of those writing, or writing recently, in the broad variety of Marxist traditions, perhaps only Perry Anderson compares to Hobsbawm, precisely because his sweeping studies, which reach from antiquity to the present, combine Hobsbawm's sense of analytic reach and a studied concern with intellectuals. But even Anderson has never quite attained the *balance* that is uniquely Hobsbawm's, of generalisation and overview, of attention to power, structure and determination as much as agency, *and* of bringing together history from below and history from above.[33]

Indeed, it is most likely Hobsbawm's commitment to the negotiation of various strands of what has too often become, politically and intellectually, the fragmentation of Marxism that situates his *oeuvre* not at the crossroads and byways of historical materialism, but at a core few choose to struggle to invigorate and revive, let alone locate. Theory and engagement, empirical recovery and speculative synthesis fuse in Hobsbawm's project of generalisation and creative adaptation of Marxist orthodoxies, most of which have withered on the abusive vine of contemporary denigration and dismissal. All of Hobsbawm's writing addresses the determinative authority of capitalism or the tensions associated with transitions to this revolutionising mode of production. He retains a language of 'the economic laws of the development of the base', albeit acknowledging that most Marxist historians have actually addressed the relations of base and superstructure.[34] As Raphael Samuel and Gareth Stedman Jones declared in 1983, 'It has been Hobsbawm's quite unusual combination of theoretical clarity, large generalising capacity and an uncanny eye for suggestive detail, pulling in seemingly unusable *faits divers* and bric-a-brac to produce imaginatively compelling and wholly unexpected syntheses that has made his approach, particularly in social history, so influential, if, of course, not at all easy to reproduce ... [O]ne thing which arguably remains most distinctively Marxist

---

33   Anderson's writing, from his earlier studies of the absolutist state and the passage from
      antiquity to feudalism to his more recent writing on social theory, has moved into increasingly less Marxist territory, although his commentaries on intellectuals and other issues
      nevertheless remain impressive. For examples only, see Anderson 1973; 1974; 1980; 1983;
      1992a; 1992b; 1998; 2004. Commentary on Anderson includes Elliott 1998 and Blackledge
      2004.
34   Abelove, et al. 1983, p. 39.

about his approach is a brilliantly illuminating but ultimately quite orthodox
Marxist approach to the old problem of the relationship between "base and
superstructure".[35]

And yet, for all his passion for rich examples, Hobsbawm demands that
the past can never be a simple reservoir of anachronism; rather, it is studied
because it provides suggestion of where we are going and why. As he noted in
a 1983 interview, historical perspective enriches the endeavour of seeing

> how society changes and when things are different and when they are
> the same. This is one big reason, one practical reason, why one should be
> Marxist. That's the way to ask those types of questions.[36]

Precisely because Hobsbawm eschews the simple art of descriptive, narrative
storytelling, which some historians now extol as a virtue compelling enough to
replace interpretation, he is demanding enough to refuse the tendency to lose
oneself in the limits of specifics and even their romanticisation. He insists on
historical writing retaining its explanatory purpose, always locating the past
and its meanings in our presents and futures.[37]

For all of these reasons, Hobsbawm is often declared to be the premier Marxist historian of our times.[38] As Genovese notes and others have also commented, Hobsbawm's strength as a Marxist is that his work stands as a powerful
defence of historical materialism and the primacy of class analysis, a consist-
ent demonstration that it is the Marxist reach for a totalising interpretive stand
which alone 'can take full account of art, science, religion, ideology, and even
social psychology', locating such forces in the contested relations of material
power and their many, varied and historicised outcomes. If Genovese scaffolded this argument on a negative assessment of the like claims of 'critical theory', 'the romance of lower-class culture' and 'assorted other fads', Samuel and
Stedman Jones made the same point by stressing that Hobsbawm has successfully integrated Marxist concerns and questions into the syllabi of economic
and social historians in general: '[P]erhaps one of Hobsbawm's most outstanding and least commented upon achievements has been his ability to bring

---

35   Samuel and Stedman Jones 1982b, p. x. In this, of course, Hobsbawm is again differentiated
     from Thompson, whose rejection of the base-superstructure model was more unorthodox.
     See Thompson 1957.

36   Abelove et al. 1983, p. 43.

37   Hobsbawm 1985, p. 72.

38   Kaye 1984, p. 130; Susman and Genovese 1978, p. 9; Cronin 1978–9, pp. 87–109; Genovese
     1984, pp. 13–36.

together the propositions of classical Marxism and the empirical preoccupations of social and economic historians into a virtually seamless web'. In the process, claim Samuel and Stedman Jones, Marxist approaches to industrialisation, popular rebellion, 'pre-industrial protest', unionisation, urbanisation and revolutionary parties and movements have become 'almost part of the "common sense" of academic inquiry and research'.[39] Hobsbawm, Genovese suggests, is a rare Marxist who reaches towards a totalising history of society, understanding class as the motor force of revolutionary possibility, but also, as so often in the conditions of its past, an inadequate vehicle for the realisation of societal transformation. In this, he is 'the man who refused to run away' from both the bourgeois apologists and ideologues as well as the utopians of the left whose wish fulfilments have, in Genovese's view, obscured our understanding of 19th- and 20th-century class formations and proletarian movements.[40]

Hobsbawm's metropolitan Marxist vision has indeed been hard-nosed and interpretively demanding, addressing proletarian defeat and inadequacy more than is the norm in left-wing scholarly circles. He has written of *labouring men* and the *worlds of labour*, even of the epoch of *revolution*, but Hobsbawm has never authored a book titled *The Age of the Proletariat*, precisely because there has not been such a period in our past. A powerful understanding of society's making in the vice grip of bourgeois culture and capitalist development animates Hobsbawm's *oeuvre*. That making has been capitalist, and Hobsbawm, the Marxist, gives the devil his due: capital has restructured the lives of generations of people and continues to do so; it has brought nations into being, fanning the flames of proletarian attachment to 'country' rather than to class, and it has altered the socio-economic, cultural and political landscape of a *world system* of globalised oppression and exploitation.

Revolution has of course threatened, not often as a *social upheaval*, but enough to indicate that Marx and Engels were not wrong to suggest the possibility that capitalism was indeed creating its own gravediggers. Why the working class has not been manning the shovels and digging that grave is, of course, a complicated question that grows more and more troubled and complex with each passing crisis. Hobsbawm suggests answers from the past, answers that apply to our present and our futures, answers that few on the left today explore all that seriously. In a brilliant chapter in perhaps his most brilliant synthetic

39   Genovese 1984, p. 13; Samuel and Stedman Jones 1982b, p. ix. See, as well, Abelove et al. 1983, pp. 39–40, in which Hobsbawm addresses the need for a dialogue between Marxists and non-Marxists.
40   Genovese 1984, especially pp. 20–34.

book, *The Age of Capital*, Hobsbawm addresses the 1848 'Springtime of Peoples' with the intellectual pessimism needed, in retrospect, to understand the class defeats that set the stage on which bourgeois hegemony would soon strut so self-confidently: 'As for the labouring poor, they lacked the organization, the maturity, the leadership, perhaps most of all the historical conjuncture, to provide a political alternative. Strong enough to make the prospect of social revolution look real and menacing, they were too weak to do more than frighten their enemies'.[41]

I want to close by suggesting that Hobsbawm's metropolitan Marxist vision was so powerful because of his creative attachment to fundamental orthodoxies, especially his conviction that capitalism was a socio-economic beast whose taming could only come with its defeat by a revolutionary working class, a process as necessary as it was likely to embody elements of violence. Like all great Marxist writers, Hobsbawm's empathy for the labouring poor emerges in his writing's antagonism to what has been done, in the name of propriety and profit, to people's bodies, feelings and dignities. Against the oppressions and exploitations that have driven capitalist progress, Hobsbawm, from a very early age and through much of his historical writing, erected such edifices as he could to understand, encourage and move forward the likelihood of revolutionary, anti-capitalist opposition. Whether it was consideration of the human wreckage of capitalism's early 'dark Satanic mills'[42] or African-American jazz singers, Hobsbawm could wax eloquent in his empathy for those who bore capitalism's disfigurements and his abhorrence of the large forces that turned them into victims. Here, for instance, are Hobsbawm's (a.k.a. Francis Newton's) closing words in a short 1959 obituary for the legendary Billie Holiday:

> To be born with both beauty and self-respect in the Negro ghetto of Baltimore in 1915 was too much of a handicap, even without rape at the age of ten and drug-addiction in her teens. But, while she destroyed herself, she sang, unmelodious, profound, and heart-breaking. It is impossible not to weep for her, or not to hate the world which made her what she was.[43]

This is the language of the revolutionary, and it was words such as these that lay behind Eric Hobsbawm's metropolitan Marxist vision, to which he added his peculiar capacity, evident in Cambridge in 1939, to know about everything.

---

41   Hobsbawm 1975, p. 21.
42   Hobsbawm 1964, pp. 105–19.
43   Hobsbawm 1998, p. 294.

Hobsbawm's vision, on this general level, produced a Marxist body of historical writing that reached, in its analytic breadth, across centuries and continents. It has come very close indeed to achieving that illusive, totalising 'history of society' that all Marxists believe is both possible and necessary. But of course the interpretation of the world is but a part of the Marxist project, and the dialectics of analysis and activity are complicated and always reciprocal.[44] Hobsbawm's construction of a metropolitan Marxism was a kind of primitive intellectual accumulation, growing out of the base of his revolutionary commitments and cosmopolitan European immersion in the canon of socialism. But this was not, sadly, sustained over time, nor was it ever entirely unencumbered by the identification with Stalinism that was part of Hobsbawm's being. Ultimately, it is possible to argue, Hobsbawm's metropolitan Marxism began to lose its moorings, culminating in a revisionist 'realism' that would derail in the difficult defeats suffered by the left in the 1980s and 1990s.[45]

---

44   For a brilliant statement, see Anderson 1976.

45   I pick up on this theme in the next chapter, which was paired with this essay when it was originally delivered as a two-part lecture: 'Hobsbawm's Politics: The Forward March of the Popular Front Halted' (B. Palmer 2005). Hobsbawm has referred to Stalinism as 'the hypertrophy of the bureaucratized, dictatorial state', but he has spent little time analysing it in a sophisticated way. See Hobsbawm 1973, p. 85. Hobsbawm 2002 and 1994 are not much help on Stalinism, for which see the acutely insightful review of the former title by Perry Anderson, 'The Age of EJH', *London Review of Books*, 3 October 2002.

CHAPTER 11

Hobsbawm's Politics: The Forward March of the Popular Front Halted*

To be a historian of the Left is a responsibility and a burden. Few write with breadth of vision, critical engagement, passion for evidence and commitment to reason, embracing as well revolutionary social change – foundations all of a calling as difficult as any to realise. It is one thing to research deeply, theorise imaginatively, orchestrate materials from the past to construct its blazing colours in all of their glory *and* despair and write with creativity and flair. Quite another to tend the garden of politics, where the blooms of one month fade and the foliage of another can be overtaken by weeds, some of which are quite compelling in their attractiveness. Figures honoured for their labours in certain tasks, can be, quite uncharitably, taken to task for their toils in another. Thus Perry Anderson once wrote of E.P. Thompson as 'our finest socialist writer today', concluding in 1980 that Thompson's oeuvre constituted 'the most declared political history of any of his generation'. Yet for all such praise, Thompson still lacked, in Anderson's view, 'either an intermediate or a long-term programme of objectives for a *socialist* movement'.[1] To be a Marxist historian, as is undeniably Eric Hobsbawm's touchstone of identity, is to court political critique.

I enter into that project aware of the twin pitfalls that inevitably plague the revolutionary left – arrogance and sectarianism – but insistent that avoiding the hard and often harsh questions and findings posed in an examination of Hobsbawm's life as a historian *and* a Marxist is no service to either historiography or politics. As much as Hobsbawm's historical range and depth, his reach and his interpretive vision, are indeed daunting, they were always, in some senses, compromised and brought back to the densely packed, sometimes barren terrain of 20th-century politics, in which the kind of leftism he

---

* 'Las politicas de Hobsbawm: se ha detnindo la marcha hacia adelante del Frente Popular', in *Los Historioadores y La Historia para el Sigo XXI: Homenaje a Eric J. Hobsbawm*, edited by Gumersindo Vera Hernandez and José Patoja (Mexico City: Escuela Nacional de Antropolíga e Historia, 2006), 93–104. Published here under the title 'Hobsbawm's Politics: The Forward March of the Popular Front Halted'.

1 Anderson 1980, pp. 1, 204.

embraced called out for rejoinder. In Hobsbawm's life and in the conceptualisation of the world that ordered his histories, however rich and varied, Stalinism
and, in particular, the Popular Front of the 1930s loomed large and left the mark
of deformation, one that became increasingly visible in the cauldron of the
1980s, when so much of the so-called communism of the 20th century crashed
and burned, leaving in its wake the scorched earth of a revolutionary left seemingly vanquished from the politics of our time.

There is, I will suggest, a disjuncture in the *histories* and the *politics* of
Hobsbawm. To some extent such a radical separation is evident in all of us
on the left who are historians. To research and write, guided by the insights
of Marxism, is, however difficult, easier than to struggle against capitalism and
realise another world. But in Hobsbawm's case, ironically, the rift is all the more
evident because of the rich range of his historical practice, one that throws
shortcomings of political engagement into sharp relief. One leftist actually
suggested in the mid-1990s that there were two Hobsbawms, a schizophrenic
congealment that was difficult to reconcile.

On the one hand, Eric the Red was ending his *The Age of Extremes* (1994)
with an assessment of capitalism's threatening drive to destruction:

> We live in a world captured, uprooted and transformed by the titanic eco-
> nomic and techno-scientific process of the development of capitalism,
> which has dominated the past two or three centuries. We know, or at
> least it is reasonable to suppose, that it cannot go on *ad infinitum*. The
> future cannot be a continuation of the past, and there are signs, both
> externally, and, as it were, internally, that we have reached a point of his-
> toric crisis. The forces generated by the techno-scientific economy are
> now great enough to destroy the environment, that is to say, the material
> foundations of human life. The structures of human societies themselves,
> including even some of the social foundations of the capitalist economy,
> are on the point of being destroyed by the erosion of what we have inher-
> ited from the human past. Our world risks both explosion and implosion.
> It must change.[2]

On the other, Eric of Radical Reconciliation was serving as the intellectual
and political brains trust of political accommodation to the processes he so
decried in *Age of Extremes*. Hobsbawm's mid-1980s assault on 'retreating into
extremism' and his insistence that the Labour Party needed to reconstitute

---

2 Hobsbawm 1994, pp. 584–5.

itself as a popular-frontist body attractive to the broad anti-Thatcher coalition that might turn back the tide of reaction would, in actuality, culminate in a rightward trajectory that was truly destructive of socialist possibility and alternative. Blairism and New Labour would emerge out of the jettisoning of even the mildest of social-democratic programmatic vocabulary to become the rhetorical ballast of George Bush's imperial presidency and a New World Order that was defined by its explosive and implosive ruptures. The march to historic crisis continued apace, with Hobsbawm seemingly having tipped his hat to the carnage.[3]

Antonio Polito's interviews with Hobsbawm, conducted at the end of the 1990s and published in English in 2000, bring together these two Hobsbawms. Capable of insightful commentary on inequality's world reach and the threat of environmental degradation, Hobsbawm's radical pessimism unfolded with little sense of security as to what the new millennium would bring. Scathing in his mild-mannered refusal to concede to 'Western experts' much credit for how to bring about 'development' on a global scale, blunt in his assessment of the costs extracted in the transition from a problematised 'socialism' in the Soviet Union to a bandit capitalism in Russia, feeding voraciously off the primitive accumulation of a revolutionary workers' state that had long ago succumbed to hostile pressures and the internal drift into bureaucratised Stalinisation, Hobsbawm remained capable of staking out left positions. His commentary on war and nationalism or the oppressive terror waged on the Palestinians by the Israeli state made this abundantly clear. But in his discussions of what remains of the left, Hobsbawm proved disturbingly accommodating, to the point of considering, albeit critically, both Tony Blair and Bill Clinton to be leaders of the left. He seemed unable to face up to his own role in paving the road to Blairism, oblivious to his christening as 'Neil Kinnock's Favourite Marxist'.[4]

Hobsbawm's autobiographical *Interesting Times: A Twentieth-Century Life* (2002) allows us entry into this problematic bifurcation of past and present, history and politics. Few autobiographies are as internally differentiated, in style, in sensitivity, indeed in truth. His memoir commences with a flourish: a riveting account of Hobsbawm's youth which draws on its author's unrivalled historical imagination, fusing the particularities of growing up marked as something

---

3 The notion of two Hobsbawms introduces Harman 2002. On the developments of the mid-1980s see, among many possible sources, Miliband 1985, pp. 5–28; Norris 1993, pp. 5–14. Hobsbawm's politico-journalistic writings of this period appear in Hobsbawm 1989. Particularly useful is the survey of Pimlott 2005.

4 Hobsbawm with Polito 2000, esp. pp. 106–7, 113.

of a cosmopolitan outsider – Jewish and without roots of place and national identity – with a sensitivity to the tumultuous events that unfolded across his own early age of extremes. Born in the year of proletarian revolution, 1917, Hobsbawm's first two decades were ones of personal trauma that included the death of both parents, difficult adjustments into kinship networks of cultured caring that were always nevertheless perched on the edge of economic insecurity and a forced march from Alexandria to Vienna to Berlin to London that reverberated with the echoes of fascism's jackboot advances. Only a historian of Hobsbawm's immense range could craft such a portrait, in which his childhood and adolescence is woven into the texture of the first third of the 20th century, a period 'surrounded by the debris of defeat, ruined empires, and economic collapse', contextualising his formative years as 'the most murderous as well as the most revolutionary era in history'.[5]

Hobsbawm's remembrances of his recruitment to Communism in Berlin in the last days of the KPD are an extraordinary portrayal, combining literary elegance and surprisingly candid political judgment, anything but uncritical of the Comintern's suicidal structuring of its German revolutionary ranks into a sectarian refusal of the need to rally anti-fascists together rather than cut them into corpses to be fed, one by one, to Hitler's Nazis. In the outline of the libidinal charge of participating in the last Communist parade in Berlin, Hobsbawm provides an eloquent accounting of the exuberance of youthful revolutionary spirit: 'We belonged together', he writes of himself at age 16 and his comrades, swept in 'mass ecstasy' into the aesthetics of a comprehensive intellectual system that cared for the exploited, was animated by the Blakean vision of the New Jerusalem, and revelled in the possibilities of dialectical materialism and a relentless anti-philistinism.[6] In this opening 100 pages Hobsbawm offers an evocative construction of the dream of revolutionary possibility, one in which experience, not words, was his guide. He had read little more than the *Communist Manifesto*. These introductory chapters stand, disappointingly, as the most politically charged and convincing of the entire 450-page text.

What follows is draped in the defeats of Stalinism and the Popular Front, which condition in Hobsbawm a defensiveness that masks the meaning of Communist politics in evasions that register in an increasingly terse tone. It is as if incorporation into the ideology of 'socialism in one country' has narrowed not only the interpretive and political but also the aesthetic vision of 'world revolution'. There is a hint of this in his treatment of the Parisian events of 1936–7, a

---

5   Hobsbawm 2002, p. 7.
6   Hobsbawm 2002, pp. 73–4.

small piece of which Hobsbawm witnessed on Bastille Day from the back of a Socialist Party camera truck. He reduces the left achievement to its early festive bacchanalia, shorn of any sustained assessment of the strike movements and popular struggles that were associated with the electoral victory. More importantly, the debacle of decisive defeat that followed is all but eclipsed. 'It was one of the rare days when my mind was on autopilot', Hobsbawm recalls of the parade of June 1936. 'I only felt and experienced'. It was a celebration of social boundaries transcended that did not end until dawn. It also 'introduced both the first national paid holidays and cheap railway fares'.[7] No doubt the fires of the Popular Front burned brightly in June 1936. Yet Hobsbawn barely touches on the fall of Leon Blum's socialist government and the French Communist Party's sad role in disciplining workers who wanted to take the struggle to another revolutionary level, just as he avoids confronting the problematic outcomes of so many Popular Front endeavours. Sadly, his *Interesting Times* winds down in political denouement that is all the more anti-climactic for its unbending lack of self-reflection.

As Perry Anderson has suggested, in a stunning essay reviewing Hobsbawm's 20th-century life, the Popular Front once galvanised the masses in genuine enthusiasm for radical alternative, but it was a dream destined to end in the anguish of nightmare. Even at its height in France and Spain in the 1930s, the Popular Front, with its commitment to the revolutionary left participating in a process of bourgeois governance that had as one of its fundamental class purposes the unambiguous erosion and indeed suffocation of all left popular appeal, 'lacked any realistic calculus of power, and ended in disaster'. It was but one of many Stalinist turns that the Comintern engineered only to have the practitioner ranks discover, too late, that the backfiring was not some minor fireworks but rather the deadly direct and on-target fusillade of the class enemy's firing squad.

Yet this was, as Hobsbawm makes abundantly clear, the politics that has always guided his strategic thinking.[8] He revels in the Popular Front electing the left to power; much leeway is given implicitly to the means licenced in the achievement of this end. Yet, if it had any saving grace in the Red upturns of the 1930s, which is certainly debatable, the Popular Front could promise no gain in the post-World War II years, which saw a stark demobilisation of popular left resistance. The illusion in it, grasped with sentimentality by so many leftists like Hobsbawm, proves an unseemly concession on the part of a man who has

---

7   Hobsbawm 2002, pp. 323–4.
8   For Hobsbawm's most explicit statement, see Hobsbawm 1989, pp. 103–17.

resolutely brooked no romanticism on the left. To chalk up the consequences of a long-standing faith in the Popular Front in the years that Hobsbawm covers in the last half of his *Interesting Times* is to find oneself mired in paradises that were not so much lost as never really very much in the cards. Much of the defeat was relatively banal: the Communist Parties turfed out of continental European governments in the aftermath of World War II; the exercise in futility that was Euro-communism and, especially in Hobsbawm's beloved Italy, the demise of the Historic Compromise in the 1970s. But there were places where the toll was exacted in bloodier tragedies: in Indonesia an appetite for the Popular Front conditioned the Communist Party (PKI) playing up to Sukharno and his politics of nationalism. This led directly to the slaughter of upwards of one million Indonesian militants in 1965–6 as the PKI, then the world's third largest Communist Party and one poised to actually take state power, given its widening reach in trade unions and progressive organisations, was destroyed in a vicious campaign of mass murder and brutal suppression.[9]

Tellingly, Hobsbawm's memoirs offer a detailed look at his efforts to popular-frontise the Labour Party in the 1980s, saving it from the sectarians, bringing it in line with coalition politics and dispensing with the traditional Labour left that, he claims, no longer exists. He won, although it is not at all clear that the outcome would have been different had Hobsbawm and others writing for *Marxism Today*, the 1980s forum of slick communist accommodation to benign reformism and post-modern mumbo-jumbo, simply stayed home and watched the video. Tony Benn was dispatched to the back benches, having been dragged through the mud by every conventional newspaper from the *Sun* to the *Guardian*; Neil Kinnock was ensconced in Labour's leadership, whatever his failings, which were made all too evident in his campaigning and which Hobsbawm himself had suggested were a not-inconsiderable barrier to parliamentary victory in an earlier period; the dreaded Trotsky*ites* were made even more marginal amidst mainstream rants against the loony left. The reification of electoral victory that Popular-Frontism always entails ran rampant, especially after the failure of the revamped Labour Party to win the 1992 election brought Blairism and New Labour to the fore. Hobsbawm himself became a casualty of the realpolitik of Popular-Frontism, a rather deep irony given the extent to which he armed his cause in the Labour Party debates of the 1980s with a rhetoric of realism. 'We wanted a reformed Labour, not Thatcher in trousers', Hobsbawm complained when it was all over but the New Labour shouting, noting that his efforts to address actual conditions ('the real') rather than cling to emotionally

9   Perry Anderson, 'The Age of EJH', *London Review of Books*, 3 October 2002.

attractive sloganeering (he quoted, 'Let cowards flinch and traitors sneer, we'll keep the red flag flying here') was not an acceptance of the logic and practical results of New Right governance. Yet, with Kinnock's defeat and Blair's rise, this is what ensued as the reconfigured party of the 'left' 'abandoned everything that might remind the decisive middle-class voters of workers, trade unions, publicly owned industry, social justice, equality, let alone socialism'. 'The narrow failure of Labour to win the 1992 election' thus eliminated, seemingly decisively and without question, the possibility of the kind of reformed Labour party that Hobsbawm wanted and instead over-determined the politics of the left in the direction of its ultimate demise in Blairism and New Labour. 'The time had come for the political realists and the technicians of government. And both must operate in the market economy and fit in with its requirements. True enough'. This is Hobsbawm's sadly truncated commentary on the destruction of even a moderate social-democratic programme. He regarded the defeat of Labour in 1992 as 'the saddest and most desperate in my political experience'.[10]

Such chagrin is illuminating. What kind of Marxist would register this sense of political defeat in 1992 with Kinnock losing a Labour Party election, but not in 1933, or 1937, or 1956, or any number of other benchmarks of defeat and despair? It is almost unfathomable, and in its hyperbole shifts responsibility away from Hobsbawm, Stuart Hall, Gareth Stedman Jones, Raphael Samuel, Beatrix Campbell and a host of others who had considered the Labour Party to be in a mess in the 1980s and did what they could to reform it out of its ineffectiveness. In the process they assailed class politics, downplayed a language and a programme that gestured only (but at least!) weakly in the direction of socialism, railed against the hegemony of the unions, demanded a 'realistic' politics that acknowledged the market as an arbiter of parliamentary possibilities, castigated and caricatured those of the left who disagreed with this wholesale transformation, from Benn and Arthur Scargill's miners to the Militant Tendency, and called, as all popular-frontists always have, for *unity*.[11] In the end the unity they got was not quite enough to sate the lust for an electoral win, but it was more than sufficient to turn the Labour Party into something very distant from what it had been since its founding. New Labour was the unwelcome result. To extend a metaphor of Perry Anderson's 'the forlorn attempt to put the cracked shell of Labourism together in the 1980s' may have been a pipe dream, but in the process what was smashed, probably

---

10   Hobsbawm 2002, pp. 276–7. This contrasts somewhat with his cautions in 'The Retreat into Extremism' (1985), reprinted in Hobsbawm 1989, especially p. 95.

11   On unity, see Hobsbawm 1989, pp. 108–9.

forever, was certainly more than was intended. Hobsbawm admits as much, confessing that he and his co-thinkers at *Marxism Today* could barely envisage the post-1994 development of Blairism. Realism had its blinkers.[12]

More than one commentator has concluded that Hobsbawm's political accounting of what was at stake in the 1980s remaking of Labourism, and above all its tragic outcome, was a realism reduced, in the final analysis, to a loss of contact with anything approximating reality. But few have offered suggestions as to how this happened. Let me close with gestures in this direction.

First, we cannot discount the extent to which Hobsbawm's accommodation to Stalinism was a central feature in the derailing of his sense of Marxist strategy in the politics of the 1980s. There are many dimensions to this. As *Interesting Times* makes absolutely clear, of all the so-called British Marxist historians, Hobsbawm, more than any other, was able to make his peace with the deforming power of the programme of 'socialism in one country' *and* the tyranny of Stalinist authoritarianism and worse. At various points in his memoir he confirms what is evident in other writings, such as his collection of essays, *Revolutionaries* (1973): Stalinism can be, in Hobsbawmian flourish, swept aside as 'that hypertrophy of the bureaucratised dictatorial state', but it remains largely a descriptive term of almost no political, programmatic significance. Destalinisation, in the 1953–6 years, according to Hobsbawm, did not call into being a sense amongst Communists that they needed to change very much in their political lives; a bad man at the pinnacle of Soviet world power had been toppled, and that was enough. Freedoms in the realm of ideas meant a flowering of unrecognised Marxisms, both in terms of past writings being uncovered and promoted and new writings made possible, but the politics of Communism remained largely unaltered. This perhaps explains, in part, why Hobsbawm stayed in the Communist Party of Great Britain when his counterparts in the Historians' Group largely left, along with thousands of others. When pressed as to why he remained in the CP, Hobsbawm reaches for an ironic explanation. He had joined out of loyalty to the 1917 October Revolution, as a European with a deep commitment to world revolution. How, one asks in bewilderment, did he then not question the very programmatic foundation of Stalinism, the jettisoning of world revolution in favour of narrowing the political focus to the needs

---

12   For fuller critical accounts see Miliband 1985; Pimlott 2005; Perry Anderson, 'The Age of EJH', *London Review of Books*, 3 October 2002; Hobsbawm 2002, p. 276. Important texts relating to the reform impulse in the 1980s include Hobsbawm 1989; Jones 1983, pp. 239–56; Campbell 1984b; 1984a; Raphael Samuel, 'Benn Past and Benn Present', *New Statesman*, 28 September 1984.

of socialism in one country? And how could an historian of the short 20th century not appreciate this shift in the ground of revolutionary politics, bloodied
as it was by the Comintern's sad role in Germany in 1923, in China in 1926–7,
in the Hitler-Stalin Pact of 1939–41 and so on and so forth? His answer would
be a further unreflective embrace of the Popular Front: 'I belong to the era of
anti-fascist unity and the Popular Front. It continues to determine my strategic
thinking in politics to this day'.[13]

Yet to explore Hobsbawm's writings is to be confronted with an immense
gulf between his seeming historical capacities to analyse the price paid in the
Stalinist suppression of the original revolutionary proletarian internationalist
impulses of 1917 and the actual analytic atrophy evident in his sparse commentary on this vital matter. Covering it is the façade of mass mobilisation and unity
that flowered briefly in the Popular Fronts of France and Spain in the mid- to
late 1930s, political movements that collapsed within a few years. This demise
in left involvement in governance, programmatically predictable from within
a range of dissident communist writings, registers negligibly with Hobsbawm,
who remains committed to a rather decisive wall in Stalinism's architecture of
defeat. It brought him, in his twilight years as a leftist, face to face with Blairism.

Second, if Hobsbawm's inadequate confronting of Stalinism is related centrally to a long-standing political myopia, the specific failures of strategic sensibility evident in the 1980s were prefaced by a faltering of historical insight. Hobsbawm's metropolitan Marxism, with its uncharacteristic range of vision and
synthetic sweep, had, as I have suggested earlier, significant strengths. Subjects
somewhat removed from the contemporary political terrain where someone
like Hobsbawm might intervene with some effectiveness were especially likely
to accent the vitality of his long-term historical reconnaissance, all the more
so if they were not subjected directly to his blinkered Popular-Frontism. The
closer such subjects came to the present and to the politics of pressured 'unity'
in the face of an unambiguously ugly enemy, however, the more likely were
they to be historicised in ways that highlighted Hobsbawm's problematic politics.

This of course was precisely what occurred when Hobsbawm was invited
to deliver the Marx Memorial Lecture in 1978 and chose as his subject 'The
Forward March of Labour Halted?' Intellectually, few analyses from the Marxist left have spring-boarded so decisively into the political arena. Hobsbawm's
argument, which posited the end of a long half-century of Labourist political

---

13   Hobsbawm 2002, p. 218; Hobsbawm 1973, especially p. 85, but also pp. 23, 27, 29, 111, 134,
      144–6, 218.

presence, coincided with the election within a year of Margaret Thatcher's first government, with all the threats that her 'regime' entailed. This bleak electoral context was compounded by worries that the Labour Party, whose vote fell to its lowest level since 1931, was about to be eclipsed and its class constituency overcome with unemployment, deindustrialisation and the erosion of its historically secured entitlements in the trade unions and the expansive arenas of the welfare state. In addition, the Communist Party of Great Britain, like all such parties around the world, was in the beginning stages of a free-fall into the oblivion that would finally gather speed at the end of the 1980s, spiralling into the black hole of 1989. To reverse this threat (which, if not quite fascistic, was certainly unprecedented in the post-World War II period with respect to the *dangers* it posed) panicked the politics of the left and unleashed a Pandora's box of popular-frontist initiatives, the most conscious and most politically left of which were undoubtedly those of Hobsbawm himself.[14]

Hobsbawm's account of labour's forward march winding down by about 1950 was suggestive, but it is surprising, in retrospect, how thin was its evidence and how sketchy its argumentation. Certainly it lacked depth as an historical statement and was more of a sociological gloss than a deeply researched and considered articulation of trends. It tended to present brief summaries of areas of working-class fragmentation – the decline of manual occupations and the complexity of class/union formation; the erosion of a common working-class culture; the shifting nature of British capitalism; the growth in women's employment; a proliferation of sectionalism within the working class; the emergence of an 'underclass' of impoverished and underemployed workers; the drop in union density and the percentage of the popular vote going to the Labour Party (the only 'measures' of class consciousness that Hobsbawm provided); and the economistic character of militancy – and draw from them pessimistic conclusions about the traditional strength of British labour. Concluding that the old standards of Labour Party support were waning fast, and could no longer be relied upon to secure the electoral victory of even the most moderate of social-democratic machines, Hobsbawm was armed with perhaps the most effective ammunition in his call for yet another, final popular-frontist unity against the Thatcherite enemy. It seemed so obvious.

---

14   Hobsbawm's essay 'The Forward March of Labour Halted?' first appeared in *Marxism Today* (September 1978) and was reprinted with a number of rejoinders that had appeared in *Marxism Today* along with some that were commissioned, as well as other documents and a final observation on the debate by Hobsbawm in Jacques and Mulhern 1981, and is further reprinted in Hobsbawm 1989, pp. 9–22.

And so Hobsbawm's politics risked all on a toss of the electoral dice. He wagered the project of socialism on the rallying cry of unity, a seven or an eleven that would bring together all of those committed to Democracy, Decency, and Development. It was less of a bet, in Hobsbawm's mind, than a fore-gone political conclusion: all should recognise what was needed to turn back the Thatcherite tide. Only a broad alliance could do this, and to oppose this shift in the terms of the Labour Party and its potential constituencies, even to raise questions about what it would mean, was little more than unbelievable, an 'infant-school theory', yet another 'ideological sermon', more 'baloney'. No quarter was given to the 'left sectarians' who would reduce the Labour Party to yet another 'marginalised socialist chapel'. The 'Trotskyites' could look forward to 'proletarian revolution' but it was not coming.[15] And so the old popular-frontist went to the table, shook the dice in his fist and – dropped a snake eyes.

It was another popular-frontist move that backfired, one in a long line. The outcome was not determined by Hobsbawm alone, of course; indeed, it could be argued that the dice were so loaded that nothing good for the left could possibly have come out of the sordid global politics of the 1980s. It was a bad time indeed. And the 1990s would be worse. In rebuilding in the new century the left can, however, learn from Hobsbawm. His short 20th century has left us with one very clear and very vital political lesson, although it is not one that Hobsbawm himself has taught us purposively or willingly: what has halted is the forward march of the Popular Front.

---

15   Hobsbawm 1989, pp. 88–98; Hobsbawm 2002, pp. 270–5.

CHAPTER 12

James Patrick Cannon: Revolutionary Continuity and Class-Struggle Politics in the United States, 1890–1974[*]

The history of the United States revolutionary left is one of intense bouts of activism and momentous upheavals, punctuated by periods of repression and seeming retreat. The bloody 1886 confrontation with police in Chicago's Haymarket Square, occasioned by protests of coercive suppression of factory strikers and the mobilisation for the eight-hour day, was followed by the country's first Red Scare, the state execution of four anarcho-communists, and the economic depression and political doldrums of the 1890s. Two decades later, animated by revolution in Russia, widespread working-class resistance to war, the proliferation of radical organisations, the spreading politics of socialism and a wave of class struggle encompassing general strikes, American revolutionaries faced the Palmer raids, deportations of alien radicals, outlawing of specific organisations, a sheaf of new criminal syndicalist legislation, state trials of leftist luminaries and the defeat of industrial union drives in pivotal sectors of manufacturing like the steel industry. What went up with a bang from 1917 to 1919 came down with something of a whimper in the open-shop drives, political witch-hunts and vigilante violence that followed, stamping the 1920s as a decade of setbacks. It was not all that dissimilar to the 1950s of McCarthyism. This era wrote *finis* to many of the gains registered by communist-led proletarian militancy in the epoch of early 1930s 'class against class' battles or Popular Frontist agitations and the drive to mass-production unionism in the late 1930s and World War II years. In the roller-coaster ride that constitutes the American revolutionary tradition, then, continuity is an illusive feature of the landscape of class struggles and oppositional political formations.

Perhaps more than any other figure on the revolutionary left, James Patrick Cannon constitutes a red thread of continuity, reaching from the Industrial Workers of the World of the early 20th century through left currents in the Socialist Party and the nascent communist underground of the 1917–20 years,

---

[*] 'James Patrick Cannon: Revolutionary Continuity and Class Struggle Politics in the United States, 1890–1974', originally published in Italian in *The Other Twentieth Century: Heretical Communism and Critical Thinking*, edited by Michele de Gregorio (Milan: Jaca Book, 2013).

and into the formation and development of a Communist International-affiliated Bolshevism in the early 1920s. As this Workers (Communist) Party underwent Stalinisation in the mid- to late 1920s, Cannon struggled, often uncertainly, to preserve what was revolutionary in an organisation that he saw lurching erratically in the stormy seas of class struggle. Eventually, in 1928, he found his way to Trotskyism, and for the remainder of his life he intervened in the struggles of the American working class on the basis of principles that he felt were true to his origins as a militant dedicated to advancing the possibility of working-class revolution. Central to this purpose was building a proletarian party that could implement a politics of class struggle. If at times Cannon's history seemed consumed in the factional infighting that characterised a fissi-parous Left Opposition, he also figured forcefully in momentous mass uprisings like the Minneapolis teamsters' strikes of 1934. During World War II, Cannon and others associated with these successful working-class initiatives faced the direct attack of ossified trade-union bureaucracies and state agencies, whose response to a revolutionary challenge to their hegemony was to jail those who provided left-wing alternatives. Cannon and others were tried and convicted under the Smith Act, sentenced to prison terms for their ostensible acts of sedi-tious treason. Even in the midst of this difficult, repressive climate, a harbinger of the Cold War McCarthyism that lay just around the corner, Cannon helped to chart a principled strategy of defence, providing a model for future generations of how to conduct oneself against red-baiting state attack.

It is the continuity of Cannon's revolutionary commitments, which never bartered away the idealism of his youthful conversion to the left, that marks his life as noteworthy. As he commented before an assembly of comrades on the occasion of his 60th birthday, 'The mark of a man's life is his capacity to march to the music of his youth'. Everyone's younger self, Cannon believed, is the 'better self'. 'In my own youth I saw the vision of a new world', the old revolutionary recalled in 1950, 'and I have never lost it. I came out of Rosedale, Kansas, forty years ago, looking for truth and justice. I'm still looking for it'.[1]

Cannon grew up in a poor, almost rural working-class enclave not far from the meat-packing plants of Kansas City. He was born 11 February 1890, the middle child of an Irish-American couple. A radical republican who grew up opposed to England's domination of his homeland, Cannon's father, John, joined the Knights of Labor and then the Socialist Party after settling in the United States. He became a supporter of Eugene Debs and a subscriber to the popular left-wing *Appeal to Reason*. It was John who first introduced Jim

---

1 Cannon 1971, pp. 257, 259.

Cannon to the ideas and principles of the revolutionary movement. Cannon's mother, Ann, was entirely different, a devout Catholic antagonistic to socialism who was the stoic anchor of the family's day-to-day struggles to eke an existence out of her husband's meagre earnings. Ann died in 1904, however, and young Jim Cannon was forced to leave school and home, find lodgings in a boarding house and work in the rail yards. 'Very unhappy, melancholy, at loose ends', Cannon spent much of his free time in dissolute youth gang activities, gaining a reputation as a 'sharp' at the local pool hall.[2]

Around the age of 16, Jim Cannon began to read the radical newspapers that were scattered about his father's house. He picked up copies of books by Jack London, Upton Sinclair and Edward Bellamy at public libraries. Soon he was working avidly in the labour-defence campaign of Charles Moyer, 'Big Bill' Haywood and George Pettibone. The trio, all centrally involved in violent battles between the Western Federation of Miners and the mining operatives, was accused of assassinating the anti-union ex-governor of Idaho, Frank Steunenberg. All would be acquitted or have their charges of murder dropped, and the successful mobilisation to secure their freedom was Cannon's introduction to the movement politics of the American left. The importance of labour defence was impressed on Cannon as a young socialist, and he always held it a revolutionary responsibility to keep the cause of class-war prisoners paramount in the collective consciousness of the workers' movement.

Cannon tried briefly to congeal his father's radicalism and his mother's religion into the politics of Christian socialism, but he could never quite fit the square of revolutionary materialism into the round dogma of Catholicism. He was drawn, however, to reading, debating and the values of education, returning to high school and struggling to graduate even as he supported himself with a variety of poorly remunerated employments. In the end it proved impossible, but the older student was drawn to a young teacher, Lista Makimson, whom he would later marry; during the World War I years they would have two children, Carl and Ruth.

By 1911 Cannon's politics were evolving quickly. He flirted briefly with the Democratic Party's Pendergast machine in Kansas City, but moved more comfortably in circles where his father was well known, particularly the Socialist Party and the Industrial Workers of the World (IWW). The former seemed too staid and complacent; it was the IWW that captivated Cannon's allegiance, put-

---

2   Harry Ring, interview with James P. Cannon, unpublished typescript in possession of the
    author, 4 April 1973, p. 10; Harry Ring, interview with James P. Cannon, unpublished typescript
    in possession of the author, 11 April 1973, p. 5.

ting him on the road to his life-long commitment to working-class revolution. Soapboxing on Kansas City's skid row, Cannon put his now-refined skills of oratory to proletarian purpose. He caught the attention of older Wobblies, who sent him to Chicago in 1912 to serve as a Kansas City delegate to the seventh national convention of the IWW. There he was taken under the wing of the revered Wobbly centraliser Vincent St. John. St. John soon dispatched Cannon to New Castle, Pennsylvania, where he worked on the Ben Williams-edited newspaper *Solidarity*. Cannon wrote short articles for the agitational paper and organised incoming speakers, including Emma Goldman, whose fiery talk on 'Marriage and Love' had the local bourgeoisie up in moralistic arms.

As one of St. John's chosen roving agitators, Cannon also criss-crossed strike-torn states, riding the rails and co-habiting in jail cells with the likes of the legendary Native American Wobbly rabble-rouser Frank Little. Igniting the flames of class conflict in Akron, Ohio, rubber plants, on Duluth, Minnesota, docks or in free-speech fights in Peoria, Illinois, Cannon became part of an incendiary group of 'hobo rebels' who lent credence to the myth that the mere presence of the IWW in seemingly peaceful industrial settings could result in unprecedented social conflagration. Now a seasoned strike leader, Cannon felt himself transformed by his brief career in what he jokingly called 'the Soapboxers' Union'.

The IWW in this period contained two camps: the hobos and the home guard. With his marriage to Lista and the birth of their children in 1914 and 1916, Cannon joined the latter contingent. Domestic responsibilities necessitated his return to Kansas City, where he did his best to put food on the table with a regular job in a boring office (which he hated) and keep his hat in the ring of radical politics through involvement in memorial meetings for Wobbly martyrs like Joe Hill and defence campaigns such as that mobilised to free Tom Mooney, sentenced to death as a result of the bombing of a 1916 San Francisco 'Preparedness Day' parade. As the Mooney case revealed, war was now the issue of the hour amongst radicals. Like the Russian Revolution of 1917, it necessitated debate and realignment on the revolutionary left. The political issues raised by war and revolution pushed Cannon to see that while industrial organising was obviously critically important, it was never, in and of itself, going to be sufficient to displace the ultimate class enemy of entrenched capitalist power.

Gradually Cannon drifted away from the IWW. He moved back into Socialist Party circles, albeit as part of a decidedly left-wing current. Having no illusions in the right-wing leadership of the Socialist Party (SP), Cannon nonetheless looked at the growing mass movement of socialist opposition to war and the ways in which the IWW failed to develop a coherent strategy of dealing with the war-fuelled state repression that incapacitated it in a series of 1918 political trials. Reading revolutionary journals and magazines like Max Eastman's *Liberator* or Louis Fraina's *Class Struggle* or *Revolutionary Age*, Cannon became re-energised as to the possibilities of revolution. He hooked up with another Kansas City revolutionary, Earl Browder, to launch his own journal, *Workers' World*. In 1919, Cannon made his way to New York, one of 94 delegates to attend a national conference of the Socialist Party's increasingly rebellious left wing. Soon these nascent 'Reds' would be expelled from the SP at a raucous Chicago conference, but they themselves were factionally divided into different camps. Cannon found himself, almost by default, aligned with John Reed, Benjamin Gitlow and others in what would be designated the Communist Labor Party (CLP). Attracted to the new body's more positive orientation towards the necessity of developing a presence in the trade unions, Cannon found himself catapulted into the position of district organiser of Nebraska, Missouri and Kansas. Within months, as a result of his soapboxing amongst insurgent miners in Kansas and publishing articles about their defiant strikes, Cannon was arrested, jailed and indicted for conspiracy to obstruct the production of coal, still judged a 'wartime' necessity. Cannon cooled his heels in a cell for 60 days but was eventually bailed out by his Kansas City comrades, a contingent of socialist Jewish tailors putting up what property and cash they could to post the necessary bond. Meanwhile, across the nation Cannon's CLP counterparts were being rounded up by police forces, beaten and driven into retreat by vigilante mobs and deported if they lacked the credentials of citizenship. Literature was seized and destroyed, halls broken into and trashed and newspapers like *Workers' World* shut down. Attorney General A. Mitchell Palmer had unleashed an anti-Bolshevik Red Scare that literally wiped organisations like the Communist Labor Party off the American political map. The injunction under which Cannon had been arrested was but the tip of an iceberg of political repression that aimed at nothing less than the obliteration of the new bodies of revolutionary communists that first surfaced in the United States in 1919.

The Communist Labor Party was one of these left organisations. All were driven into retreat by 1920. Some found the underground congenial: as immigrant revolutionaries with stronger ties to Old World Russia than New World New York, let alone frontier states like Kansas, and speaking little English, theoretically acute but socially isolated communists were actually more comfortable working in clandestine cells than they would have been leading mass political agitations and building class-struggle currents within established unions. Others, long-standing left-wingers in the Socialist Party, like Charles Emil Ruthenberg, envied the CLP's native-born American revolutionaries but could not quite bring themselves into the same camp; they formed a Communist Party with ties to the largely foreign-language underground. Cannon, as a young and relatively inexperienced Kansas revolutionary from the IWW tradition, could not have immediately brokered a regroupment of these divided communist forces. But within a relatively short period of time he emerged as a pivotal mechanic in the machinery of revolutionary reunification.

What was most noteworthy about Cannon's involvement in the emerging communist underground was how much his Wobbly experience with class struggle marked him as special. For the most part, communism in 1919 America was entirely separated from the basic organisations of working-class defence, and there were only a handful of leading revolutionaries in this period with any connection to the trade unions. Cannon was thus forced into prominence in the revolutionary movement. Over the course of 1919 to 1921 he was dispatched to the coal fields of southern Illinois to organise amongst miners; sent to Cleveland to edit a revolutionary newspaper, *The Toiler*, which was expected to build up the political presence of an emerging communist movement; and eventually moved to New York, where he became arguably the central moving force in uniting the divided ranks of American communism.

Cannon championed the necessity of amalgamating particularistic communist factions, long separated into warring groups and distinct, if nascent, political 'parties' based as much in linguistic and cultural distinctions as they were in decisive programmatic difference. Melding together a contingent of native-born English-speaking militants and once-contentious groupings of left-wing and communist Jews, Cannon used his New York base to proselytise for 'unity' amongst American revolutionaries. Eventually Cannon, alongside others like Ruthenberg, Jay Lovestone and Alexander Bittelman, forged a fragile political coalition that encompassed – even if it never truly integrated – ultra-left and underground Letts; pragmatic Finns and their network of co-operative societies, socialist halls and extensive publishing enterprises; expatriate Russian Marxists, whose sense of themselves was coloured more by the experience of czarism than by encounters with the more ambiguous democratic order of the United States; remnants of the Workers' Council movement and English-speaking radicals who had cut their political teeth in labour-defence campaigns, trade-union organising, and free-speech mobilisations. Bittelman remembered a 30-year-old Cannon, charming in personality and astute in political skills, breaking the ice of distrust with his humour and wit, as something of an organisational caretaker. His image of Cannon was of someone 'moving about various machines, tools, gadgets, testing tubes, etc., making sure they operate properly, oiling, fixing, changing, improving, and adjusting'.[3] When, in

---

3   Alexander Bittelman, 'Things I Have Learned: An Autobiography', Boxes 1–2, Collection 62,

December 1921, the Workers' Party formed, Cannon chaired the historic convention's proceedings, lauding the formation for the first time in the history of the American revolutionary left of a disciplined, centralised party. 'We have come together to face the future', Cannon told the roughly 110 delegates representing bodies like the underground Communist Party, the United Communist Party, the Proletarian Party, the African Blood Brotherhood, the Workers' Education Society, the IWW Committee for the Red Trade Union International, the American Labor Alliance and the Marx-Engels Institute of New York.[4]

Facing the future in the newly established Workers' Party posed a series of problems for Cannon and other American revolutionaries. How an avowedly Leninist organisation would negotiate the minefields of class relations and political strategy in the world's most buoyant bourgeois democracy was tested in debates over how to orient to the struggles of African Americans, build militancy in the trade unions, and relate to third-party mobilisations like the Farmer-Labor initiatives of the 1920s. In all of these areas the struggling communist movement, with Cannon occupying a particular space within it as leader of a faction especially concerned with issues of the trade unions, made advances and experienced setbacks, charted new paths for revolutionary perspectives and committed elementary blunders that demanded correction and realignments of party direction. At times Cannon worked in tandem with another Party leader, William Z. Foster, whose connections to trade-union officialdom in the American Federation of Labor were more developed than was healthy for a revolutionary. Cannon was more closely and resolutely linked to figures like the former editor of the radical *Butte Bulletin*, William F. Dunne; a precocious and urbane New York Jew, Max Shachtman; the youth leader and office functionary, Martin Abern; and Cannon's future partner, Rose Karsner, a Romanian immigrant and former secretary of the Max Eastman-edited journal *Masses*, who went on to be a founding member of the American communist movement and a mainstay of bodies such as the Friends of Soviet Russia and Workers International Relief. As Jim and his first wife, Lista, drifted apart in 1922–3, he and Rose, who had a daughter, Walta, from a previous marriage, consolidated what would be a life-long relationship. This group, concentrated around Cannon, provided the backbone of some of American communism's most impressive accomplishments in the 1920s, including the founding of

pp. 357–9, unpublished typescript in Alexander Bittelman Papers, Tamiment Institute, New York, New York.

4   Cannon's speech to the founding convention of the Workers' Party appeared in *The Toiler*, 7 January 1922, and is reprinted in Cannon 1992, pp. 90–4.

the party's largest united-front organisation, the International Labor Defense (ILD). This body and its aesthetically innovative propaganda organ, the *Labor Defender*, advanced Cannon's long-standing commitment to class-war prisoners. It pioneered the principled development of non-partisan labour defence, calling for freedom for Nicola Sacco and Bartolomeo Vanzetti, Tom Mooney and scores of lesser-known figures who found themselves facing execution, deportation or prison sentences. Through his direction of the ILD, Cannon retained old connections to the Wobblies and to partisans of freedom such as the civil libertarian Roger Baldwin and the anarchist Carlo Tresca, both of whom he would work with on campaigns that reached out of the 1920s and into the 1930s and 1940s, when Cannon's relationship to the Communist International no longer existed. The ILD became something of a haven for Cannon and like-minded members of the renamed Workers (Communist) Party in the later 1920s, although it proved increasing difficult to sustain the kinds of mass campaigns needed to promote labour defence effectively as the communist movement became increasingly balkanised into competing factions.

Stalinisation, emanating from the Communist International, disfigured relations amongst the leading cadre of the Workers (Communist) Party. It deepened the bureaucratisation of a movement still struggling to find its political way, producing some astounding political sensibilities that seemed remarkably distanced from Marxist fundamentals. A Comintern emissary, Joseph Pogany, a.k.a. John Pepper, would be the personal embodiment of this process. Pogany was the kind of Communist functionary who destroyed Bolshevism internationally as well as in its home base of Soviet Russia, having had a hand in failed revolutions in his homeland, Hungary, and in Germany. He found a convenient resting place in the Communist International, where he adapted to Stalin's bureaucratising tendencies and programmatic degenerations, but it was not long before Comintern head Grigory Zinoviev decided that putting Pogany out to pasture was necessary if revolutionary stability was to be consolidated in the Moscow-based International. Pogany ended up in the United States, where he almost immediately transformed himself into John Pepper, a slick operator playing on his 'revolutionary credentials' and stature within the Comintern, adept in the 'arts' of consolidating political power, bludgeoning opponents until their influence was annihilated and promoting weaker capitulators. A quick study if ever there was one, Pepper's climb up the Workers Party ladder was swift and, for a time, largely unobstructed. Amazingly, Pepper soon consolidated what Cannon called a 'personal dictatorship', establishing himself as 'czar and commissar over a somewhat bewildered party' and ruling with 'an iron hand'. 'This room shakes when that man talks', Foster once conceded in awe, Pepper being a dazzling orator. 'A phony', in Cannon's judgment, Pepper was nonetheless 'the most brilliant phony' the Kansas revolutionary had ever known: 'He sparkled like an Arkansas diamond'. But Pepper's glitter would not last. He overstepped his political reach with his endorsement of the Farmer-Laborite 'LaFollette revolution', which Pepper lauded as a cross-class struggle of 'the well-to-do and exploited farmers, small businessmen, and workers'. This initial stage of the next American Revolution, Pepper prophesied, would contain 'elements of the great French Revolution, and the Kerensky Revolution. In its ideology it will have elements of Jeffersonianism, Danish co-operatives, Ku Klux Klan and Bolshevism'. Such rhetorical pyrotechnics were eventually revealed as nothing more than theoretical charlatanism, but for a time Pepper exercised his sway over the ranks of American communism.[5]

For much of the mid- to late 1920s, however, Cannon battled Pepper's stranglehold over the Party, confronting as well one of the Hungarian exile's protégés, Jay Lovestone. The factionalism of these years was debilitating and, for the rank-and-file, almost incomprehensible. So stalemated had the executive corps of the Workers (Communist) Party become under Pepper's misdirection that Cannon pressed for a 'collective leadership', stressing within his group the necessity of a faction against factionalism. For all of his efforts, however, Cannon was ground down in the debilitating day-to-day jockeying for power that coloured so much of the time and decision-making of the leaders of American communism. By 1928, this had left Cannon somewhat disillusioned and uncertain about how to continue as a revolutionary. He was increasingly disturbed by the changed context of what was now manifesting itself as blatant interference in the routine affairs of the American Party by a bureaucratised Comintern given to substituting its own dictates as to who should be validated amongst the leadership, on occasion overturning decisions democratically arrived at during properly convened conventions. The usual means of conveying these orders was a transatlantic cable or telegram from Moscow, which gave rise to the famous revolutionary joke: 'Why is the Communist Party of the United States like the Brooklyn Bridge? Because it is suspended on cables'.[6]

All of this was anything but a laughing matter for Cannon. Pressured to attend the Sixth Congress of the Communist International in Moscow over the course of the summer of 1928, Cannon had little appetite for the proceedings. With 'so many disappointments in Moscow', Cannon had trouble working up any enthusiasm that the depressing state of United States communism could

---

5   See Cannon 1962, pp. 74–83; Harry Ring, interview with James P. Cannon, unpublished type-
    script in possession of the author, 12 April 1974, pp. 13–16; Pepper 1923, pp. 9–12.
6   Gitlow 1940, p. 187.

be changed, and he was 'a more or less sullen participant in the business'.[7] Still, he made the trek to Moscow. There he would discover, not only answers to a variety of perplexing questions, but also solutions to what had seemed to him the inexplicable impasse of communism in his homeland.

Cannon was one of 29 American delegates attending the Sixth Congress, many of them arriving in July 1928. Historically, the Congress of 1928 proved a major step towards subordinating the *world* communist movement, with its diversity of struggles and needs, to the dominance of the Soviet Union and, in hindsight, to the consolidation of Stalin's unquestioned rule and the elevation to a theoretical maxim of the contradictory notion of 'socialism in one country'. Comparable gatherings of the world communist movement in the early 1920s had bristled with debate and productive exchanges, with the early leaders of the Communist International trusted as guides on a range of practical matters, insightful commentators on how Marxist ideas could be translated into revolutionary practice in different national settings. But they were not dogmatists, nor did they seek reverence and obeisance. At the Sixth Congress there was a different tone to the proceedings. International figures shook their heads in despair at the arrogance of the Russian leaders, who obviously demanded and received 'dull and sad parades of loyalty'. It made the Italian Marxist Palmiro Togliatti feel like 'hanging oneself', while the French communist Maurice Thorez thought the mood of Moscow one of 'uneasiness, discontent and scepticism'.[8] Leon Trotsky had been banished from power and the Left Opposition expelled from the Communist Party of the Soviet Union; Zinoviev had been driven from Moscow and the arrests of dissidents such as Victor Serge had begun. Even the rising star of the Comintern, Nikolai Bukharin, had recently fallen out of favour with the ruling *apparatchiks*, for whom Cannon had, in past visits to the Soviet Union, developed a healthy dislike. A Minnesota trade unionist and old friend of Cannon's, Clarence Hathaway, was ensconced in the Lenin School and briefed his long-time comrade on the lay of the Soviet land, where Stalin was beginning to plant the seeds of doubt about Bukharin by encouraging gossip in the corridor about the young Bolshevik's 'right-wing' proclivities. Cannon understood how things worked, lapsed into acceptance of this socially constructed type-casting and stayed well within the boundaries of conventional behaviour, appreciating that it was diplomatic to keep one's distance from Bukharin at the same time that it was not yet safe to publicly and directly attack him.

---

7   Cannon 1962, pp. 200–1; 1944, pp. 48–9.
8   Deutscher 1959, p. 444.

In any case, so familiar was Cannon with this Stalinist mode of tarring factional enemies with the brush of innuendo that he failed at first to see anything repugnant in this practice. Like his factional counterparts, led by the
Bukharin-aligned Jay Lovestone and William Z. Foster, with whom Cannon
had temporarily united to form an American opposition, this was all peri-
pheral to the struggle within the US Communist Party. Lovestone's endorsement by Bukharin sealed his fate, and Cannon, had he played his factional
cards right, could well have displaced Foster, whose fortunes in his own group
were at a low ebb. Cannon, had he continued in the old ways, might well have
risen to unprecedented power within American communism. This was not to
be.

Elected to the Program Commission, 'a sort of honor without substance',
Cannon encountered – whether by accident or design has never been fully
established – a copy of Trotsky's *Draft Program of the Communist International:
A Criticism of Fundamentals*. A withering assault on the draft of a Comintern
program pieced together by Bukharin, Stalin and a host of hangers-on, Trotsky's
rejoinder laid bare the false nature of Stalinist claims about Soviet economic
life. More importantly, Trotsky assailed the Comintern's embrace of the politics of 'socialism in one country', counter-posing the long-standing commitment
to world revolution. In the imperialist epoch, moreover, Trotsky demonstrated
that the consequences of a parochial counter-revolutionary 'protectionism', in
which socialism in the Soviet Union was privileged over the struggles of workers in China, the United Kingdom and elsewhere, would dead-end in defeat, as
it had in the bloody suppression of the Chinese Revolution of 1926–7. Finally, in
what hit decisively home for Cannon, Trotsky railed against American Pepper-
ism and its embrace of LaFollette's Farmer-Laborism, deploring this reliance
on a politics of cross-class collaboration. Trotsky insisted that such attempts
to substitute the struggles of the landed masses for the class struggles of the
working class and, above all, to skip over the Party of class-conscious workers
would inevitably end in disaster. Along with a Canadian revolutionary dissident, Maurice Spector, Cannon was won over to Trotsky's ideas. The two col-
laborators decided not to make their fight against Stalinism in an open way in
Moscow, but to smuggle Trotsky's document out of the Soviet Union and back
to Canada and the United States.

Appreciating that Stalinism meant the degeneration of the revolutionary
vision and the repudiation of basic Marxism, Cannon and Spector resolved
to keep their new ideas to themselves for a time, return to their respective
countries and there take up the struggle to build a Left Opposition and right
the course of their respective parties. For Cannon, Trotsky's *Draft Program* also
prompted an inner look at what Stalinism was conditioning him to be:

The foot-loose Wobbly rebel that I used to be had imperceptibly begun to fit comfortably into a swivel chair, protecting himself in his seat by small maneuvers and evasions, and even permitting himself a certain conceit about his adroit accommodations to this shabby game. I saw myself for the first time as another person, as a revolutionist who was on the road to becoming a *bureaucrat*. The image was hideous, and I turned away from it in disgust.[9]

After years of struggling to build a communist movement, Cannon had slowly and somewhat reluctantly come to the conclusion, articulated in his earthy Rosedalian way, that the American revolution could not be advanced by further accommodations to Stalinism. 'Stalin makes shit out of leaders', he told Alexander Bittelman, 'and leaders out of shit'.[10]

Having smuggled Trotsky's draft programme back to the United States, Cannon showed it to Karsner, Shachtman and Abern, all of whom were convinced by its Left Opposition politics. Bill Dunne, Cannon's closest friend and the single individual with whom he had worked most closely in executive committees and the inner circles of the communist movement, refused to be moved away from loyalty to Stalin's Comintern, and his falling out with Cannon was irrevocable. Gradually, however, others around the Cannon group in the American Party were shown the document and had their political eyes opened. Within a matter of weeks, however, the Jay Lovestone and William Z. Foster forces flushed the clandestine oppositionists out, levelling charges of Trotskyism against Cannon, Shachtman and Abern in October 1928 political committee meetings of the Central Executive Committee of the now-renamed Communist Party USA (CPUSA). Dubbed 'three generals without an army', Cannon, Shachtman and Abern were soon summarily expelled from the communist movement they had helped to found and build in the 1920s.

Over the course of October and November 1928 and into the first months of 1929, the Lovestone leadership of the CPUSA (which was soon subject to expulsion itself, rejected by Moscow as a Right Opposition) hounded dissidents out of the Party, often driving them towards Cannon and the nascent American Trotskyist Left Opposition. In Chicago, Boston, Toronto and Minneapolis, Lovestone's heavy-handed emissaries and Stalinist 'statesmen' recently gradu-

---

9   Cannon 1962, p. 225.
10   Alexander Bittelman, 'Things I Have Learned: An Autobiography', Boxes 1–2, Collection 62, p. 210, unpublished typescript in Alexander Bittelman Papers, Tamiment Institute, New York, New York.

ated from the Lenin School, like Cannon's former friend Clarence Hathaway or the Canadian Stewart Smith, imposed a wooden and anti-democratic discipline on all Party members, many of whom ended up expelled because they had the temerity to question kangaroo-court proceedings or declare the necessity of studying documents to determine their positions rather than simply accept the politics of fiat. Cannon and his emerging group, which would soon be named the Communist League of America (Opposition) (CLA), drew approximately 150 activists and supporters to their ranks. Committed to winning former comrades back to the politics of revolutionary Leninism, Cannon and others struggled over the course of 1930 to build up an external tendency of the CPUSA, conceiving of themselves as an expelled faction that nonetheless still oriented itself to the Party and its membership. To this end, they put out a propaganda organ, the *Militant*, and embarked on an ambitious publication programme of a basic library of books and pamphlets outlining Trotsky's criticisms of the degeneration of the revolutionary programme of the Communist International.

For a time Cannon's spirits were high and his enthusiasm for the project of revolutionary revival within the CPUSA boundless. By the end of 1930 and into 1931, however, things changed. First, Cannon's particular material and domestic circumstances hit rock bottom. He and Rose, long-time paid functionaries of the communist movement, were now without the even modest remuneration of professional revolutionaries. Cannon's first wife Lista died, leaving him with economic responsibility for two children and the acute tensions of integrating blended families that had never quite managed to consolidate new relationships. The debilitating and on-going poverty of the Cannon-Karsner household and the troubling frictions of bringing three strong-willed teenagers into the fold of an already precarious domesticity weighed heavily on the leader of the CLA. Rose had a breakdown and ended up confined to bed for long periods of time. Second, amidst this bleak set of private-life experiences, the politics of the moment also shifted for the worse: the American Left Opposition was undercut in its attempts to promote a critique of the rightward degeneration of the CPUSA and its Comintern allies. Stalin lurched to the left, ushering in the Third Period of 'class against class', in which an ultra-left and sectarian insistence on refusing all united-front work with 'social fascists' in the political sphere paralleled the industrial work of building revolutionary unions separate from the mainstream American Federation of Labor. This made it difficult to recruit CPers to the Left Opposition – all the more so when Stalinist leaders, threatened by a sense that Cannon and company were making inroads, promoted fresh and quite violent rounds of thuggery and hooliganism, as well as upping the decibel level of slandering all Trotskyists as counter-revolutionaries.

Third, as the American Left Opposition grew more isolated and shut out of mass work, the internal regime of the CLA degenerated. An original crisis developing out of Shachtman's adaptation to the politics of cliquism consolidating in the European ranks of the Left Opposition engulfed the nascent CLA, threatening the capacity of its small leadership to consolidate itself and advance its work. Cannon, depressed with the prospects for the newly established League, retreated from his leadership role, often drinking to excess, and neglected his duties; Shachtman and Abern mobilised an anti-Cannon faction that descended into a politics of personal recrimination. Making little headway, the Communist League of America entered 1933 seemingly stillborn. Cannon would later dub these difficult times 'the dog days' of Trotskyism in the United States.

Throughout this worsening situation, Cannon found his isolation from mass working-class struggles debilitating. He especially disliked the hot-house atmosphere of cliquish New York, in which factionalism and endless debate and discussion seemed to dominate League activities and where recruits to Trotskyism seemed to be increasingly petty bourgeois. All of this was far removed from the more proletarian and down-to-earth relations of other areas where the CLA was making inroads, including the Illinois coal fields.

Gradually, by the end of 1933 and into 1934, Cannon and the American Left Opposition, with Trotsky's guidance, moved out of the factionalism of the early 1930s and began to intervene more directly in the mass movements of the United States. Central to this widening influence was the role of Cannon and other League leaders in the emerging anti-war movement, which necessarily addressed the extent to which the rise of Hitler threatened the powerful German workers' movement. Soon, with developments in Spain and Germany indicating how Stalinism's Third Period sectarianism was marginalising the Communist International and inhibiting united fronts of opposition to fascism, Trotsky and the International Left Opposition concluded that it was no longer either possible or productive to continue functioning as an external faction of the official international communist movement. The Left Opposition thus finally broke decisively from the Comintern and proposed the necessity of the formation of a Fourth International, which eventually came into being in France in 1938. Now free to pursue mobilisations and intervene in labour-defence campaigns, the unemployed struggle and the trade unions without having to orient directly to the CPUSA, Cannon and the League soon gained a second lease on political life. Cannon, in particular, was energised by trips to the Illinois coal fields, where the Progressive Miners of America (PMA) were led by Gerry Allard, an on-again/off-again Left Oppositionist. The class struggle commitments of dissident miners who battled bosses and their armed thugs, local police forces, National Guardsmen and the corrupt machine of John L. Lewis and the then-conservative United Mine Workers of America provided Cannon with an important perspective that all the world of revolutionary politics was not ordered around New York cliques and factional imbroglios. Cannon saw the PMA pioneer new paths, through which women of the mining community could play a militant role in the often tumultuous battles of one-industry towns, and he became a firm advocate of the model of Women's Auxiliaries he saw emerging in southern Illinois. As the Free Tom Mooney movement heated up in this period, Cannon was also centrally involved, as he was in state-wide agitations of the unemployed in New York. When a major New York hotel and restaurant workers' strike erupted in the winter of 1933–4 with a mercurial CLA-figure, B.J. Field, at its head, Cannon found himself addressing working-class audiences of thousands of militants, and the Left Opposition's periphery of sympathising literary figures, journalists and progressives expanded significantly.

Few of these mobilisations ended in unambiguous victories for the Communist League of America, but all of them raised the profile of the struggling Trotskyist movement. The single most decisive step forward Cannon and the Left Opposition took, however, would register in a major advance for American workers. When the Lovestone leadership of the Workers (Communist) Party expelled Cannon, Shachtman and Abern in November 1928, it demanded prompt and unequivocal obeisance from all Party members. In Minneapolis a contingent of communists balked at the order to denounce Cannon, largely because they had never, in the factional impasse of the communist movement in the 1920s, trusted Lovestone. They also had no fundamental grasp of what was at stake in the animosity to Trotsky and his critique of the Communist International. When these figures, led by Vincent Ray Dunne and Carl Skoglund, asked for clarifications and demanded an open discussion of the issues, they were given the heave-ho by the Lovestone leadership, expelled from the Comintern and its American affiliate. They became, in the ensuing encounter with the political issues, confirmed Trotskyists and convinced Cannonists.

Employed in the coal yards of Minneapolis, a transportation hub of the Midwest, these nascent Trotskyists talked union amongst themselves and strategised as to how best to make a breakthrough in a viciously anti-union environment where employers were organised in a powerful Citizen's Alliance; found no interest in the moribund International Brotherhood of Teamsters (IBT), led by the Boston-based trucker leader Daniel Tobin, in organising the unorganised; and built up a reserve of good-will and trust amongst the workers. Dunne, a respected figure in the trucking sector who had galvanised the union organisation of office workers and dispatchers, was eventually fired from his job after he took the day off to speak at an anti-fascist rally in the morning and lead an unemployed delegation to City Hall in the afternoon. This only gave the organising drive of the Minneapolis truckers a full-time functionary. Over the course of 1934, Dunne and Skoglund, with the help of the New York offices of the Communist League of America and key figures like Cannon and Shachtman, led three major strikes that polarised Minneapolis and made the mobilising Teamsters the focus of articles in the *New York Times, Fortune* and *Harper's*, not to mention progressive journals like the *Nation* and the *New Republic*. Mass pickets of thousands confronted police and armed advocates of the Citizens' Alliance while flying squadrons of striking workers shut down Minneapolis and forced the hand of progressive Farmer-Labor governor, Floyd B. Olson, who called out the National Guard, invaded the headquarters of the General Drivers Union and arrested strike leaders. In the pitched battles that ensued, two 'special deputies' of the Citizens' Alliance were killed, as were two workers. The strikers, struggling to establish an *industrial* union in the shell of an ineffective craft structure, demanded that the entitlements of organised labour be extended to coal heavers and market labourers as well as those who could claim the credentials of the 'truck-driving fraternity'. In the end the strikes were a considerable success and built up the Minneapolis Local 574 of the International Brotherhood of Teamsters from a weak shadow of a union, with barely 75 members in 1933, into a vibrant, democratic body of class struggle encompassing 7,000 within its ranks, supplemented by tens of thousands of supporters, including strong backers amongst other trade unionists and a growing unemployed movement. With a strike headquarters that would have been the envy of military commanders in wartime, the Trotskyist leadership of Local 574 perfected strike mechanisms and pioneered class-struggle innovations that included a dedicated Women's Auxiliary movement, a daily strike newspaper, the *Organizer*, and a disciplined system of dispatching to coordinate the city-wide movement of pickets. Local leaders like Dunne and Skoglund drew on the knowledge and perspective, as well as the journalistic talents, of Cannon and Shachtman, who found themselves under arrest, confined to a stockade patrolled by bayonet-wielding National Guardsmen. New recruits to Trotskyism, like strike leaders Farrell Dobbs and Harry DeBoer, became lifelong converts to the cause of revolutionary politics.

Dobbs catapulted the Minneapolis truckers' victories of 1934 into a startlingly effective campaign to mobilise long-distance truckers in 11 states. By 1940 the achievements in this realm had revitalised a flagging International Brotherhood of Teamsters, which grew from a national membership of 75,000 in 1933 to roughly 400,000. With World War II breaking out and the Trotskyist Teamster leadership of Minneapolis an irksome thorn in the side of the IBT, an array of forces, including the United States Attorney General, the Federal Bureau of

Investigation and Teamster patriarch Tobin, led a war against the successful Left Opposition labour leadership in the Midwest trucking sector. The Smith Act, also known as the Alien Registration Act, was passed on 29 June 1940, establishing criminal penalties for those advocating the overthrow of the United States government. After a trial and an appeal, Cannon, Dunne, Skoglund and 15 other leaders of the Minneapolis teamsters and the Cannon-led Socialist Workers Party were sentenced to jail terms. Cannon spent all of 1944 and most of January 1945 in Minnesota's Sandstone Prison.

Between the Minneapolis truckers' strikes and his trial and imprisonment in the 1940s, Cannon was a central player in the making of the politics and programme of American Trotskyism. After his agitational stint in Minneapolis, Cannon returned to the CLA's New York offices, where he helped to orchestrate a series of political mergers, entries and party-building developments that culminated in the founding of the Socialist Workers Party in 1938. Convinced, in 1934, that the A.J. Muste-led American Workers Party (AWP) was gravitating to the politics of revolution and that its leadership of the Toledo Auto-Lite strike had championed the same industrial-unionist orientation that the CLA had adopted in Minneapolis, Cannon promoted a fusion between the CLA and the AWP. In December 1934, the two bodies merged, making the resulting Workers Party an organisation far larger than the CLA, with membership estimated to be around 1,000. This development was in the making at the same time that Trotsky was advocating the 'French Turn', entry of the Left Opposition forces into the larger Section Francais de l' International Ouvrière (SFIO) in order to gain recruits. The SFIO, led by Léon Blum, was the equivalent of Norman Thomas's SP in the United States, and in the mid-1930s Thomas was open to the idea of a broad, inclusive Party of the left. Cannon and comrades close to him inside the newly established Workers Party thought that a French Turn in America might well pay huge dividends, bolstering the leftward course of a youthful contingent of SPers known as Militants. The eventual entry of the Workers Party into the Socialist Party, formally announced in a 6 June 1936 call for all revolutionary workers to join the SP, was not without its fallout; long-time Cannon allies and talented organisers such as Hugo Oehler and Tom Stamm resisted entryism and formed their own organisation, the Revolutionary Workers League. Even Muste could not make the French Turn and left revolutionary politics as he reconnected to his religious past.

The energies that Cannon directed to mergers and fusions in 1934–7 bore considerable fruit as revolutionary Trotskyism expanded its ranks considerably. Just as Cannon had drawn together revolutionaries of various backgrounds and inclinations in building the above-ground Workers Party in the early 1920s, so too, in the mid-1930s, did he bring into a common space an impressive array of individuals who, in the turmoil of class struggle, showed signs of embracing anti-capitalist politics. One measure of this success was the mass appeal of the Leon Trotsky Defense Committee, which organised 'hearings' in Coyoacán, Mexico, headed by Columbia University philosopher John Dewey, inquiring into the Stalinist allegations that Trotsky and his son Leon Sedov had committed atrocities against the Soviet Union, including involvement in assassination conspiracies. The sub-commission found the verdicts of trials held in Moscow, in which Trotsky was declared guilty of sabotage, conspiracy with fascists and other crimes intended to restore capitalism in the USSR, to be without foundation. As in Minneapolis, Trotskyism gained credibility and sympathisers, with the Trotsky Defense Campaign cutting a swath of support through progressive America.

For all of this, Cannon and his growing body of revolutionary Trotskyists never found their fit in the Socialist Party all that seamless. Acute differences separated revolutionaries and reformists. Trotsky himself was cognisant that in both Europe and America the French Turn had, after a period of education, regroupment and political clarification, crystallised those forces that could be won to the politics of the Left Opposition. He urged a course of increasingly hard-nosed exposure of Socialist compromise and conciliation, all of which led to expulsions of individuals and branches, culminating in the United States in a 1937 dictate by the National Executive Committee of the Socialist Party to clean its house of all confirmed revolutionists. A few months later, on 31 December 1937 and 1 January 1938, Cannon presided over the founding of the Socialist Workers Party.[11]

From a membership of less than 200 on the eve of the Minneapolis truckers' strikes of 1934, Cannon's corps of Trotskyist revolutionaries had expanded to more than 1,000; the periphery of this steeled contingent was now reinforced by a significant body of sympathetic writers that included James T. Farrell, Phillip Rahv, James Rorty, Dwight Macdonald and Mary McCarthy. Irving Howe later noted that Trotskyism in these years was 'marked by an abundance of intellectual pride'; Cannon himself saw the prospects of the Socialist Workers Party as bright indeed. As the only truly revolutionary party on the horizon of the American left, the SWP was, in Cannon's view, 'heir of the rich traditions of the past and herald of the future'.[12]

One component of the rich traditions of the American revolutionary left's past, however, was factionalism, and this would factor decisively in Cannon's

---

11   Cannon 1944, pp. 250–2; 1938a, pp. 4–6.
12   Le Blanc 1996, p. 23, quoting Howe 1982, pp. 53, 57; Cannon 1938b, pp. 41–2.

future. The Socialist Workers Party, assailed by the state during the 1940s, was also wracked by internal battles that led to splits, expulsions and defections in its ranks. Amongst those who parted company with Cannon and the SWP were the patrician philosopher James Burnham; Cannon's former protégé Max Shachtman; the brilliant but mercurial Trinidadian dialectician C.L.R. James; the talented revolutionary lawyer Albert Goldman and his ally, the writer-activist Felix Morrow; future mainstay of the radical publishing house Monthly Review Press, Harry Braverman; and Bert Cochran, later to become a research fellow at Columbia University and around whom many SWPers in the Cleveland and Detroit auto industry rallied.

Between 1940 and 1954 Cannon faced three major factional wars and a number of other internal skirmishes that turned on fundamental questions of revolutionary principles and programme. At issue was the nature of the Soviet Union. Did it retain any features of a workers' state that demanded defending, or had it so fundamentally changed that it constituted a new kind of bureaucratic collectivist order that necessitated thorough-going revolutionary criticism? In 1940 Cannon opted for the former position, with Shachtman taking up the cudgels of the latter; the resulting factional impasse led to an irreconcilable break between the two founding figures of American Trotskyism. The departure of Goldman and Morrow from the SWP occurred six years later, a consequence of the duo's opposition to Cannon's understanding of revolutionary possibilities in the United States. Goldman and Morrow insisted that the SWP and Cannon were overestimating the prospects for revolutionary advances in the post-World War II period, conjuring up prospects of crisis and failing to appreciate that in both Europe and the US bourgeois democracy rather than proletarian insurrection was the likely course for the immediate future. In addition, Goldman and Morrow suggested the need for a rapprochement with the Shachtman-led Workers Party, having concluded that any reasons once given for defending the Soviet Union had, by the mid-1940s, disappeared. Eventually Goldman joined the Shachtman camp while Morrow hung on within the SWP, arguing for his positions until he was expelled in November 1946 for unauthorised collaboration with the Workers Party. Six years later a fresh round of factional dispute yet again convulsed the SWP. This time the voices of dissent were even more pessimistic. So distant was revolutionary possibility in the United States and so dire the threat of fascism and an outbreak of war that some claimed the SWP should essentially liquidate its position of political independence and unite with whatever forces of radical progressivism, even Stalinism, could be convinced to resist the tide of reaction associated with McCarthyism. The so-called Cochran group, which promoted these kinds of views heterogeneously, eventually split from the SWP, its loose components making their marks in a variety of ways in the late 1950s and early 1960s. For a time Cochran and Braverman put out an impressive and freewheeling monthly magazine, the *American Socialist*. A politics of strategic realignment that bore some resemblance to the Cochran group's stress on liquidation was being promoted in Europe by Michel Pablo, Ernest Mandel, Pierre Frank and Livio Maitan, who claimed that in the dark times of the 1950s Trotskyists could do little more than enter into the mass Stalinist and social-democratic movements. Cannon, Gerry Healy in Britain and France's Pierre Lambert opposed such a course, but Trotskyism, in the United States and globally, was divided against itself in the difficult and increasingly reactionary climate of the 1950s. Cannon thus stayed a particular course, one in which orthodoxy was perhaps valued over adaptation to the pressures of the moment, a stand that kept alive the promise of socialism even as its realisation seemed increasingly distant.[13]

However plagued Cannon and the SWP were by state repression and internal division over the course of the 1940s and 1950s, and however bleak the prospects seemed for revolutionary advances, there were positive accomplishments to brighten the undeniably difficult times. Cannon and his co-defendants in the Smith Act trials conducted an impeccable and principled defence. The books and pamphlets that resulted, such as Goldman's *In Defense of Socialism* (1941) and Cannon's *Socialism on Trial* (1942), remain classics of education in the revolutionary movement. Membership in the SWP in 1946, despite losses to factional haemorrhaging, remained at around 1,500, and the Party had important bases in industrial unions in the auto, steel, rubber, aircraft and maritime sectors. It registered gains in recruiting African Americans; SWPers earned reputations as staunch and reliable advocates of the emerging civil rights movement. While the Communist Party failed to defend Cannon and others in the first Smith Act trials later in the 1940s and 1950s, with Stalinist leaders indicted under the same anti-communist legislation, the SWP stood firm in demanding that its hardest critics on the left be afforded their democratic rights. In a famous refusal to knuckle under to McCarthyist witch-hunting, the SWP led the battle to secure the clerical job of one of its members, James Kutcher, who had been fired from his position in the Veterans Administration in 1948 because of his Trotskyist politics. Kutcher, who lost his legs during the Italian campaign of World War II, fought the anti-communist hysteria of the era, resisting the blacklist through 11 hearings that eventually won him his job back, a victory celebrated in the SWP pamphlet *The Case of the Legless Veteran* (1953).

---

13   James P. Cannon, 'The Coming American Revolution', *Fourth International*, February 1947; Cannon 1947.

Unlike so many once active in the revolutionary cause, Cannon's spirit was never broken. During the depths of McCarthyism he spoke to a 1953 Los Angeles forum on the subject of 'What Socialist America Will Look Like'. His talk accented the necessity of living as a revolutionary along the arc of anticipation:

> We cannot be citizens of the socialist future, except by anticipation. But it is precisely this anticipation, this vision of the future, that fits us for our role as soldiers of the revolution, soldiers of the liberation war of humanity. And that, I think, is the highest privilege today, the occupation most worthy of a civilized man. No matter whether we personally see the dawn of socialism or not, no matter what our personal fate may be, the cause for which we fight has social evolution on its side and is therefore invincible. It will conquer and bring all mankind a new day. It is enough for us, I think, if we do our part to hasten on the day. That's why we're here. That's all the incentive we need.

Cannon thus left his audience with the words of the socialist poet William Morris:

> Join in the only battle
> Wherein no man can fail,
> For whoso fadeth and dieth,
> Yet his deeds shall still prevail.[14]

Morris was also fond of reminding audiences to whom he spoke that he was there so that they could not be contented with a little. From the moment he joined the revolutionary movement in Kansas City with his 1911 entry into the ranks of the hobo rebels of the Industrial Workers of the World, Cannon never settled for little and never let his comrades think that they could do less. Moving slowly and reluctantly into retirement from his leadership of the SWP, Cannon took a back seat to a new generation of Trotskyist leaders in the mid-1950s and 1960s, replaced by Farrell Dobbs and Jack Barnes. He lived uncomfortably with the trajectory of the SWP that he had founded decades before but would not publicly criticise those who were taking American Trotskyism in different, and ultimately quite unhealthy, directions, in which the central role and revolutionary potential of US workers was routinely downplayed. The American Left Opposition never quite recaptured the drama and national impact of its leader-

---

14   Cannon 1971, pp. 423–4.

ship of the 1934 Minneapolis truckers' strikes, but it left a legacy of class-struggle politics that Cannon, more than any other figure, exemplified.

Living out his last years in Los Angeles with Rose Karsner, who preceded him in death in 1968, Cannon was a vital living continuity with a revolutionary working-class past that had been largely obliterated in the memory of American radicalism. Through his father and his active cultivation of the labour-defender tradition, Cannon was connected directly to the early 20th-century socialism of Eugene Debs and to Lucy Parsons, anarchist agitator and indefatigable proselytising wife of Haymarket martyr Albert Parsons. Few Marxists commanded the respect and regard that Cannon did amongst revolutionary syndicalists and anarchists such as Carlo Tresca, with whom Jim and Rose were close personal friends. He provided a direct link that ran through the militancy of the Wobblies into the proletarian internationalism of post-World War 1 Bolshevism, resurfacing with the Trotskyist critique of Stalinism's betrayal of revolutionary principles. Jailed as a consequence of his activism in both world wars, Cannon was the perennial objector who never relinquished his critical opposition to capitalism, imperialism and the suppression of fundamental freedoms of speech.

One measure of Cannon's continuity was that he never sacrificed the ideals of his youth. When he died on 21 August 1974, the 'Old Man' of American Trotskyism, Jim Cannon remained convinced that there was a future for the American revolution because its youth would always struggle for a better world. 'The young relate the word to the deed', he wrote from prison in the mid-1940s:

> They are moved and inspired by *example*. That is why they demand *heroes*; nobody can talk them out of it. The young have better eyes, they see farther. Youth is not petty, timid, or calculating. Far goals and grandiose ideals seem attainable to the young, as in fact they are. They see the truth beckoning in the distance and run to meet her.[15]

For the youth of the future, the hope of socialist anticipation who seek *examples* of American revolutionary activism, Cannon is worthy of a close look.

---

15   Barnes et al. 1976, p. 31.

CHAPTER 13

Paradox and the Thompson 'School of Awkwardness'*

E.P. Thompson offered all who would listen many words on the complications crucial to understanding the past. He put this with the flourish of metaphorical simplicity in his 'The Poverty of Theory', proclaiming, 'History knows no regular verbs'. By this he meant:

> In investigating history we are not flicking through a series of 'stills', each of which shows us a moment of social time transfixed into a single eternal pose: for each one of these 'stills' is not only a moment of being but also a moment of becoming: and even within each seemingly-static section there will be found contradictions and liaisons, dominant and subordinate elements, declining or ascending energies. Any historical moment is both a result of prior process and an index towards the direction of its future flow.

'Oh, but one must be a dialectician to understand how this world goes!' he wrote in his open letter to Leszek Kolakowski.[1]

In what follows I do not so much address Thompson's positions on a wide variety of topics over a significant number of decades of change as look, in this appreciative overview, for something rather different – an explication that is, at the same time, a plea for caution. Moreover, while I allude to most of Thompson's major writings, I rely less on these canonical texts – most of which are of course widely discussed by a range of scholars, as well as in my past discussions of Thompson – than on writings more likely to be unfamiliar, including a body of spirited reviews. I try to approach Thompson through a discussion of his general approach, which I maintain was characterised by a coherence that nonetheless defies easy categorisation precisely because it was often paradoxical. This was the awkward school in which Thompson insisted on placing himself. Its instruction has an urgency that, through time, remains

---

* 'Paradox and the Thompson "School of Awkwardness"', in *E.P. Thompson and English Radicalism*, edited by Roger Fieldhouse and Richard Taylor (Manchester: Manchester University Press, 2013), 205–28.

1 Thompson 1978c, pp. 238–9, 183.

relevant to all of those who refuse to adapt complacently to power's many incursions on freedom and its infinite capacity to define lives subject to its governance in disfiguring restraints.

Like William Blake, whom he so admired, Thompson articulated a way 'of breaking out from received wisdom and moralism, and entering upon new possibilities'. This was done through 'attack' and, as in Blake, the ways that Thompson did this grew out of 'thought and feeling' that were 'unique'. Thompson's concluding assessment of Blake was in some ways an apt self-portrait. Blake had his own way of keeping 'the divine vision in time of trouble', wrote Thompson, and he took characteristic and received positions of dissent 'into more esoteric ways'. In this there was 'obscurity and perhaps even some oddity' as 'incompatible traditions' met. The resulting intellectual system was a creative historical hybrid: past systems of thought blurred into present concerns, 'tried to marry – argued as contraries – were held in polarized tension'. And yet there was a foundation of continuity: 'there is never ... [any] sign of submission to "Satan's Kingdom". Never, on any page of Blake, is there the least complicity with the kingdom of the Beast'.[2]

Dialectics and Argument, Sensibility and Tone

All learning 'worthy of the name involves a relationship of mutuality, a dialectic', Thompson once declared. He envisioned extending democracy through adult education. But this lofty ideal would only be realised by introducing into the lesson plan 'the abrasion of different worlds of experience, in which ideas are brought to the test of life'. Empirical evidence and abstract theorisation had to be made to converse with one another. Out of the clash of seeming opposites and contradictory difference, Thompson fashioned fresh ways of utilising a tired language to address the needs and aspirations of men and women situated amongst particular kinds of tension-ridden social relations, erecting a new interpretive edifice within which such relations could be analytically housed. As Thompson once said of the ways in which Christopher Caudwell enriched and illuminated Marxism's varied understandings, 'What then is communicated is not just a new "idea" (or an old idea freshly communicated) but a new way of seeing ... a rupture with a whole received view of the world'. All of this, for Thompson, was a 'dialectics of historical knowledge'.[3]

---

2 Thompson 1993c, pp. 20–1, 228–9.
3 Thompson 1968, pp. 1, 22–3; 1978c, pp. 235, 112; 1963a, especially pp. 10–12. Thompson's rich

Its movement was *argument*. Thompson self-deprecatingly likened himself to an earth-bound bustard who might yet give high-flying intellectual eagles 'a peck or two about their gizzards'. An oppositionist, he refused to be silenced by criticism and pressures to conform.[4] Indeed, what might be called Thompsonian analytic sensibilities invested a great deal of significance in the form in which intellectual and political stands were posed. When Perry Anderson was writing in the *London Review of Books* on Michael Oakeshott, whom he appraised as an 'outstanding European theorist of the intransigent right', Thompson let it be known that he disapproved – not of the subject, but of the *ways* in which Anderson was writing about the conservative. 'Oakeshott was a scoundrel', he said with feeling, advising Anderson to 'stiffen his tone'.[5] Often devastatingly brutal, Thompson's remarkable rhetoric of reconsideration was also strikingly effective, charged as it was with charisma *and* commitment. Most often associated with *The Making of the English Working Class*, which one transatlantic commentator would later describe as sending 'a quenching shower of spring rain across a parched landscape', this fertile prose passion was evident in almost all of Thompson's writing.[6] In finding fault with histories in which '[t]he blind alleys, the lost causes, and the losers themselves are forgotten', Thompson exposed the centrality of contingency in historical process, reminding us that the imbalances of power relations must be appreciated as influencing outcomes which were themselves contested. History's seeming ends are seldom if ever inevitable; reversals are potentially always in the making. What Thompson thus taught was that the everyday lives of people struggling to survive within, and sometimes to transform, their social order should never be suppressed in an unreflective privileging of 'subsequent preoccupations'.[7]

Reviews and Critique

Commenting on two 1970s books on family history, Lawrence Stone's *The Family, Sex, and Marriage in England, 1500–1800* and Edward Shorter's *The Making of*

---

but difficult essay 'Caudwell' first appeared in Thompson 1977a, pp. 228–76, and is reprinted in Thompson 1994b, pp. 78–140, quote at pp. 89, 125.

4   Thompson 1978c, p. 110; 1999, pp. 59, 80–1.

5   Perry Anderson, 'Diary', *London Review of Books*, 21 October 1993.

6   Dawley 1978–9, p. 39. See also Hobsbawm 1996, pp. 521–39; B. Palmer 1994b, pp. 1–5.

7   Thompson 1963a, pp. 12–13.

the Modern Family, Thompson made his dissatisfactions with skewed present-ations of the past clear:

> I am persuaded that we are different, as parents or as lovers, from those in the past; but I am not persuaded that we are so much better, more companionate, more caring, than our forefathers and mothers. It may depend, somewhat, upon class and occupation, then and now ... It annoys me that both Professor Stone and Professor Shorter leave their readers to feel so complacent about their own modernity. It annoys me even more that both should indict the poor, on so little evidence, of indifference to their children and of callous complicity in their high rate of mortal-ity.

Where Stone saw liberal affective individualism moving, osmosis-like, in a creep of modernisation's beneficence, from the elite downwards to the ple-beian masses, Shorter imagined liberated sexuality coming about as the 'lads and lasses set free by the industrial revolution' charted new territories of libid-inal adventure, not unlike contemporary fashion trends working their way out of the ghetto and into club scenes frequented by teenage celebrities and jet-setting 'trust funders'. One view was paternalist, another populist. No matter, Thompson concluded, 'neither ... is supported by any relevant evidence'. Each, in its own way, was ordered by 'culture-bound assumption, an expectation learned within our own immature but sexually overstimulated time'. Present-ing this as historical interpretation made Thompson 'cross'.[8]

Equally vexing were literary productions like D.N. Furbank's 1985 *The Unholy Pleasure: The Idea of Social Class*. Thompson thought the book a good example of a kind of 'English intellectual amateurism' in which stimulating digressions and sardonic witticisms were used to deflate the pretensions of professional academics. So far, so good, but Furbank could not quite bring himself to believe that 'the historical events of class' even existed, or that the object of enquiring into them was valid. Thompson likened the enterprise to a voyeuristic exercise in which Furbank and a few friends crash a 'banqueting hall' of 'historians, soci-ologists, critics and some (but not all) novelists', carrying on a 'garrulous and boring discourse about class'. They observe the proceedings, 'making wry faces and ridiculing the gaudy feast'. Thompson thought the result a 'complacent pharisaism', the chit-chat's trajectory one of boring declension. 'Mr Furbank

---

8   E.P. Thompson, 'Happy Families', *New Society*, 8 September 1977, reprinted in Thompson 1994b, pp. 301–11. See also Thompson 1976b, pp. 328–60; 1993b.

has talked himself out', Thompson concluded, 'hiccupping scraps of Joyce and Proust, sprawled on the table where he and his readers fall asleep'.[9]

Someone regarded as an 'old colleague and mentor' might find himself exposed in embarrassing vulnerabilities by Thompson's cutting considerations. George Rudé, hounded from academic positions in England during the Cold War, was driven into exile in Australia and Canada: researches beckoned into the lot of those 19th-century 'industrial and political felons' sent by the state to Van Diemen's Land. The resulting book, *Protest and Punishment*, angered Thompson. He thought Rudé insufficiently attentive to the extant historical evidence, prone to lapse into 'criminological generalisation' based on inadequate statistics. Enticed into a convenient evidentiary lair, Rudé relied on reports of what the transported *said* they had been exiled for upon their obligatory arrival interrogation in the penal colony. Thompson was incredulous that Rudé proved so willing to accept statements that riots had been motivated solely by demands for '*an increase in wages*'. Failing to understand that these were words the prison officers might want to hear, Rudé seemed unable to fathom that such depositions would rarely voice more defiant aspirations, such as 'any high-flying bourgeois democratic false consciousness', including 'staying on strike until the Charter was the law of the land'. Shed the condescension of posterity, rid oneself of the notion that working-class people are pure and simple response mechanisms to the wage relation, however important that relation may be, and a more rounded understanding of proletarian life as something other than 'brutish, instrumental, casual or almost unstructured' emerged. 'The only adequate critic' for many of Rudé's pages, Thompson snorted, 'would be a pair of scissors'.[10]

This sensibility (and irreverent tone) was the genius of *The Making of the English Working Class*, which rejected the conventional chronicle of class formation as a static equation in which 'steam power plus the factory system equals the working class'.[11] Central to Thompson's success was his admonition to *listen* to voices seldom admitted to the High Table of university-generated research. This was elevated to an injunction that informed all questions of method and interpretation. Beginning with his encounter with Wordsworth in his adult-education teaching, Thompson took inspiration from the romantic poet's com-

---

9   E.P. Thompson, 'Table Talk about Class', *Listener*, 6 June 1985.

10   Thompson 1963a, p. 12; E.P. Thompson, 'Sold like a Sheep for a Pound', *New Society*, 14 December 1978, reprinted in Thompson 1994b, pp. 193–200, a review of Rudé 1978. Emphasis in original.

11   Abelove et al. 1983, pp. 6–7.

passion and capacity to hear 'From mouths of lowly men and of obscure / A tale of honour'. Thompson turned this into a necessity charged with political and intellectual import:

> When I began to inquire,
> To watch and question those I met, and held
> Familiar talk with them, the lonely roads
> Were schools to me in which I daily read
> With most delight the passions of mankind
> There saw into the depths of human souls,
> Souls that appear to have no depth at all
> To vulgar eyes. And now convinced at heart
> How little that to which alone we give
> The name of education hath to do
> With real feeling and just sense[12]

Nowhere, perhaps, was this revealed more tellingly than in a lengthy, seldom-cited review of a sociological work on religion at the coal face, Robert Moore's *Pit-Men, Preachers and Politics: The Effects of Methodism in a Durham Mining Community.*

Thompson was adamant that Moore had missed an important part of how miners negotiated lives of oppression and exploitation. 'The weapons of the weak' included rude, ribald or risqué mockery. Laughter, in this context, might serve as 'a kind of criticism, a kind of self-defence'; the social balloon of hegemony's expectation of deference could be pricked in ways that destabilised the self-confidence of the powerful. 'Dr. Moore's book altogether lacks the control of this laughter', Thompson concluded, and as a result the sociologist was blind to all manner of other behaviours and class responses that modified the impact of nonconformist religious dominance: back-sliding, agnosticism, boredom, humour, irreverence, sarcasm, even the gritty earthiness of blasphemy. 'People are more paradoxical in their behaviour than typologies allow', Thompson concluded. When he saw too little of these dialectics of abrasion in Moore's account he grew exasperated.[13]

---

12   Thompson 1968, quoting Wordsworth, pp. 6, 8. Note as well Thompson's discussion of Wordsworth in Thompson 1969, pp. 149–82; E.P. Thompson, 'Wordsworth's Crisis', *London Review of Books*, 8 December 1988; Thompson 1997.

13   Thompson 1976c, pp. 387–402. See also J.C. Scott 1985.

A close reading of Thompson's texts reveal that if his designated opponents were many and varied, his indignation at a superficial gloss on subjects
deserving a more sustained, perhaps empathetic, engagement produced prose
passages that bristled with insight. In his many refusals, be they of the optimistic school that excused the tragedy and the alienating imperatives of England's Industrial Revolution with a satisfied calculation of increased caloric
intake over the course of the 1840s or of the constitutionalist quarter of the
emerging labour movement that justified its reform-minded concessions to
capitalist triumphalism with a smug, social-democratic dismissal of night
marauders and machine breakers, Thompson reconstructed his sense of the
working-class past with unrivalled brio. Who can forget Thompson's account
of the 'average' working man's share in the 'benefits of economic progress',
nurtured in the shadows of the dark Satanic mills of early capitalism: 'more
potatoes, a few articles of cotton clothing for his family, soap and candles,
some tea and sugar, and a great many articles in the *Economic History Review*'.
Or, alternatively, his rebuttal to those conservative economic historians like
R.M. Hartwell, whose judgment on child labour and early industrialism was
deformed by a misplaced relativism. Hartwell, writing in 1959, insisted that
modern readers, 'well disciplined by familiarity with concentration camps',
were 'comparatively unmoved' by unduly sentimental tales of the ways in
which children were harnessed to the machine age of the early 1800s.
Thompson's rejoinder was a gruff refusal: 'We may be allowed to reaffirm a more
traditional view: that the exploitation of little children, on this scale and with
this intensity, was one of the most shameful events in our history'.[14]

Refusing Assimilation: In a School of Awkwardness

Thompson had no truck with what he once referred to as the 'conservative bias
of the orthodox academic tradition'.[15] It was given the political equivalent of a
rough musicking in his contribution to a critique of the business university,
Warwick University, Ltd. An account of student protest at a 'new university'
located in the industrial West Midlands, where Thompson taught in the late
1960s, this edited collection was produced in the aftermath of the youth radicalism that exploded across campuses in England, Europe, North America
and elsewhere. Thompson was not necessarily impressed with a great deal of

---

14   Thompson 1963a, pp. 318, 349.
15   Thompson 1963a, p. 592.

what passed for political agitation in this era. Nonetheless, he found the pomposity, instinctual caution and inclination to retreat from argument and controversy of many university-based colleagues even more difficult to stomach. Shown 'the last ditch for the defence of liberty', Thompson railed, and these sorts would 'walk backwards into the sea, complaining that the ditch is very ill dug, that they cannot possibly be asked to defend it alongside such a ragged and seditious-looking set of fellows, and, in any case, it would surely be better to write out a tactful remonstrance and present it on inscribed vellum, to the enemy'. Living in 'awe of propriety', *academici superciliosi* encouraged 'an atmosphere of institutional loyalty' which defrauded students 'of some of the essential intellectual dialectic from which their own orientations should be worked out'.[16]

A committed contrarian, Thompson believed deeply that it was absolutely necessary to guard relentlessly against the myriad forces that drew one into 'the infinitely assimilative culture'.[17] When Conor Cruise O'Brien penned a 1979 rant in *The Observer*, denouncing Labour Party Marxists for ostensibly luring striking lorry workers into their 'hateful' lair, leading society 'towards the abyss', Thompson's response was a sharp and scathing indictment. He defended labouring people's legitimate right to strike, suggesting that in spite of the inconvenience to the public and rare instances of real suffering, the picketing workers were exercising an understandable withdrawal of services with 'surprising good humour and self control'. Thompson chastised O'Brien's imploding irrationality, warning of the dangers that could come of unbridled bigotry and political narrow-mindedness. He thus rejected the social construction of class crisis concocted in O'Brien's great fear of a 'Nauseous Marxist-Methodist Cocktail'.[18]

Thompson could thus not forgo stressing how imperative it was to strain 'at every turn in one's thought and to resist the assumption that what one observes and what one is is the very course of nature'.[19] In the opening line

---

16   Thompson 1970, pp. 153–4.

17   Thompson 1978c, p. 183; E.P. Thompson, 'The Segregation of Dissent', *New University*, 6 May 1961.

18   E.P. Thompson, 'The Acceptable Faces of Marxism', *Observer*, 4 February 1979, republished as 'The Great Fear of Marxism' in Thompson 1980b, pp. 181–6.

19   Thompson 1978c, pp. 183–4. This is central to other discussions relating to disenchantment, on the one hand, and apostasy, on the other. See Thompson 1969, pp. 149–82, reprinted in Thompson 1997, pp. 107–55, which also contains Thompson's reflections on Coleridge. In contrast to Thelwall, Coleridge was a sadder case of apostasy: 'the impotence of his own self-isolation' was 'an excuse for a reconciliation with the status quo' (p. 131). See

of his 1960 essay 'Revolution', Thompson declared, 'At every point the way out of apathy leads us outside the conventions within which life is confined'. This principled separation from all manner of compromise made it mandatory, in Thompson's view, to place oneself, repeatedly and routinely, 'into a school of awkwardness'. Thompson's peace activism, which highlighted the necessity to step outside of one's received education in any national culture, demanded a critical interrogation of the official, proselytising state curriculum, replete with its socio-political primers.[20] 'One must make one's sensibility all knobbly – all knees and elbows of susceptibility and refusal – if one is not to be pressed through the grid into the universal mish-mash of the received assumptions of the intellectual culture', Thompson concluded.[21]

The Personal Assessment not Quite Political Enough

So what? Can not all of this be 'explained' with acknowledgement that Thompson was just 'difficult'? The accounts of Thompson and the fissiparous years of the rise and fall of the British New Left are replete with reference to him as, however inspirational and creative, a movement 'problem'. He was given to 'venting his personal anger' (Chun); a 'persistent behind-the-scenes critic' who besieged co-workers like Stuart Hall with 'highly critical and sometimes angry letters', a barrage of 'ceaseless pressure' and worse (Dworkin); 'volatile, suspicious and disinclined to compromise', a 'prima donna' who tended to 'hit out' 'in anger without expecting the victim not to take it too seriously' (Newman).[22] In published polemics that took aim at a younger cohort of New Leftists associated with Hall and those around him in the dissident journal *Universities and Left Review*, and later, in a brilliant but decisively critical reaction to Raymond Williams's *The Long Revolution*, Thompson raised predictable objections.[23] Madeleine Davis has recently characterised Thompson's response to

---

Thompson 1994a, pp. 94–140, reprinted in Thompson 1997, pp. 156–217. For the 1930s, see Thompson 1978c, pp. 211–44, which is discussed at length in S. Hamilton 2011, pp. 49–92.

20   The classic statement is Thompson 1980a, pp. 3–31, reprinted, along with other statements of importance in Thompson's 1980s peace campaigning, in Thompson 1982a. See as well the widely influential Thompson and Smith 1980.

21   Thompson 1978c, pp. 183–4. See also Christopher Hill, 'From the Awkward School', *Guardian*, 30 August 1993; Thompson 1960b, p. 287.

22   Chun 1993, p. 64; Dworkin 1997, p. 68; Newman 2002, pp. 68–9.

23   Thompson 1959a, pp. 50–5; 1961a, pp. 24–33; 1961b, pp. 34–9.

the *Universities and Left Review* discussion of 'classlessness' as a 'furious outburst' that 'had the effect of closing down rather than opening up debate within the New Left about the critical issue of class', but it must be noted that she provides no evidence for this interpretive assertion. Williams implied that Thompson's review caused tensions between two senior figures associated with the early New Left, etching lines in the sand of dissent that separated others into specific camps, but he accepted much of the critique and would soon collaborate with Thompson on the 1967 May Day Manifesto Committee.[24]

My own small cache of Thompson letters from three different decades, which I have spilled out onto my desk in writing this paragraph, will confirm, if read piecemeal, a sense of Thompson as combative, hasty in his condemnations and capable of brusque dismissals and wounding caricature.[25] Thompson *was* difficult, *very difficult*.[26] Yet being difficult, incomprehensible though this may be to most academics, is a part of what building movements of resistance entails, however regrettable. Individuals in positions of leadership and responsibility find themselves in conflict over tactics, strategies and even such a basic issue as what an oppositional mobilisation is about. Exchanges amongst such people are on occasion private for a reason: they were never intended to be 'open' to the public.[27] Historians benefit from seeing such correspondence. Few advocate ignoring or suppressing material of this kind. But this internal documentary record needs to be assessed with care, harsh sentences set against recognition of the kinds of behaviour and failures of responsibility that might well have prompted lashing language. Thompson had the commitment of the old communist to the discipline of the organisation, and he valued those who

---

24   Madeleine Davis 2011, pp. 25–6; R. Williams 1979, pp. 135–6; 1968.

25   There is allusion to this in Givertz and Klee 1993, pp. 112–13.

26   I am indebted to Wade Matthews, who has shared with me his research into Thompson, including important material in the John Saville Papers, Hull University Archives, U DJS/109, especially Thompson's extraordinarily pointed attack on the direction of the *New Left Review*, a wide-ranging, detailed and lengthy document entitled 'Where Are We Now?' (no date, but c. March–April 1963) and a detailed letter outlining his reasons for resignation from the editorial board, in Thompson to Saville, 12 May (1963?).

27   Thompson commented on the issue of private/public correspondence, writing of how the minefield of 'personal' letters available to those studying William Godwin and Mary Wollstonecraft was 'fortunate ... for biographers'. But as Thompson noted, 'We have scarcely begun to establish the facts before we begin to mix them up with our own moralising additives: scandalised, or apologetic, or admiring or condescending ... I doubt how far any of us would wish to be judged – or judged in a public sense – on evidence of this casual, and essentially unconsidered kind'. See Thompson 1994b, pp. 2–4.

could be counted on to carry out their assignments responsibly; he imposed on himself the same expectations he had of others.[28]

Moreover, there were often political issues extending well beyond Thompson's personal style, centrally important in disputes within particular mobilisations and movements. Consider, for instance, his devastating 1963 document of departure from the *New Left Review*. His objections and oppositions to the *Review*'s drift into certain stands on internationalism and a kind of abdication before the 'Third Worldist' glorification of violence evident in Jean-Paul Sartre's preface to Frantz Fanon's *Les damnés de la terre* were posed seriously and with some insight. He was demanding of the *Review* something more than a First World political tailism. Thompson wondered aloud (and his words seem eerily prophetic in 2012, however abstract and hypothetical) about casting the New Left's lot with an 'ardent Moslem militarist, of feudal stock, who at the same time' as he was righteously opposing imperialist occupation and colonial subordination was also more than willing to lock up 'trade unionists and peasant agitators' and suppress 'birth control propaganda'. Knowing well the sorry denouement of Stalinism, Thompson declared that '[t]he clothes of revolution only too easily become the habit of pious scoundrels'. He thus argued again the awkward nature of political responsibility:

> We have a task which is difficult, easily misrepresented, and quite probably one that will not quickly be understood in the Third World itself. We have at one and the same time to see (and interpret) the great liberating impulses of the Soviet and Chinese revolutions, and of the emergent nationalisms of Asia and Africa; and to adopt a critical and at times uncompromising stand as to certain socialist principles and humanist values. It is the critical standpoint which is truly that of internationalism. The execution of Communist trade unionists in Iraq and of intellectuals (again, often Communist) in China is no prettier because these events happen in a third world: they happen also in our world, and the victims have the right to expect from us the duties of solidarity. Because one's heart has leapt at the Cuban revolution, and because one pukes at the libels upon Ghana in the *Daily Express*, this does not mean that one can pass over in silence offensive ideological or authoritarian tendencies in

---

28   Note Eric Hobsbawm's jocular account of the organisationally dishevelled mode of work of one New Left figure of this period, Raphael Samuel, in Hobsbawm 2002, pp. 210–14. One Thompson critique of the conduct and style of work of Hall and others from the *Universities and Left Review* is in Thompson 1963b.

these countries. If the 'third world consciousness' appears to us to be compounded of truth and of illusion, we do poor service, to them and to ourselves, if we propagate the illusion as well as the truth.

Thompson also tried to pull his younger comrades back into recognition of what remained available in Britain:

> Attention, internationalists and intellectual workers! The old mole, revolution, may still be at work in Battersea and Fife, in Tyneside and Ebbw Vale. It may manifest itself in conflicts far removed from your scheme ... Perhaps something 'real' could happen ... even in Britain? Perhaps, if we turn away from our own people, this might be the worst way in which we could also betray the First, the Second, and the Third World?

'Internationalism', Thompson stressed, 'should imply, not a translating agency working one way, but a discourse in which we participate'. One route into such exchange was argument.[29]

Beyond Reductionism

Thompson found himself in his perennial school of awkwardness, this time standing in the corner, pondering how he was to be sent home for his bad behaviour in the New Left class. What meaning, beyond a personal proclivity to be difficult, can we draw out of this sensibility?

Little is to be gained by classifying Thompson according to a variety of social constructivist projects firmly embedded in the polemics of a particular period, be they associated with the mid-1960s, when Perry Anderson situated Thompson in an 'impressionist, inspirational tradition' that harboured 'brilliant, imaginative' histories as well as 'a vacuous political analysis';[30] the late

---

29 The above paragraphs draw on E.P. Thompson, 'Where Are We Now?', [no date but c. March–April 1963], especially pp. 2, 5–7, 15–16, in the John Saville Papers, Hull University Archives, U DJS/109. Thompson took exception to Buchanan 1963, pp. 5–23.

30 Anderson 1966, p. 39, a harsh judgment tempered years later in Anderson 1980, which nonetheless concluded on terms which yet again accented a gulf in Thompson between the inspirational and the programmatic, pp. 204, 206. Bernard Crick was, in contrast, describing the Thompson of this period as 'the best political essayist today in the tradition of Swift, Hazlitt, Cobbett, and Orwell'. Bernard Crick, 'Thompson and Liberty!', *Manchester Guardian Weekly*, 11 May 1980.

1970s 'culturalist' critique of Richard Johnson and his allies in cultural studies
at Birmingham,[31] which precipitated Thompson into the 'gladiatorial combat'
of the infamous History Workshop debate at Oxford;[32] or the recent reading
of Scott Hamilton, which sees in this anti-Althusserian moment a divide fragmenting Thompson's political life course.[33] Thompson responded to such classifying criticism repeatedly, insisting that he had been engaged in a project
quite different than these schematic orderings suggested. He was struggling
to rehabilitate 'lost categories and a lost vocabulary in the Marxist tradition',
attempting to fill a void in Marx's own undertaking, bringing back to life the
'unarticulated assumptions and unrealised mediations' of the plebeian and
labouring people. 'I am examining the dialectic of interaction, the dialectic
between "economics" and "values"', Thompson explained in 1976, adding, 'This
preoccupation has run through all my work, historical and political'.[34]

Thompsonian Provincialism: Metaphorical Geographies of Awkwardness

Arguably the most impressive and stimulating of recent attempts to fix Thompson's meaning in a particular analytics is Wade Matthews's refusal of the standard claims that Thompson was, in the phrasing of W.L. Webb's obituary, 'a
thoroughly English dissident'.[35] At its most scapegoating, this classification, originating in the Anderson-Nairn critique of the mid-1960s, impaled Thompson
on a tradition of 'messianic nationalism', altogether too English in its aversion
to theory; quick to reduce the difficulties of socialist initiative to a populist
faith in 'the British people's' capacity to realise its transformative destiny; and
prone to inflate 'living English traditions' into self-delusional and moralising
claims of dissenting possibilities that bore no relationship to reality.[36] Hobsbawm offered a benevolent, refining version: Thompson's persona was that of
'the traditional English (not British) country gentleman of the radical left'. 'Big
cities', Hobsbawm remarked of Thompson's tastes, 'were places to visit, not for

---

31   R. Johnson 1978, pp. 79–100; Clarke, Critcher and Johnson 1979.

32   Succinct overviews appear in Dworkin 1997, pp. 232–45, which is not particularly sym-
      pathetic to Thompson, and Samuel 1981, pp. 375–408.

33   S. Hamilton 2011, especially pp. 268–78, containing many contentious claims.

34   Abelove et al. 1983, pp. 14–15, 21.

35   W.L. Webb, 'A Thoroughly English Dissident', *Guardian*, 30 August 1993.

36   Anderson 1966, pp. 35–6; Nairn 1977, pp. 303–4.

living'.[37] A man of the provinces, with an aversion to what he once called 'intellectual metropolitomania', Thompson was convinced that much of what was of value in the history of dissenting opposition had come out of 'indistinct nether regions', places like the Yorkshire that had nurtured a 'forgotten "provincial"' of English socialism, Tom Maguire.[38]

As Matthews shows, however, Thompson could hardly be confined to any kind of English provincialism, however positive a reading one might offer of such a space, both physical and intellectual. Thompson's provincialism was, paradoxically, profoundly internationalist. Nowhere does this appear more forcefully than in Thompson's appreciation of two American dissidents, neither of whom fit comfortably in easily constructed containers: the larger-than-life sociological star-gazer and gadfly C. Wright Mills,[39] whom Thompson recognised as inconsistent, impatient and incorruptible in his commitments, and the North Dakotan outlaw poet Tom McGrath. Of McGrath's oeuvre, Thompson wrote: 'It is true that McGrath's *politics* are given a very distinct American location; they are not the extrapolation of some theorised cosmopolitan prescription. But these are interpreted through his poetic grid of reference which, if not universal, is as universal as his selection of poetic values allows it to be'. Thompson's provinces were places where men and women laboured, the ground on which love and loss occurs, through which relationships to nature are forged in thwarted aspirations for 'communitas', where oppression, exploitation and resistance are ever-present forces. Such places have proven, historically, to be geographies of a 'common imbrication in the capitalist nexus'.[40] Matthews provides a brilliant travelogue of how Thompson's thinking was formed in 'provinces' like his father's India, his brother's Yugoslavia and the West Riding woollen district. The birthplace of much that Thompson valued was in just such shadowy metaphorical peripheries and, as Matthews notes, the 'tracer beams' of his polemics, the rich texture of his argued histories and much of the immediacy of his political interventions came out of such places. 'Socialist internationalism, the "spirit of Europe", the tradition of the "freeborn Englishman" – each makes some sense of Thompson', concludes Matthews, '[b]ut only if it is remembered that he approached all three awkwardly'.[41]

37　Eric J. Hobsbawm, 'Obituary: E.P. Thompson', *Independent*, 30 August 1993; Hobsbawm 1996, pp. 521–39.

38　Thompson 1965, pp. 330, 332; Thompson 1960a, p. 315.

39　Thompson 1979, pp. 61–73, especially p. 63.

40　Thompson 1987, pp. 158–92, especially pp. 133–4.

41　See Chapter 3 of Matthews 2013.

Awkwardness and the Dialectic of Paradox

It is this awkwardness that is crucial in understanding Thompson, and that produces what is undeniably the dialectic of paradox that defeats any simplified attempt to locate him within a singular sighting. For even as Thompson was indeed an internationalist, he was also a characteristic English radical. Matthews perhaps too easily sidesteps the tension always pulling at Thompson's polemics and politics, perhaps even his histories, in which internationalism and Englishness (with its allusions to 'our people' and its ostensibly identifiable empirical idiom) are engaged in a tug-of-war of allegiance.[42]

In 'Where Are We Now', this paradox of internationalism and Englishness jostled awkwardly on every page:

> What is surely required – and here I burn my last boat – is that socialists of our kind should now be somewhat more plain-spoken and less clever: more willing to break our demands down into programmes: more willing to defend our positions, and less willing to drop them at the first hint that they ain't respectable, or that something *far* cleverer has been published in Paris or said in Balliol ... to put our boots into the British scene and walk around among British people; listen to them a bit more; have a touch of humility before their experience, without a precious fear that the least contact with programmes or slogans will soil our intellectual integrity ... [W]e can surely see the British people bumping up against facts: and we should surely be in there with them, helping to draw conclusions? Because if in our muddled way we were able to break or grow through to a new kind of socialist society, this would be an event of comparable importance for Europe with 1789 ... There will be no way out of the Cold War, except through the consummation of fire, unless somewhere in the advanced capitalist world, one nation can move. From the very per-

---

42   Thompson's brother Frank was executed by fascists as he marched with Bulgarian partisans in May 1944. His internationalism is commemorated in the edited collection of letters and poems, extolling the anti-fascist spirit that was arising throughout war-torn Europe, Thompson and Thompson 1947, and later in Thompson 1977a. But Frank had written to Edward (1941?): 'To Palmer. Looking forward to the time when we shall be back among our own people, doing the job that we were cut out to do'. Inscription in Ilya Ehrenburgh, *The Fall of Paris* (London: Hutchinson, n.d.), front endpaper (in possession of the author), a book that Frank purchased and read while stationed in Cairo. On Frank Thompson's time in Cairo and his high regard for the journalism of Ehrenburgh, see Conradi 2012, pp. 179–206, 342.

versity of historical development, that nation might be our own. If we fail to enlarge what slender possibilities there are, we fail ourselves *and* we fail the world ... we are not finished ... the world is tied in a contradiction, one of whose knots lies across London, Paris and Rome. And English Socialists! Insular, moralistic, empirical, affluent, compromised – nevertheless, three worlds might be waiting for us.[43]

Such a perspective congealed the solidarities of internationalism and the particularities of Englishness.

Paradoxes of other kinds also cut through Thompson's presence in intellectual and political circles. His nature as a polymath, like the Caudwell he so admired,[44] meant that he approached knowledge, politics and the productions of the writing desk from a variety of vantage points, none of which could be comfortably slotted into the conventional boxes of contemporary critical theory, orthodoxies and movements of the left or 'university standards'. Thompson's romanticism, with its critique of the cash nexus,[45] reached from William Blake and the 1790s into William Morris and the late 19th-century socialist movement. It also infused his writing with passions that seemed perpetually out of step with many dissenting traditions. More tellingly, all of this meant that Thompson wrote history in ways that were not unrelated to his intense desire to change its course, to actually *make* history. This imperative often left Thompson awkwardly situated, appreciative of radical history's necessity but aware of the ways in which it could be 'hemmed in' by 'playing safe', constrained by failures of originality and vitality. In a 1985 New York lecture Thompson discussed all of this, stressing the need always to bring to bear on academic scholarship some consideration of the relations of such work and 'active experience' that promotes 'distrust of easy assimilation by the [h]ost society', whose institutional and ideological determinations are not only weighty, but 'founded upon unreason, or on the reasons of power and the reasons of money'.[46]

In the realm of theory Thompson's paradoxical nature was patently obvious and could well seem quite heretical. He was a theorist quick to offer denials of his contributions and capacities. This was often done tongue-in-cheek, as

---

43   E.P. Thompson, 'Where Are We Now?', [no date but c. March–April 1963], p. 20, in the John Saville Papers, Hull University Archives, U DJS/109.20; Thompson 1965.

44   Thompson 1994b, pp. 78–142.

45   An entrée into this aspect of Thompson is the close analysis of Blake's poem *London* in Thompson 1993c, pp. 174–94.

46   Thompson 1994b, pp. 360–6.

in his 'Notes on Exterminism', where he declares, 'I cannot, as is well known, understand economics'.[47] Nonetheless, whatever Thompson's vulnerabilities and jaundiced appraisals of his theoretical acumen, he had a particular sense of theory that enriched not only historical writing but other scholarly realms as well. At times Thompson abandoned his self-denigration and back-pedaling and became quite insistent that he was addressing theoretical questions with rigour and sophistication. 'I have presented myself to you as a more muddled and Anglo-Saxon character than is quite true', he told an interviewer in New York in 1976, answering a question about why he had not written about the culture industry of advanced capitalism and its impact on the radicalism of the 19th century. 'I have always written about this', Thompson replied, 'but I have written about it mainly at the level of theory'.[48] The Reasoners of 1956 and the social historians of the 1970s and 1980s, attending to class and customary cultures, were always oriented by Thompson to consider their subject, be it a political movement or a historical research endeavour, as emanating in part from theoretical concerns, indeed, out of theoretical necessity.[49] His political commitment to socialist humanism, for instance, entailed not only a repudiation of Stalinism but a thorough-going questioning and rejection of the base-superstructure metaphor.[50] Thompson thus entered endlessly into theoretical debate, far more so than most conventional historians, often taking on the heaviest of philosophical thinkers – whom he engaged on *their* terms, not his.

This relationship to theory was again awkward, because Thompson saw theory not so much as being self-generating and free-standing but as being relational, extended and developed in critique and polemic. Argument was theory's engine, driving understanding to new realisations, quickening the pace of conceptualisation and its refinement. And precisely because of Thompson's resolute insistence that theory mattered *because* it could contribute to changing the world, there were times when theory took a backseat to popular mobilisations, when the theoreticians either had to move in light of social circumstances or be left very much behind. Thompson felt that the disarmament mobilisations of the 1980s were just such a radical moment of re-education.[51] As

---

47   Thompson 1982b, p. 17. See also Thompson 1978c, p. 197.
48   Abelove et al. 1983, p. 15.
49   See, for instance, Thompson 1994b, pp. 201–27, 360–6; Abelove et al, 1983, pp. 15–22.
50   Thompson 1957, pp. 105–43; 1958, pp. 89–106; Thompson 1959b, pp. 1–8, a theoretical discussion that he developed in Thompson 1978c.
51   Thompson 1980a, p. 31.

a polymath, moreover, he had come to think as early as the 1970s that not only was theory provisional, dependent always on establishing its claims through argument and counter-argument, but that the very notion of being guided by any 'all-embracing theory' was itself wrong-headed.[52] This was not the standard stance of theorists.

The awkward school in which Thompson found it necessary to place himself produced paradox and, driven by argument, difference. This did not mean that there were no continuities and no fundamental overall unifying features in his political and intellectual activity. There was such continuity and unity, but they persevered through decades of different political and intellectual circumstance; Thompson inevitably reacted to such developments and in the process changed, albeit not so strikingly that we can actually locate ruptures of meaning. The most obvious area in which he shifted his perspective relates to the politics of Marxism, within which Thompson underwent a series of reconstructions associated with the 1950s, 1960s, 1970s and 1980s.[53] Yet the causes in which he invested political activity in the 1970s and 1980s, defending democratic institutions and practices in the face of state encroachments and erosions[54] and then lending his energies and engagements, on a full-time basis, to an internationalist discourse on peace, disarmament and the nature of freedoms in the East and the West as well as the India of the Emergency (1975–7),[55] represented no break with long-standing commitments. Rather, they proved an extension of them into new historical periods and challenges. They took an English radical to a score of countries. There Thompson addressed hundreds of meetings and attended countless committees, some of them, in situations of authoritarian repression, clandestine gatherings of the underground.

In his homeland, Thompson became a public figure whose popularity was surpassed only by the Queen, the Queen Mother and Margaret Thatcher. Hobsbawm notes that Thompson's death in 1993 was 'probably received with more personal grief than that of any other British historian of his time'.[56] Hundreds

---

52   Abelove et al. 1983, pp. 18–19.

53   One of Thompson's last abbreviated statements on his shifting relationship to Marxism is Thompson 1994b, pp. 360–6.

54   See Thompson 1980b.

55   Much could be cited on this development, but of particular note are Thompson 1976a, pp. 119–38; Thompson 1985; and the unpublished (for the safety of Indian dissidents) 'Strictly Confidential: Six Weeks in India', (no date), in the John Saville Papers, Hull University Archives.

56   Hobsbawm, 'Obituary: E.P. Thompson', *Independent*, 30 August 1993; Hobsbawm 1996, p. 537.

of thousands had grown accustomed to his theatrical presentations before the mass rallies of the 1980s peace movement, aware that as he bounded on to the stage, his white hair flying, his lanky body leaning into an historical allusion to William Blake, his passion exploding no longer on the page but across a sea of listeners, they were being treated to refusals and arguments and oppositions to the consolidating 'doomsday consensus'. It all hearkened back to the best oratorical traditions of the English working class in the early 19th century. If Paine had changed the world with a pamphlet, Thompson's *Protest & Survive*, with its sales in the hundreds of thousands, failed to have the same impact, but it came as close as any comparable modern publication.

Thompson as Historical Happening

Thompson's negotiation of the related processes of making and writing history, of living complex acts of refusal and translating them into both art and a form of dissenting, combative truth, has few modern precedents. He was in many ways, *sui generis* and, to complicate matters, his uniqueness was often paradoxical. Thompson managed to translate his awkwardness into a kind of genius, his being difficult into appreciations and reverence. It was an alchemy no other figure of his generation managed in quite the same way or with the same intensity. How is all of this to be understood?

We can perhaps appreciate Thompson and his meaning by turning to his own understandings of class. 'The finest-meshed sociological net cannot give us a pure specimen of class, any more than it can give us one of deference or of love',[57] Thompson wrote, and, similarly, no classification, category or analytic label can capture the totality of Thompson's being. Always situated inside historical developments, Thompson could engage only by active interventions that brought him *into* argument, opposition and resolution. Thompson's substance, like that of class, is therefore inseparable from *historically* constituted relations: with individuals and their ideas, as well as Thompson's sense of their responsibilities and duties; with movements and mobilisations, and Thompson's contributions to these collectivities and his expectations of them; and with research and its dialogue of evidence and theory, a dance of the dialectic in which past, present and future are brought into mutual consideration.

Made inside history but always refusing to be made *only* by it, Thompson reminds us of one of his favoured passages in William Morris's *A Dream of*

---

57   Thompson 1963a, p. 9.

John Ball: '[M]en fight and lose the battle, and the thing they fought for comes about in spite of their defeat, and when it comes turns out to be not what they meant, and other men had to fight for what they meant under another name'.[58] Thompson's meaning, then, can never be titled, except in rather clumsy ways. It 'owes as much to agency as to conditioning' and unifies 'disparate and seemingly unconnected' aspects of 'experience and consciousness'. Thompson, like class, had a 'fluency which evades analysis if we attempt to stop it dead at any given moment and atomise its structure'.[59] We might do no better, then, in understanding Thompson than to see him as he often saw his subject: as an immensely creative *historical happening.*

---

58   William Morris, *A Dream of John Ball*, pp. 19–20, quoted in Thompson 1977b, p. 722; Thompson 1958, p. 106.

59   Thompson 1963a, p. 9.

References

AA.VV. 1980, *Ross Dawson v. RCMP: A Vivid Episode of the Ongoing Struggle for Freedom of Thought and Social Justice in Canada*, Toronto: Forward Publications.

——— 1991, *Tessera*, 10, Summer.

——— 1995–6, *Left History*, 3–4: 205–48.

——— 2003, 'Symposium: The American Worker', special issue of *Historical Materialism*, 11, December.

——— 2006, 'Symposium: What Is Left History?', *Left History: An Interdisciplinary Journal of Historical Enquiry & Debate*, 11, Spring: 12–68.

——— 2008, 'Revisiting "Gender: A Useful Category of Historical Analysis"', *American Historical Review*, 113: 1344–430.

Aaron, Daniel 1959, *Writers on the Left: Episodes in American Literary Communism*, New York: Harcourt, Brace and World.

Abella, Irving M. 1973, *Nationalism, Communism, and Canadian Labour: The CIO, the Communist Party, and the Canadian Congress of Labour, 1935–1956*, Toronto: University of Toronto Press.

——— (ed) 1975, *On Strike: Six Key Labour Struggles in Canada, 1919–49*, Toronto: James Lorimer.

——— 1982, 'Labour and Working-Class History' in *A Reader's Guide to Canadian History, Vol. 2: Confederation to the Present*, edited by J.L. Granatstein and Paul Stevens, Toronto: University of Toronto Press.

Abella, Irving M. and David Millar (eds) 1978, *The Canadian Worker in the Twentieth Century*, Toronto: Oxford University Press.

Abelove, Henry, et al. (eds) 1983, *Visions of History: Interviews with E.P. Thompson*, New York: Pantheon.

Adam, Barry D. 1997, 'Post-Marxism and the New Social Movements' in *Organizing Dissent: Contemporary Social Movements in Theory and Practice*, edited by William K. Carroll, Toronto: Garamond.

Adamson, Nancy, Linda Briskin and Margaret McPhail 1988, *Feminist Organizing for Change: The Contemporary Women's Movement in Canada*, Toronto: Oxford University Press.

Ahmad, Aijaz 1992, *In Theory: Classes, Nations, and Literatures*, New York: Verso.

Alexander, Robert J. 1981, *The Right Opposition: The Lovestoneites and the International Communist Opposition of the 1930s*, Westport: Greenwood.

Alexander, Sally, Anna Davin and Eve Hostettler 1979, 'Labouring Women: A Reply to Eric Hobsbawm', *History Workshop Journal*, 8, Autumn: 174–82.

Ali, Tariq 1990, *Redemption*, London: Chatto and Windus.

——— 2009, 'Foreword' in *Ernest Mandel: A Rebel's Dream Deferred*, London: Verso.

Almond, Gabriel A. 1954, *The Appeals of Communism*, Princeton, NJ: Princeton University Press.

Anbinder, Tyler 2002, *Five Points: The Nineteenth Century New York City Neighborhood that Invented Tap Dance, Stole Elections, and Became the World's Most Notorious Slum*, New York: Plume.

Anderson, Perry 1966, 'Socialism and Pseudo-Empiricism', *New Left Review*, 35, January–February: 2–42.

———— 1973, *Passages from Antiquity to Feudalism*, London: New Left Books.

———— 1974, *Lineages of the Absolutist State*, London: New Left Books.

———— 1976, *Considerations on Western Marxism*, London: New Left Books.

———— 1980, *Arguments within English Marxism*, London: Verso.

———— 1981, 'Communist Party History' in *People's History and Socialist Theory*, edited by Raphael Samuel, London: Routledge & Kegan Paul.

———— 1983, *In the Tracks of Historical Materialism*, London: Verso.

———— 1984, *In the Tracks of Historical Materialism*, Chicago: University of Chicago Press.

———— 1992a, *English Questions*, London: Verso.

———— 1992b, *A Zone of Engagement*, London: Verso.

———— 1998, *The Origins of Postmodernity*, London: Verso.

———— 2004, *Extra Time: World Politics since 1989*, London: Verso.

———— 2005, *Spectrum*, London: Verso.

Angus, Ian 1981, *Canadian Bolsheviks: The Early Years of the Communist Party of Canada*, Montreal: Vanguard.

Appel, Alfred Jr. 1974, 'The Director: Fritz Lang's American Nightmare', *Film Comment*, 10, November–December: 12–17.

Arnesen, Eric et al. 2001, 'Whiteness and Historians' Imagination', *International Labor and Working-Class History*, 60: 1–92.

Asbury, Herbert 1928, *The Gangs of New York: An Informal History of the Underworld*, New York: Knopf.

Ashman, Sam 1998, 'The Communist Party Historians' Group' in *Essays on Historical Materialism*, edited by John Rees, London: Bookmarks.

Ashton, T. and C.H.E. Philpin (eds) 1987, *The Brenner Debate: Agrarian Class Structure and Economic Development in Pre-Industrial Europe*, New York: Cambridge University Press.

Avery, Donald 1979, *'Dangerous Foreigners': European Immigrant Workers and Labour Radicalism in Canada, 1896–1932*, Toronto: McClelland and Stewart.

Babcock, Robert H. 1974, *Gompers in Canada: A Study in American Continentalism before the First World War*, Toronto: University of Toronto Press.

Bannerji, Himani 2000, *The Dark Side of the Nation: Essays on Multiculturalism, Nationalism, and Gender*, Toronto: Scholar's Press.

Barnes, Jack et al. (eds) 1976, *James P. Cannon as We Knew Him: By Thirty-Three Comrades, Friends, and Relatives*, New York: Pathfinder.

Barrett, James R. 1994, 'William Z. Foster' in *The American Radical*, edited by Mari Jo Buhle, Paul Buhle and Harvey J. Kaye, New York: Routledge.

———— 1999, *William Z. Foster and the Tragedy of American Radicalism*, Urbana: University of Illinois Press.

———— 2004, 'Class Act: An Interview with David Montgomery', *Labor: Studies in Working-Class History of the Americas*, 1: 23–54.

Barrett, Michèle 1980, *Women's Oppression Today: Problems in Marxist Feminist Analysis*, London: New Left Books.

———— 1988, *Women's Oppression Today: The Marxist/Feminist Encounter*, London: Verso.

Barrett, Michèle and Roberta Hamilton (eds) 1986, *The Politics of Diversity: Feminism, Nationalism, and Marxism*, London: Verso.

Barros, James 1986, *No Sense of Evil: Espionage, The Case of Herbert Norman*, Toronto: Deneau.

Barthes, Roland 1983, *Mythologies*, London: Fontana.

Bartolovich, Crystal and Neil Lazarus (eds) 2002, *Marxism, Modernity, and Postcolonial Studies*, Cambridge: Cambridge University Press.

Baskerville, Peter and Eric W. Sager 1998, *Unwilling Idlers: The Urban Unemployed and Their Families in Late Victorian Canada*, Toronto: University of Toronto Press.

Baxandall, Rosalyn 1993, 'The Question Seldom Asked: Women and the CPUSA' in *New Studies in the Politics and Culture of U.S. Communism*, edited by Michael E. Brown et al., New York: Monthly Review Press.

Beal, Fred 1937, *Proletarian Journey: New England, Gastonia, Moscow*, New York: Hillman-Curl.

Beck, Louis Joseph 1898, *New York's Chinatown: An Historical Presentation of Its People and Places*, New York: Bohemia Pub. Co.

Belanger, Noël et al. 1975, *Les travailleurs québecois, 1851–96*, Montréal: Les Presses de l'Université du Québec.

Belfrage, Sally 1994, *Un-American Activities: A Memoir of the Fifties*, New York: HarperPerennial.

Benson, Ed 1983, '*Martin Guerre*, the Historian and the Filmmakers: An Interview with Natalie Zemon Davis', *Film and History*, 13: 49–65.

Bercuson, David Jay 1974, *Confrontation at Winnipeg: Labour, Industrial Relations, and the General Strike*, Kingston: McGill-Queen's University Press.

———— 1977, 'Labour Radicalism and the Western Industrial Frontier, 1897–1919', *Canadian Historical Review*, 48: 154–75.

———— 1981, 'Through the Looking Glass of Culture: An Essay on the New Labour History and Working-Class Culture in Recent Canadian Historical Writing', *Labour/Le Travailleur*, 7, Spring: 95–112.

———— 1983, review of *Dreaming of What Might Be* by Gregory S. Kealey and Bryan D. Palmer, *Business History Review*, 57: 589–91.

———— 1990, *Confrontation at Winnipeg: Labour, Industrial Relations, and the General Strike*, Kingston: McGill-Queen's University Press.

Bercuson, David Jay and Kenneth McNaught 1974, *The Winnipeg General Strike: 1919*, Toronto: Longman.

Bercuson, David Jay and David Bright (eds) 1984, *Canadian Labour History: Selected Readings*, Toronto: Copp, Clark, Longman.

Berger, Carl 1976, *The Writing of Canadian History: Aspects of English-Canadian Historical Writing, 1900–70*, Toronto: Oxford University Press.

———— 1986, *The Writing of Canadian History: Aspects of English-Canadian Historical Writing since 1900*, Toronto: University of Toronto Press.

Berlin, Isaiah 1963, *Karl Marx*, Oxford: Oxford University Press.

Berman, Marshall 1982, *All that Is Solid Melts into Air: The Experience of Modernity*, New York: Simon and Schuster.

Bernstein, Iver 1990, *The New York City Draft Riots: Their Significance for American Society and Politics in the Age of the Civil War*, Oxford: Oxford University Press.

Best, Varpu Lindström 1988, *Defiant Sisters: A Social History of Finnish Immigrant Women in Canada, 1890–1930*, Toronto: Multicultural History Society of Ontario.

Billington, Ray (ed) 1966, *The Frontier Thesis: Valid Interpretation of American History?*, New York: Holt, Rinehart, and Winston.

Binder, Frederick M. and David M. Reimers 1995, *All the Nations under Heaven: An Ethnic and Racial History of New York City*, New York: Columbia University Press.

Biskind, Peter 1976, '*They Live by Night* by Daylight,' *Sight and Sound*, 45, Autumn.

Black, Gregory D. 1994, *Hollywood Censored: Morality Codes, Catholics, and the Movies*, Cambridge: Cambridge University Press.

Blackledge, Paul 2004, *Perry Anderson, Marxism and the New Left*, London: Merlin.

Bliss, Michael 1991–2, 'Privatizing the Mind: The Sundering of Canadian History, the Sundering of Canada', *Journal of Canadian Studies*, 26, Winter: 5–17.

Bloom, James D. 1992, *Left Letters: The Culture Wars of Mike Gold and Joseph Freeman*, New York: Columbia University Press.

Borde, Raymond and Etienne Chaumeton 1996, 'Towards a Definition of *Film Noir*' in *Film Noir Reader*, edited by Alain Silver and James Ursini, New York: Limelight Editions.

Bottomore, Tom (ed) 1983, *A Dictionary of Marxist Thought*, Cambridge, MA: Harvard University Press.

Bowen, Roger W. 1986, *Innocence Is Not Enough: The Life and Death of Herbert Norman*, Vancouver: Douglas & McIntyre.

Bradbury, Bettina 1987, 'Women's History and Working-Class History', *Labour/Le Travail*, 19, Spring: 23–44.

————— 1993, *Working Families: Age, Gender, and Daily Survival in Industrializing Montreal*, Toronto: McClelland and Stewart.

Braverman, Harry 1959, 'Labor and Politics' in *American Labor in Mid-Passage*, edited by Bert Cochran, New York: Monthly Review Press.

————— 1974, *Labor and Monopoly Capital: The Degradation of Work in the Twentieth Century*, New York: Monthly Review Press.

Breitman, George 1976, 'Harry Braverman: Marxist Author', *Militant*, 27, August: 12.

Brier, Stephen 1988, 'A History Film without Much History', *Radical History Review*, 41: 120–8.

Briskin, Linda and Linda Yanz (eds) 1983, *Women in the Labour Movement*, Toronto: Women's Press.

Browder, Earl 1938, *The People's Front*, New York: International.

————— 1967, 'The American Communist Party in the Thirties' in *As We Saw the Thirties: Essays on Social and Political Movements of a Decade*, edited by Rita James Simon, Urbana: University of Illinois.

Browder, Lara 1998, *Rousing the Nation: Radical Culture in Depression America*, Amherst: University of Massachusetts Press.

Brown, Kathleen A. 1999, 'The "Savagely Fathered and Unmothered" World of the Communist Party, U.S.A.: Feminism, Maternalism, and "Mother" Bloor', *Feminist Studies*, 25, Fall: 537–70.

Brown, Kathleen A. and Elizabeth Faue 2000, 'Social Bonds, Sexual Politics, and Political Community in the U.S. Left, 1920s–1940s', *Left History*, 7, Spring: 9–45.

Bubis, Mordecai Donald 1985, 'The Soviet Union and Stalinism in the Ideological Debates of American Trotskyism (1937–1951)', PhD dissertation, London School of Economics and Political Science.

Buchanan, Keith 1963, 'The Third World – Its Emergence and Contours', *New Left Review*, 18, January–February: 5–23.

Buhle, Mari Jo, Paul Buhle and Dan Georgakas (eds) 1992, *Encyclopedia of the American Left*, Urbana: University of Illinois Press.

Buhle, Paul 1981, 'Historians and American Communism: An Agenda', *International Labor and Working-Class History*, 20, Fall: 38–45.

————— 1982, 'Young People's Socialist League' in *Encyclopedia of the American Left*, edited by Mari Jo Buhle, Paul Buhle and Dan Georgakis, Urbana: University of Illinois Press.

————— 1987, *Marxism in the USA: From 1870 to the Present Day*, London: Verso.

————— 1989, 'Isn't It Romantic: E.P. Thompson's Global Agenda', *Voice Literary Supplement*, 76, July: 24–6.

————— (ed) 1990, *History and the New Left: Madison, Wisconsin, 1950–1970*, Philadelphia: Temple University Press.

————— 1991, *Marxism in the United States: Remapping the History of the American Left*, 2nd edition, London: Verso.

Buhle, Paul and Edward Rice-Maximin 1995, *William Appleman Williams: The Tragedy of Empire*, London: Routledge.

Burgess, Joanne 1977, 'L'industrie de la chaussure à Montréal (1840–1870): Le passage de l'artisanal à la fabrique', *Revue d'histoire de l'Amérique français*, 31: 187–210.

——— 1990, 'Exploring the Limited Identities of Canadian Labour: Recent Trends in English Canada and Quebec', *International Journal of Canadian Studies*, 1–2: 149–73.

Burr, Christina 1999, *Spreading the Light: Work and Labour Reform in Late Nineteenth-Century Toronto*, Toronto: University of Toronto Press.

Butler, Jeremy G. 1996, 'Miami Vice, the Legacy of Film Noir' in *Film Noir Reader*, edited by Alain Silver and James Ursini, New York: Limelight Editions.

Cadigan, Sean T. 1990, 'Battle Harbour in Transition: Merchants, Fisherman, and the State in the Struggle for Relief in a Labrador Fishing Community during the 1930s', *Labour/Le Travail*, 26: 125–50.

——— 1995, *Hope and Deception in Conception Bay: Merchant-Settler Relations in Newfoundland, 1785–1855*, Toronto: University of Toronto Press.

——— 2009, *Newfoundland and Labrador: A History*, Toronto: University of Toronto Press.

Callinicos, Alex 1988, *Making History: Agency, Structure and Change in Social Theory*, Ithaca, NY: Cornell University Press.

——— 1990, *Against Postmodernism: A Marxist Critique*, New York: St. Martin's Press.

Callow, Alexander B. Jr. 1966, *The Tweed Ring*, Oxford: Oxford University Press.

Campbell, Beatrix 1984a, 'Politics, Pyramids – and People', *Marxism Today*, December.

——— 1984b, *Wigan Pier Revisited: Poverty and Politics in the 1980s*, London: Virago.

Campbell, J. Peter 1999, *Canadian Marxists and the Search for a Third Way*, Kingston: McGill-Queen's University Press.

Cannon, James P. 1938a, 'The Convention of the New Party', *New International*, 4, January: 4–6.

——— 1938b, 'The New Party is Founded', *New International*, 4, February: 41–2.

——— 1944, *The History of American Trotskyism: Report of a Participant*, New York: Pioneer.

——— 1947, *The Coming American Revolution*, New York: Pioneer.

——— 1953, *Speeches to the Party: The Revolutionary Perspective and the Revolutionary Party*, New York: Pathfinder.

——— 1962, *The First Ten Years of American Communism: Report of a Participant*, New York: Lyle Stuart.

——— 1970, *Socialism on Trial*, New York: Pathfinder.

——— 1971, *Speeches for Socialism*, New York: Pathfinder.

——— 1972a, *The History of American Trotskyism: From Its Origins (1928) to the Founding of the Socialist Workers Party (1938)*, New York: Pathfinder.

——— 1972b, *The Struggle for a Proletarian Party*, New York: Pathfinder.

———— 1973a, *The First Ten Years of American Communism – Report of a Participant*, New York: Pathfinder.

———— 1973b, *Letters from Prison*, New York: Pathfinder.

———— 1973c, *Notebook of an Agitator*, New York: Pathfinder.

———— 1975, *The Socialist Workers Party in World War II: Writings and Speeches, 1940–43*, New York: Pathfinder.

———— 1977, *The Struggle for Socialism in the 'American Century': Writings and Speeches, 1945–47*, New York: Pathfinder.

———— 1992, *James P. Cannon and the Early Years of American Communism: Selected Writings and Speeches, 1920–1928*, New York: Prometheus Research Library.

Careless, J.M.S. 1969, '"Limited Identities" in Canada', *Canadian Historical Review*, 40: 1–10.

Carr, E.H. 1982, *Twilight of the Comintern, 1930–1935*, New York: Pantheon.

Carroll, William K. (ed) 1997, *Organizing Dissent: Contemporary Social Movements in Theory and Practice*, Toronto: Garamond.

Carter, Dan 1969, *Scottsboro: A Tragedy of the American South*, Baton Rouge: Louisiana State University Press.

———— 1971, *Scottsboro: A Tragedy of the American South*, New York: Oxford University Press.

Caspary, Vera 1979, *The Secrets of Grown-Ups*, New York: McGraw-Hill.

Caute, David 1979, *The Great Fear: The Anti-Communist Purge under Truman and Eisenhower*, New York: Touchstone Books.

Ceplair, Larry and Steven Englund 1983, *The Inquisition in Hollywood: Politics in the Film Community, 1930–60*, Berkeley: University of California Press.

Chandler, Raymond 1976 [1939], *The Big Sleep*, New York: Vintage.

Charbonnier, G. 1973, *Conversations with Claude Lévi-Strauss*, London: Jonathan Cape.

Charney, George 1968, *A Long Journey*, Chicago: Quadrangle.

Charpentier, Alfred 1971, *Cinquante ans d'action ouvrière: les memoirs d'Alfred Charpentier*, Québec: Les Presses de l'Université Laval.

Chauncey, George 1994, *Gay New York: Gender, Urban Culture, and the Making of the Gay Male World, 1890–1940*, New York: Basic Books.

Cherny, Robert W. 2002, 'Prelude to the Popular Front: The Communist Party in California, 1931–35', *American Communist History*, 1: 5–42.

Cherwinski, W.J.C. and Gregory S. Kealey (eds) 1985, *Lectures in Canadian Labour and Working-Class History*, St. John's: Canadian Committee on Labour History.

Christopher, Nicholas 1997, *Somewhere in the Night: Film Noir and the American City*, New York: Free Press.

Chun, Lin 1993, *The British New Left*, Edinburgh: Edinburgh University Press.

Clark, Christopher 1986, 'Politics, Language and Class', *Radical History Review*, 34: 78–86.

Clarke, John, Chas Critcher and Richard Johnson (eds) 1979, *Working-Class Culture: Studies in History and Theory*, London: Hutchinson.

Claudin, Fernando 1975, *The Communist Movement: From Comintern to Cominform*, Harmondsworth: Penguin.

Clement, Wallace (ed) 1997, *Understanding Canada: Building on the New Canadian Political Economy*, Montreal: McGill-Queen's University Press.

Clement, Wallace and Glen Williams (eds) 1989, *The New Canadian Political Economy*, Montreal: McGill-Queen's University Press.

Clement, Wallace and Leah F. Vosko (eds) 2003, *Changing Canada: Political Economy as Transformation*, Montreal: McGill-Queen's University Press.

Cochran, Bert 1977, *Labor and Communism: The Conflict that Shaped American Unions*, Princeton, NJ: Princeton University Press.

Coe, Tony 1983, 'Hobsbawm and Jazz' in *Culture, Ideology, and Politics: Essays for Eric Hobsbawm*, edited by Raphael Samuel and Gareth Stedman Jones, London: Routledge.

Cohen, G.A. 1978, *Karl Marx's Theory of History: A Defence*, Princeton, NJ: Princeton University Press.

Coldwell, M.J. 1945, *Left Turn, Canada*, London: Victor Gollancz.

Cole, Lester 1981, *Hollywood Red: The Autobiography of Lester Cole*, Palo Alto, CA: Ramparts Press.

Colletti, Lucio 1972, *From Rousseau to Lenin: Studies in Ideology and Society*, London: New Left Books.

———— 1973, *Marxism and Hegel*, London: New Left Books.

Connable, Alfred and Edward Silberfarb 1967, *Tigers of Tammany: Nine Men Who Ran New York*, New York: Holt, Rinehart, and Winston.

Connelly, Marie Katheryn 1991, *Martin Scorsese: An Analysis of His Feature Films with a Filmography of His Entire Directorial Career*, Jefferson: McFarland.

Conradi, Peter J. 2012, *A Very English Hero: The Making of Frank Thompson*, London: Bloomsbury.

Cook, Adrian 1974, *The Armies of the Streets: The New York City Draft Riots, 1863*, Lexington: University of Kentucky Press.

Cook, Ramsay 1967, 'Canadian Centennial Cerebrations', *International Journal*, 31: 663.

———— 1983, 'The Making of Canadian Working-Class History', *Historical Reflections*, 10, Spring: 115–26.

Copjec, Joan 1993, 'The Phenomenal Nonphenomenal: Private Space in Film Noir' in *Shades of Noir: A Reader*, edited by Joan Copjec, London: Verso.

Copp, Terry 1974, *The Condition of the Working Class in Montreal, 1897–1929*, Toronto: McClelland and Stewart.

Corber, Robert J. 1997, *Homosexuality in Cold War America: Resistance and the Crisis of Masculinity*, Durham, NC: Duke University Press.

Cowie, Elizabeth 1993, '*Film Noir* and Women' in *Shades of Noir: A Reader*, edited by Joan Copjec, London: Verso.

Craven, Paul (ed) 1995, *Labouring Lives: Work and Workers in Nineteenth-Century Ontario*, Toronto: University of Toronto Press.

Creese, Gillian 1999, *Contracting Masculinity: Gender, Class, and Race in a White Collar Union, 1944–1994*, Toronto: Oxford University Press.

Creighton, Donald G. 1937, *The Commercial Empire of the St. Lawrence, 1760–1850*, Toronto: Ryerson Press.

Cronin, James 1978–9, 'Creating a Marxist Historiography: The Contribution of Hobsbawm', *Radical History Review*, 19, Winter: 87–109.

Cross, Michael 1973, 'The Shiners' War: Social Violence in the Ottawa Valley in the 1930s', *Canadian Historical Review*, 44: 1–26.

———— (ed) 1974a, *The Decline and Fall of a Good Idea: CCF-NDP Manifestoes, 1932–1969*, Toronto: New Hogstown Press.

———— (ed) 1974b, *The Workingman in the Nineteenth Century*, Toronto: Oxford University Press.

Crossman, Richard (ed) 1949, *The God that Failed: A Confession*, New York: Harper & Brothers.

Cruse, Harold 1964, *The Crisis of the Negro Intellectual*, New York: Morrow.

Danysk, Cecilia 1995, *Hired Hands: Labour and the Development of Prairie Agriculture, 1880–1930*, Toronto: McClelland and Stewart.

Darwin, Charles 2009, *On the Origin of Species*, edited by Jim Endersby. Cambridge: Cambridge University Press.

Darwin, Francis (ed) 1888, *The Life and Letters of Charles Darwin including an Autobiographical Chapter*, Volume II, London: John Murray.

Davis, Madeleine 2011, 'Arguing Affluence: New Left Contributions to the Socialist Debate, 1957–1963', *Twentieth-Century British History*: 25–6.

Davis, Mike 1986, *Prisoners of the American Dream: Politics and Economy in the History of the US Working Class*, London: Verso.

———— 1992, *City of Quartz: Excavating the Future in Los Angeles*, New York: Vintage Books.

———— 1999, 'Magical Urbanism: Latinos Reinvent the US Big City', *New Left Review*, I, 234 (March–April), 3–43.

———— 2003, 'History: The Bloody Streets of New York', *Socialist Review*, 270, January.

Davis, Natalie Zemon 1987, 'Any Resemblance to Persons Living or Dead: Film and the Challenge of Authenticity', *Yale Review*, 76: 461–77.

———— 1988, 'On the Lame', *American Historical Review*, 93: 572–603.

———— 2000, *Slaves on Screen: Film and Historical Vision*, Toronto: Vintage Canada.

Dawley, Alan 1976, *Class and Community: The Industrial Revolution in Lynn*, Cambridge, MA: Harvard University Press.

————— 1978–9, 'E.P. Thompson and the Peculiarities of the Americans', *Radical History Review*, 19, Winter: 33–60.

————— 1994, *Struggles for Justice: Social Responsibility and the Liberal State*, Cambridge, MA: Harvard University Press.

Dawley, Alan and Paul Faler 1976, 'Working-Class Culture and Politics in the Industrial Revolution: Sources of Loyalism and Rebellion', *Journal of Social History*, 9: 466–80.

Debord, Guy 1990, *Comments on the Society of the Spectacle*, London: Verso.

Dechêne, Louise 1992, *Habitants and Merchants in Seventeenth-Century Montreal*, Kingston: McGill-Queen's University Press.

DeMarco, Gordon 1979, *October Heat*, San Francisco: Germinal Press.

————— 1982, *The Canvas Prison*, San Francisco: Germinal Press.

————— 1985, *Frisco Blues*, London: Pluto.

Denning, Michael 1996, *The Cultural Front: The Laboring of American Culture in the Twentieth Century*, London: Verso.

Dennis, Peggy 1977, *The Autobiography of an American Communist: A Personal View of a Political Life, 1925–75*, Westport/Berkeley, CA: Lawrence Hill/Creative Arts.

Derrida, Jacques 1978, *Writing and Difference*, Chicago: University of Chicago Press.

————— 1994, *Spectres of Marx: The State of the Debt, the Work of Mourning, and the New International*, New York: Routledge.

Deutscher, Isaac 1953, *Russia after Stalin*, London: Hamish Hamilton.

————— 1959, *The Prophet Unarmed: Trotsky, 1921–29*, London: Oxford University Press.

————— 1964, *The Prophet Armed: Trotsky, 1879–1921*, London: Oxford University Press.

————— 1969a, *Heretics and Renegades and Other Essays*, Indianapolis: Bobbs-Merrill.

————— 1969b, *Russia after Stalin*, London: Jonathan Cape.

————— 1984, *Marxism, Wars and Revolutions: Essays from Four Decades*, London: Verso.

Dews, Peter 1987, *Logics of Disintegration: Post-Structuralist Thought and the Claims of Critical Theory*, London: Verso.

Diawara, Manthia 1993, 'Noir by Noirs: Towards a New Realism in Black Cinema' in *Shades of Noir: A Reader*, edited by Joan Copjec, London: Verso.

Dixler, Elsa Jane 1974, 'The Woman Question: Women and the American Communist Party, 1929–41', PhD dissertation, Yale University.

Dofny, Jacques and Paul Bernard 1972, *Le syndicalisme au Québec: structure et movement*, Ottawa: Bureau du Conseil Privé.

Doss, Erika 1983, 'Edward Hopper, Nighthawks, and Film Noir', *Postscript: Essays in Film and the Humanities*, 2, Winter: 14–36.

Drache, Daniel (ed) 1972, *Quebec – Only the Beginning: The Manifestoes of the Common Front*, Toronto: New Press.

————— 1976, 'Rediscovering Canadian Political Economy', *Journal of Canadian Studies*, 11, August: 3–18.

Drachkovitch, Milorad M. 1966, *The Revolutionary Internationals, 1864–1943*, Stanford, CA: Stanford University Press.

Draper, Theodore 1957, *The Roots of American Communism*, New York: Viking.

———— 1960, *American Communism and Soviet Russia*, New York: Viking.

———— 1973, 'Preface' in *The First Ten Years of American Communism – Report of a Participant*, by James P. Cannon, New York: Pathfinder.

———— 1986, *American Communism and Soviet Russia*, New York: Vintage.

Drucker, Peter 1994, *Max Shachtman and His Left: A Socialist's Odyssey Through the 'American Century'*, Atlantic Highlands, NJ: Humanities Press.

Dubinsky, Karen 1993, *Improper Advances: Rape and Heterosexual Conflict in Ontario, 1880–1929*, Chicago: University of Chicago Press.

Dubofksy, Melvyn 1990, 'Matewan', *Labor History*, 31: 488–90.

Dubuc, Alfred 1978, 'L'influence de l'école des "Annales" au Québec', unpublished mimeograph, Université du Québec à Montréal.

Dummitt, Christopher 2007, *The Manly Modern: Masculinity in Postwar Canada*, Vancouver: UBC Press.

Durgnat, Raymond 1996, 'Paint It Black: The Family Tree of Film Noir' in *Film Noir Reader*, edited by Alain Silver and James Ursini, New York: Limelight Editions.

Durham, Philip 1963, *Down These Mean Streets a Man Must Go: Raymond Chandler's Knight*, Chapel Hill: University of North Carolina Press.

Dworkin, Dennis 1997, *Cultural Marxism in Postwar Britain: History, the New Left, and the Origins of Cultural Studies*, Durham, NC: Duke University Press.

Eagleton, Terry 1981, *Walter Benjamin, or, Towards a Revolutionary Criticism*, London: Verso.

———— 1991, *Ideology: An Introduction*, London: Verso.

———— 2003, *After Theory*, New York: Basic Books.

Eastman, Max 1964, *Love and Revolution: My Journey Through an Epoch*, New York: Random House.

Edenbaum, Robert I. 1968, 'The Poetics of the Private-Eye: The Novels of Dashiell Hammett' in *Tough Guy Writers of the Thirties*, edited by David Madden, Carbondale: Southern Illinois University Press.

Eley, Geoff 1986, 'International Communism in the Heyday of Stalin', *New Left Review*, 157, January–February: 92.

———— 2002, *Forging Democracy: The History of the Left in Europe, 1850–2000*, New York: Oxford University Press.

Eley, Geoff and Keith Nield 2007, *The Future of Class in History: What's Left of the Social?*, Ann Arbor: University of Michigan Press.

Eliot, T.S. 1971, *The Complete Poems and Plays, 1909–50*, New York: Harcourt, Brace & World.

Elliott, Gregory 1998, *Perry Anderson: The Merciless Laboratory of History*, Minneapolis: University of Minnesota Press.

Ellroy, James 1997, *My Dark Places*, New York: Knopf.

Engelhardt, Tom 1995, *The End of Victory Culture: Cold War America and the Disillusioning of a Generation*, New York: BasicBooks.

Engels, Frederick 1941, *Ludwig Feuerbach and the Outcome of Classical German Philosophy*, New York: International.

————— 1943, *Condition of the Working Class in England in 1844*, London: George Allen and Unwin.

————— 1968, 'Introduction to *Dialectics of Nature*' in *Karl Marx and Frederick Engels: Selected Works*, Moscow: Progress.

Epstein, James 1986, 'Rethinking the Categories of Working-Class History', *Labour/Le Travail*, 18, Fall: 195–208.

————— 1989, 'Understanding the Cap of Liberty: Symbolic Practice and Social Conflict in Early Nineteenth-Century England', *Past & Present*, 122, February: 75–118.

Erickson, Glenn 1996, 'Expressionist Doom in Night in the City' in *Film Noir Reader*, edited by Alain Silver and James Ursini, New York: Limelight Editions.

Erickson, Todd 1996, 'Movement Becomes Genre' edited by Alain Silver and James Ursini, New York: Limelight Editions.

Ernst, Robert 1965, *Immigrant Life in New York City, 1825–1863*, Port Washington: Ira J. Friedman.

Espeset, Hélène, Jean-Pierre Hardy and David-Thiery Ruddel 1972, 'Le monde du travail au Québec au XVIIe et au XIXe siècles: historiographie et état de la question', *Revue d'histoire de l'Amérique français*, 25: 499–539.

Fahrni, Magdalena 2005, *Household Politics: Montreal Families and Post-War Reconstruction*, Toronto: University of Toronto Press.

Ferns, H.S. 1983, *Reading from Left to Right: One Man's Political History*, Toronto: University of Toronto Press.

Fingard, Judith 1974, 'The Winter's Tale: Contours of Poverty in British North America, 1815–60', Canadian Historical Association, *Annual Papers*: 65–94.

————— 1977, 'The Decline of the Sailor as a Ship Labourer in 19th Century Timber Ports', *Labour/Le Travailleur*, 2: 35–53.

————— 1982, *Jack in Port: Sailortowns of Eastern Canada*, Toronto: University of Toronto Press.

Finlay, Robert 1988, 'The Refashioning of Martin Guerre', *American Historical Review*, 93: 533–71.

Fischer, Ruth 1948, *Stalin and German Communism: A Study in the Origins of State Policy*, Cambridge, MA: Harvard University Press.

Foner, Eric 1984, 'Why Is There No Socialism in the United States', *History Workshop Journal*, 17, Spring: 57–80.

————— 1999, *The Story of American Freedom*, New York: Norton.

Foner, Philip S. and Herbert Shapiro (eds) 1991, *American Communism and Black Americans: A Documentary History*, Philadelphia: Temple University Press.

Foster, John 1985, 'The Declassing of Language', *New Left Review*, 150, March–April: 29–46.

Fournier, Louis 1984, *F.L.Q.: The Anatomy of an Underground Movement*, Toronto: New Press.

Fox, Bonnie (ed) 1980, *Hidden in the Household: Women's Domestic Labour Under Capitalism*, Toronto: Women's Education Press.

Frager, Ruth 1992, *Sweatshop Strife: Class, Ethnicity, and Gender in the Jewish Labour Movement of Toronto, 1900–1939*, Toronto: University of Toronto Press.

————— 1999, 'Labour History and the Interlocking Hierarchies of Class, Ethnicity, and Gender: A Canadian Perspective', *International Review of Social History*, 44: 217–47.

Francoeur, J., J.P. Lefebvre, P. Vadeboncoeur and J.L. Roux 1963, *En grève: L'histoire de la c.s.n. et des luttles menées par ses militants de 1937 à 1963*, Montréal: Les Éditions du Jour.

Frank, David 1999, *J.B. McLachlan: A Biography*, Toronto: James Lorimer.

Frank, David and Gregory S. Kealey (eds) 1995, *Labour and Working-Class History in Atlantic Canada: A Reader*, St. John's: Institute of Social and Economic Research.

Frank, David and John Manley 1992, 'The Sad March to the Right: J.B. McLachlan's Resignation from the Communist Party of Canada, 1936', *Labour/Le Travail*, 30: 115–34.

Frank, Pierre 1979, *The Fourth International: The Long March of the Trotskyists*, London: Links.

Freeman, Joseph 1936, *An American Testament: A Narrative of Rebels and Romantics*, New York: Farrar & Rinehart.

Freeman, Joshua B. 2000, *Working-Class New York: Life and Labor since World War II*, New York: New Press.

Fried, Albert 1997, *Communism in America: A History in Documents*, New York: Columbia University Press.

Fried, Richard M. 1990, *Nightmare in Red: The McCarthy Era in Perspective*, New York: Oxford University Press.

Friedman, Gerald 1998, *State-Making and Labor Movements: The United States and France, 1876–1914*, Ithaca: Cornell University Press.

Fryer, Peter 1957, 'Lenin as Philosopher', *Labour Review*, 2, September–October: 136–47.

Fudge, Judy and Eric Tucker 2001, *Labour before the Law: The Regulation of Workers' Collective Action in Canada, 1900–48*, Toronto: Oxford University Press.

Fukuyama, Francis 1989, 'The End of History', *National Interest*, 16, Summer: 3–18.

————— 1992, *The End of History and the Last Man*, New York: Free Press.

Fund for the Republic 1955, *Bibliography on the Communist Problem in the United States*, New York: Fund for the Republic.

Gabaccia, Donna and Franca Iacovetta (eds) 2002, *Women, Gender, and Transnational Lives: Italian Workers of the World*, Toronto: University of Toronto Press.

Gallafent, Edward 1992, 'Echo Park: Film Noir in the "Seventies"' in *The Movie Book of Film Noir*, edited by Ian Alexander Cameron, London: Studio Vista.

Gates, John 1958, *The Story of an American Communist*, New York: Thomas Nelson.

Genovese, Eugene D. 1979, *From Rebellion to Revolution: Afro-American Slave Revolts in the Making of the Modern World*, Baton Rouge: Louisiana State University Press.

———— 1984, 'The Politics of Class Struggle in the History of Society: An Appraisal of the Work of Eric Hobsbawm' in *The Power of the Past: Essays for Eric Hobsbawm*, edited by Pat Thane, Geoffrey Crossick and Roderick Floud, Cambridge: Cambridge University Press.

Geras, Norman 1978, 'Althusser's Marxism: An Assessment' in *Western Marxism: A Critical Reader*, edited by New Left Review, London: Verso.

———— 1990, *Discourses of Extremity: Radical Ethics and Post-Marxist Extravagances*, London: Verso.

Gerstle, Gary 1984, 'Mission from Moscow: American Communism in the 1930s', *Reviews in American History*, 12, December: 559–66.

Gifford, Barry 1988, *Devil Thumbs a Ride, and Other Unforgettable Movies*, New York: Groves Press.

Gitlow, Benjamin 1940, *I Confess: The Truth about American Communism*, New York: Dutton.

Givertz, A.M. and Marcus Klee 1993, 'Historicizing Thompson: An Interview with Bryan D. Palmer', *Left History*, 1, Fall: 111–20.

Glotzer, Albert 1989, *Trotsky: Memoir & Critique*, Buffalo: Prometheus Books.

Goldfield, Michael 1985, 'Recent Historiography of the Communist Party, U.S.A.' in *The Year Left: An American Socialist Yearbook, 1985*, edited by Mike Davis, Fred Pfeil and Michael Sprinker, London: Verso.

Golz, Annalee 1993, 'Family Matters: The Canadian Family and the State in the Postwar Period', *Left History*, 1: 9–50.

Gordon, Max 1976, 'The Communist Party of the 1930s and the New Left', *Socialist Revolution*, 6, January–March: 11–66.

Gornick, Vivian 1977, *The Romance of American Communism*, New York: Basic Books.

Gosse, Van 1991, '"To Organize in Every Neighbourhood, in Every Home": The Gender Politics of American Communists between the Wars', *Radical History Review*, 50: 110–41.

Gramsci, Antonio 1971, *Selections from the Prison Notebooks*, edited and introduced by Quintin Hoare and Geoffrey Nowell Smith, New York: International.

Granatstein, J.L. 1998, *Who Killed Canadian History?*, Toronto: Harper Collins.

Grant, George 2005 [1965], *Lament for a Nation: The Defeat of Canadian Nationalism*, Montreal: McGill-Queen's University Press.

Gray, Robert 1986, 'The Deconstructing of the English Working Class', *Social History*, 11, October: 363–73.

Greer, Allan 1995, '1837–38: Rebellion Reconsidered', *Canadian Historical Review*, 76, March: 1–18.

Grella, George 1968, 'The Gangster Novel: The Urban Pastoral' in *Tough Guy Writers of the Thirties*, edited by David Madden, Carbondale: Southern Illinois University Press.

Grist, Leighton 1992, 'Moving Targets and Black Widows: Film Noir in Modern Hollywood' in *The Movie Book of Film Noir*, edited by Ian Alexander Cameron, London: Studio Vista.

Guard, Julie 1996, 'Fair Play or Fair Pay: Gender Relations, Class Consciousness, and Union Solidarity in the Canadian UE', *Labour/Le Travail*, 37: 149–77.

―――― 2004, 'Authenticity on the Line: Women Workers, Native "Scabs", and the Multi-Ethnic Politics of Identity in a Left-Led Strike in Cold War Canada', *Journal of Women's History*, 15: 117–40.

Guilbault, Serge 1983, *How New York Stole the Idea of Modern Art: Abstract Expressionism, Freedom, and the Cold War*, Chicago: University of Chicago Press.

Guillet, Edwin C. 1938, *The Lives and Times of the Patriots: An Account of the Rebellion in Upper Canada, 1837–1838 and of the Patriot Agitation in the United States, 1837–42*, Toronto: University of Toronto Press.

Gutman, Herbert G. 1976, *Work, Culture, and Society in Industrializing America*, New York: Knopf.

Hamelin, Jean and Fernand Harvey 1976, *Les Travailleurs Québecois, 1941–71*, Québec: Institut superieur des sciences humaines, Université Laval.

Hamelin, Jean, Paul Larocque and Jacques Rouillard 1970, *Répertoire des grèves dans la province de Québec au XIXe siècle*, Montréal: Les Presses de l'École des Hautes Études Commerciales.

Hamilton, Roberta and Michèle Barrett (eds) 1986, *The Politics of Diversity: Feminism, Marxism and Nationalism*, London: Verso.

Hamilton, Scott 2011, *The Crisis of Theory: E.P. Thompson, the New Left, and Post-War British Politics*, Manchester: Manchester University Press.

Hann, Russell and Gregory S. Kealey 1977, 'Documenting Working-Class History: North American Traditions and New Approaches', *Archivaria*, 4: 92–114.

Hann, Russell, Gregory S. Kealey, Linda Kealey and Peter Warrian (eds) 1973, *Primary Sources in Canadian Working Class History, 1860–1930*, Kitchener: Dumont Press.

Hardy, Jean-Pierre and David-Thiery Ruddel 1977, *Les apprentis artisans à Québec, 1660–1825*, Montréal: Les Presses de l'Université du Québec.

Harman, Chris 2002, review of *Interesting Times: A Twentieth-Century Life* by Eric J. Hobsbawm, *Socialist Review*, 267, October.

Hartz, Louis 1964, *The Founding of New Societies*, New York: Harcourt, Brace and World.

Harvey, David 1989, *The Condition of Postmodernity: An Enquiry into the Origins of Cultural Change*, New York: Blackwell.

Harvey, Fernand 1978, *Révolution industrielle et travailleurs: une enquêsur les rapports entre le capital et le travail au Québec à la fin du 19e siècle*, Montréal: Boréal Express.

——— 1979, 'L'histoire des travailleurs québécois: les variations de la conjuncture et de l'historiographie' in *Le movement ouvrier au Québec*, edited by Fernand Harvey, Montréal: Boréal Express.

Haynes, John Earl 1984, *Dubious Alliance: The Making of Minnesota's DFL Party*, Minneapolis: University of Minnesota Press.

——— 1987, *Communism and Anti-Communism in the United States: An Annotated Guide to Historical Writings*, New York: Garland.

——— 1996, *Red Scare or Red Menace? American Communism and Anti-Communism in the Cold War Era*, Chicago: Ivan R. Dee.

——— 2000, 'The Cold War Debate Continues: A Traditionalist View of Historical Writing on Domestic Communism and Anti-Communism', *Journal of Cold War Studies*, 2: 76–115.

——— 2003, 'Poison or Cancer: Stalinism and American Communism', *American Communist History*, 2, December: 183–91.

Haywood, Harry 1978, *Black Bolshevik: Autobiography of an Afro-American Communist*, Chicago: Liberator Press.

Healey, Dorothy and Maurice Isserman 1990, *Dorothy Healey Remembers: A Life in the American Communist Party*, New York: Oxford University Press.

Heaton, Herbert 1938, review of *The Commercial Empire of the St. Lawrence, 1760–1850* by Donald G. Creighton, *Canadian Journal of Economics and Political Science*, 4, November: 565–70.

Heffer, Jean and Jeanine Rovet (eds) 1988, *Why Is There No Socialism in the United States?*, Paris: L'École des Hautes Études en Sciences Sociales.

Hegel, Georg Wilhelm Friedrich 1961, *Hegel's Science of Logic*, translated by W.H. Johnston and L.G. Struthers, London: Allen and Unwin.

Heron, Craig 1980, 'The Crisis of the Craftsman: Hamilton's Metal Workers in the Early Twentieth Century', *Labour/Le Travailleur*, 6: 7–49.

——— 1984, 'Labourism and the Canadian Working Class', *Labour/Le Travail*, 13: 45–76.

——— 1988, *Working in Steel: The Early Years in Canada, 1883–1935*, Toronto: McClelland and Stewart.

——— 1996, *The Canadian Labour Movement: A Short History*, Toronto: Lorimer.

——— (ed) 1998, *The Workers' Revolt in Canada, 1917–25*, Toronto: University of Toronto Press.

——— 2003, *Booze: A Distilled History*, Toronto: Between the Lines.

Heron, Craig and Bryan D. Palmer 1977, 'Through the Prism of the Strike: Industrial Conflict in Southern Ontario, 1901–14', *Canadian Historical Review*, 58, December: 423–58.

Heron, Craig and Robert Storey (eds) 1986, *On the Job: Confronting the Labour Process in Canada*, Kingston: McGill-Queen's University Press.

Heron, Craig and Steven Penfold 2006, *The Workers' Festival: A History of Labour Day in Canada*, Toronto: University of Toronto Press.

Hewitt, Steve 2002, *Spying 101: The RCMP's Secret Activities at Canadian Universities, 1917–97*, Toronto: University of Toronto Press.

High, Steven 1996, 'Native Wage Labour and Independent Production during the "Era of Irrelevance"', *Labour/Le Travail*, 37: 243–64.

———— 2003, *Industrial Sunset: The Making of North America's Rost Belt, 1969–1984*, Toronto: University of Toronto Press.

Higham, Charles and Joel Greenberg 1968, *Hollywood in the Forties*, New York: A.S. Barnes.

Hill, Christopher 1972a, *God's Englishman: Oliver Cromwell and the English Revolution*, New York: Dial Press.

———— 1972b, *The World Turned Upside Down: Radical Ideas during the English Revolution*, New York: Viking Press.

———— 1984, *The Experience of Defeat: Milton and Some Contemporaries*, London: Bookmarks.

Hilton, Rodney (ed) 1978, *The Transition from Feudalism to Capitalism*, New York: Verso.

Himes, Chester 1976, *My Life of Absurdity: The Later Years*, New York: Paragon House.

Himmelfarb, Gertrude 1987, *The New History and the Old: Critical Essays and Reappraisals*, Cambridge, MA: Harvard University Press.

Hobbs, Margaret and Joan Sangster (eds) 1999, *The Woman Worker, 1926–29*, St. John's: Canadian Committee on Labour History.

Hobsbawm, Eric J. 1948, *Labour's Turning Point, 1880–1900*, Hassocks: Harvester.

———— 1954a, 'The Crisis of the Seventeenth Century, Part I', *Past & Present*, 5: 33–53.

———— 1954b, 'The Crisis of the Seventeenth Century, Part II', *Past & Present*, 6: 44–65.

———— 1955, 'The Economics of the Gangster', *Quarterly Review*, 604: 243–56.

———— 1959, *Primitive Rebels: Studies in Archaic Forms of Social Movement in the 19th and 20th Centuries*, Manchester: The University Press.

———— 1960, 'The Seventeenth Century in the Development of Capitalism', *Science & Society*, 24, Spring: 97–112.

———— 1962, *The Age of Revolution, 1789–1848*, London: Abacus.

———— 1964, *Labouring Men: Studies in the History of Labour*, New York: Basic Books.

———— 1967, 'The Crisis of the Seventeenth Century' in *Crisis in Europe, 1560–1660*, edited by Trevor Aston, Garden City: Doubleday.

———— 1968, 'Karl Marx's Contribution to Historiography', *Diogenes*, 64: 37–56.

————— 1969, *Bandits*, New York: Delacrote Press.

————— 1970, 'Guerillas in Latin America' in *The Socialist Register 1970*, edited by Ralph Miliband and John Saville, London: Merlin Press.

————— 1971a, 'Class Consciousness in History' in *Aspects of History and Class Consciousness*, edited by István Mészaros, London: Routledge and K. Paul.

————— 1971b, 'From Social History to the History of Society', *Daedalus*, 100, Winter: 20–45.

————— 1973, *Revolutionaries: Contemporary Essays*, New York: Pantheon.

————— 1975, *The Age of Capital, 1848–1875*, New York: Scribner.

————— 1977a, 'Gramsci and Political Theory', *Marxism Today*, 21: 205–13.

————— 1977b, *The Italian Road to Socialism: An Interview with Giorgio Napolitano of the Italian Communist Party*, New York: Whirlwind Book Co.

————— 1978a, 'The Historians' Group of the Communist Party' in *Rebels and Their Causes: Essays in Honour of A.L. Morton*, edited by Maurice Cornforth, London: Lawrence and Wishart.

————— 1978b, 'Man and Woman in Socialist Iconography', *History Workshop Journal*, 6, Autumn: 121–38.

————— 1981, *The Forward March of Labour Halted?*, edited by Martin Jacques and Francis Mulhern, London: New Left Books in association with *Marxism Today*.

————— 1982a, 'The Fortunes of Marx's and Engels' Writings' in *The History of Marxism, Volume 1: Marxism in Marx's Day*, edited by Eric Hobsbawm, Bloomington.

————— 1982b, 'Marx, Engels and Pre-Marxian Socialism' in *The History of Marxism, Volume 1: Marxism in Marx's Day*, edited by Eric J. Hobsbawm, Bloomington: Indiana University Press.

————— 1983a, 'Introduction: Inventing Traditions' in *The Invention of Tradition*, edited by E.J. Hobsbawm and Terence Ranger, Cambridge: Cambridge University Press.

————— 1983b, 'Mass-Producing Traditions: Europe, 1870–1914' in *The Invention of Tradition*, edited by E.J. Hobsbawm and Terence Ranger, Cambridge: Cambridge University Press.

————— 1984, *Workers: Worlds of Labor*, New York: Pantheon Books.

————— 1985, 'History from Below – Some Historical Reflections' in *History from Below: Studies in Popular Protest and Popular Ideology in Honour of George Rudé*, edited by Frederick Krantz, Montreal: Concordia University.

————— 1987, *The Age of Empire, 1875–1914*, London: Weidenfeld and Nicolson.

————— 1989, *Politics for a Rational Left: Political Writing, 1977–1988*, London: Verso.

————— 1990, *Nations and Nationalism since 1780: Programme, Myth, Reality*, Cambridge: Cambridge University Press.

————— 1993, *The Jazz Scene*, New York: Pantheon Books.

————— 1994, *The Age of Extremes: The Short Twentieth Century, 1914–1991*, London: Michael Joseph.

———— 1996, 'Edward Palmer Thompson, 1924–1933', *Proceedings of the British Academy*, 90: 521–39.

———— 1998, *Uncommon People: Resistance, Rebellion, and Jazz*, London: Weidenfeld & Nicolson.

———— 2002, *Interesting Times: A Twentieth-Century Life*, London: Allen Lane.

Hobsbawm, Eric and Antonio Polito 2000, *On the Edge of the New Century*, New York: New Press.

Hollinger, Karen 1996, 'Film Noir, Voice-Over, and the Femme Fatale' in *Film Noir Reader*, edited by Alain Silver and James Ursini, New York: Limelight Editions.

Hopkin, Deian R. and Gregory S. Kealey (eds) 1989, *Class, Community, and the Labour Movement: Wales and Canada, 1850–1930*, Llafur/CCLH.

Horne, Gerald 1993, 'The Red and the Black: The Communist Party and African Americans in Historical Perspective' in *New Studies in the Politics and Culture of U.S. Communism*, edited by Michael E. Brown et al., New York: Monthly Review Press.

Horowitz, Gad 1968, *Canadian Labour in Politics*, Toronto: University of Toronto Press.

Howe, Irving 1982, *A Margin of Hope: An Intellectual Biography*, New York: Harcourt, Brace, Jovanovich.

———— 1985, *Socialism in America*, New York: Harcourt, Brace, Jovanovich.

———— 1991, 'The Value of the Canon', *New Republic*, 18, February: 40–7.

Howe, Irving and Lewis Coser 1957, *The American Communist Party: A Critical History (1919–57)*, Boston: Beacon Press.

———— 1962, *The American Communist Party: A Critical History*, New York: Praeger.

Hughes-Warrington, Marnie (ed) 2009, *The History on Film Reader*, London and New York: Routledge.

Hunt, Karen 2001, 'Dora Montefiore: A Different Communist', in *Party People, Communist Lives: Exploration in Biography*, edited by John McIlroy, Kevin Morgan and Alan Campbell, London: Lawrence and Wishart, pp. 29–50.

Iacovetta, Franca 1992, *Such Hardworking People: Italian Immigrants in Postwar Toronto*, Montreal: McGill-Queen's University Press.

———— 2006, *Gatekeepers: Reshaping Immigrant Lives in Cold War Canada*, Toronto: Between the Lines.

Ignatiev, Noel 1995, *How the Irish Became White*, London: Routledge.

Inman, Mary 1941, *In Woman's Defense*, Los Angeles: Committee to Organize the Advancement of Women.

Irving, Terry and Allen Seager 1996, 'Labour and Developments to 1960', *Labour/Le Travail*, 38: 239–77.

Isserman, Maurice 1982, *Which Side Were You On? The American Communist Party during the Second World War*, Middletown: Wesleyan University Press.

———— 1985, 'Three Generations: Historians View American Communism', *Labor History*, 26, Fall: 517–45.

———— 1987, *If I Had a Hammer: The Death of the Old Left and the Birth of the New Left*, New York: Basic Books.

Jacobson, Julian 2000, 'Revising the History of Cold War Liberals', *New Politics*, 7, Winter.

Jacoby, Russell 1987, *The Last Intellectuals: American Culture in the Age of Academe*, New York: Basic Books.

Jacques, Martin and Francis Mulhern (eds) 1981, *The Forward March of Labour Halted?*, London: Verso.

Jaffe, Philip J. 1975, *The Rise and Fall of American Communism*, New York: Horizon Press.

James, C.L.R. 1980 [1948], *Notes on Dialectics: Hegel, Marx, Lenin*, London: Allison and Busby.

———— 1993, *American Civilization*, edited by Anna Grimshaw and Keith Hart, Cambridge: Blackwell.

Jameson, Fredric 1981, *The Political Unconscious: Narrative as a Socially Symbolic Act*, Ithaca: Cornell University Press.

———— 1991, *Postmodernism: or the Cultural Logic of Late Capitalism*, Durham, NC: Duke University Press.

———— 1993, 'The Synoptic Chandler' in *Shades of Noir: A Reader*, edited by Joan Copjec, London: Verso.

Jenkins, Keith (ed) 1997, *The Postmodern History Reader*, London and New York: Routledge.

Johanningsmeier, Edward P. 1994, *Forging American Communism: The Life of William Z. Foster*, Princeton, NJ: Princeton University Press.

Johnson, Diane 1983, *Dashiell Hammett: A Life*, New York: Random House.

Johnson, Richard 1978, 'Edward Thompson, Eugene Genovese, and Socialist-Humanist History', *History Workshop*, 6, Autumn: 79–100.

———— 1979, 'Culture and the Historians' in *Working-Class Culture: Studies in History and Theory*, edited by John Clarke, Chas Critcher and Richard Johnson, London: Hutchinson, in association with the Centre for Contemporary Cultural Studies, University of Birmingham.

Johnson, Richard et al. (eds) 1982, *Making Histories: Studies in History-Writing and Politics*, London: Hutchinson.

Joyce, Patrick 1980, *Work, Society, and Politics: The Culture of the Factory in Later Victorian Britain*, New Brunswick: Rutgers University Press.

———— 1991, *Visions of the People: Industrial England and the Question of Class, 1848–1914*, Cambridge: Cambridge University Press.

Kaplan, E. Ann (ed) 1978, *Women in Film Noir*, London: BFI Publishing.

Kaplan, Judy and Linn Shapiro (eds) 1998, *Red Diapers: Growing Up in the Communist Left*, Urbana: University of Illinois Press.

Katz, Michael B. 1975, *The People of Hamilton, Canada West: Family and Class in a Mid-Nineteenth Century City*, Cambridge, MA: Harvard University Press.

———— 1978, 'Origins of the Institutional State', *Marxist Perspectives*, 1: 6–23.

Katz Michael B., Michael J. Doucet and Mark J. Stern 1982, *The Social Organization of Early Industrial Capitalism*, Cambridge, MA: Harvard University Press.

Katznelson, Ira and Aristide Zolberg (eds) 1986, *Working-Class Formation: Nineteenth-Century Patterns in Western Europe and the United States*, Princeton, NJ: Princeton University Press.

Kaye, Harvey J. 1984, *The British Marxist Historians: An Introductory Analysis*, Cambridge: Polity.

———— 1992, *The Education of Desire: Marxists and the Writing of History*, New York: Routledge.

Kealey, Gregory S. 1973a, 'Artisans Respond to Industrialism: Shoemakers, Shoe Factories, and the Knights of St. Crispin in Toronto', Canadian Historical Association, *Historical Papers*: 137–57.

———— (ed) 1973b, *Canada Investigates Industrialism: The Royal Commission on the Relations of Labor and Capital, 1889*, Toronto: University of Toronto Press.

———— 1976, 'The "Honest Workingman" and Workers' Control: The Experience of Toronto Skilled Workers', *Labour/Le Travailleur*, 1: 32–68.

———— 1980, *Toronto Workers Respond to Industrial Capitalism, 1867–1892*, Toronto: University of Toronto Press.

———— 1981a, 'Labour and Working-Class History in Canada: Prospects in the 1980s', *Labour/Le Travail*, 7: 95–126.

———— 1981b, 'Looking Backward: Reflections on the Study of Class in Canada', *The History and Social Science Teacher*, 16: 213–22.

———— 1982a, 'Stanley Bréhaut Ryerson: Canadian Revolutionary Intellectual', *Studies in Political Economy*, 9: 103–31.

———— 1982b, 'Stanley Bréhaut Ryerson: Marxist Historian', *Studies in Political Economy*, 9: 133–71.

———— 1984, '1919: The Canadian Labour Revolt', *Labour/Le Travail*, 13: 11–44.

———— 1992, 'State Repression of Labour and the Left in Canada, 1914–20: The Impact of the First World War', *Canadian Historical Review*, 73: 281–314.

———— 1995, *Workers and Canadian History*, Toronto: University of Toronto Press.

———— 1999, 'The Empire Strikes Back: The Nineteenth-Century Origins of the Canadian Secret Service', *Journal of the Canadian Historical Association*, 10: 3–18.

Kealey, Gregory S. and Bryan D. Palmer 1981, 'The Bonds of Unity: The Knights of Labor in Ontario, 1880–1900', *Histoire Sociale/Social History*, 28: 369–411.

———— 1982, *Dreaming of What Might Be: The Knights of Labor in Ontario, 1880–1900*, New York: Cambridge University Press.

———— 1983, '"The Bonds of Unity": Some Further Reflections', *Histoire Sociale/Social History*, 31: 175–89.

Kealey, Gregory S. and Greg Patmore (eds) 1990, *Canadian and Australian Labour History: Towards a Comparative Perspective*, St. John's: CCLH.

Kealey, Gregory S. and Peter Warrian (eds) 1976, *Essays in Canadian Working Class History*, Toronto: McClelland and Stewart.

Kealey, Linda (ed) 1979, *A Not Unreasonable Claim: Women and Reform in Canada, 1880s to 1920s*, Toronto: Women's Press.

———— 1998, *Enlisting Women for the Cause: Women, Labour and the Left in Canada, 1890–1920*, Toronto: University of Toronto Press.

Keeran, Roger 1980, *The Communist Party and the Auto Workers Unions*, Bloomington: Indiana University Press.

Kelley, Robin D.G. 1990, *Hammer and Hoe: Alabama Communists during the Great Depression*, Chapel Hill: University of North Carolina Press.

———— 1994, *Race Rebels: Culture, Politics, and the Black Working Class*, New York: Free Press.

Kelly, Mary Pat 1980, *Martin Scorsese: The First Decade*, Pleasantville: Redgrave.

Kessler-Harris, Alice 1975, 'Where Are the Organized Women Workers?', *Feminist Studies*, 3: 92–110.

Kiernan, Victor 1984, 'Making Histories', *Our History Journal*, 8: 7–10.

Kimmage, Ann 1996, *An Un-American Childhood: A Young Woman's Secret Life behind the Iron Curtain*, Athens: University of Georgia Press.

Kingsley, E.T. 1916, *The Genesis and Evolution of Slavery: Showing How the Chattel Slaves of Pagan Times Have Been Transformed into the Capitalist Property of Today*, Vancouver.

Kinsman, Gary 1987, *The Regulation of Desire: Sexuality in Canada*, Montreal: Black Rose.

Kirk, Neville 1987, 'In Defence of Class: A Critique of Recent Revisionist Writing on the Nineteenth-Century Working Class', *International Review of Social History*, 32: 2–47.

———— 2000, 'American "Exceptionalism" Revisited: The Case of Samuel Gompers', *Socialist History*, 16: 1–26.

Klehr, Harvey 1978, *Communist Cadre: The Social Background of the American Communist Party Elite*, Stanford: Hoover Institution Press.

———— 1984, *The Heyday of American Communism: The Depression Decade*, New York: Basic Books.

Klehr, Harvey and John Earl Haynes 1992, *The American Communist Movement: Storming Heaven Itself*, New York: Twayne.

———— 1999, *Venona: Decoding Soviet Espionage in America*, New Haven, CT: Yale University Press.

Klehr, Harvey, John Earl Haynes, and Fridrikh Irorevich Firsov 1995, *The Secret World of American Communism*, New Haven, CT: Yale University Press.

Klehr, Harvey, John Earl Haynes and Kryill M. Anderson 1998, *The Soviet World of American Communism*, New Haven, CT: Yale University Press.

Klehr, Harvey and Ronald Radosh 1996, *The Amerasia Spy Case: Prelude to McCarthyism*, Chapel Hill: University of North Carolina Press.

Klein, Norman M. 1997, *The History of Forgetting: Los Angeles and the Erasure of Memory*, London: Verso.

Knight, Rolf 1978, *Indians at Work: An Informal History of Native Indian Labour in British Columbia, 1858–1930*, Vancouver: New Star Books.

Kofsky, Frank 1970, *Black Nationalism and the Revolution in Music*, New York: Pathfinder Press.

Koonz, Claudia 1989, 'Post Scripts', *Women's Review of Books*, 6, January: 19–20.

Kristofferson, Robert B. 2007, *Craft Capitalism: Craftworkers and Early Industrialization in Hamilton, Ontario, 1840–72*, Toronto: University of Toronto Press.

Krutnik, Frank 1991, *In a Lonely Street: Film Noir, Genre, Masculinity*, London: Routledge.

Kuo Wei Tchen, Jack 1990, 'New York Chinese: The Nineteenth-Century Pre-Chinatown Settlement' in *Chinese America: History and Perspectives*, San Francisco: Chinese Historical Society of America.

Kutulas, Judy 1995, *The Long War: The Intellectual People's Front and Anti-Stalinism, 1930–40*, Durham, NC: Duke University Press.

Lacan, Jacques 1968, *Speech and Language in Psychoanalysis*, translated by Anthony Wilden. Baltimore: Johns Hopkins University Press.

Ladies of the Mission 1854, *The Old Brewery and the New Mission House at the Five Points*, New York: Stringer and Townsend.

Landis, Arthur 1967, *The Abraham Lincoln Brigade*, New York: Citadel Press.

Laslett, John H.M. and Seymour Martin Lipset (eds) 1974, *Failure of a Dream? Essays in the History of American Socialism*, Garden City, NY: Anchor Press.

Lasswell, Harold D. and Dorothy Blumenstock 1939, *World Revolutionary Propaganda: A Chicago Study*, New York: Knopf.

Laurie, Bruce 1980, *Working People of Philadelphia, 1800–50*, Philadelphia: Temple University Press.

Lavigne, Marie and Yolande Pinard (eds) 1983, *Travailleuses et feminists: les femmes dans la société québecois*, Montréal: Boréal Express.

Laxer, Robert M. 1973, *Canada, Ltd: The Political Economy of Dependency*, Toronto: McClelland and Stewart.

Leab, Daniel J. 2000, *I Was a Communist for the FBI: The Unhappy Life and Times of Matt Cvetic*, University Park: Pennsylvania State University Press.

LeBlanc, André E. and James D. Thwaites 1973, *Le Monde Ourvier au Québec: bibliographie retrospective*, Montréal: Les Presses de l'Université du Québec.

Le Blanc, Paul 1996, 'Trotskyism in the United States: The First Fifty Years' in *Trotskyism in the United States: Historical Essays and Reconsiderations*, edited by George Breitman, Paul Le Blanc and Alan Wald, Atlantic Highlands: Humanities Press.

Le Blanc, Paul n.d., 'The Rise of American Communism', unpublished manuscript.

Leier, Mark 1995, *Red Flags and Red Tape: The Making of a Labour Bureaucracy*, Toronto: University of Toronto Press.

———— 1996a, 'Response to Professors Palmer, Strong-Boag, and McDonald', *BC Studies*, 111: 93–8.

———— 1996b, 'W[h]ither Class: Regionalism, Class, and the Writing of BC History', *BC Studies*, 111: 61–75.

———— 1999, *Rebel Life: The Life and Times of Robert Gosden – Revolutionary, Mystic, Labour Spy*, Vancouver: New Star Books.

Lenin, V.I. 1960, *Lenin: Selected Works*, Volume I, Moscow: Foreign Languages Publishing House.

Levenstein, Harvey 1981, *Communism, Anticommunism and the CIO*, Westport: Greenwood Press.

Lévesque, Andrée 1984, *Virage à gauche interdit: les communists, les socialistes, and leur enemies au Québec, 1929–39*, Montréal: Boréal Express.

———— 1989, *La norme et les déviantes: les femmes au Québec pendant l'entre-deux-guerres*, Montréal: Éditions Remue-menage.

———— 1999, *Scènes de la Vie en Rouge: L'époque de Jeanne Corbin, 1906–44*, Montréal: Boréal Express.

Levin, Gail 1980a, *Edward Hopper: The Art and the Artist*, New York: Norton: Whitney Museum of American Art.

———— 1980b, 'Edward Hopper: The Influence of Theatre and Film', *Arts Magazine*, 55, October: 123–7.

———— 1995, *Edward Hopper: An Intimate Biography*, New York: Knopf.

Levine, Bruce 1986, 'In the Heat of Two Revolutions: The Forging of German-American Radicalism' in *'Struggle a Hard Battle': Essays on Working-Class Immigrants*, edited by Dirk Hoerder, DeKalb: University of Northern Illinois Press.

Levitt, Kari 1970, *Silent Surrender: The Multinational Corporation in Canada*, Toronto: Macmillan.

Lichtenstein, Nelson 2001, *State of the Union: A Century of American Labor*, Princeton, NJ: Princeton University Press.

Lichtheim, George 1965, *Marxism: An Historical and Critical Study*, New York: Praeger.

Lippe, Richard 1996, 'At the Margins of Film Noir: Preminger's Angel Face' in *Film Noir Reader*, edited by Alain Silver and James Ursini, New York: Limelight Editions.

Lipset, Seymour Martin 1971 [1950], *Agrarian Socialism: The Cooperative Commonwealth Federation in Saskatchewan: A Study in Political Sociology*, Berkeley: University of California Press.

Lipsitz, George 1994, *Rainbow at Midnight: Labor and Culture in the 1940s*, Urbana: University of Illinois Press.

Lorwin, Lewis L. 1929, *Labor and Internationalism*, New York: Macmillan.

Lott, Eric 1996, 'The Whiteness of Film Noir' in *Whiteness: A Critical Reader*, edited by Mike Hill, New York: New York University Press.

Lovestone, Jay 1939–40, 'Testimony of Jay Lovestone, Secretary, Independent Labor League of America' in *Investigation of Un-American Propaganda Activities in the United States: Hearings Before a Special Committee on Un-American Activities (Dies Committee), House of Representatives, 75th–76th Congresses*, Washington, DC: Government Printing Office.

Lower, A.R.M. 1929, 'Some Neglected Aspects of Canadian History', Canadian Historical Association, *Report*: 66.

Löwy, Michael 1981, *The Politics of Combined and Uneven Development: The Theory of Permanent Revolution*, London: Verso.

Lukács, Georg 1968, *History and Class Consciousness: Studies in Marxist Dialectics*, Cambridge, MA: MIT Press.

―――― 2000, *A Defense of History and Class Consciousness: Tailism and the Dialectic*, London: Verso.

Lumsden, Ian (ed) 1970, *Close the 49th Parallel, Etc.: The Americanization of Canada*, Toronto: University of Toronto Press.

Luxton, Meg 1980, *More Than a Labour of Love: Three Generations of Women's Work in the Home*, Toronto: Women's Educational Press.

―――― 2001, 'Feminism as a Class Act: Working-Class Feminism and the Women's Movement in Canada', *Labour/Le Travail*, 48: 63–88.

Luxton, Meg and June Corman 2001, *Getting By in Hard Times: Gendered Labour at Home and on the Job*, Toronto: University of Toronto Press.

Lyon, Peyton V. 1991, 'The Loyalties of E. Herbert Norman', *Labour/Le Travail*, 28, Fall: 219–59.

Lyons, Deborah and Adam D. Weinberg 1995, *Edward Hopper and the American Imagination*, New York: W.W. Norton.

Lyons, Paul 1982, *Philadelphia Communists, 1936–56*, Philadelphia: Temple University Press.

MacDowell, Laurel Sefon 2001, *Renegade Lawyer: The Life of J.L. Cohen*, Toronto: University of Toronto Press.

Macintyre, Stuart 1980, *A Proletarian Science: Marxism in Britain, 1917–33*, London: Lawrence and Wishart.

Macpherson, C.B. 1953, *Democracy in Alberta: Social Credit and the Party System*, Toronto: University of Toronto Press.

―――― 1962, *The Political Theory of Possessive Individualism: Hobbes to Locke*, Oxford: Clarendon Press.

Madden, David (ed) 1968, *Tough Guy Writers of the Thirties*, Carbondale: Southern Illinois University Press.

Malin, Irving 1968, 'Focus on "The Maltese Falcon": The Metaphysical Falcon' in *Tough*

Guy Writers of the Thirties, edited by David Madden, Carbondale: Southern Illinois University Press.

Mandel, Ernest 1963, 'The Dialectic of Class and Region in Belgium', *New Left Review*, 20, Summer: 5–31.

—— (ed) 1968, *50 Years of World Revolution, 1917–67*, New York: Merit.

—— 1984, *Delightful Murder: A Social History of the Crime Story*, London: Pluto Press.

Mandelbaum, Seymour J. 1990, *Boss Tweed's New York*, Chicago: Ivan R. Dee.

Manley, John 1992, 'Preaching the Red Stuff: J.B. McLachlan, Communism, and the Cape Breton Coal Miners, 1922–1935', *Labour/Le Travail*, 30: 65–114.

—— 2005, 'Moscow Rules? "Red" Unionism and "Class against Class" in Britain, Canada, and the United States', *Labour/Le Travail*, 56: 9–50.

Marcuse, Herbert 1960, *Reason and Revolution: Hegel and the Rise of Social Theory*, Boston: Beacon Press.

—— 1961, *Soviet Marxism: A Critical Analysis*, New York: Vintage.

Marks, Lynne 1996, *Revivals and Roller Rinks: Religion, Leisure, and Identity in Late-Nineteenth-Century Small-Town Ontario*, Toronto: University of Toronto Press.

—— 2001, 'Heroes and Hallelujahs – Labour History and the Social History of Religion in English Canada: A Response to Bryan Palmer', *Histoire Sociale/Social History*, 34: 169–86.

Maroney, Heather Jon 1983, 'Feminism at Work', *New Left Review*, 141: 51–71.

Maroney, Heather Jon and Meg Luxton (eds) 1987, *Feminism and Political Economy: Women's Work, Women's Struggles*, Toronto: Methuen.

Marx, Karl n.d. [1847] *The Poverty of Philosophy; Answer to the 'Philosophy of Poverty' by M. Proudhon*, New York: International.

—— 1941, *The Class Struggles in France (1848–1850)*, New York: International.

—— 1947, *The German Ideology*, New York: International.

—— 1959, *Capital*, 3 Volumes, Moscow: Foreign Language Publishing House.

—— 1962, 'Critique of the Gotha Program' in *Karl Marx and Frederick Engels: Selected Works in Two Volumes*, Moscow: Foreign Languages Publishing House.

—— 1968, 'The Eighteenth Brumaire of Louis Bonaparte' in *Marx and Engels: Selected Works*, Moscow: Progress.

—— 1969, *Pre-Capitalist Economic Formations*, edited and introduced by Eric J. Hobsbawm, London: Lawrence and Wishart.

—— 1980, *Economic and Philosophic Manuscripts of 1844*, New York: International.

Marx, Karl and Frederick Engels 1935, *Correspondence, 1846–95: A Selection with Commentary and Notes*, New York: International.

—— 1947, *The German Ideology*, New York: International.

—— 1956, *The Holy Family or Critique of Critical Critique*, Moscow: Foreign Language Publishing House.

———— 1968, 'Manifesto of the Communist Party' in *Marx and Engels: Selected Works*, Moscow: Progress.

Matthews, Wade 2013, *International of the Imagination: The New Left, National Identity, and the Break-Up of Britain*, Leiden: Brill.

Maynard, Steven 1994, 'Through a Hole in the Lavatory Wall: Homosexual Subcultures, Police Surveillance, and the Dialectics of Discovery, 1890–1930', *Journal of the History of Sexuality*, 5: 207–42.

———— 1997, '"Horrible Temptations": Sex, Men, and Working-Class Male Youth in Urban Ontario, 1890–1935', *Canadian Historical Review*, 78: 191–235.

McCalla, Douglas 2008, review of *Craft Capitalism: Craftworkers and Early Industrialization in Hamilton, Ontario, 1840–1872* by Robert B. Kristofferson, *American Historical Review*, 113: 1513–14.

McCallum, Todd 2005, 'The Reverend and the Tramp, Vancouver, 1931: Andrew Roddan's *God in the Jungles*', *BC Studies*, 147: 51–88.

———— 2006, 'The Great Depression's First History? The Vancouver Archives of Major J.S. Matthews and the Writing of Hobo History', *Canadian Historical Review*, 87, March: 79–107.

———— 2007, 'Vancouver Through the Eyes of a Hobo: Experience, Identity, and Value in the Writing of Canada's Depression-Era Tramps', *Labour/Le Travail*, 59: 43–68.

McCarney, Joseph 1992, 'Shaping Ends: Reflections on Fukuyama', *New Left Review*, 202, November–December: 37–54.

McCormack, A.R. 1977, *Reformers, Rebels, and Revolutionaries: The Western Canadian Radical Movement, 1899–1919*, Toronto: University of Toronto Press.

McDonald, Robert A.J. 1996, '"The West is a Messy Place"', *BC Studies*, 111: 88–92.

McDougall, Brian 1981, 'Stanley Ryerson and the Materialist Conception of History: A Study in the Stalinist Distortion of Marxism', MA thesis, Carleton University.

McGilligan, Patrick and Paul Buhle (eds) 1997, *Tender Comrades: A Backstory of the Hollywood Blacklist*, New York: St. Martin's Press.

McHenry, Dean E. 1950, *The Third Force in Canada: The Cooperative Commonwealth Federation, 1932–48*, Toronto: Oxford University Press.

McIlroy, John and Alan Campbell 2002a, '"For a Revolutionary Workers' Government": Moscow, British Communism and Revisionist Interpretations of the Third Period, 1927–1934', *European Historical Quarterly*, 32: 535–69.

———— 2002b, '"Nina Ponomareva's Hats": The New Revisionism, the Communist International, and the Communist Party of Great Britain', *Labour/Le Travail*, 49, Spring: 147–87.

McIlroy, John, Kevin Morgan and Alan Campbell (eds) 2001, *Party People, Communist Lives: Exploration in Biography*, London: Lawrence and Wishart.

McInnis, Peter 2002, *Harnessing Labour Confrontation: Shaping the Postwar Settlement in Canada*, Toronto: University of Toronto Press.

McKay, Ian 1978, 'Capital and Labour in the Halifax Baking and Confectionary Industry in the Last Half of the Nineteenth Century', *Labour/Le Travailleur*, 3: 63–108.

———— 1981–2, 'Historians, Anthropology, and the Concept of Culture', *Labour/Le Travailleur*, 8/9: 185–241.

———— 1987, 'The Three Faces of Canadian Labour History', *History Workshop*, 24: 172–9.

———— 1994, *The Quest of the Folk: Antimodernism and Cultural Selection in Twentieth-Century Nova Scotia*, Kingston: McGill-Queen's University Press.

———— 2000, 'The Liberal Order Framework: A Prospectus for a Reconnaissance of Canadian History', *Canadian Historical Review*, 81, December: 617–45.

———— 2005, *Rebels, Reds, Radicals: Rethinking Canada's Left History*, Toronto: Between the Lines.

———— 2008, *Reasoning Otherwise: Leftists and the People's Enlightenment in Canada, 1890–1920*, Toronto: Between the Lines.

McKillop, A.B. 1999, 'Who Killed Canadian History? A View from the Trenches', *Canadian Historical Review*, 80: 269–99.

McLennan, Gregor 1981, *Marxism and the Methodologies of History*, London: Verso.

McNally, David 1981, 'Staples Theory as Commodity Fetishism: Marx, Innis, and Canadian Political Economy', *Studies in Political Economy*, 6, Autumn: 35–63.

McNaught, Kenneth 1959, *A Prophet in Politics: A Biography of J.S. Woodsworth*, Toronto: University of Toronto Press.

———— 1981, 'E.P. Thompson vs. Harold Logan: Writing about Labour and the Left in the 1970s', *Canadian Historical Review*, 62: 141–68.

———— 1999, *Conscience and History: A Memoir*, Toronto: University of Toronto Press.

McPherson, Kathryn 1996, *Bedside Matters: The Transformation of Canadian Nursing, 1900–90*, Toronto: Oxford University Press.

McPherson, Kathryn, Cecilia Morgan and Nancy M. Forestell (eds) 1999, *Gendered Pasts: Historical Essays in Femininity and Masculinity in Canada*, Toronto: Oxford University Press.

McShane, Frank 1976, *The Life of Raymond Chandler*, London: Jonathan Cape.

Mealing, S.R. 1965, 'The Concept of Social Class and the Interpretation of Canadian History', *Canadian Historical Review*, 46, September: 201–18.

Megill, Allan 1985, *Prophets of Extremity: Nietzsche, Heidegger, Foucault, Derrida*, Berkeley: University of California Press.

Mico, Ted, et al. (eds) 1995, 'A Conversation between Eric Foner and John Sayles', *Past Imperfect: History According to the Movies*, Oxford: Oxford University Press.

Miliband, Ralph 1985, 'The New Revisionism in Britain', *New Left Review*, 150, March–April: 5–28.

Miliband, Ralph and Leo Panitch (eds) 1990, *Socialist Register, 1990: The Retreat of the Intellectuals*, London: Merlin Press.

Minc, P. (Aleksander) 2002, *The History of a False Illusion: Memoirs on the Communist Movement in Poland 1918–1938*, translated and edited by Robert Michaels, Lewiston, NY: Edwin Mellen Press.

Mitchell, Juliet 1974, *Psychoanalysis and Feminism: Freud, Reich, Laing, and Women*, New York: Pantheon.

—— 1986, 'Reflections on Twenty Years of Feminism' in *What is Feminism?*, edited by Juliet Mitchell and Ann Oakley, Oxford: Basil Blackwell.

Montgomery, David 1967, *Beyond Equality: Labor and the Radical Republicans, 1862–72*, New York: Knopf.

Moogk, Peter 1971, 'Apprenticeship Indentures: A Key to Artisan Life in New France', Canadian Historical Association, *Annual Report*: 65–83.

Moretti, Franco 1988, *Signs Taken for Wonders: Essays in the Sociology of Literary Forms*, London: Verso.

Morgan, Kevin 2001, 'Parts of People and Communist Lives' in *Party People, Communist Lives: Exploration in Biography*, edited by John McIlroy, Kevin Morgan and Alan Campbell, London: Lawrence and Wishart.

Morgan, Ted 1999, *A Covert Life: Jay Lovestone: Communist, Anti-Communist, and Spymaster*, New York: Random House.

Morrow, Felix 1974, *Revolution & Counter-Revolution in Spain*, New York: Pathfinder.

Morton, Desmond 1983, 'E.P. Thompson dans les arpents de neige: les historiens Canadiens-Anglais et la classe ouvrière', *Revue d'Histoire de l'Amérique français*, 37: 165–84.

—— 1990, *Working People: An Illustrated History of the Canadian Labour Movement*, Toronto: Summerhill Press.

—— 2000, 'Some Millennial Reflections on the State of Canadian Labour History', *Labour/Le Travail*, 46: 11–36.

Morton, Suzanne 1995, *Ideal Surroundings: Domestic Life in a Working-Class Suburb in the 1920s*, Toronto: University of Toronto Press.

Mumford, Ken J. 1997, *Interzones: Black/White Sex Districts in Chicago and New York in the Early Twentieth Century*, New York: Columbia University Press.

Muszynski, Alicia 1996, *Cheap Wage Labour: Race and Gender in the Fisheries of British Columbia*, Montreal: McGill-Queen's University Press.

Nairn, Tom 1977, *The Break-Up of Britain: Crisis and Neo-Nationalism*, London: New Left Books.

Naison, Mark 1983, *Communists in Harlem during the Depression*, Urbana: University of Illinois Press.

Navasky, Victor S. 1980, *Naming Names*, New York: Viking Press.

Naylor, James 1991, *The New Democracy: Challenging the Social Order in Industrial Ontario, 1914–25*, Toronto: University of Toronto Press.

Neis, Barbara 1993, 'From "Shipped Girls" to "Brides of the State": The Transition from

Familial to Social Patriarchy in the Newfoundland Fishing Industry', *Canadian Journal of Regional Science*, 16: 185–202.

Nelles, H.V. 1980, 'Creighton's Seminar', *Canadian Forum*, September: 6.

Nelson, Steve, James R. Barrett and Rob Ruck 1981, *Steve Nelson: American Radical*, Pittsburgh: University of Pittsburgh Press.

Newman, Michael 2002, *Ralph Miliband and the Politics of the New Left*, Halifax: Merlin Press.

Newsinger, John 1995, '*Matewan*: Film and Working-Class Struggle', *International Socialism Journal*, 66: 89–107.

Newton, Janice 1995, *The Feminist Challenge to the Canadian Left, 1900–1918*, Montreal: McGill-Queen's University Press.

Nolan, William F. 1983, *Hammett: A Life at the Edge*, New York: Congdon & Weed.

Norris, Christopher 1993, *The Truth About Postmodernism*, Oxford: Blackwell.

Nove, Alec 1975, *Stalinism and After*, London: George Allen and Unwin.

O'Toole, Roger 1977, *The Precipitous Path: Studies in Political Sects*, Toronto: P. Martin Associates.

Oates, Joyce Carol 1968, 'Man under Sentence of Death: The Novels of James M. Cain' in *Tough Guy Writers of the Thirties*, edited by David Madden, Carbondale: Southern Illinois University Press.

Oneal, James and G.A. Werner 1947, *American Communism: A Critical Analysis of its Origins, Development and Programs*, New York: E.P. Dutton.

Oshinsky, David M. 1983, *A Conspiracy So Immense: The World of Joe McCarthy*, New York: Free Press.

Ottanelli, Fraser M. 1991, *The Communist Party of the United States: From the Depression to World War II*, New Brunswick, NJ: Rutgers University Press.

Ouellet, Fernand 1985, 'La modernization de l'historiographie et l'emergence de l'histoire sociale', *Recherches Sociographiques*, 26: 11–83.

Owram, Doug 1996, *Born at the Right Time: A History of the Baby Boom Generation*, Toronto: University of Toronto Press.

Painter, Nell Irvin 1979, *The Narrative of Hosea Hudson, His Life as a Negro Communist in the South*, Cambridge, MA: Harvard University Press.

Palmer, Bryan D. 1975, 'Class, Conception, and Conflict: The Thrust for Efficiency, Managerial Views of Labor, and Working-Class Rebellion, 1903–22', *Review of Radical Political Economics*, 7, Summer: 31–49.

——— 1976, 'Modernizing History', *Bulletin of the Committee on Labour History*: 16–25.

——— 1978, 'Discordant Music: Charivaris and Whitecapping in Nineteenth-Century North America', *Labour/Le Travailleur*, 3: 5–62.

——— 1979, *A Culture in Conflict: Skilled Workers and Industrial Capitalism in Hamilton, Ontario, 1860–1914*, Kingston: McGill-Queen's University Press.

——— 1979–80, 'Working-Class Canada: Recent Historical Writing', *Queen's Quarterly*, 86: 594–616.

——— 1981a, *The Making of E.P. Thompson: Marxism, Humanism, and History*, Toronto: New Hogtown Press.

——— 1981b, 'They Ride Horses Don't They? Historical Musings on the Canadian State and Its Agents', *Our Generation*, 14: 28–41.

——— 1983, *Working-Class Experience: The Rise and Reconstitution of Canadian Labour, 1800–1980*, Toronto: Butterworth's.

——— 1984a, 'Emperor Katz's New Clothes; or with the Wizard in Oz', *Labour/Le Travail*, 13, Spring: 190–7.

——— 1984b, 'Social Formation and Class Formation in Nineteenth-Century North American' in *Proletarianization and Family History*, edited by David Levine, New York: Academic Press.

——— 1987, 'Response to Joan Scott', *International Labor and Working-Class History*, 31, April: 14–23.

——— (ed) 1988a, *A Communist Life: Jack Scott and the Canadian Workers Movement, 1927–85*, St. John's: Committee on Canadian Labour History.

——— 1988b, *Solidarity: The Rise and Fall of an Opposition in British Columbia*, Vancouver: New Star.

——— 1990a, *Descent into Discourse: The Reification of Language and the Writing of Social History*, Philadelphia: Temple University Press.

——— 1990b, 'The Eclipse of Materialism: Marxism and the Writing of Social History in the 1980s' in *Socialist Register, 1990: The Retreat of the Intellectuals*, edited by Ralph Miliband and Leo Panitch, London: Merlin, 111–46.

——— 1992, *Working-Class Experience: Rethinking the History of Canadian Labour, 1800–1991*, Toronto: McClelland and Stewart.

——— 1993a, 'The Condition of Postmodernity and the Poststructuralist Challenge to Political and Historical Meaning', *Maryland Historian*, 24, 1: 54–70.

——— 1993b, 'Poststructuralism/Postmodernism, Internationalism, and Socialism', *Socialist Alternatives*, 2, Winter: 48–62.

——— 1993c, 'The Poverty of Theory Revisited: Or, Critical Theory, Historical Materialism, and the Ostensible End of Marxism', *Left History*, 1, Spring: 6–101.

——— 1994a, 'La Teoria Critica, el Materialismo Historico y el Supuesto Fin del Marxismo: Retorno a *La Miseria de la Teoria*', *Historia Social*, 18, invierno: 125–51.

——— 1994b, *E.P. Thompson: Objections & Oppositions*, London: Verso.

——— 1996, 'Class and the Writing of History: Beyond BC', *BC Studies*, 111: 76–84.

——— 1997, 'Old Positions, New Necessities: History, Class, and Marxist Metanarrative', in *In Defense of History: Marxism and the Postmodern Agenda*, edited by Ellen Meiksins Wood and John Bellamy Foster, New York: Monthly Review, 65–73.

——— 1999, 'Of Silences and Trenches: A Dissident View of Granatstein's Meaning', *Canadian Historical Review*, 80: 676–86.

——— 2000a, *Cultures of Darkness: Night Travels in the Histories of Transgression*, New York: Monthly Review Press.

——— 2000b, 'Historiographic Hassles: Class and Gender, Evidence and Interpretation', *Histoire Sociale/Society History*, 33, May: 105–44.

——— 2001, 'Marxism and Radical History' in *Encyclopedia of European Social History from 1350 to 2000*, Volume I, edited by Peter Stearns, New York: Charles Scribner.

——— 2002, 'Reasoning Rebellion: E.P. Thompson, British Marxist Historians, and the Making of Dissident Political Mobilization', *Labour/Le Travail*, 50, Fall: 187–216.

——— 2003, '40 Years of Class Struggle', *Canadian Dimension*, 37, November–December: 37–9.

——— 2004, 'Preface to the Korean Edition': *Descent into Discourse: In Defense of Historical Materialism*, Hanshin: Hanshin University Press.

——— 2005, 'Hobsbawm's Politics: The Forward March of the Popular Front Halted', lecture delivered at the Congreso Eric Hobsbawm, Instituto Nacional de Antropologia e Historia Mexico, Mexico City, October.

——— 2006, 'Fin-de-Siècle Labour History in Canada and the United States: A Case for Tradition' in *Global Labour History: A State of the Art*, edited by Jan Lucassen, Bern: Peter Lang.

——— 2007, *James P. Cannon and the Origins of the American Revolutionary Left, 1920–1928*, Urbana: University of Illinois Press.

Palmer, Bryan D. and Joan Sangster (eds) 2008, *Labouring Canada: Class, Gender, and Race in Canadian Working-Class History*, Toronto: Oxford University Press.

Palmer, Jerry 1978, *Thrillers: Genesis and Structure of a Popular Genre*, London: E. Arnold.

——— 1991, *Potboilers: Methods, Concepts, and Case Studies in Popular Fiction*, London: Routledge.

Palmer, R. Barton 1994, *Hollywood's Dark Cinema: The American Film Noir*, New York: Twayne Publishers.

Palmer, William G. 1979, 'The Burden of Proof: J.H. Hexter and Christopher Hill', *Journal of British Studies*, 19, Autumn: 122–29.

Panitch, Leo (ed) 1977, *The Canadian State: Political Economy and Political Power*, Toronto: University of Toronto Press.

——— 1981, 'Dependency and Class in Canadian Political Economy', *Studies in Political Economy*, 6, Autumn: 7–33.

Panitch, Leo and Colin Leys (eds) 2005, *Socialist Register, 2006: Telling the Truth*, London: Merlin Press.

Panitch, Leo and Donald Swartz 1984, 'Towards Permanent Exceptionalism: Coercion and Consent in Canadian Industrial Relations', *Labour/Le Travail*, 13: 133–57.

——— 1988, *The Assault on Trade Union Freedoms: From Consent to Coercion Revisited*, Toronto: Garamond Press.

——— 2003, *From Consent to Coercion: The Assault on Trade Union Freedoms*, Aurora: Garamond Press.

Parker, D. 1997, 'The Communist Party and Its Historians', *Socialist History*, 12: 33–58.

Parnaby, Andrew 2008, *Citizen Docker: Making a New Deal on the Vancouver Waterfront, 1919–39*, Toronto: University of Toronto Press.

Parr, Joy 1990, *The Gender of Breadwinners: Women, Men, and Change in Two Industrial Towns, 1880–1950*, Toronto: University of Toronto Press.

——— 1995, 'Gender History and Historical Practice', *Canadian Historical Review*, 76: 354–76.

Parr, Joy and Mark Rosenfeld (eds) 1996, *Gender and History in Canada*, Toronto: Copp Clark.

Pelling, Henry 1958, *The British Communist Party: A Historical Profile*, London: A. & C. Black.

Penfold, Steven 1994, '"Have You No Manhood in You?": Gender and Class in the Cape Breton Coal Towns, 1920–26', *Acadiensis*, 23: 21–44.

——— 1995–6, letter to *Left History* editors, *Left History*, 3–4: 238.

Penner, Norman (ed) 1973, *The Strikers' Own History of the Winnipeg General Strike*, Toronto: James Lewis and Samuel.

Pentland, H. Clare 1974, 'Marx and the Canadian Question', *Canadian Forum*, 54, January: 26–8.

——— 1981, *Labour and Capital in Canada, 1650–1860*, edited and introduced by Paul Phillips, Toronto: Lorimer.

Pepper, John 1923, 'Facing the Third American Revolution', *Liberator*, September: 9–12.

Pernicone, Carol Groneman 1973, '"The Bloody Old Sixth": A Social Analysis of a New York City Working-Class Community in the Mid-Nineteenth Century', PhD dissertation, University of Rochester.

Perry, George 1998, *Steven Spielberg*, London: Orion.

Pfeil, Fred 1990, *Another Tale to Tell: Politics and Narrative in Postmodern Culture*, London: Verso.

——— 1993, 'Home Fires Burning: Family Noir in Blue Velvet and Terminator 2' in *Shades of Noir: A Reader*, edited by Joan Copjec, London: Verso.

——— 1995, *White Guys: Studies in Postmodern Domination and Difference*, London: Verso.

Phelps, Christopher 1997, *Young Sidney Hook: Marxist and Pragmatist*, Ithaca: Cornell University Press.

Pickering, Paul 1986, 'Class without Words: Symbolic Communication in the Chartist Movement', *Past & Present*, 112, August: 144–62.

Pimlott, Herbert 2005, 'From "Old Left" to "New Labour": Eric Hobsbawm and the Rhetoric of "Realistic Marxism"', *Labour/Le Travail*, 56, Fall: 175–98.

Piva, Michael 1979, *The Condition of the Working Class in Toronto*, Ottawa: University of Ottawa Press.

———— 1983, '"The Bonds of Unity": A Comment', *Histoire Sociale/Social History*, 31: 169–74.

Place, Janey 1978, 'Women in Film Noir' in *Women in Film Noir*, edited by E. Ann Kaplan, London: BFI Publishing.

Place, Janey and Lowell Peterson 1996, 'Some Visual Motifs of Film Noir' in *Film Noir Reader*, edited by Alain Silver and James Ursini, New York: Limelight Editions.

Polan, Dana 1986, *Power and Paranoia: History, Narrative and the American Cinema, 1940–1950*, New York: Columbia University Press.

Polito, Robert 1995, *Savage Art: A Biography of Jim Thompson*, New York: Knopf.

Porfirio, Robert 1979, 'The Dark Age of American Film: A Study of the American Film Noir', PhD dissertation, Princeton.

———— 1996, 'No Way Out: Existential Motifs in the Film Noir' in *Film Noir Reader*, edited by Alain Silver and James Ursini, New York: Limelight Editions.

Porter, Anne 2003, *Gendered States: Women, Unemployment Insurance and the Political Economy of the Welfare State in Canada, 1945–97*, Toronto: University of Toronto Press.

Porter, Cathy 1980, *Alexandra Kollontai*, London: Virago.

Porter, Marilyn 1985, '"She Was Skipper of the Shore Crew": Notes on the Sexual Division of Labour in Newfoundland', *Labour/Le Travail*, 15: 105–23.

Poster, Mark 1989, *Critical Theory and Poststructuralism: In Search of a Context*, Ithaca, NY: Cornell University Press.

Postgate, R.W. 1920, *The Workers' International*, New York: Harcourt, Brace & Howe.

Preis, Art. 1964, *Labor's Giant Step: Twenty Years of the CIO*, New York: Pioneer Publishers.

Preliminary Commission of Inquiry into the Charges Made against Trotsky in the Moscow Trials 1937, *The Case of Leon Trotsky: Report of Hearings on the Charges Made Against Him in the Moscow Trials*, New York: Harper and Brothers.

———— 1938, *Not Guilty*, New York: Harper and Brothers.

Prometheus Research Library (ed) 2002, *Dog Days: James P. Cannon vs. Max Shachtman in the Communist League of America, 1931–33*, New York: Prometheus Research Library.

Rabinbach, Anson 1987, 'Rationalism and Utopia as Languages of Nature: A Note', *International Labor and Working-Class History*, 31, April: 30–6.

Radforth, Ian 1987, *Bush Workers and Bosses: Logging in Northern Ontario, 1900–80*, Toronto: University of Toronto Press.

Radforth, Ian and Laurel Sefton (eds) 1992, *Canadian Working-Class History: Selected Readings*, Toronto: Canadian Scholars' Press.

Radosh, Ronald and Joyce Milton 1984, *The Rosenberg File: A Search for the Truth*, New York: Vintage.

Ramirez, Bruno 1999, 'Clio in Words and in Motion: Practices of Narrating the Past', *Journal of American History*, 86: 987–1014.

Rebick, Judy 2005, *Ten Thousand Roses: The Making of a Feminist Revolution*, Toronto: Penguin.

Record, Wilson 1951, *The Negro and the Communist Party*, Chapel Hill: University of North Carolina Press.

Reddy, William M. 1987, *Money and Liberty in Modern Europe: A Critique of Historical Understanding*, Cambridge: Cambridge University Press.

Reid, David and Jayne L. Walker 1993, 'Strange Pursuit: Cornell Woolrich and the Abandoned City of the Forties' in *Shades of Noir: A Reader*, edited by Joan Copjec, London: Verso.

Reshef, Yonatan and Sandra Rastin 2003, *Unions in the Time of Revolution: Government Restructuring in Alberta and Ontario*, Toronto: University of Toronto Press.

Rice, Richard 1983, 'Sailortown: Theory and Method in Ordinary People's History', *Acadiensis*, 13: 154–68.

Richardson, Carl 1992, *Autopsy: An Element of Realism in Film Noir*, Metuchen, NJ: Scarecrow Press.

Richmond, Al 1973, *A Long View from the Left: Memoirs of an American Revolutionary*, Boston: Houghton Mifflin.

Riley, Denise 1988, *'Am I That Name'?: Feminism and the Category of 'Women' in History*, London: Macmillan.

Robbins, Bruce 1991, 'Tenured Radicals, the New McCarthyism, and "PC"', *New Left Review*, 188, July–August: 151–57.

Roberts, Wayne 1976a, 'Artisans, Aristocrats, and Handymen: Politics and Unionism Among Toronto Skilled Building Trades Workers, 1896–1914', *Labour/Le Travailleur*, 1: 92–121.

——— 1976b, *Honest Womanhood: Feminism, Femininity and Class Consciousness among Toronto Working Women, 1893–1914*, Toronto: New Hogtown Press.

——— 1980, 'Toronto Metal Workers and the Second Industrial Revolution, 1896–1914', *Labour/Le Travailleur*, 6: 49–72.

Roberts, Wayne and Alice Klein 1974, 'Besieged Innocence: The "Problem" and Problems of Working Women, Toronto, 1896–1914' in *Women at Work: Ontario, 1880–1930*, edited by Janice Acton et al., Toronto: Canadian Women's Educational Press.

Robinson, Cedric J. 1983, *Black Marxism: The Making of the Black Radical Tradition*, London: Zed.

Rogers, Nicholas 1987, 'Chartism and Class Struggle', *Labour/Le Travail*, 19, Spring: 143–52.

Romney, Paul 1999, *Getting It Wrong: How Canadians Forgot Their Past and Imperiled Confederation*, Toronto: University of Toronto Press.

Rosengarten, Theodore 1974, *All God's Dangers: The Life of Nate Shaw*, New York: Alfred Knopf.

Rosenstone, Robert A. 1995, *Visions of the Past: The Challenge of Film to Our Idea of History*, Cambridge: Harvard University Press.

———— 2012, *History on Film/Film on History*, Harrow, England: Pearson Education Limited.

Rosenzweig, Roy 1976, 'Organizing the Unemployed: The Early Years of the Great Depression', *Radical America*, 10, July–August: 37–62.

———— 1983, 'Oral History and the Old Left', *International Labor and Working-Class History*, 24, Fall: 32–3.

Ross, Becki L. 2000, 'Bumping and Grinding on the Line: Making Nudity Pay', *Labour/Le Travail*, 46: 221–50.

Ross, Steve 1998, *Working-Class Hollywood: Silent Film and the Shaping of Class in America*, Princeton, NJ: Princeton University Press.

———— 2011, *Hollywood Left and Right: How Movie Stars Shaped American Politics*, New York: Oxford University Press.

Rosswurm, Steve (ed) 1992, *The CIO's Left-Led Unions*, New Brunswick, NJ: Rutgers University Press.

Rouillard, Jacques 1974, *Les travailleurs du cotton au Québec*, Montréal: Les Presses de l'Université du Québec.

———— 1979, *Les Syndicats nationaux au Québec de 1900 à 1930*, Montréal: Les Presses de l'Université Laval.

———— 1981, *Histoire de la CSN, 1921–81*, Montréal: Boréal Express.

Rudé, George 1978, *Protest and Punishment: The Study of the Social and Political Protesters Transported to Australia, 1788–1868*, Oxford: Clarendon Press.

Rudin, Ronald 1997, *Making History in Twentieth-Century Quebec*, Toronto: University of Toronto Press.

Rudy, Jarrett 2005, *The Freedom to Smoke: Tobacco Consumption and Identity*, Montreal: McGill-Queen's University Press.

Ruhm, Herbert 1968, 'Raymond Chandler: From Bloomsbury to the Jungle – and Beyond' in *Tough Guy Writers of the Thirties*, edited by David Madden, Carbondale: Southern Illinois University Press.

Ruth, David E. 1996, *Inventing the Public Enemy: The Gangster in American Culture, 1918–34*, Chicago: University of Chicago Press.

Ryan, James G. 1997, *Earl Browder: The Failure of American Communism*, Tuscaloosa: University of Alabama Press.

———— 2002, 'Socialist Triumph as a Family Virtue: Earl Browder and Soviet Espionage', *American Communist History*, 2: 125–42.

Ryerson, Stanley 1937, *1837: The Birth of Canadian Democracy*, Toronto: Francis White.

——— 1943, *French Canada: A Study in Canadian Democracy*, Toronto: Progress.

——— 1946, *A World To Win: An Introduction to the Science of Socialism*, Toronto: Progress Books.

——— 1947, 'Marxism and the Writing of Canadian History', *National Affairs*, 4: 46–51.

——— 1962, 'Conflicting Approaches to the Social Sciences', *Marxist Quarterly*, 1: 46–64.

——— 1963, *The Founding of Canada: Beginnings to 1815*, Toronto: Progress.

——— 1973, *Unequal Union: Roots of Crisis in the Canadas, 1815–73*, Toronto: Progress.

Said, Edward W. 1979, *Orientalism*, New York: Vintage.

Samuel, Raphael (ed) 1981, *People's History and Socialist Theory*, London: Routledge and Kegan Paul.

——— 1985, 'The Lost World of British Communism', *New Left Review*, 154, November–December: 3–53.

——— 1986, 'Staying Power: The Lost World of British Communism' (Part II), *New Left Review*, 156, March–April: 63–133.

——— 1987, 'Class Politics: The Lost World of British Communism' (Part III), *New Left Review*, 165, September–October: 52–91.

——— 1991, 'Reading the Signs', *History Workshop: A Journal of Socialist and Feminist Historians*, 32, Autumn: 105–7.

Samuel, Raphael and Gareth Stedman Jones (eds) 1982a, *Culture, Ideology, and Politics: Essays for Eric Hobsbawm*, London: Routledge.

——— (eds) 1982b, 'Preface' in *Culture, Ideology, and Politics: Essays for Eric Hobsbawm*, edited by Raphael Samuel and Gareth Stedman Jones, London: Routledge.

Sanbonmatsu, John 2004, *The Postmodern Prince: Critical Theory, Left Strategy, and the Making of a New Political Subject*, New York: Monthly Review Press.

Sangster, Joan 1989, *Dreams of Equality: Women on the Canadian Left, 1920–50*, Toronto: McClelland and Stewart.

——— 1995a, 'Beyond Dichotomies: Re-Assessing Gender History and Women's History in Canada', *Left History*, 3: 109–21.

——— 1995b, *Earning Respect: The Lives of Working Women in 'Small-Town' Ontario, 1920–60*, Toronto: University of Toronto Press.

——— 1995–6, 'Reconsidering Dichotomies', *Left History*, 3–4: 239–48.

——— 2000, 'Feminism and the Making of Canadian Working-Class History: Exploring the Past, Present, and Future', *Labour/Le Travail*, 46: 127–65.

——— 2004, '"We No Longer Respect the Law": The Tilco Strike, Labour Injunctions, and the State', *Labour/Le Travail*, 53: 47–88.

Sante, Luc 1991, *Low-Life: Lures and Snares of Old New York*, New York: Farrar, Strauss, Giroux.

Sayles, John 1987, *Thinking in Pictures: The Making of the Movie 'Matewan'*, Boston: Houghton Mifflin.

Scher, Len 1992, *The Un-Canadians: True Stories of the Blacklist Era*, Toronto: Lester.

Schmied, Wieland 1995, *Edward Hopper: Portraits of America*, New York: Prestel.

Schneider, Dorothee 1994, *Trade Unions and Community: The German Working Class in New York City, 1870–1900*, Urbana: University of Illinois Press.

Schrader, Paul 1996, 'Notes on Film Noir' in *Film Noir Reader*, edited by Alain Silver and James Ursini, New York: Limelight Editions.

Schrecker, Ellen 1998, *Many Are the Crimes: McCarthyism in America*, Boston: Little, Brown and Company.

Schwartz, Bill 1990, '"The People" in History: The Communist Party Historians' Group, 1946–1956' in *Making Histories: Studies in History-Writing and Politics*, edited by Richard Johnson et al., London: Hutchinson, in association with the Centre for Contemporary Cultural Studies, University of Birmingham.

Schwartz, Lawrence 1980, *Marxism and Culture: The CPUSA and Aesthetics in the 1930s*, Port Washington: Kennikat Press.

Scorsese, Martin 2002, *Gangs of New York: Making the Movie*, New York: Miramax.

Scott, Jack 1974, *Sweat and Struggle: Working Class Struggles in Canada, Volume I: 1789–1899*, Vancouver: New Star.

Scott, James C. 1985, *Weapons of the Weak: Everyday Forms of Peasant Resistance*, New Haven, CT: Yale University Press.

Scott, Joan Wallach 1974, *The Glassworkers of Carmaux: French Craftsmen and Political Action in a Nineteenth-Century City*, Cambridge, MA: Harvard University Press.

———— 1986, 'Gender: A Useful Category of Historical Analysis,' *American Historical Review*, 91, 1053–75.

———— 1987, 'On Language, Gender, and Working-Class History', *International Labor and Working-Class History*, 31, April: 1–13.

———— 1988, *Gender and the Politics of History*, New York: Columbia University Press.

Seccombe, Wally 1983, 'Marxism and Demography', *New Left Review*, 137, January–February: 22–47.

———— 1992, *A Millennium of Family Change: Feudalism to Capitalism in Northwestern Europe*, London: Verso.

———— 1993, *Weathering the Storm: Working-Class Families from the Industrial Revolution to the Fertility Decline*, London: Verso.

Sedgwick, Peter 1976, 'The Two New Lefts' in *The Left in Britain, 1956–68*, edited by David Widgery, Harmondsworth: Penguin.

Segal, Lynne 1987, *Is the Future Female? Troubled Thoughts on Contemporary Feminism*, London: Virago.

———— 1990, *Slow Motion: Changing Masculinities, Changing Men*, London: Virago.

Seidman, Joel 1969, *Communism in the United States: A Bibliography*, Ithaca, NY: Cornell University Press.

Sen, Amartya 2006, *Identity and Violence: The Illusion of Destiny*, New York: W.W. Norton.

Seve, Lucien 1978, *Man in Marxist Theory and the Psychology of Personality*, Atlantic Highlands: Humanities Press.

Sewell, William H. 2005, *Logics of History: Social Theory and Social Transformation*, Chicago: University of Chicago Press.

Shachtman, Max 1962, *The Bureaucratic Revolution: The Rise of the Stalinist State*, New York: Donald Press.

——— 1967, 'Radicalism in the Thirties: The Trotskyist View' in *As We Saw the Thirties: Essays on Social and Political Movements of a Decade*, edited by Rita James Simon, Urbana: University of Illinois Press.

Shaffer, Robert 1979, 'Women and the Communist Party, USA: 1930–40', *Socialist Review*, 45, May–June: 73–118.

Shapiro, Charles 1968, '"Nightmare Alley": Geeks, Cons, Tips, and Marks' in *Tough Guy Writers of the Thirties*, edited by David Madden, Carbondale: Southern Illinois University Press.

Silver, Alain 1996, 'Introduction' in *Film Noir Reader*, edited by Alain Silver and James Ursini, New York: Limelight Editions.

Silver, Alain and Elizabeth Ward (eds) 1979, *Film Noir: An Encyclopedic Reference to the American Style*, Woodstock: Overlook Press.

Silverman, Victor 1999, *Imagining Internationalism in American and British Labor*, Urbana and Chicago: University of Illinois.

Skelton, O.D. 1911, *Socialism: A Critical Analysis*, Boston: Houghton Mifflin.

Slaughter, Cliff (ed) 1974, *Trotskyism versus Revisionism: A Documentary History: Volume 1: The Fight against Pabloism in the Fourth International*, London: New Park.

Smith, Matthew Hale 1868, *Sunshine and Shadow in New York*, Hartford: J.B. Burr.

Smith, Murray E.G. 1994, *Invisible Leviathan: The Marxist Critique of Market Despotism Beyond Postmodernism*, Toronto: University of Toronto Press.

——— 1996–7, 'Revisiting Trotsky: Reflections on the Stalinist Debacle and Trotskyism as Alternative', *Rethinking Marxism*, 9, 3: 40–67.

——— 2000, 'Political Economy and the Canadian Working Class: Marxism or Nationalist Reformism?', *Labour/Le Travail*, 46, Fall: 343–68.

Solomon, Mark 1998, *The Cry was Unity: Communists and African Americans, 1917–36*, Jackson: University of Mississippi Press.

Sombart, Werner 1976 [1906], *Why Is There No Socialism in the United States?*, White Plains: M.E. Sharpe.

Soper, Kate 1990, *Troubled Pleasures: Writings on Politics, Gender and Hedonism*, London: Verso.

REFERENCES

Stalin, Joseph 1940, *Dialectical and Historical Materialism: A Succinct Presentation of the Philosophic Foundations of Marxism*, New York: International.

Stansell, Christine 1986, *City of Women: Sex and Class in New York, 1789–1860*, New York: Knopf.

——— 1987, 'A Response to Joan Scott', *International Labor and Working-Class History*, 31, April: 24–9.

——— 2000, *American Moderns: Bohemian New York and the Creation of a New Century*, New York: Henry Holt.

Starobin, Joseph R. 1972, *American Communism in Crisis, 1943–57*, Berkeley: University of California Press.

Stedman Jones, Gareth 1971, *Outcast London: A Study in the Relationship between Classes in Victorian Society*, Oxford: Clarendon Press.

——— 1973, 'History: The Poverty of Empiricism' in *Ideology and Social Science: Readings in Critical Social Theory*, edited by Robin Blackburn, New York: Vintage.

——— 1978, 'The Marxism of the Early Lukács' in *Western Marxism: A Critical Reader*, edited by New Left Review, London: Verso.

——— 1983, *Languages of Class: Studies in English Working Class History, 1832–1982*, Cambridge: Cambridge University Press.

——— 1989a, '"The Cockney" and the Nation: 1780–1988' in *Metropolis London: Histories and Representations*, edited by David Feldman and Gareth Stedman Jones, London: Routledge.

——— 1989b, 'The Crisis of Communism' in *New Times: The Changing Face of Politics in the 1990s*, edited by Stuart Hall and Martin Jacques, London: Lawrence and Wishart.

——— 2001, 'History and Theory: An English Story', *Historein: A Review of the Past and Other Stories*, 3: 103–24.

Steedman, Mercedes 1997, *Angels of the Workplace: Women and the Construction of Gender Relations in the Canadian Clothing Industry, 1900–40*, Toronto: Oxford University Press.

Storch, Randi 2007, *Red Chicago: American Communism at its Grassroots, 1928–33*, Urbana and Chicago: University of Illinois Press.

Strange, Carolyn 1995, *Toronto's Girl Problem: The Perils and Pleasures of the City, 1880–1930*, Toronto: University of Toronto Press.

Strong-Boag, Veronica 1988, *The New Day Recalled: The Lives of Girls and Women in English Canada, 1919–39*, Toronto: Copp Clark.

——— 1996, 'Moving Beyond Tired "Truths": Or, Let's Not Fight the Old Battles', *BC Studies*, 111: 84–7.

Struthers, James 1994, *The Limits of Affluence: Welfare in Ontario, 1920–70*, Toronto: University of Toronto Press.

Sturak, Thomas 1968, 'Horace McCoy's Objective Lyricism' in *Tough Guy Writers of the Thirties*, edited by David Madden, Carbondale: Southern Illinois University Press.

Stutje, Jan Willem 2009, *Ernest Mandel: A Rebel's Dream Deferred*, London: Verso.

Sugiman, Pamela 1994, *Labour's Dilemma: The Gender Politics of Automobile Workers in Canada, 1937–79*, Montreal: McGill-Queen's University Press.

Susman, Warren I. and Eugene D. Genovese 1978, 'Editorial Statement', *Marxist Perspectives*, 1, Spring: 9–43.

Teeple, Gary (ed) 1972, *Capitalism and the National Question in Canada*, Toronto: University of Toronto Press.

Telotte, J.P. 1989, *Voices in the Dark: The Narrative Patterns of Film Noir*, Urbana: University of Illinois Press.

Thomas, Deborah 1992, 'Psychoanalysis and Film Noir' in *The Movie Book of Film Noir*, edited by Ian Alexander Cameron, London: Studio Vista.

Thompson, Dorothy 1986, 'The Languages of Class', *Bulletin of the Society for the Study of Social History*, 52, 1: 54–7.

Thompson, E.P. 1957, 'Socialist Humanism: An Epistle to the Philistines', *New Reasoner*, 1, Summer: 105–43.

——— 1958, 'Agency and Choice: A Reply to Criticism', *New Reasoner*, 5, Summer: 89–106.

——— 1959a, 'Commitment and Politics', *Universities and Left Review*, 6, Spring: 50–55.

——— 1959b, 'A Psessay in Ephology', *New Reasoner*, 10, Autumn: 1–8.

——— 1960a, 'Homage to Tom Maguire' in *Essays in Labour History: In Memory of G.D.H. Cole, 25 September 1889–14 January 1959*, edited by Asa Biggs and John Saville, London: Macmillan.

——— 1960b, 'Revolution' in *Out of Apathy*, edited by E.P. Thompson, London: New Left Books.

——— 1961a, 'The Long Revolution', *New Left Review*, 9, May–June: 24–33.

——— 1961b, 'The Long Revolution II', *New Left Review*, 10, July–August: 34–9.

——— 1963a, *The Making of the English Working Class*, New York: Vintage.

——— 1963b, personal correspondence with John Saville, 12 May.

——— 1965, 'The Peculiarities of the English' in *The Socialist Register, 1965*, edited by Ralph Miliband and John Saville, London: Merlin.

——— 1968, *Education and Experience: Fifth Mansbridge Memorial Lecture*, Leeds: Leeds University Press.

——— 1969, 'Disenchantment or Default? A Lay Sermon' in *Power and Consciousness: The Schweitzer Lectures*, edited by Conor Cruise O'Brien and William Dean Vanech, New York: New York University Press.

——— (ed) 1970, *Warwick University Ltd*, Harmondsworth: Penguin.

——— 1972, 'Anthropology and the Discipline of Historical Context', *Midland History*, 1, Spring: 41–55.

——— 1976a, 'Détente and Dissent' in *Détente & Socialist Democracy: A Discussion with Roy Medvedev*, edited by Ken Coates, New York: Monad Press.

———— 1976b, 'The Grid of Inheritance: A Comment' in *Family and Inheritance: Rural Society in Western Europe, 1200–1800,* edited by Jack Goody, Joan Thirsk and E.P. Thompson, London: Cambridge University Press.

———— 1976c, 'On History, Sociology and Historical Relevance', *British Journal of Sociology,* 27, September: 387–402.

———— 1977a, 'Caudwell' in *Socialist Register, 1977,* edited by John Saville and Ralph Miliband, London: Merlin.

———— 1977b, *William Morris: Romantic to Revolutionary,* New York: Pantheon.

———— 1978a, 'Eighteenth-Century English Society: Class Struggle without Class?', *Social History,* 3, May: 133–65.

———— 1978b, 'Folklore, Anthropology, and Social History', *Indian Historical Review,* 3: 247–66.

———— 1978c, *The Poverty of Theory and Other Essays,* London: Merlin.

———— 1979, 'C. Wright Mills: The Responsible Craftsman', *Radical History Review,* 13, July–August: 61–73.

———— 1980a, 'Notes on Exterminism: The Last Stage of Civilization', *New Left Review,* 121, May–June: 3–31.

———— 1980b, *Writing by Candlelight,* London: Merlin.

———— 1981, 'The Politics of Theory' in *People's History and Socialist Theory,* edited by Raphael Samuel, London: Routledge & Kegan Paul.

———— 1982a, *Beyond the Cold War: A New Approach to the Arms Race and Nuclear Annihilation,* New York: Pantheon.

———— 1982b, 'Notes on Exterminism, the Last Stage of Civilization' in *Exterminism and Cold War,* edited by New Left Review, London: Verso.

———— 1985, *Double Exposure,* London: Merlin.

———— 1987, 'Homage to Thomas McGrath', *Triquarterly,* 70, Fall: 158–92.

———— 1988, *The Sykaos Papers,* New York: Pantheon.

———— 1993a, *Alien Homage: Edward Thompson and Rabindranath Tagore,* New Delhi: Oxford University Press.

———— 1993b, *Customs in Common: Studies in Traditional Popular Culture,* New York: New Press.

———— 1993c, *Witness against the Beast: William Blake and the Moral Law,* New York: New Press.

———— 1994a, 'Hunting the Jacobin Fox', *Past & Present,* 142, February: 94–140.

———— 1994b, *Persons & Polemics: Historical Essays,* London: Merlin.

———— 1997, *The Romantics: England in a Revolutionary Age,* edited by Dorothy Thompson, New York: New Press.

———— 1999, *Collected Poems,* edited by Fred Inglis, Newcastle-upon-Tyne: Bloodaxe Books.

Thompson, E.P. and Dan Smith (eds) 1980, *Protest and Survive,* Harmondsworth: Penguin.

Thompson, T.J. and E.P. Thompson 1947, *There Is a Spirit in Europe: A Memoir of Frank Thompson*, London: Victor Gollancz.

Thorpe, Andrew 2000, *The British Communist Party and Moscow, 1920–43*, Manchester: Manchester University Press.

Timpanaro, Sebastiano 1975, *On Materialism*, London: New Left Books.

Tremblay, Louis-Marie 1968, *Évolution de la philosophie du syndicalisme au Québec, 1940–65*, Ottawa: Éditions de l'Université d'Ottawa.

—— 1972, *Le syndicalisme québécois: ideologies de la c.s.n. et de la f.t.q., 1940–70*, Montréal: Les Presses de l'Université de Montréal.

Tremblay, Robert 1979, 'La formation materielle de la classe ouvrière à Montréal entre 1790 et 1830', *Revue d'histoire de l'Amérique français*, 33: 301–35.

Trevor-Roper, H.R. (ed) 1968, *The Crisis of the Seventeenth Century*, New York: Harper and Row.

Trofimenkoff, Susan Mann 1977, 'One Hundred and One Muffled Voices: Canada's Industrial Women of the 1880s', *Atlantis*, 3: 67–82.

Trotsky, Leon 1937, *The Revolution Betrayed: What is the Soviet Union and Where is it Going?*, New York: Doubleday, Doran.

—— 1941, *Stalin: An Appraisal of the Man and His Influence*, New York: Harper & Brothers.

—— 1973, *In Defense of Marxism*, New York: Pathfinder.

Ursini, James 1996, 'Angst at Sixty Fields per Second' in *Film Noir Reader*, edited by Alain Silver and James Ursini, New York: Limelight Editions.

Vachss, Andrew 1985, *Flood*, New York: Vintage Books.

—— 1987, *Strega*, New York: Vintage Books.

—— 1988, *Blue Belle*, New York: Vintage Books.

—— 1989, *Hard Candy*, New York: Vintage Books.

—— 1990, *Blossom*, New York: Vintage Books.

—— 1991, *Sacrifice*, New York: Vintage Books.

—— 1993, *Shella*, New York: Vintage Books.

—— 1994a, *Born Bad*, New York: Vintage Books.

—— 1994b, *Down in the Zero*, New York: Vintage Books.

—— 1995a, *Another Chance to Get It Right: A Children's Book for Adults*, Milwaukie, OR: Dark Horse.

—— 1995b, *Batman: The Ultimate Evil*, Warner Books.

—— 1995c, *Footsteps of the Hawk*, New York: Vintage Books.

—— 1996, *False Allegations*, New York: Vintage Books.

Vallières, Pierre 1971, *White Niggers of America: The Precocious Autobiography of a Quebec 'Terrorist'*, New York: Monthly Review Press.

Valverde, Mariana 2000, 'Some Remarks on the Rise and Fall of Discourse Analysis', *Histoire Sociale/Social History*, 33: 59–77.

Vance, Catherine 1962, 'Early Trade Unionism in Quebec: The Carpenters and Joiners General Strike of 1833–34', *Marxist Quarterly*, 3: 26–42.

Wald, Alan M. 1978, *James T. Farrell: The Revolutionary Socialist Years*, New York: New York University Press.

———— 1983, *The Revolutionary Imagination: The Poetry and Politics of John Wheelwright and Sherry Mangan*, Chapel Hill: University of North Carolina Press.

———— 1987, *The New York Intellectuals: The Rise and Decline of the Anti-Stalinist Left from the 1930s to the 1980s*, Chapel Hill: University of North Carolina Press.

———— 1992, *The Responsibility of Intellectuals: Selected Essays on Marxist Traditions in Cultural Commitment*, Atlantic Highlands, NJ: Humanities Press.

———— 1993, 'Culture and Commitment: U.S. Communist Writers Reconsidered' in *New Studies in the Politics and Culture of U.S. Communism*, edited by Michael E. Brown, et al., New York: Monthly Review Press.

———— 1994, *Writing from the Left: New Essays on Radical Culture and Politics*, London: Verso.

Walkowitz, Daniel 1985, 'Visual History: The Craft of the Historian-Filmmaker', *Public Historian*, 7, Winter: 53–64.

Walsh, David 2003a, 'Misanthropy and Contemporary American Filmmaking', *World Socialist Web Site*, 16 January, http://www.wsws.org/en/articles/2003/01/gang-j16.html.

———— 2003b 'A Conversation with Historian James M. McPherson', World Socialist Web Site, 28 February, http://www.wsws.org/en/articles/2003/02/mcph-f28.html.

Walzer, Kenneth 1983, 'The New History of American Communism', *Reviews in American History*, 11, June: 259–67.

Warshow, Robert 1962, *The Immediate Experience: Movies, Comics, Theatre and Other Aspects of Popular Culture*, Garden City, NY: Doubleday.

Watkins, Mel 1972, 'Learning to Move Left', *This Magazine Is About Schools*, 6, Spring: 68–92.

———— 1977, 'The Staple Theory Revisited', *Journal of Canadian Studies*, 12, Winter: 83–95.

———— 2006, 'Harold Innis: An Intellectual at the Edge of Empire', *Canadian Dimension*, 40, July–August: 45–7.

Watson, Alexander John 2006, *Marginal Man: The Dark Vision of Harold Innis*, Toronto: University of Toronto Press.

Weinstein, James 1969, *The Decline of Socialism in America, 1912–25*, New York: Vintage.

Weir, Robert E. 2000, *Knights Unhorsed: Internal Conflict in a Gilded Age Social Movement*, Detroit: Wayne State University Press.

Weissman, Susan 2001, *Victor Serge: The Course is Set on Hope*, London: Verso.

Werner, M.R. 1926, *Barnum*, Garden City: Doubleday.

White, Hayden 1978, *Tropics of Discourse: Essays in Cultural Criticism*, Baltimore: John Hopkins University Press.

Whitman, Walt 1993, 'Song of the Broad-Axe', *Leaves of Grass*, New York: Barnes & Noble.

Widgery, David (ed) 1976, *The Left in Britain, 1956–68*, Harmondsworth: Penguin.

Wilentz, Sean 1984a, 'Against Exceptionalism: Class Consciousness and the American Labor Movement, 1790–1920', *International Labor and Working-Class History*, 26: 1–24.

——— 1984b, *Chants Democratic: New York City and the Rise of the American Working Class, 1788–1850*, Oxford: Oxford University Press.

Williams, Glen 1976, 'Canada – The Case of the Wealthiest Colony', *This Magazine*, 10, February–March.

——— 1983, *Not For Export: Toward a Political Economy of Canada's Arrested Industrialization*, Toronto: McClelland and Stewart.

Williams, Raymond (ed) 1968, *May Day Manifesto*, Harmondsworth: Penguin.

——— 1973, 'Base and Superstructure in Marxist Cultural Theory', *New Left Review*, 82, November–December: 3–16.

——— 1976, *Keywords: A Vocabulary of Culture and Society*, London: New Left Books.

——— 1979, *Politics and Letters: Interviews with New Left Review*, London: New Left Books.

——— 1980, *Problems in Materialism and Culture: Selected Essays*, London: Verso.

——— 1989, *The Politics of Modernism: Against the New Conformists*, London: Verso.

Williams, William Appleman 1962, *The Tragedy of American Diplomacy*, New York: Dell Pub. Co.

Wittke, Carl 1952, *Refugees of Revolution: The German Forty-Eighters in America*, Philadelphia: University of Pennsylvania Press.

Wolfe, Bertram 1981, *A Life in Two Centuries: An Autobiography*, New York: Stein and Day.

Wood, Ellen Meiksins 1986, *The Retreat from Class: A New 'True' Socialism*, London: Verso.

——— 1990, 'Falling Through the Cracks: E.P. Thompson and the Debate on Base and Superstructure' in *E.P. Thompson: Critical Perspectives*, edited by Harvey J. Kaye and Keith McClelland, Philadelphia: Temple University Press.

——— 1991, *The Pristine Culture of Capitalism: An Historical Essay on Old Regimes and Modern States*, London: Verso.

——— 1997, 'What is the Postmodern Agenda?' in *In Defense of History: Marxism and the Postmodern Agenda*, edited by Ellen Meiksins Wood and John Bellamy Foster, New York: Monthly Review Press.

Wood, Ellen Meiksins and John Bellamy Foster (eds) 1997, *In Defense of History: Marxism and the Postmodern Agenda*, New York: Monthly Review Press.

Worpole, Ken 1983, *Dockers and Detectives: Popular Reading, Popular Writing*, London: Verso.

Wright, Donald 2005, *The Professionalization of History in English Canada*, Toronto: University of Toronto Press.

Wright, Miriam 2001, *A Fishery for Modern Times: The State and the Industrialization of the Newfoundland Fishery, 1934–68*, Toronto: Oxford University Press.

Yates, Charlotte 1993, *From Plant to Politics: The Autoworkers Union in Postwar Canada*, Philadelphia: Temple University Press.

Yates, James 1989, *Mississippi to Madrid: Memoir of a Black American in the Abraham Lincoln Brigade*, Seattle: Open Hand Publishers.

Young, Robert 1990, *White Mythologies: Writing History and the West*, London: Routledge.

Zipser, Arthur 1981, *Working-Class Giant: The Life of William Z. Foster*, New York: International.

Index